SiMPSONS™
COMICS

COLOSSAL COMPENDIUM

VOLUME TWO

MATT GROENING

TITAN BOOKS

SIMPSONS COMICS COLOSSAL COMPENDIUM
VOLUME TWO

Materials previously published in
Radioactive Man #100, Simpsons Comics #154, 163, 169, 180
Simpsons Super Spectacular #3, 8, The Simpsons Summer Shindig #3, 4, 6

Published in the UK by Titan Books, a division of Titan Publishing Group Ltd.,
144 Southwark St., London SE1 0UP, under licence from Bongo Entertainment, Inc.

FIRST EDITION: JULY 2014

ISBN 9781783292103

2 4 6 8 10 9 7 5 3 1

Publisher: Matt Groening
Creative Director: Nathan Kane
Managing Editor: Terry Delegeane
Director of Operations: Robert Zaugh
Art Director: Jason Ho
Art Director Special Projects: Serban Cristescu
Assistant Art Director: Mike Rote
Production Manager: Christopher Ungar
Assistant Editor: Karen Bates
Production: Nathan Hamill, Art Villanueva
Administration: Ruth Waytz, Pete Benson
Legal Guardian: Susan A. Grode

Printed by TC Transcontinental, Beauceville, QC, Canada. 06/23/2014

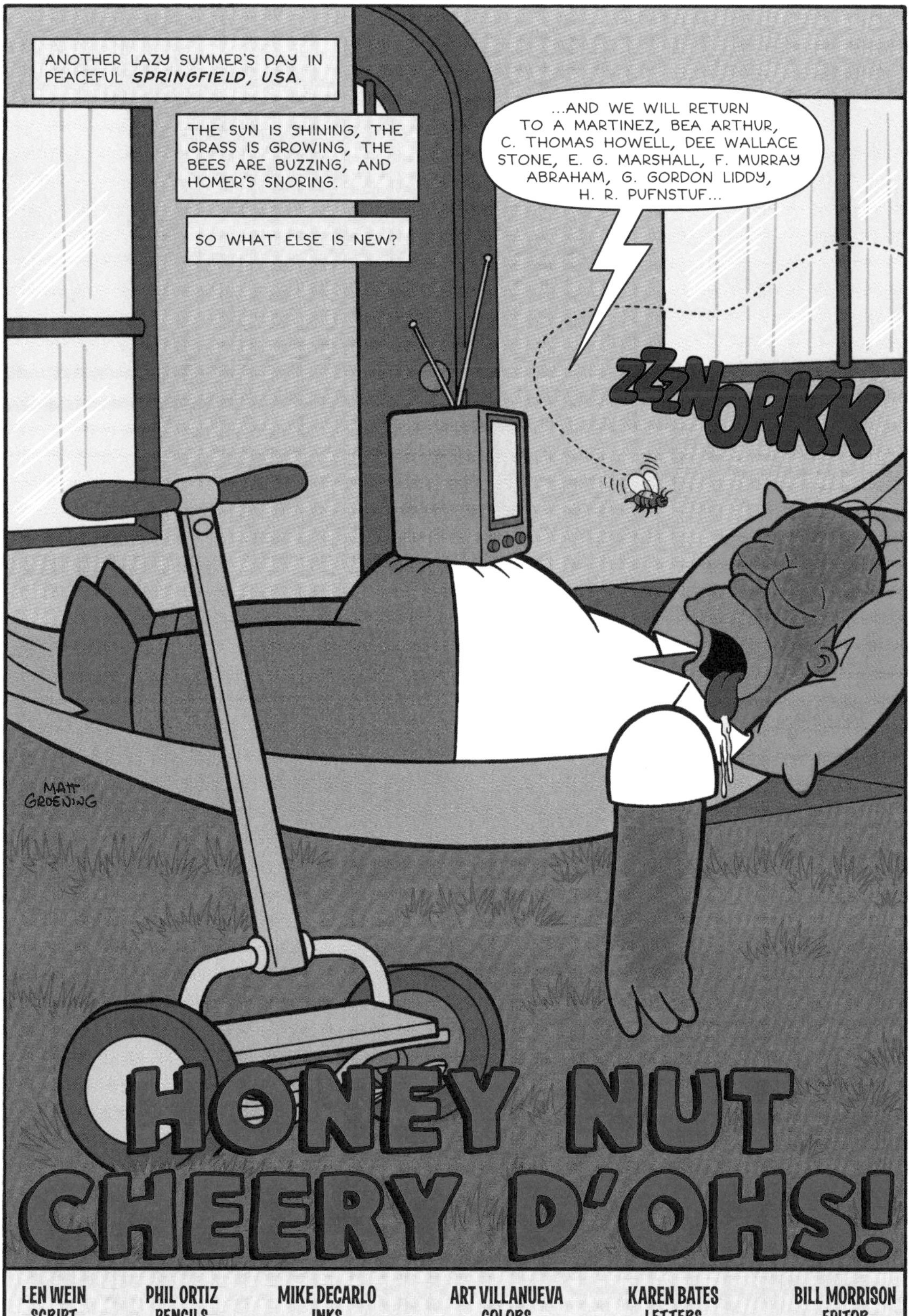
ANOTHER LAZY SUMMER'S DAY IN PEACEFUL *SPRINGFIELD, USA*.
THE SUN IS SHINING, THE GRASS IS GROWING, THE BEES ARE BUZZING, AND HOMER'S SNORING.
SO WHAT ELSE IS NEW?
...AND WE WILL RETURN TO A MARTINEZ, BEA ARTHUR, C. THOMAS HOWELL, DEE WALLACE STONE, E. G. MARSHALL, F. MURRAY ABRAHAM, G. GORDON LIDDY, H. R. PUFNSTUF...
ZZZNORKK
MATT GROENING
HONEY NUT CHEERY D'OHS!

LEN WEIN	PHIL ORTIZ	MIKE DECARLO	ART VILLANUEVA	KAREN BATES	BILL MORRISON
SCRIPT	PENCILS	INKS	COLORS	LETTERS	EDITOR

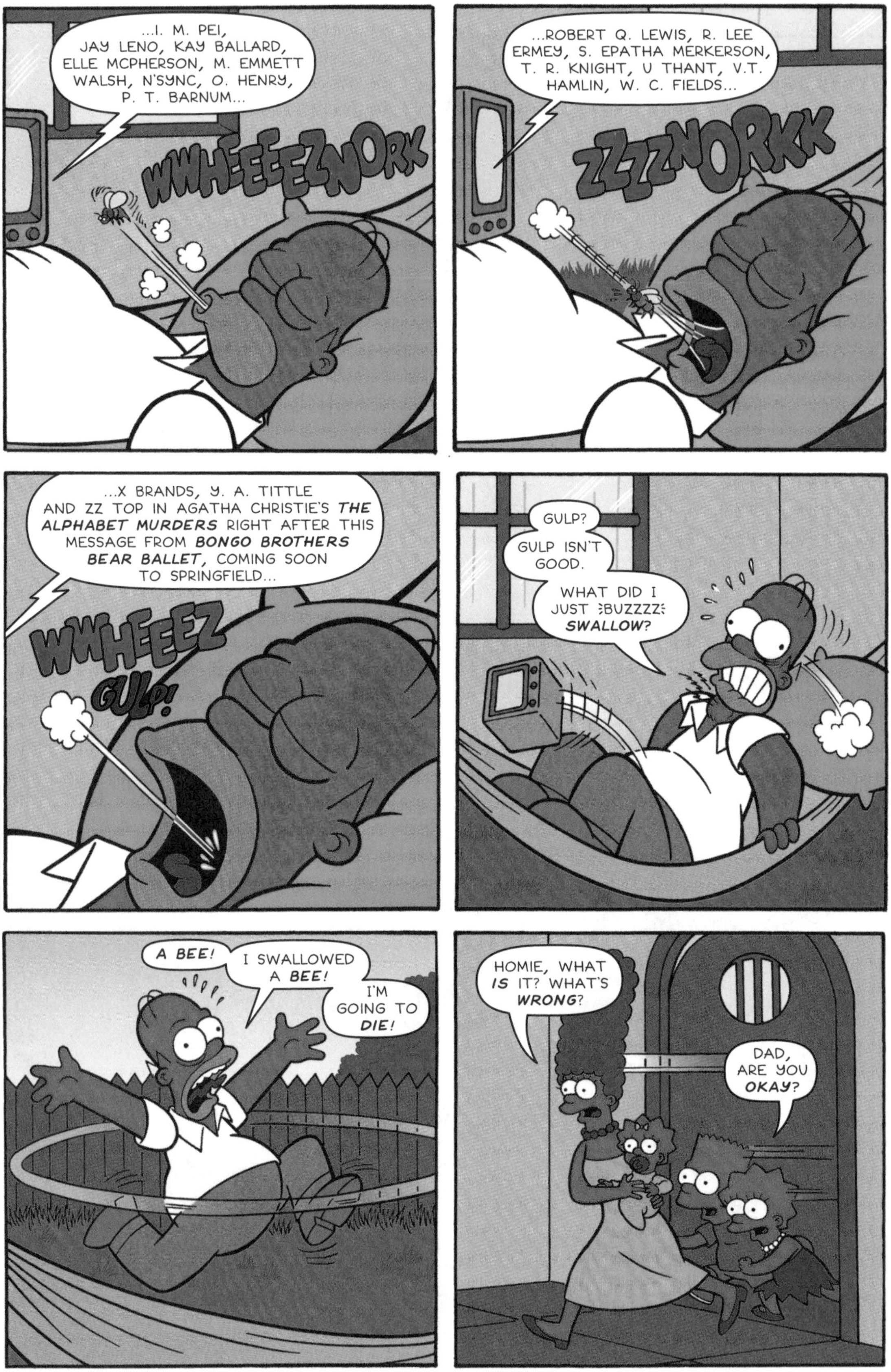
...I. M. PEI, JAY LENO, KAY BALLARD, ELLE MCPHERSON, M. EMMETT WALSH, N'SYNC, O. HENRY, P. T. BARNUM...
WWHEEEEZNORK
...ROBERT Q. LEWIS, R. LEE ERMEY, S. EPATHA MERKERSON, T. R. KNIGHT, U THANT, V.T. HAMLIN, W. C. FIELDS...
ZZZZNORKK
...X BRANDS, Y. A. TITTLE AND ZZ TOP IN AGATHA CHRISTIE'S *THE ALPHABET MURDERS* RIGHT AFTER THIS MESSAGE FROM *BONGO BROTHERS BEAR BALLET,* COMING SOON TO SPRINGFIELD...
WWHEEEZ
GULP!
GULP?
GULP ISN'T GOOD.
WHAT DID I JUST BUZZZZ *SWALLOW*?
A BEE!
I SWALLOWED A *BEE!*
I'M GOING TO *DIE!*
HOMIE, WHAT *IS* IT? WHAT'S *WRONG*?
DAD, ARE YOU *OKAY*?

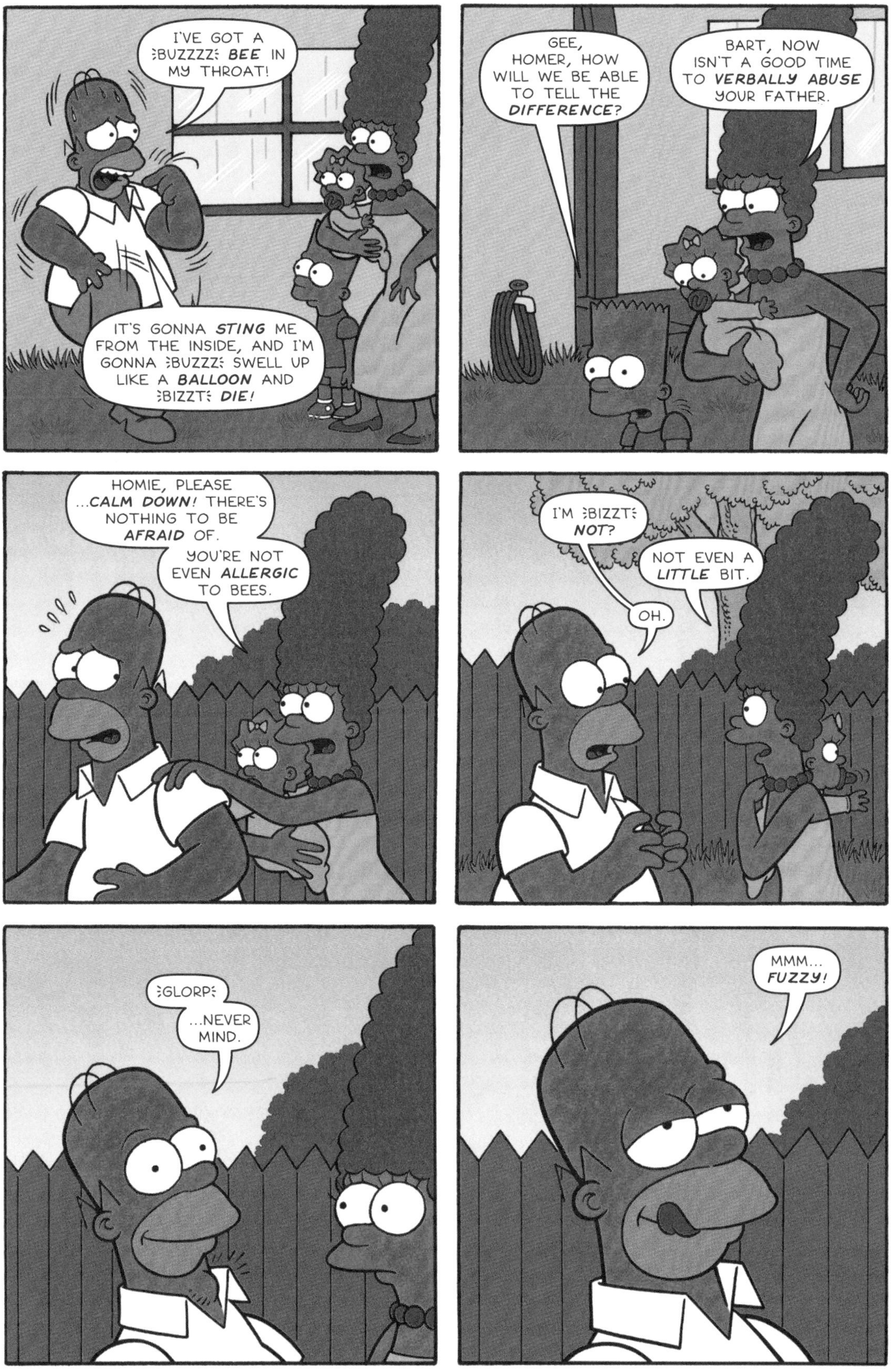
I'VE GOT A ⁝BUZZZZ⁝ BEE IN MY THROAT!
IT'S GONNA STING ME FROM THE INSIDE, AND I'M GONNA ⁝BUZZZ⁝ SWELL UP LIKE A BALLOON AND ⁝BIZZT⁝ DIE!
GEE, HOMER, HOW WILL WE BE ABLE TO TELL THE DIFFERENCE?
BART, NOW ISN'T A GOOD TIME TO VERBALLY ABUSE YOUR FATHER.
HOMIE, PLEASE ...CALM DOWN! THERE'S NOTHING TO BE AFRAID OF.
YOU'RE NOT EVEN ALLERGIC TO BEES.
I'M ⁝BIZZT⁝ NOT?
NOT EVEN A LITTLE BIT.
OH.
⁝GLORP⁝
...NEVER MIND.
MMM... FUZZY!

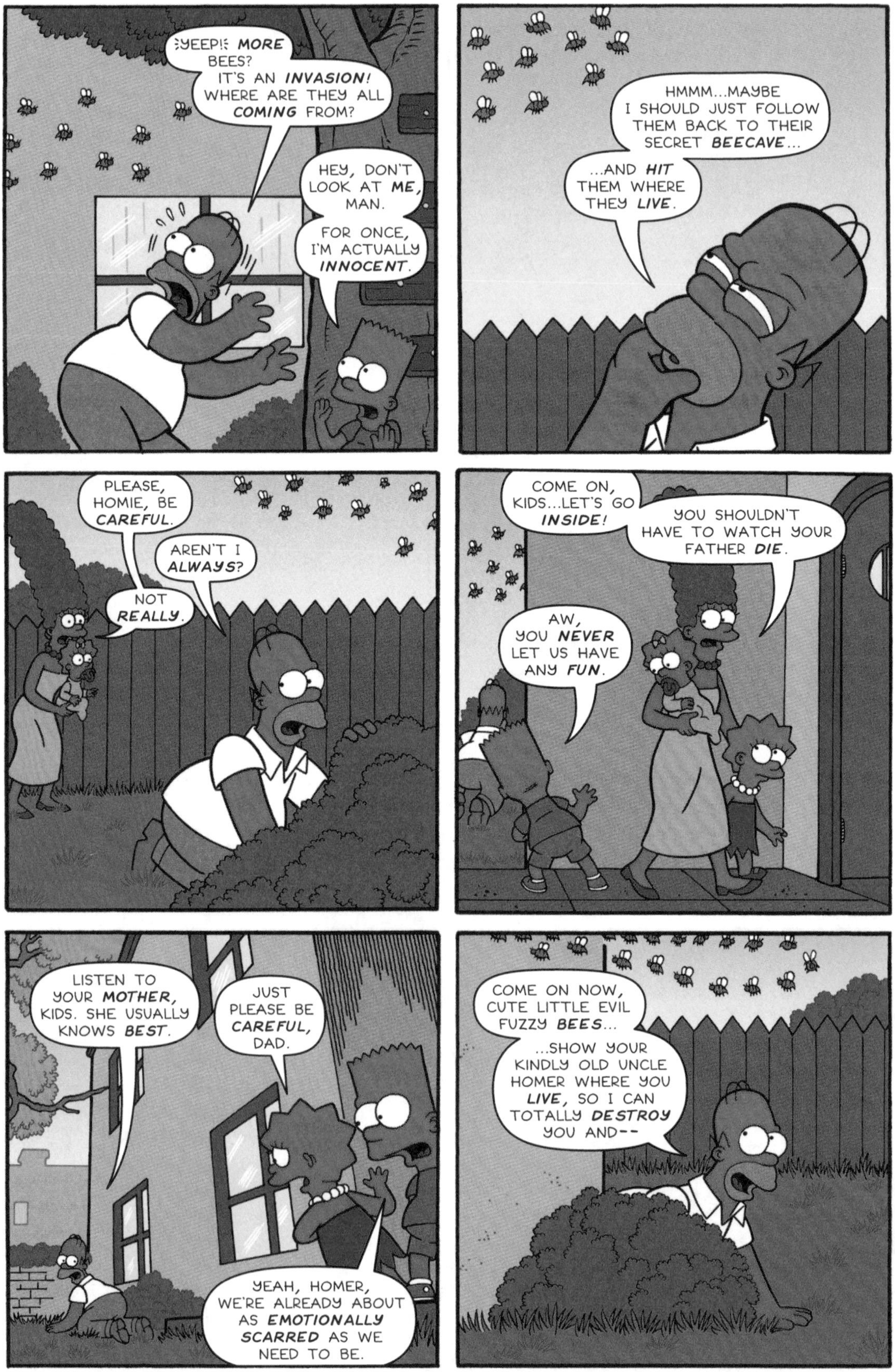
YEEP!! MORE BEES? IT'S AN INVASION! WHERE ARE THEY ALL COMING FROM?
HEY, DON'T LOOK AT ME, MAN.
FOR ONCE, I'M ACTUALLY INNOCENT.
HMMM...MAYBE I SHOULD JUST FOLLOW THEM BACK TO THEIR SECRET BEECAVE...
...AND HIT THEM WHERE THEY LIVE.
PLEASE, HOMIE, BE CAREFUL.
AREN'T I ALWAYS?
NOT REALLY.
COME ON, KIDS...LET'S GO INSIDE!
YOU SHOULDN'T HAVE TO WATCH YOUR FATHER DIE.
AW, YOU NEVER LET US HAVE ANY FUN.
LISTEN TO YOUR MOTHER, KIDS. SHE USUALLY KNOWS BEST.
JUST PLEASE BE CAREFUL, DAD.
YEAH, HOMER, WE'RE ALREADY ABOUT AS EMOTIONALLY SCARRED AS WE NEED TO BE.
COME ON NOW, CUTE LITTLE EVIL FUZZY BEES...
...SHOW YOUR KINDLY OLD UNCLE HOMER WHERE YOU LIVE, SO I CAN TOTALLY DESTROY YOU AND--

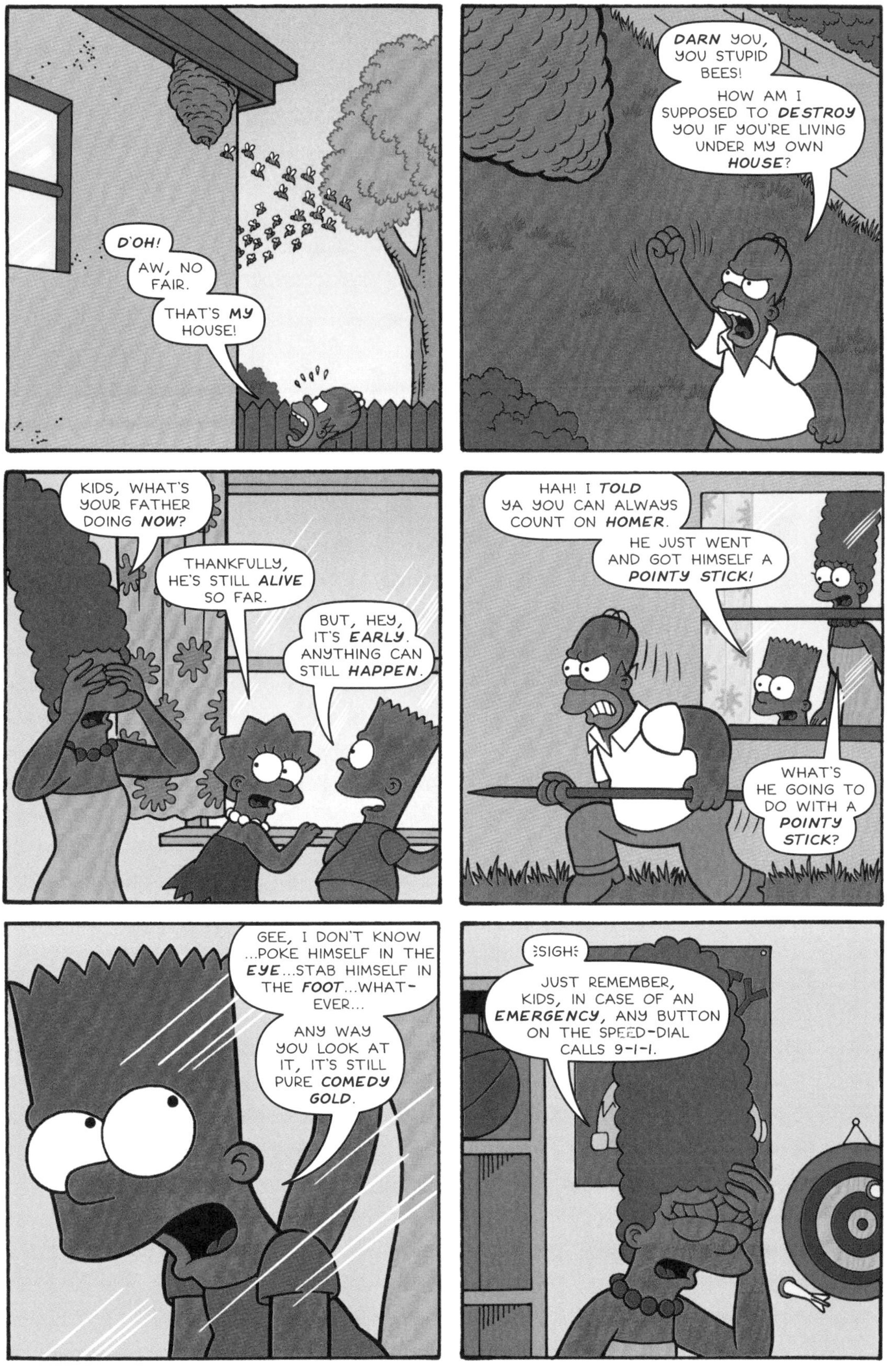
D'OH!
AW, NO FAIR.
THAT'S MY HOUSE!
DARN YOU, YOU STUPID BEES!
HOW AM I SUPPOSED TO DESTROY YOU IF YOU'RE LIVING UNDER MY OWN HOUSE?
KIDS, WHAT'S YOUR FATHER DOING NOW?
THANKFULLY, HE'S STILL ALIVE SO FAR.
BUT, HEY, IT'S EARLY. ANYTHING CAN STILL HAPPEN.
HAH! I TOLD YA YOU CAN ALWAYS COUNT ON HOMER.
HE JUST WENT AND GOT HIMSELF A POINTY STICK!
WHAT'S HE GOING TO DO WITH A POINTY STICK?
GEE, I DON'T KNOW ...POKE HIMSELF IN THE EYE...STAB HIMSELF IN THE FOOT...WHAT-EVER...
ANY WAY YOU LOOK AT IT, IT'S STILL PURE COMEDY GOLD.
SIGH
JUST REMEMBER, KIDS, IN CASE OF AN EMERGENCY, ANY BUTTON ON THE SPEED-DIAL CALLS 9-1-1.

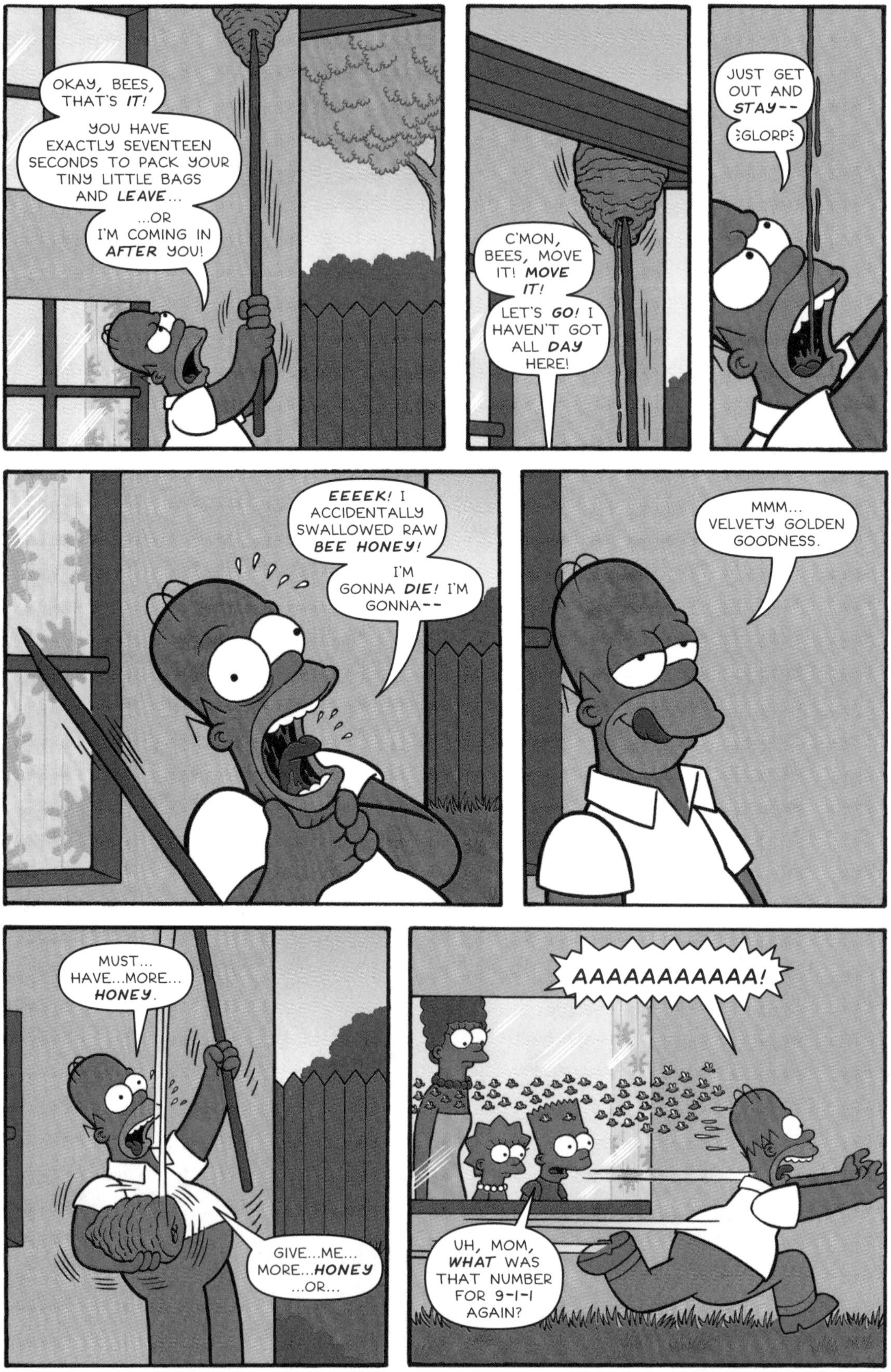
OKAY, BEES, THAT'S IT!
YOU HAVE EXACTLY SEVENTEEN SECONDS TO PACK YOUR TINY LITTLE BAGS AND LEAVE...
...OR I'M COMING IN AFTER YOU!
C'MON, BEES, MOVE IT! MOVE IT!
LET'S GO! I HAVEN'T GOT ALL DAY HERE!
JUST GET OUT AND STAY--
GLORP
EEEEK! I ACCIDENTALLY SWALLOWED RAW BEE HONEY!
I'M GONNA DIE! I'M GONNA--
MMM... VELVETY GOLDEN GOODNESS.
MUST... HAVE...MORE... HONEY.
GIVE...ME... MORE...HONEY ...OR...
AAAAAAAAAAA!
UH, MOM, WHAT WAS THAT NUMBER FOR 9-1-1 AGAIN?

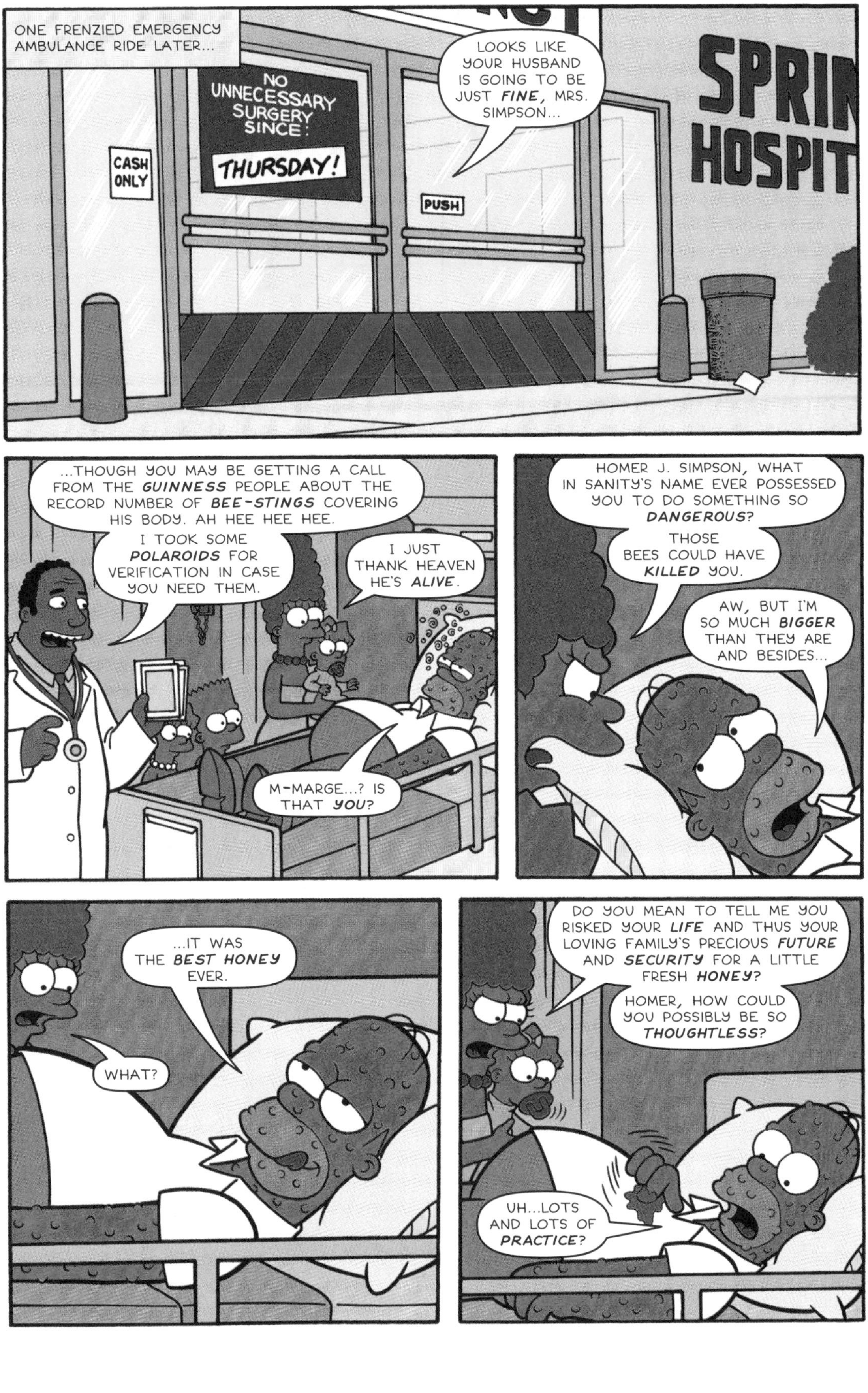

ONE FRENZIED EMERGENCY AMBULANCE RIDE LATER...
NO UNNECESSARY SURGERY SINCE: THURSDAY!
CASH ONLY
PUSH
SPRIN
HOSPIT
LOOKS LIKE YOUR HUSBAND IS GOING TO BE JUST FINE, MRS. SIMPSON...
...THOUGH YOU MAY BE GETTING A CALL FROM THE GUINNESS PEOPLE ABOUT THE RECORD NUMBER OF BEE-STINGS COVERING HIS BODY. AH HEE HEE HEE.
I TOOK SOME POLAROIDS FOR VERIFICATION IN CASE YOU NEED THEM.
I JUST THANK HEAVEN HE'S ALIVE.
M-MARGE...? IS THAT YOU?
HOMER J. SIMPSON, WHAT IN SANITY'S NAME EVER POSSESSED YOU TO DO SOMETHING SO DANGEROUS?
THOSE BEES COULD HAVE KILLED YOU.
AW, BUT I'M SO MUCH BIGGER THAN THEY ARE AND BESIDES...
...IT WAS THE BEST HONEY EVER.
WHAT?
DO YOU MEAN TO TELL ME YOU RISKED YOUR LIFE AND THUS YOUR LOVING FAMILY'S PRECIOUS FUTURE AND SECURITY FOR A LITTLE FRESH HONEY?
HOMER, HOW COULD YOU POSSIBLY BE SO THOUGHTLESS?
UH...LOTS AND LOTS OF PRACTICE?

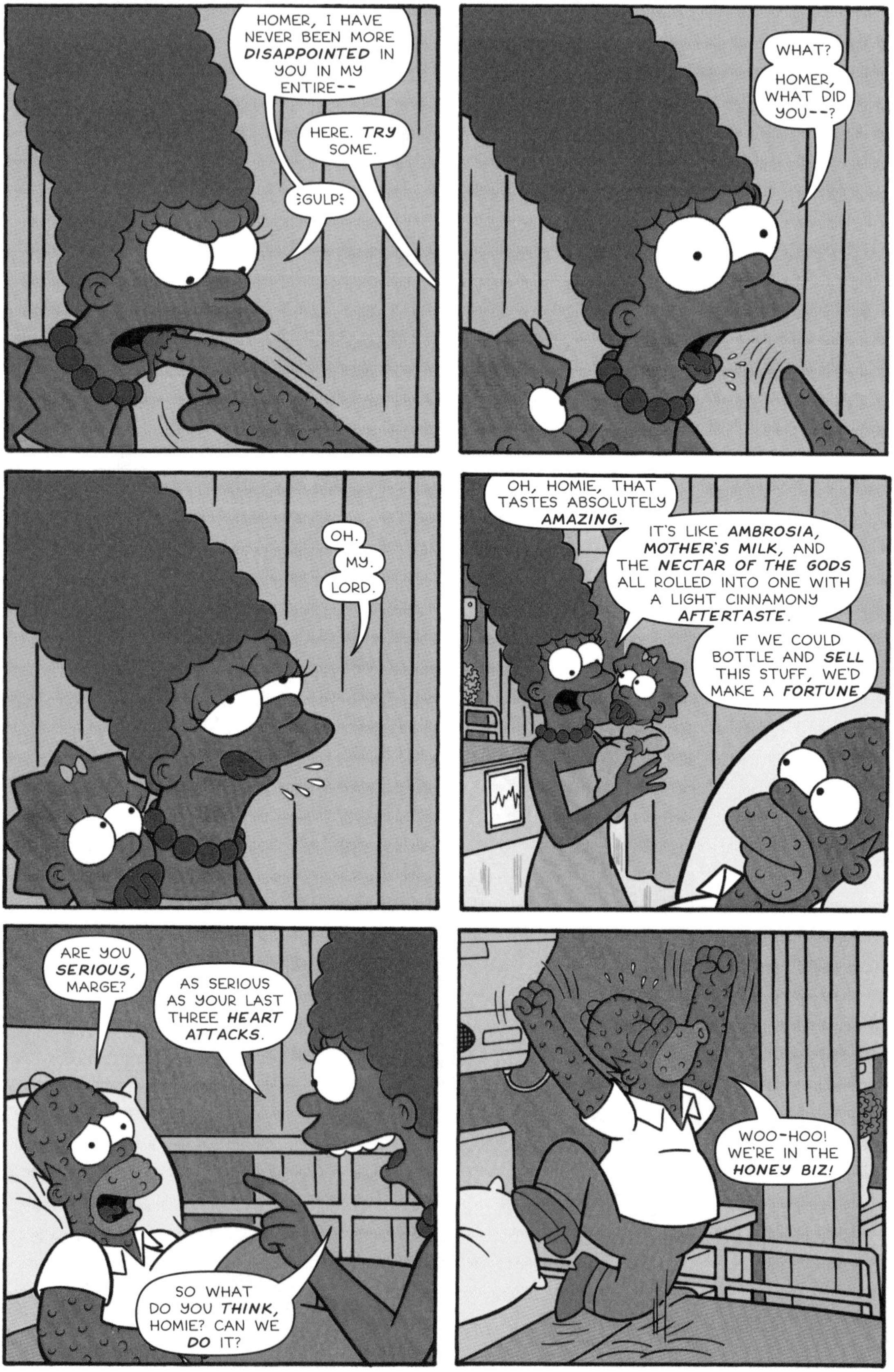

HOMER, I HAVE NEVER BEEN MORE DISAPPOINTED IN YOU IN MY ENTIRE--
HERE. TRY SOME.
GULP
WHAT?
HOMER, WHAT DID YOU--?
OH.
MY.
LORD.
OH, HOMIE, THAT TASTES ABSOLUTELY AMAZING.
IT'S LIKE AMBROSIA, MOTHER'S MILK, AND THE NECTAR OF THE GODS ALL ROLLED INTO ONE WITH A LIGHT CINNAMONY AFTERTASTE.
IF WE COULD BOTTLE AND SELL THIS STUFF, WE'D MAKE A FORTUNE.
ARE YOU SERIOUS, MARGE?
AS SERIOUS AS YOUR LAST THREE HEART ATTACKS.
SO WHAT DO YOU THINK, HOMIE? CAN WE DO IT?
WOO-HOO! WE'RE IN THE HONEY BIZ!

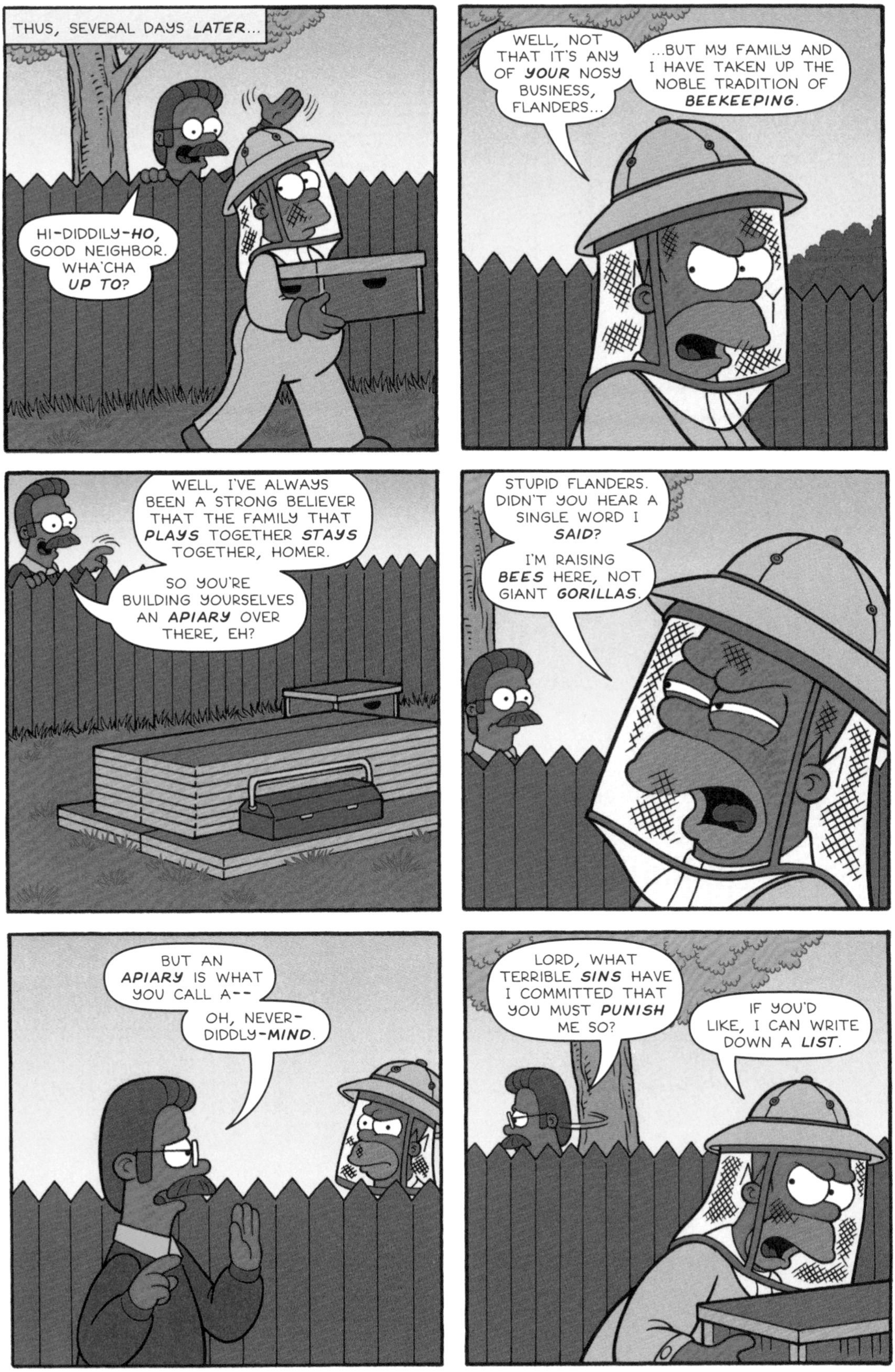
THUS, SEVERAL DAYS LATER...
HI-DIDDILY-HO, GOOD NEIGHBOR. WHA'CHA UP TO?
WELL, NOT THAT IT'S ANY OF YOUR NOSY BUSINESS, FLANDERS...
...BUT MY FAMILY AND I HAVE TAKEN UP THE NOBLE TRADITION OF BEEKEEPING.
WELL, I'VE ALWAYS BEEN A STRONG BELIEVER THAT THE FAMILY THAT PLAYS TOGETHER STAYS TOGETHER, HOMER.
SO YOU'RE BUILDING YOURSELVES AN APIARY OVER THERE, EH?
STUPID FLANDERS. DIDN'T YOU HEAR A SINGLE WORD I SAID?
I'M RAISING BEES HERE, NOT GIANT GORILLAS.
BUT AN APIARY IS WHAT YOU CALL A--
OH, NEVER-DIDDLY-MIND.
LORD, WHAT TERRIBLE SINS HAVE I COMMITTED THAT YOU MUST PUNISH ME SO?
IF YOU'D LIKE, I CAN WRITE DOWN A LIST.

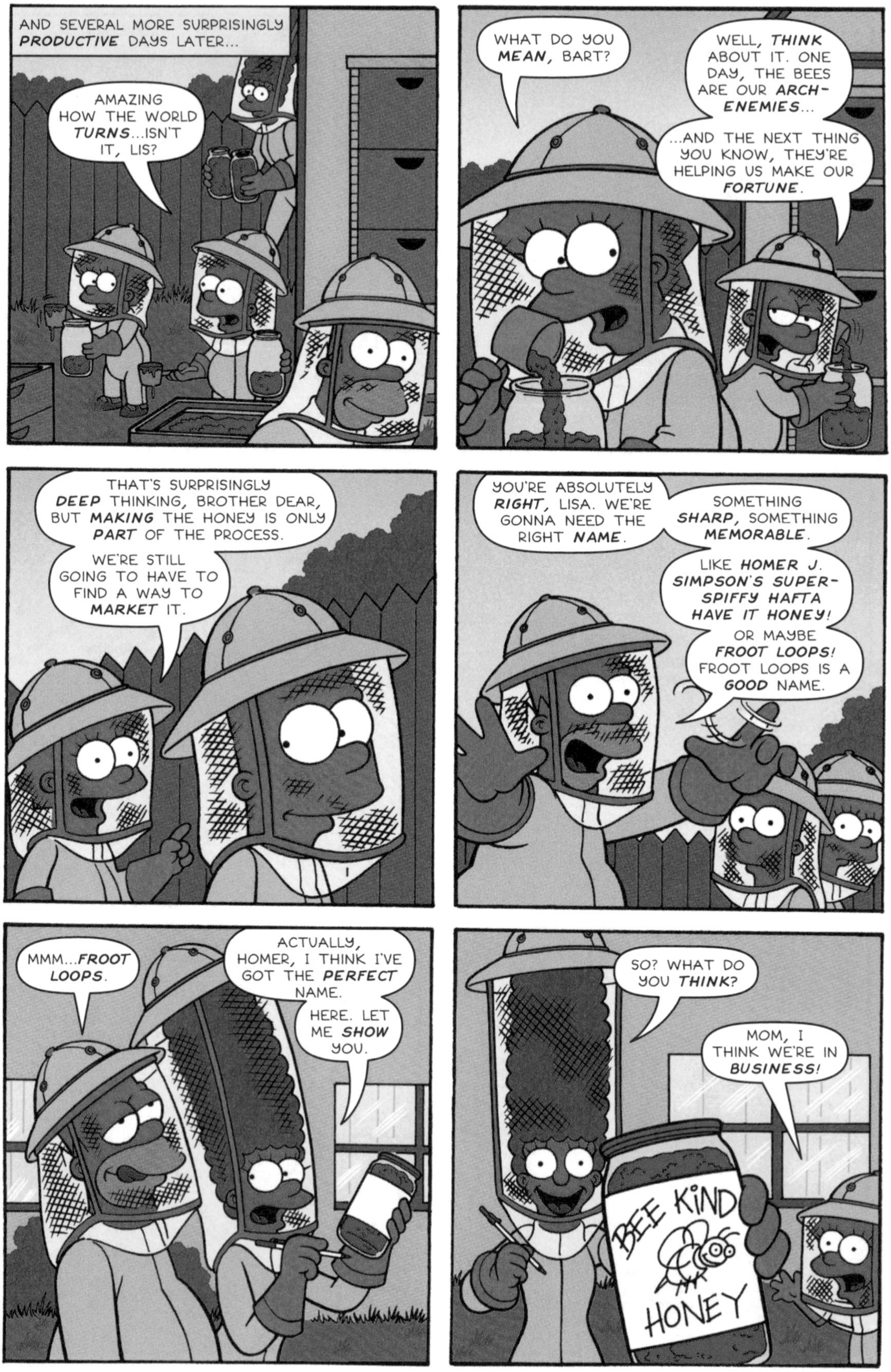
AND SEVERAL MORE SURPRISINGLY PRODUCTIVE DAYS LATER...
AMAZING HOW THE WORLD TURNS...ISN'T IT, LIS?
WHAT DO YOU MEAN, BART?
WELL, THINK ABOUT IT. ONE DAY, THE BEES ARE OUR ARCH-ENEMIES...
...AND THE NEXT THING YOU KNOW, THEY'RE HELPING US MAKE OUR FORTUNE.
THAT'S SURPRISINGLY DEEP THINKING, BROTHER DEAR, BUT MAKING THE HONEY IS ONLY PART OF THE PROCESS.
WE'RE STILL GOING TO HAVE TO FIND A WAY TO MARKET IT.
YOU'RE ABSOLUTELY RIGHT, LISA. WE'RE GONNA NEED THE RIGHT NAME.
SOMETHING SHARP, SOMETHING MEMORABLE.
LIKE HOMER J. SIMPSON'S SUPER-SPIFFY HAFTA HAVE IT HONEY!
OR MAYBE FROOT LOOPS! FROOT LOOPS IS A GOOD NAME.
MMM...FROOT LOOPS.
ACTUALLY, HOMER, I THINK I'VE GOT THE PERFECT NAME.
HERE. LET ME SHOW YOU.
SO? WHAT DO YOU THINK?
MOM, I THINK WE'RE IN BUSINESS!
BEE KIND HONEY

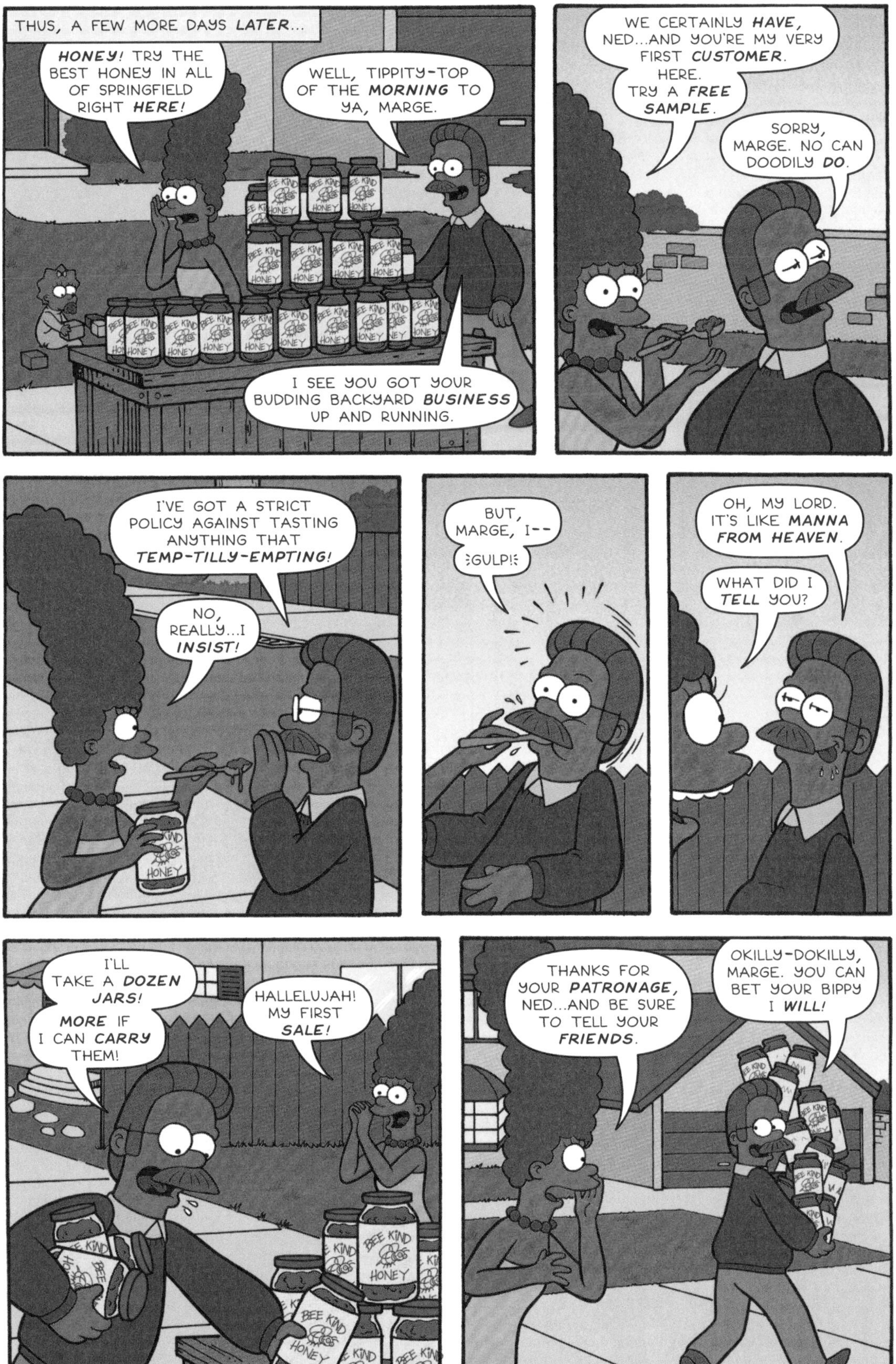
THUS, A FEW MORE DAYS LATER...
HONEY! TRY THE BEST HONEY IN ALL OF SPRINGFIELD RIGHT HERE!
WELL, TIPPITY-TOP OF THE MORNING TO YA, MARGE.
I SEE YOU GOT YOUR BUDDING BACKYARD BUSINESS UP AND RUNNING.
WE CERTAINLY HAVE, NED...AND YOU'RE MY VERY FIRST CUSTOMER. HERE. TRY A FREE SAMPLE.
SORRY, MARGE. NO CAN DOODILY DO.
I'VE GOT A STRICT POLICY AGAINST TASTING ANYTHING THAT TEMP-TILLY-EMPTING!
NO, REALLY...I INSIST!
BUT, MARGE, I--
GULP!
OH, MY LORD. IT'S LIKE MANNA FROM HEAVEN.
WHAT DID I TELL YOU?
I'LL TAKE A DOZEN JARS!
MORE IF I CAN CARRY THEM!
HALLELUJAH! MY FIRST SALE!
THANKS FOR YOUR PATRONAGE, NED...AND BE SURE TO TELL YOUR FRIENDS.
OKILLY-DOKILLY, MARGE. YOU CAN BET YOUR BIPPY I WILL!

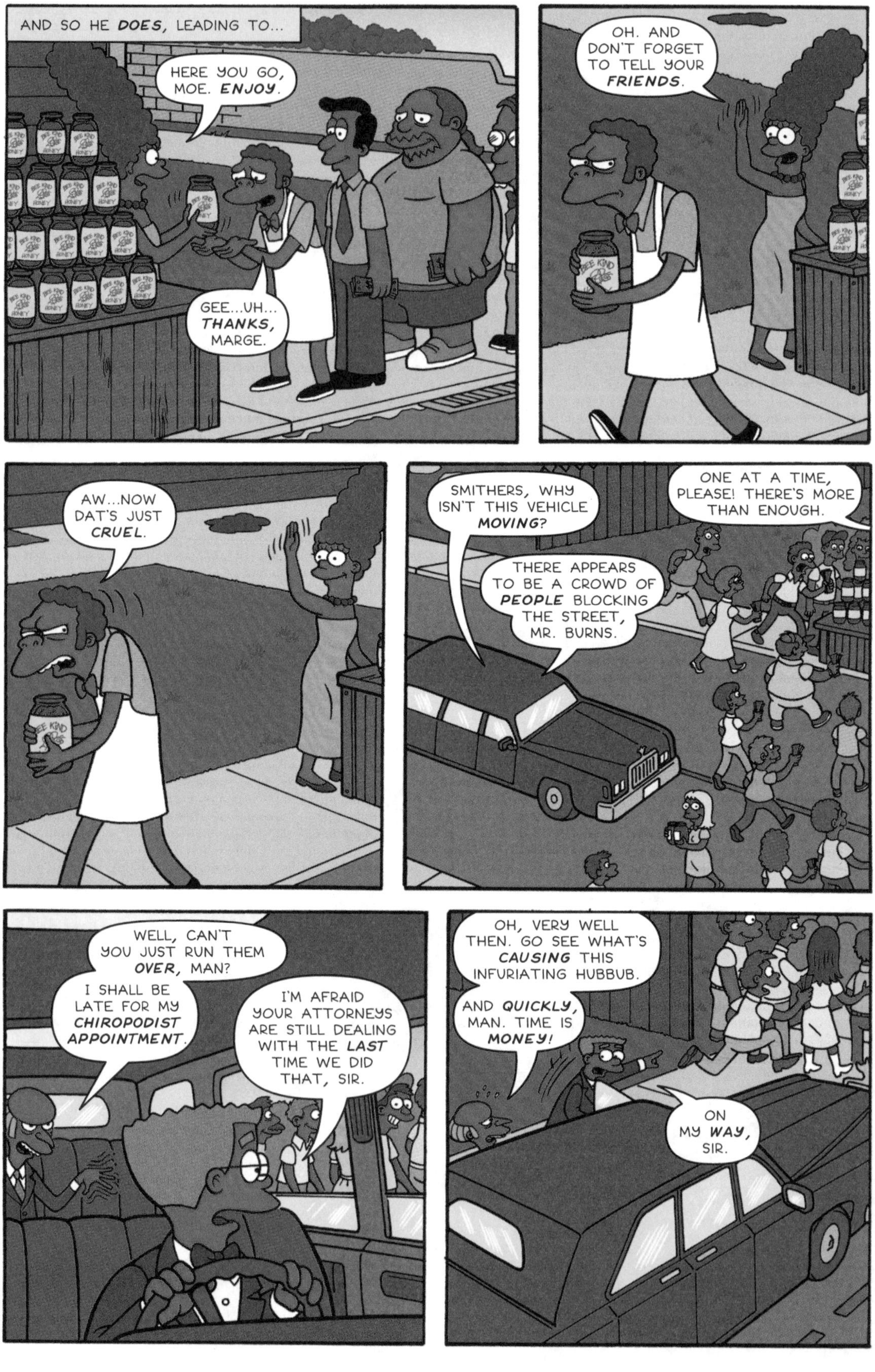
AND SO HE *DOES,* LEADING TO...
HERE YOU GO, MOE. *ENJOY*.
GEE...UH... *THANKS,* MARGE.
BEE KIND HONEY
OH. AND DON'T FORGET TO TELL YOUR *FRIENDS*.
AW...NOW DAT'S JUST *CRUEL*.
SMITHERS, WHY ISN'T THIS VEHICLE *MOVING*?
THERE APPEARS TO BE A CROWD OF *PEOPLE* BLOCKING THE STREET, MR. BURNS.
ONE AT A TIME, PLEASE! THERE'S MORE THAN ENOUGH.
WELL, CAN'T YOU JUST RUN THEM *OVER,* MAN?
I SHALL BE LATE FOR MY *CHIROPODIST APPOINTMENT*.
I'M AFRAID YOUR ATTORNEYS ARE STILL DEALING WITH THE *LAST* TIME WE DID THAT, SIR.
OH, VERY WELL THEN. GO SEE WHAT'S *CAUSING* THIS INFURIATING HUBBUB.
AND *QUICKLY,* MAN. TIME IS *MONEY!*
ON MY *WAY,* SIR.

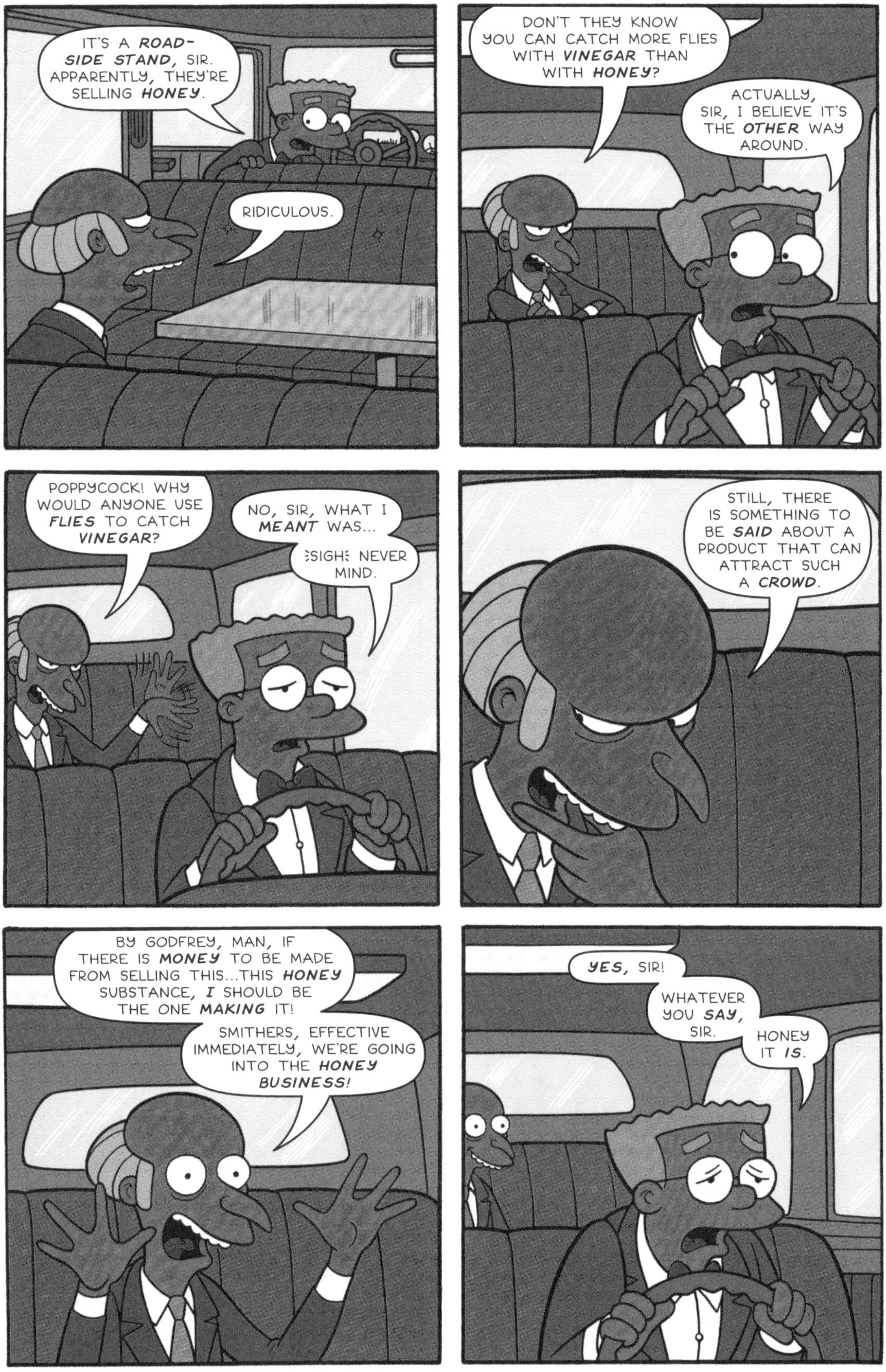
IT'S A ROAD-SIDE STAND, SIR. APPARENTLY, THEY'RE SELLING HONEY.
RIDICULOUS.
DON'T THEY KNOW YOU CAN CATCH MORE FLIES WITH VINEGAR THAN WITH HONEY?
ACTUALLY, SIR, I BELIEVE IT'S THE OTHER WAY AROUND.
POPPYCOCK! WHY WOULD ANYONE USE FLIES TO CATCH VINEGAR?
NO, SIR, WHAT I MEANT WAS...
:SIGH: NEVER MIND.
STILL, THERE IS SOMETHING TO BE SAID ABOUT A PRODUCT THAT CAN ATTRACT SUCH A CROWD.
BY GODFREY, MAN, IF THERE IS MONEY TO BE MADE FROM SELLING THIS...THIS HONEY SUBSTANCE, I SHOULD BE THE ONE MAKING IT!
SMITHERS, EFFECTIVE IMMEDIATELY, WE'RE GOING INTO THE HONEY BUSINESS!
YES, SIR!
WHATEVER YOU SAY, SIR.
HONEY IT IS.

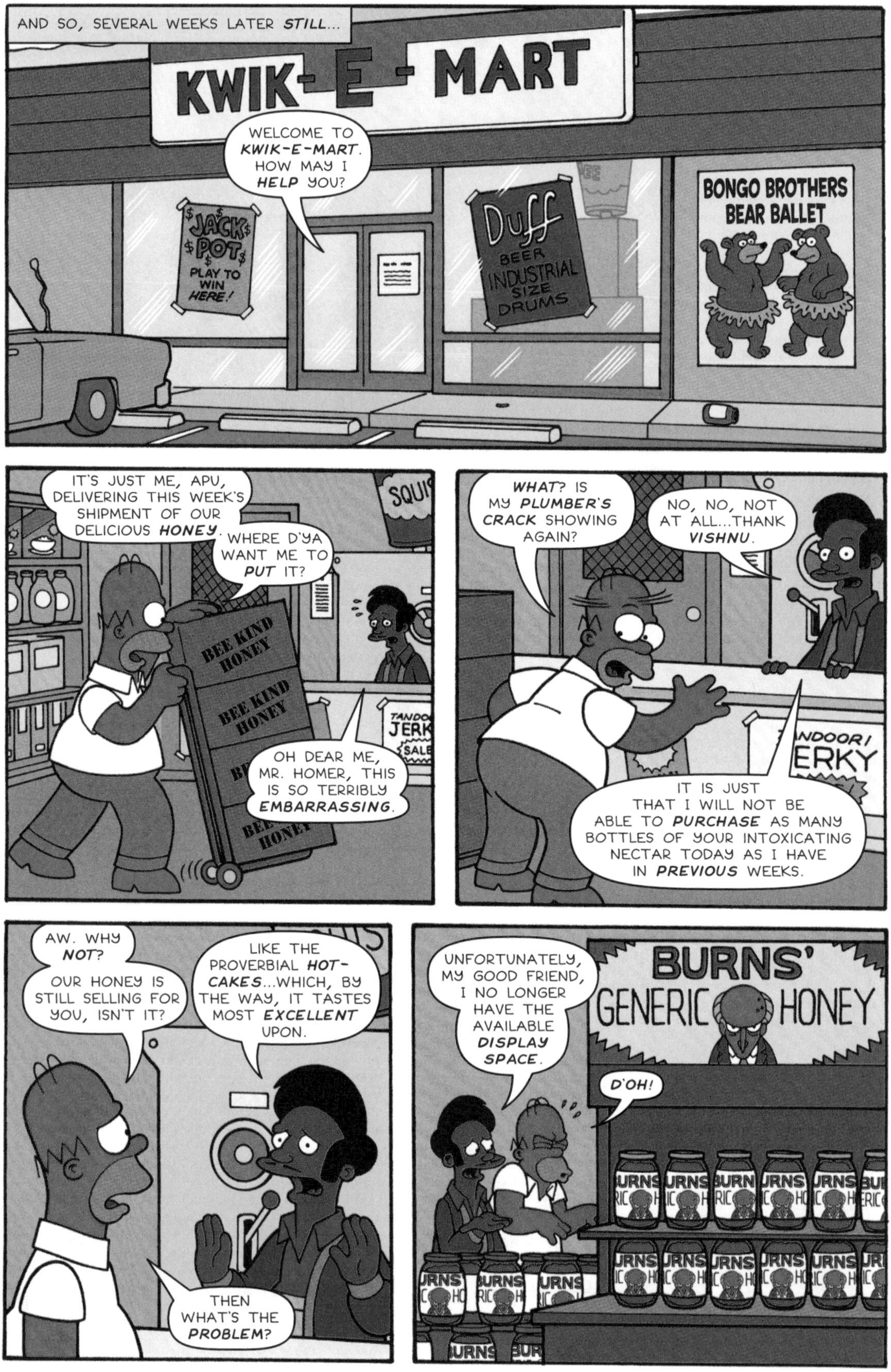
AND SO, SEVERAL WEEKS LATER STILL...
KWIK-E-MART
WELCOME TO KWIK-E-MART. HOW MAY I HELP YOU?
JACK POT PLAY TO WIN HERE!
Duff BEER INDUSTRIAL SIZE DRUMS
BONGO BROTHERS BEAR BALLET
IT'S JUST ME, APU, DELIVERING THIS WEEK'S SHIPMENT OF OUR DELICIOUS HONEY.
WHERE D'YA WANT ME TO PUT IT?
BEE KIND HONEY
BEE KIND HONEY
OH DEAR ME, MR. HOMER, THIS IS SO TERRIBLY EMBARRASSING.
WHAT? IS MY PLUMBER'S CRACK SHOWING AGAIN?
NO, NO, NOT AT ALL...THANK VISHNU.
IT IS JUST THAT I WILL NOT BE ABLE TO PURCHASE AS MANY BOTTLES OF YOUR INTOXICATING NECTAR TODAY AS I HAVE IN PREVIOUS WEEKS.
AW. WHY NOT?
OUR HONEY IS STILL SELLING FOR YOU, ISN'T IT?
LIKE THE PROVERBIAL HOT-CAKES...WHICH, BY THE WAY, IT TASTES MOST EXCELLENT UPON.
THEN WHAT'S THE PROBLEM?
UNFORTUNATELY, MY GOOD FRIEND, I NO LONGER HAVE THE AVAILABLE DISPLAY SPACE.
BURNS' GENERIC HONEY
D'OH!

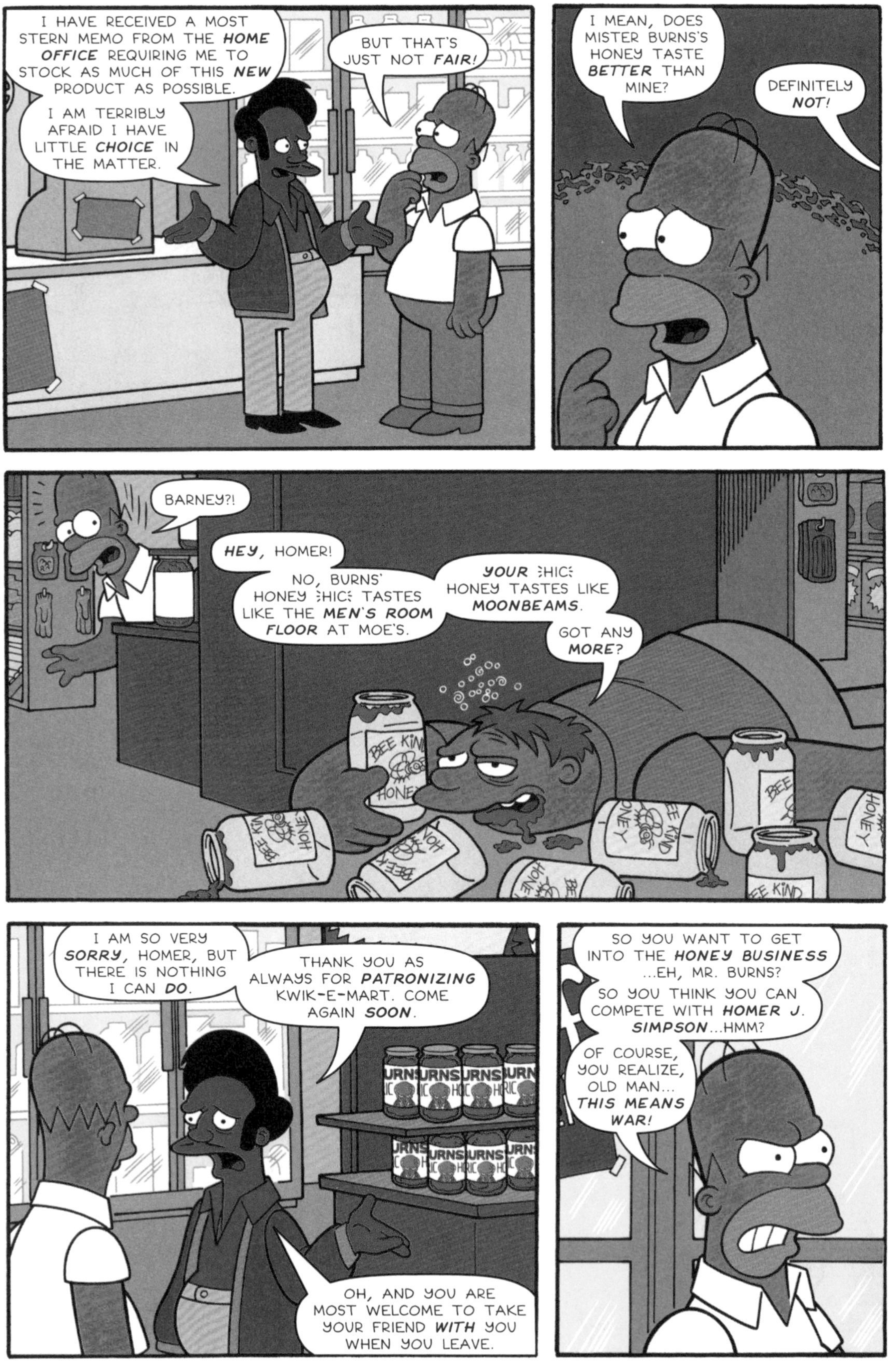

I HAVE RECEIVED A MOST STERN MEMO FROM THE HOME OFFICE REQUIRING ME TO STOCK AS MUCH OF THIS NEW PRODUCT AS POSSIBLE.
I AM TERRIBLY AFRAID I HAVE LITTLE CHOICE IN THE MATTER.
BUT THAT'S JUST NOT FAIR!
I MEAN, DOES MISTER BURNS'S HONEY TASTE BETTER THAN MINE?
DEFINITELY NOT!
BARNEY?!
HEY, HOMER!
NO, BURNS' HONEY *HIC* TASTES LIKE THE MEN'S ROOM FLOOR AT MOE'S.
YOUR *HIC* HONEY TASTES LIKE MOONBEAMS.
GOT ANY MORE?
I AM SO VERY SORRY, HOMER, BUT THERE IS NOTHING I CAN DO.
THANK YOU AS ALWAYS FOR PATRONIZING KWIK-E-MART. COME AGAIN SOON.
OH, AND YOU ARE MOST WELCOME TO TAKE YOUR FRIEND WITH YOU WHEN YOU LEAVE.
SO YOU WANT TO GET INTO THE HONEY BUSINESS ...EH, MR. BURNS?
SO YOU THINK YOU CAN COMPETE WITH HOMER J. SIMPSON...HMM?
OF COURSE, YOU REALIZE, OLD MAN... THIS MEANS WAR!

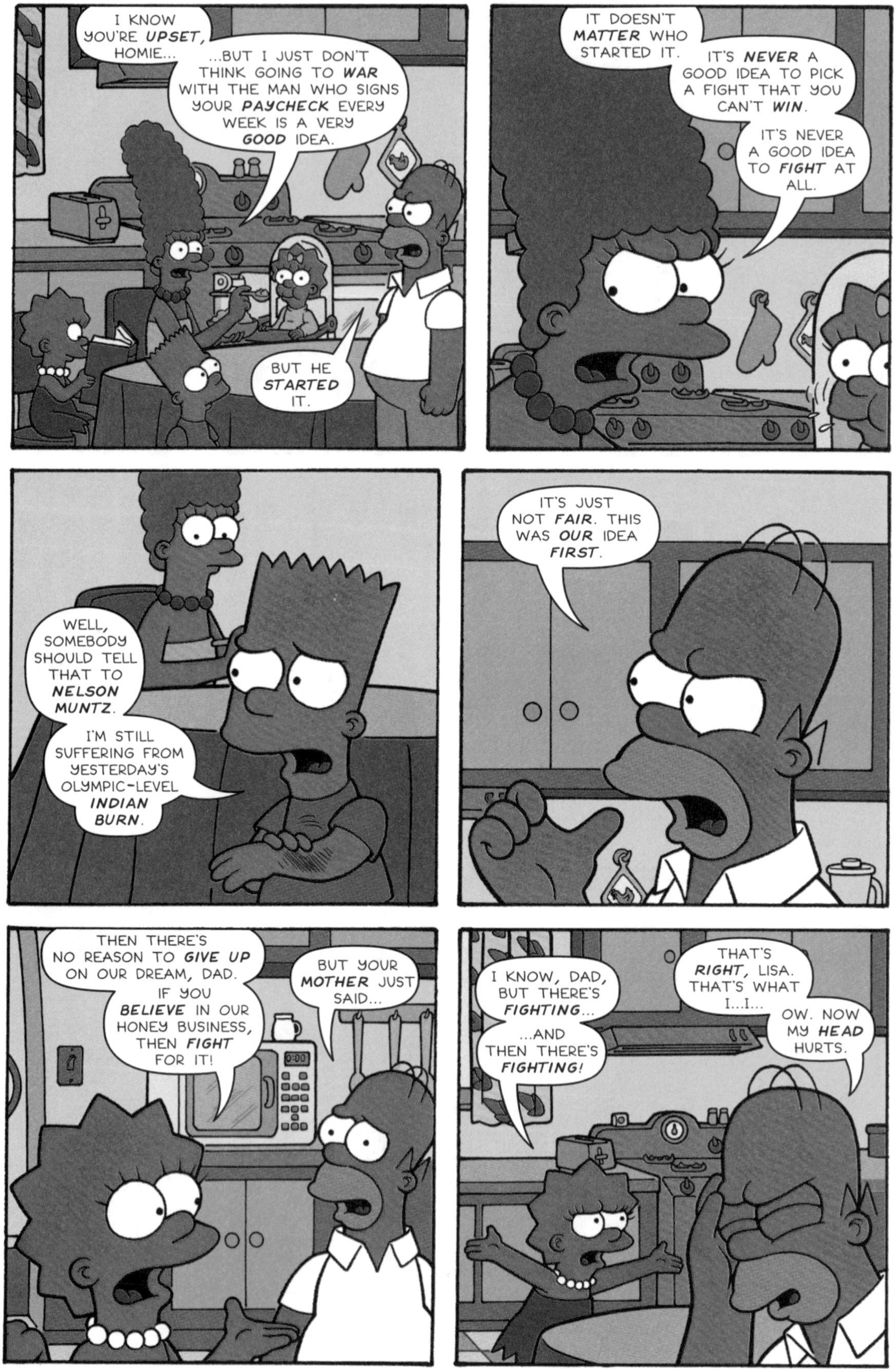
I KNOW YOU'RE **UPSET,** HOMIE...
...BUT I JUST DON'T THINK GOING TO **WAR** WITH THE MAN WHO SIGNS YOUR **PAYCHECK** EVERY WEEK IS A VERY **GOOD** IDEA.
BUT HE **STARTED** IT.
IT DOESN'T **MATTER** WHO STARTED IT.
IT'S **NEVER** A GOOD IDEA TO PICK A FIGHT THAT YOU CAN'T **WIN**.
IT'S NEVER A GOOD IDEA TO **FIGHT** AT ALL.
WELL, SOMEBODY SHOULD TELL THAT TO **NELSON MUNTZ**.
I'M STILL SUFFERING FROM YESTERDAY'S OLYMPIC-LEVEL **INDIAN BURN**.
IT'S JUST NOT **FAIR**. THIS WAS **OUR** IDEA **FIRST**.
THEN THERE'S NO REASON TO **GIVE UP** ON OUR DREAM, DAD.
IF YOU **BELIEVE** IN OUR HONEY BUSINESS, THEN **FIGHT** FOR IT!
BUT YOUR **MOTHER** JUST SAID...
I KNOW, DAD, BUT THERE'S **FIGHTING**...
...AND THEN THERE'S **FIGHTING**!
THAT'S **RIGHT,** LISA. THAT'S WHAT I...I...
OW. NOW MY **HEAD** HURTS.

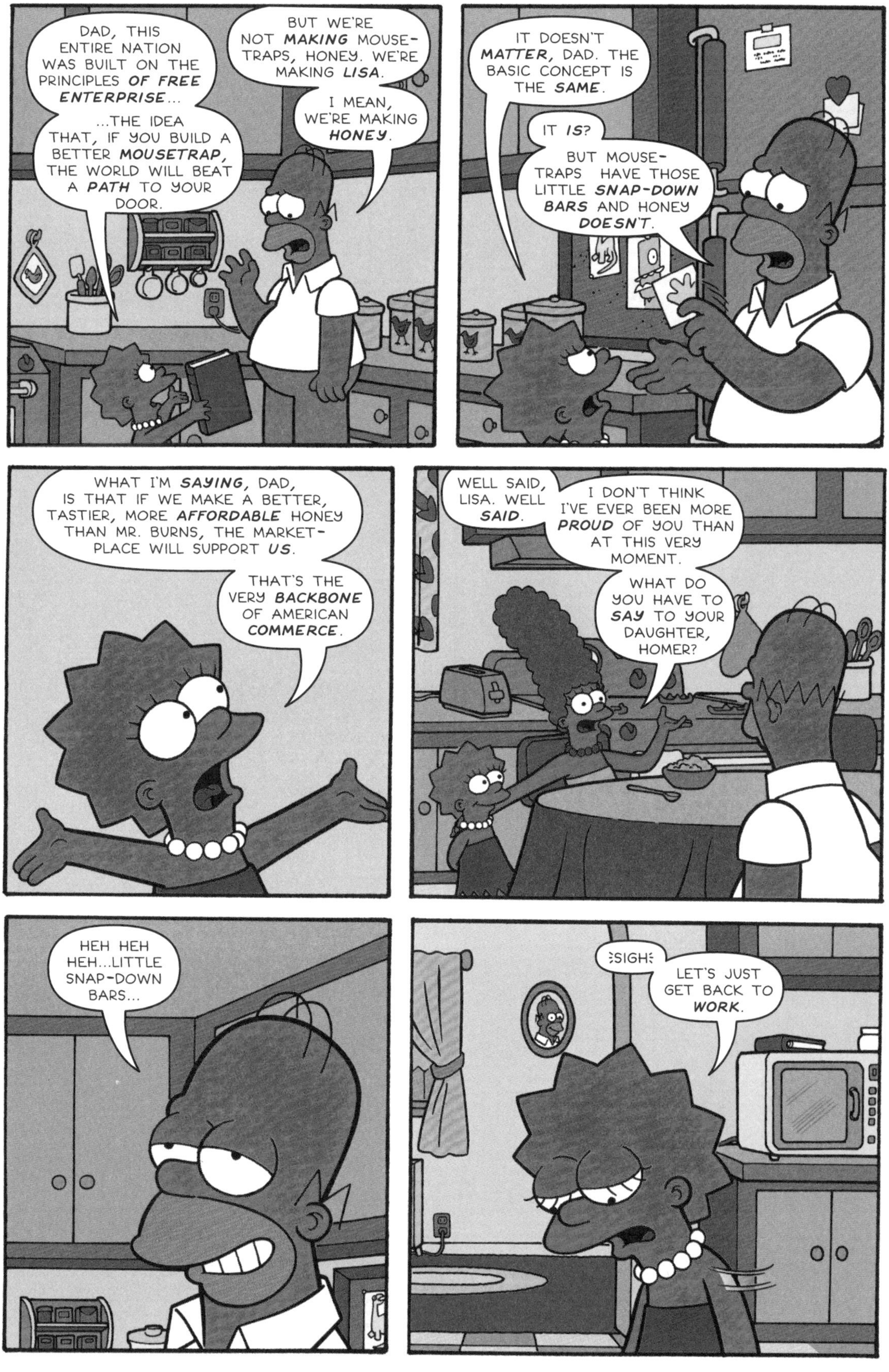
DAD, THIS ENTIRE NATION WAS BUILT ON THE PRINCIPLES OF FREE ENTERPRISE...
...THE IDEA THAT, IF YOU BUILD A BETTER MOUSETRAP, THE WORLD WILL BEAT A PATH TO YOUR DOOR.
BUT WE'RE NOT MAKING MOUSE-TRAPS, HONEY. WE'RE MAKING LISA.
I MEAN, WE'RE MAKING HONEY.
IT DOESN'T MATTER, DAD. THE BASIC CONCEPT IS THE SAME.
IT IS?
BUT MOUSE-TRAPS HAVE THOSE LITTLE SNAP-DOWN BARS AND HONEY DOESN'T.
WHAT I'M SAYING, DAD, IS THAT IF WE MAKE A BETTER, TASTIER, MORE AFFORDABLE HONEY THAN MR. BURNS, THE MARKET-PLACE WILL SUPPORT US.
THAT'S THE VERY BACKBONE OF AMERICAN COMMERCE.
WELL SAID, LISA. WELL SAID.
I DON'T THINK I'VE EVER BEEN MORE PROUD OF YOU THAN AT THIS VERY MOMENT.
WHAT DO YOU HAVE TO SAY TO YOUR DAUGHTER, HOMER?
HEH HEH HEH...LITTLE SNAP-DOWN BARS...
SIGH
LET'S JUST GET BACK TO WORK.

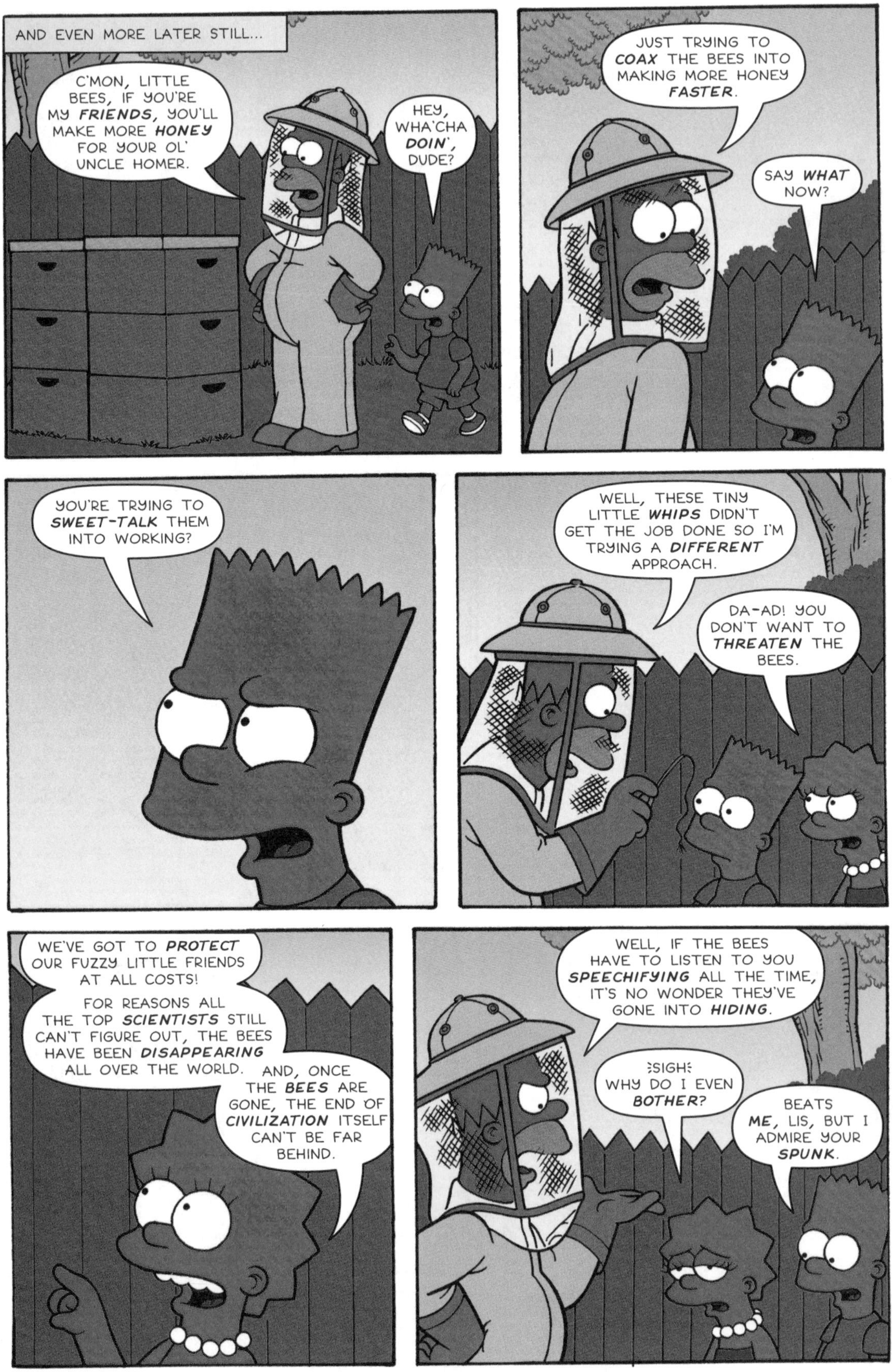
AND EVEN MORE LATER STILL...
C'MON, LITTLE BEES, IF YOU'RE MY FRIENDS, YOU'LL MAKE MORE HONEY FOR YOUR OL' UNCLE HOMER.
HEY, WHA'CHA DOIN', DUDE?
JUST TRYING TO COAX THE BEES INTO MAKING MORE HONEY FASTER.
SAY WHAT NOW?
YOU'RE TRYING TO SWEET-TALK THEM INTO WORKING?
WELL, THESE TINY LITTLE WHIPS DIDN'T GET THE JOB DONE SO I'M TRYING A DIFFERENT APPROACH.
DA-AD! YOU DON'T WANT TO THREATEN THE BEES.
WE'VE GOT TO PROTECT OUR FUZZY LITTLE FRIENDS AT ALL COSTS!
FOR REASONS ALL THE TOP SCIENTISTS STILL CAN'T FIGURE OUT, THE BEES HAVE BEEN DISAPPEARING ALL OVER THE WORLD.
AND, ONCE THE BEES ARE GONE, THE END OF CIVILIZATION ITSELF CAN'T BE FAR BEHIND.
WELL, IF THE BEES HAVE TO LISTEN TO YOU SPEECHIFYING ALL THE TIME, IT'S NO WONDER THEY'VE GONE INTO HIDING.
SIGH
WHY DO I EVEN BOTHER?
BEATS ME, LIS, BUT I ADMIRE YOUR SPUNK.

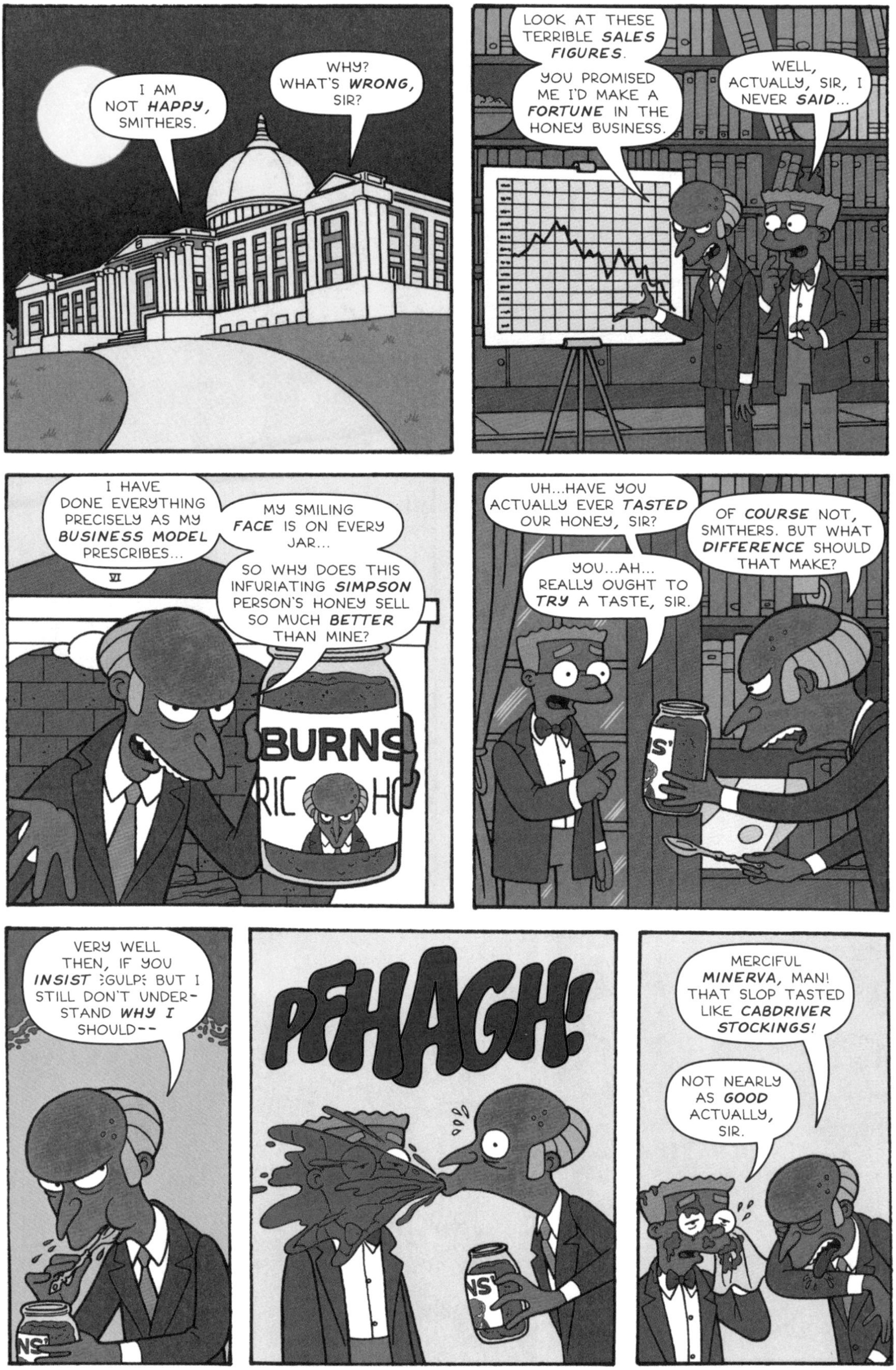
I AM NOT HAPPY, SMITHERS.
WHY? WHAT'S WRONG, SIR?
LOOK AT THESE TERRIBLE SALES FIGURES.
YOU PROMISED ME I'D MAKE A FORTUNE IN THE HONEY BUSINESS.
WELL, ACTUALLY, SIR, I NEVER SAID...
I HAVE DONE EVERYTHING PRECISELY AS MY BUSINESS MODEL PRESCRIBES...
MY SMILING FACE IS ON EVERY JAR...
SO WHY DOES THIS INFURIATING SIMPSON PERSON'S HONEY SELL SO MUCH BETTER THAN MINE?
BURNS
UH...HAVE YOU ACTUALLY EVER TASTED OUR HONEY, SIR?
YOU...AH... REALLY OUGHT TO TRY A TASTE, SIR.
OF COURSE NOT, SMITHERS. BUT WHAT DIFFERENCE SHOULD THAT MAKE?
VERY WELL THEN, IF YOU INSIST ⋮GULP⋮ BUT I STILL DON'T UNDERSTAND WHY I SHOULD--
PFHAGH!
MERCIFUL MINERVA, MAN! THAT SLOP TASTED LIKE CABDRIVER STOCKINGS!
NOT NEARLY AS GOOD ACTUALLY, SIR.

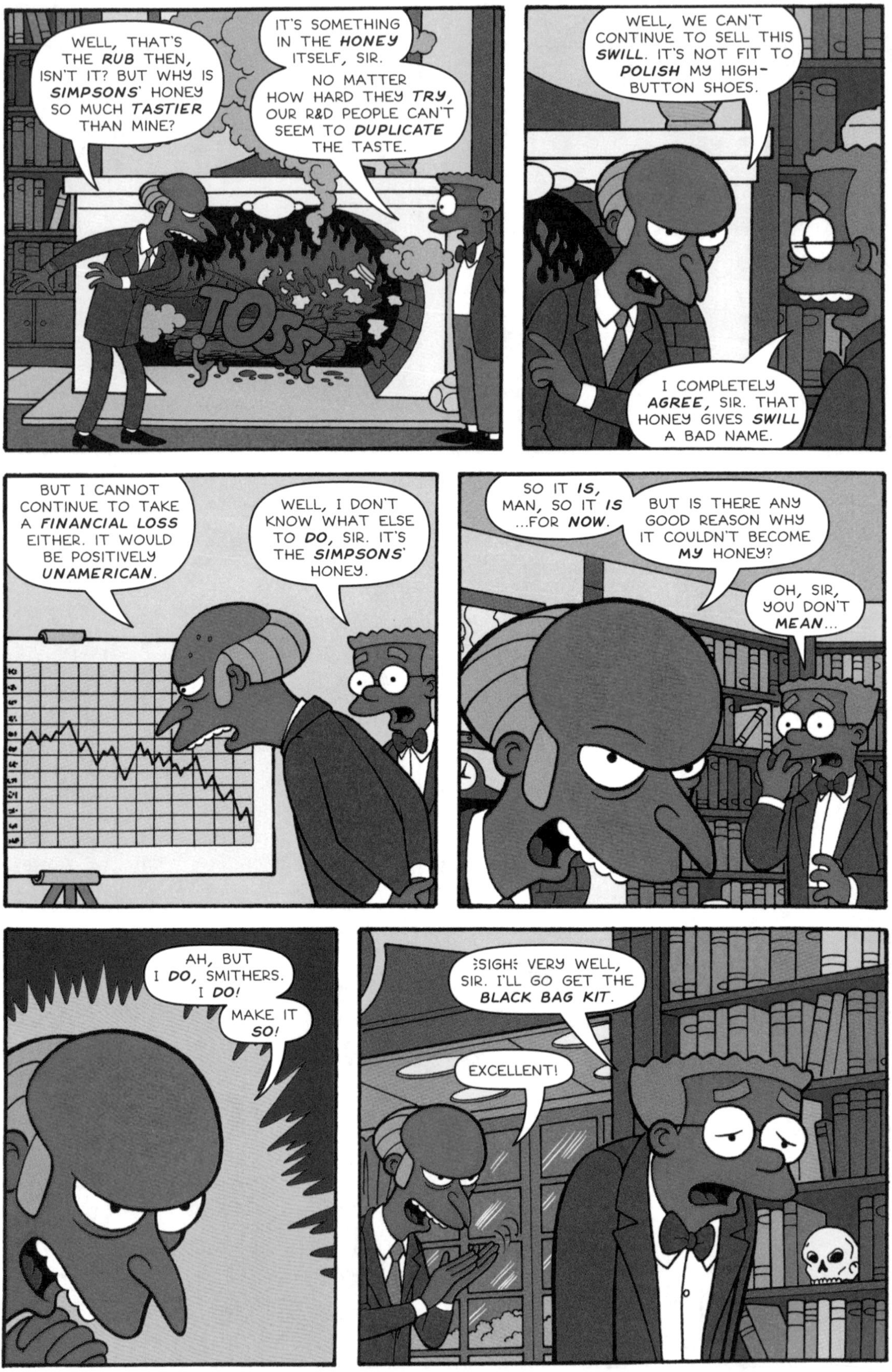
WELL, THAT'S THE RUB THEN, ISN'T IT? BUT WHY IS SIMPSONS' HONEY SO MUCH TASTIER THAN MINE?
IT'S SOMETHING IN THE HONEY ITSELF, SIR.
NO MATTER HOW HARD THEY TRY, OUR R&D PEOPLE CAN'T SEEM TO DUPLICATE THE TASTE.
TOSS!
WELL, WE CAN'T CONTINUE TO SELL THIS SWILL. IT'S NOT FIT TO POLISH MY HIGH-BUTTON SHOES.
I COMPLETELY AGREE, SIR. THAT HONEY GIVES SWILL A BAD NAME.
BUT I CANNOT CONTINUE TO TAKE A FINANCIAL LOSS EITHER. IT WOULD BE POSITIVELY UNAMERICAN.
WELL, I DON'T KNOW WHAT ELSE TO DO, SIR. IT'S THE SIMPSONS' HONEY.
SO IT IS, MAN, SO IT IS ...FOR NOW.
BUT IS THERE ANY GOOD REASON WHY IT COULDN'T BECOME MY HONEY?
OH, SIR, YOU DON'T MEAN...
AH, BUT I DO, SMITHERS. I DO!
MAKE IT SO!
:SIGH: VERY WELL, SIR. I'LL GO GET THE BLACK BAG KIT.
EXCELLENT!

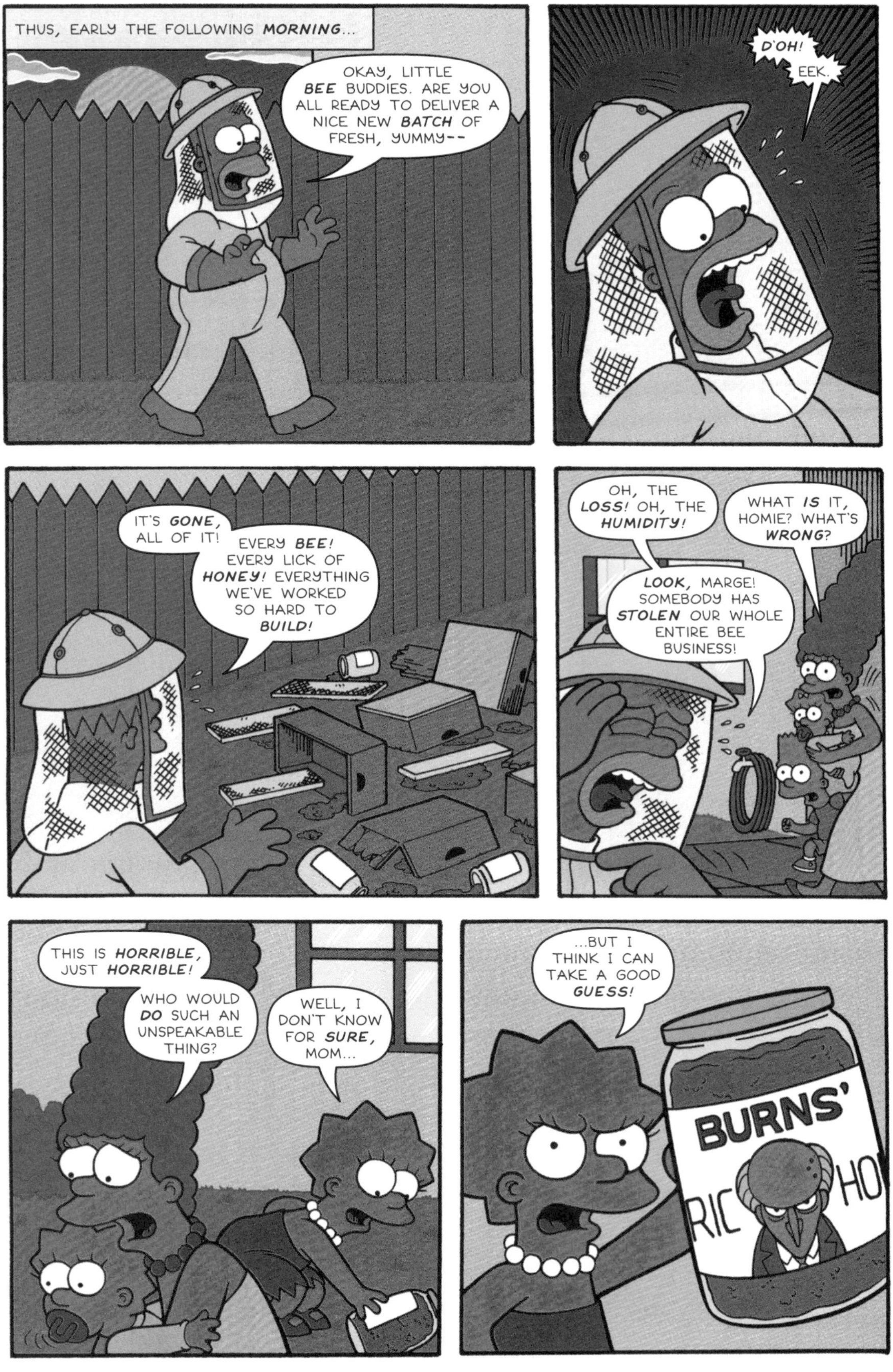
THUS, EARLY THE FOLLOWING MORNING...
OKAY, LITTLE BEE BUDDIES. ARE YOU ALL READY TO DELIVER A NICE NEW BATCH OF FRESH, YUMMY--
D'OH!
EEK.
IT'S GONE, ALL OF IT!
EVERY BEE! EVERY LICK OF HONEY! EVERYTHING WE'VE WORKED SO HARD TO BUILD!
OH, THE LOSS! OH, THE HUMIDITY!
WHAT IS IT, HOMIE? WHAT'S WRONG?
LOOK, MARGE! SOMEBODY HAS STOLEN OUR WHOLE ENTIRE BEE BUSINESS!
THIS IS HORRIBLE, JUST HORRIBLE!
WHO WOULD DO SUCH AN UNSPEAKABLE THING?
WELL, I DON'T KNOW FOR SURE, MOM...
...BUT I THINK I CAN TAKE A GOOD GUESS!
BURNS'

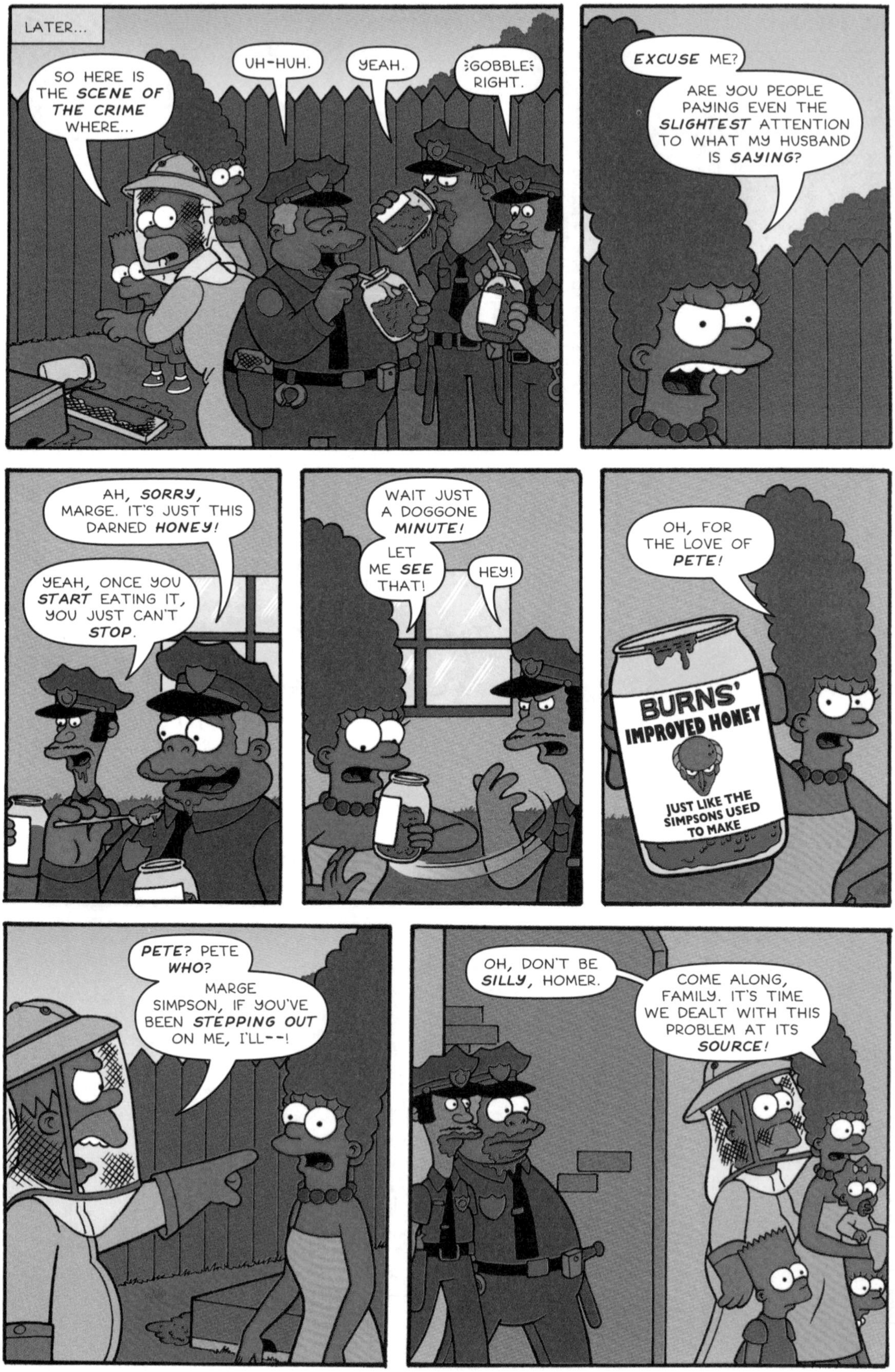
LATER...
SO HERE IS THE SCENE OF THE CRIME WHERE...
UH-HUH.
YEAH.
GOBBLE RIGHT.
EXCUSE ME?
ARE YOU PEOPLE PAYING EVEN THE SLIGHTEST ATTENTION TO WHAT MY HUSBAND IS SAYING?
AH, SORRY, MARGE. IT'S JUST THIS DARNED HONEY!
YEAH, ONCE YOU START EATING IT, YOU JUST CAN'T STOP.
WAIT JUST A DOGGONE MINUTE!
LET ME SEE THAT!
HEY!
OH, FOR THE LOVE OF PETE!
BURNS' IMPROVED HONEY
JUST LIKE THE SIMPSONS USED TO MAKE
PETE? PETE WHO?
MARGE SIMPSON, IF YOU'VE BEEN STEPPING OUT ON ME, I'LL--!
OH, DON'T BE SILLY, HOMER.
COME ALONG, FAMILY. IT'S TIME WE DEALT WITH THIS PROBLEM AT ITS SOURCE!

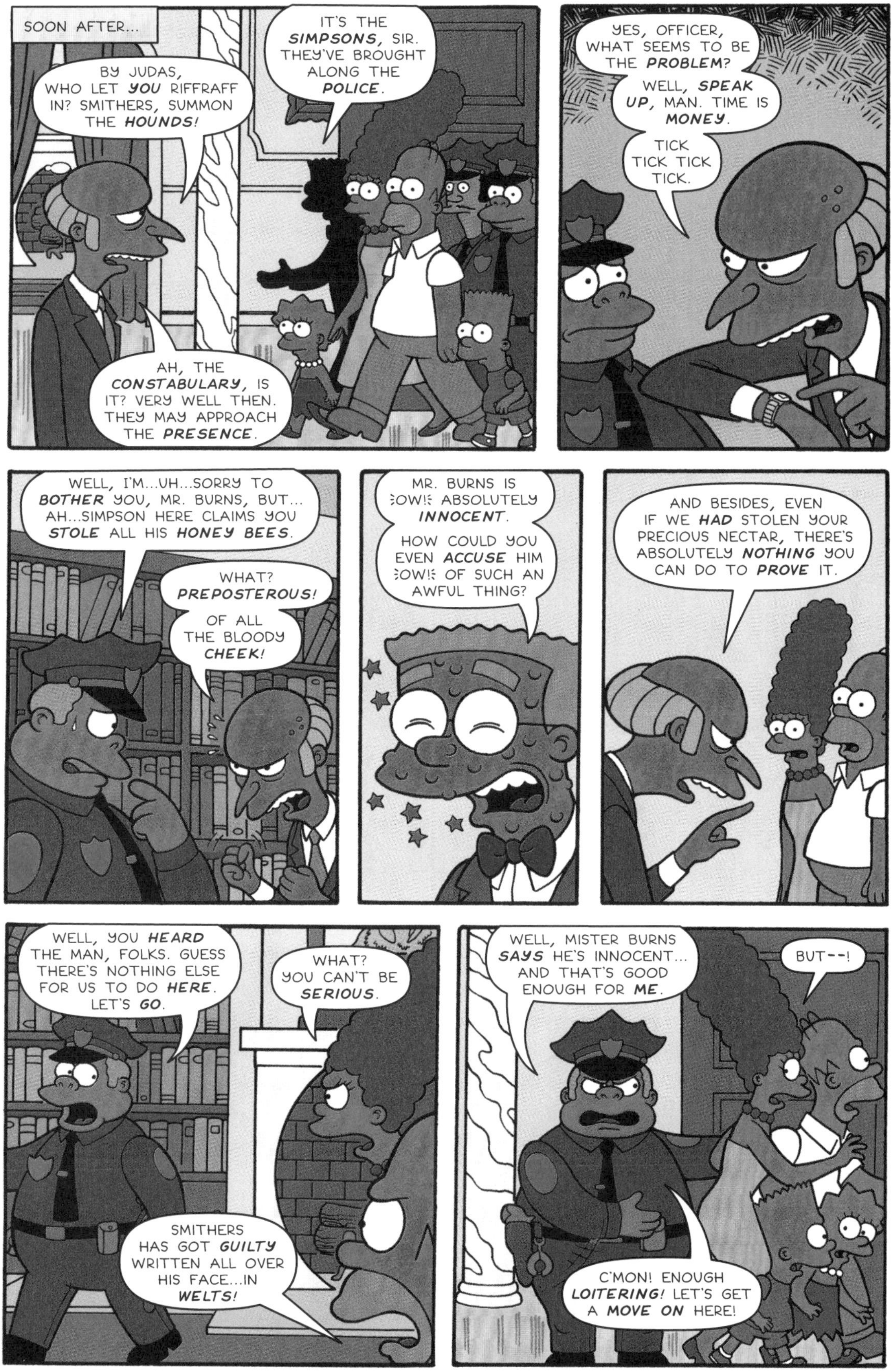
SOON AFTER...
BY JUDAS, WHO LET YOU RIFFRAFF IN? SMITHERS, SUMMON THE HOUNDS!
IT'S THE SIMPSONS, SIR. THEY'VE BROUGHT ALONG THE POLICE.
AH, THE CONSTABULARY, IS IT? VERY WELL THEN. THEY MAY APPROACH THE PRESENCE.
YES, OFFICER, WHAT SEEMS TO BE THE PROBLEM?
WELL, SPEAK UP, MAN. TIME IS MONEY.
TICK TICK TICK TICK.
WELL, I'M...UH...SORRY TO BOTHER YOU, MR. BURNS, BUT... AH...SIMPSON HERE CLAIMS YOU STOLE ALL HIS HONEY BEES.
WHAT? PREPOSTEROUS!
OF ALL THE BLOODY CHEEK!
MR. BURNS IS OW! ABSOLUTELY INNOCENT.
HOW COULD YOU EVEN ACCUSE HIM OW! OF SUCH AN AWFUL THING?
AND BESIDES, EVEN IF WE HAD STOLEN YOUR PRECIOUS NECTAR, THERE'S ABSOLUTELY NOTHING YOU CAN DO TO PROVE IT.
WELL, YOU HEARD THE MAN, FOLKS. GUESS THERE'S NOTHING ELSE FOR US TO DO HERE. LET'S GO.
WHAT? YOU CAN'T BE SERIOUS.
SMITHERS HAS GOT GUILTY WRITTEN ALL OVER HIS FACE...IN WELTS!
WELL, MISTER BURNS SAYS HE'S INNOCENT... AND THAT'S GOOD ENOUGH FOR ME.
BUT--!
C'MON! ENOUGH LOITERING! LET'S GET A MOVE ON HERE!

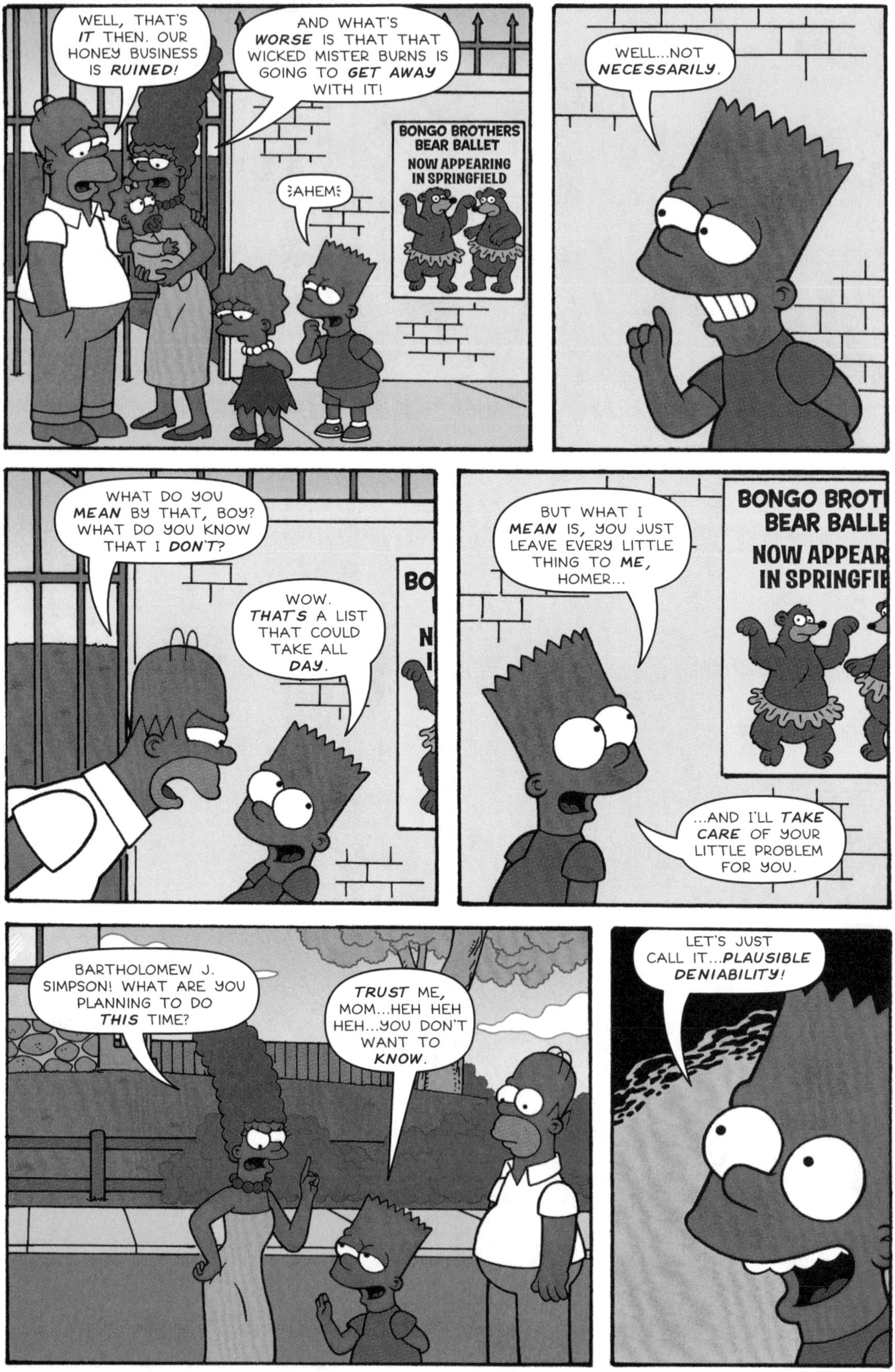

WELL, THAT'S IT THEN. OUR HONEY BUSINESS IS RUINED!
AND WHAT'S WORSE IS THAT THAT WICKED MISTER BURNS IS GOING TO GET AWAY WITH IT!
BONGO BROTHERS BEAR BALLET
NOW APPEARING IN SPRINGFIELD
AHEM
WELL...NOT NECESSARILY.
WHAT DO YOU MEAN BY THAT, BOY? WHAT DO YOU KNOW THAT I DON'T?
WOW. THAT'S A LIST THAT COULD TAKE ALL DAY.
BUT WHAT I MEAN IS, YOU JUST LEAVE EVERY LITTLE THING TO ME, HOMER...
...AND I'LL TAKE CARE OF YOUR LITTLE PROBLEM FOR YOU.
BARTHOLOMEW J. SIMPSON! WHAT ARE YOU PLANNING TO DO THIS TIME?
TRUST ME, MOM...HEH HEH HEH...YOU DON'T WANT TO KNOW.
LET'S JUST CALL IT...PLAUSIBLE DENIABILITY!

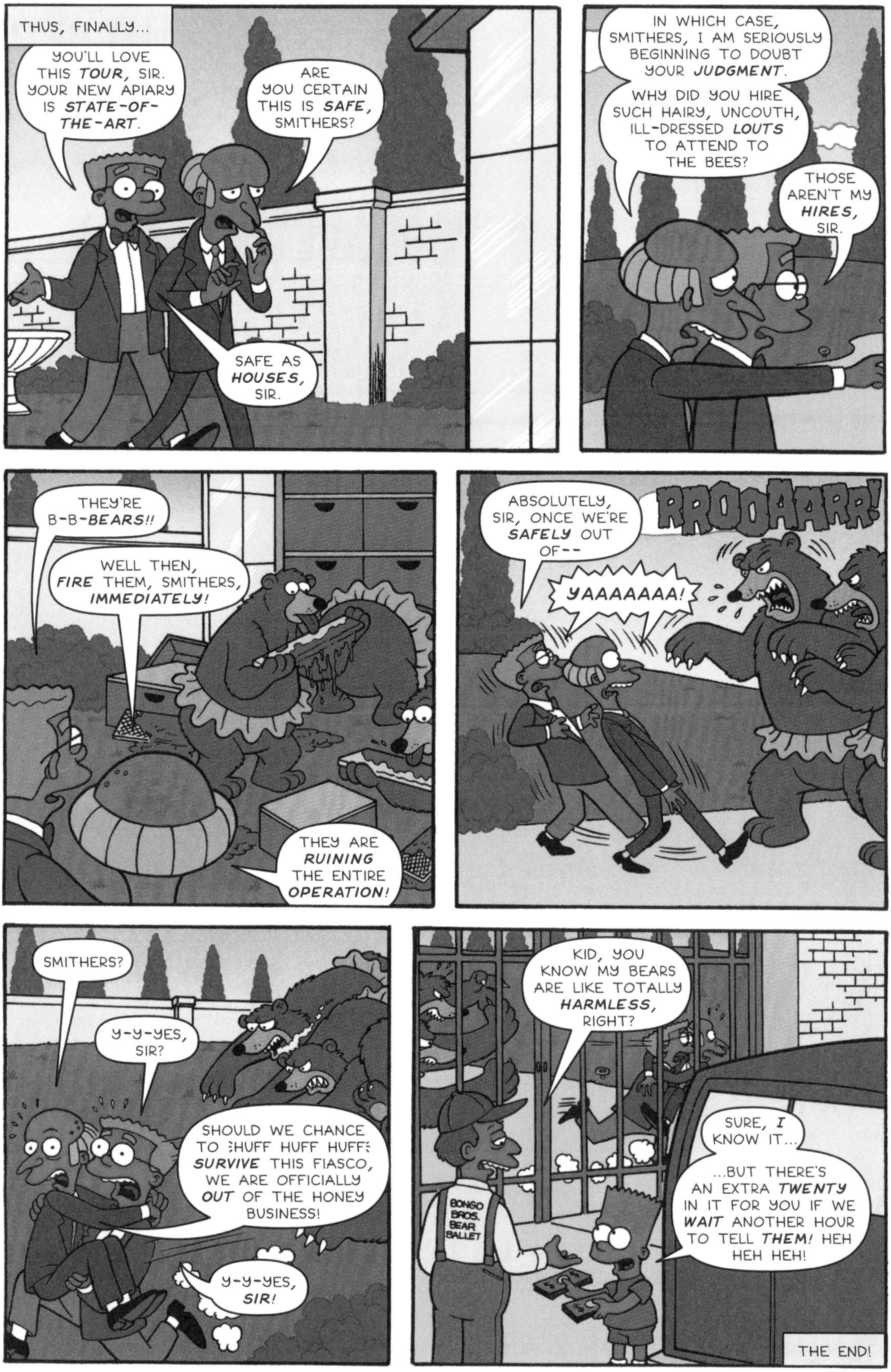
THUS, FINALLY...
YOU'LL LOVE THIS *TOUR,* SIR. YOUR NEW APIARY IS *STATE-OF-THE-ART*.
ARE YOU CERTAIN THIS IS *SAFE,* SMITHERS?
SAFE AS *HOUSES,* SIR.
IN WHICH CASE, SMITHERS, I AM SERIOUSLY BEGINNING TO DOUBT YOUR *JUDGMENT*.
WHY DID YOU HIRE SUCH HAIRY, UNCOUTH, ILL-DRESSED *LOUTS* TO ATTEND TO THE BEES?
THOSE AREN'T MY *HIRES,* SIR.
THEY'RE B-B-*BEARS!!*
WELL THEN, *FIRE* THEM, SMITHERS, *IMMEDIATELY!*
THEY ARE *RUINING* THE ENTIRE *OPERATION!*
ABSOLUTELY, SIR, ONCE WE'RE *SAFELY* OUT OF--
RROOAARR!
YAAAAAAA!
SMITHERS?
Y-Y-YES, SIR?
SHOULD WE CHANCE TO :HUFF HUFF HUFF: *SURVIVE* THIS FIASCO, WE ARE OFFICIALLY *OUT* OF THE HONEY BUSINESS!
Y-Y-YES, *SIR!*
KID, YOU KNOW MY BEARS ARE LIKE TOTALLY *HARMLESS,* RIGHT?
BONGO BROS. BEAR BALLET
SURE, *I* KNOW IT...
...BUT THERE'S AN EXTRA *TWENTY* IN IT FOR YOU IF WE *WAIT* ANOTHER HOUR TO TELL *THEM!* HEH HEH HEH!
THE END!

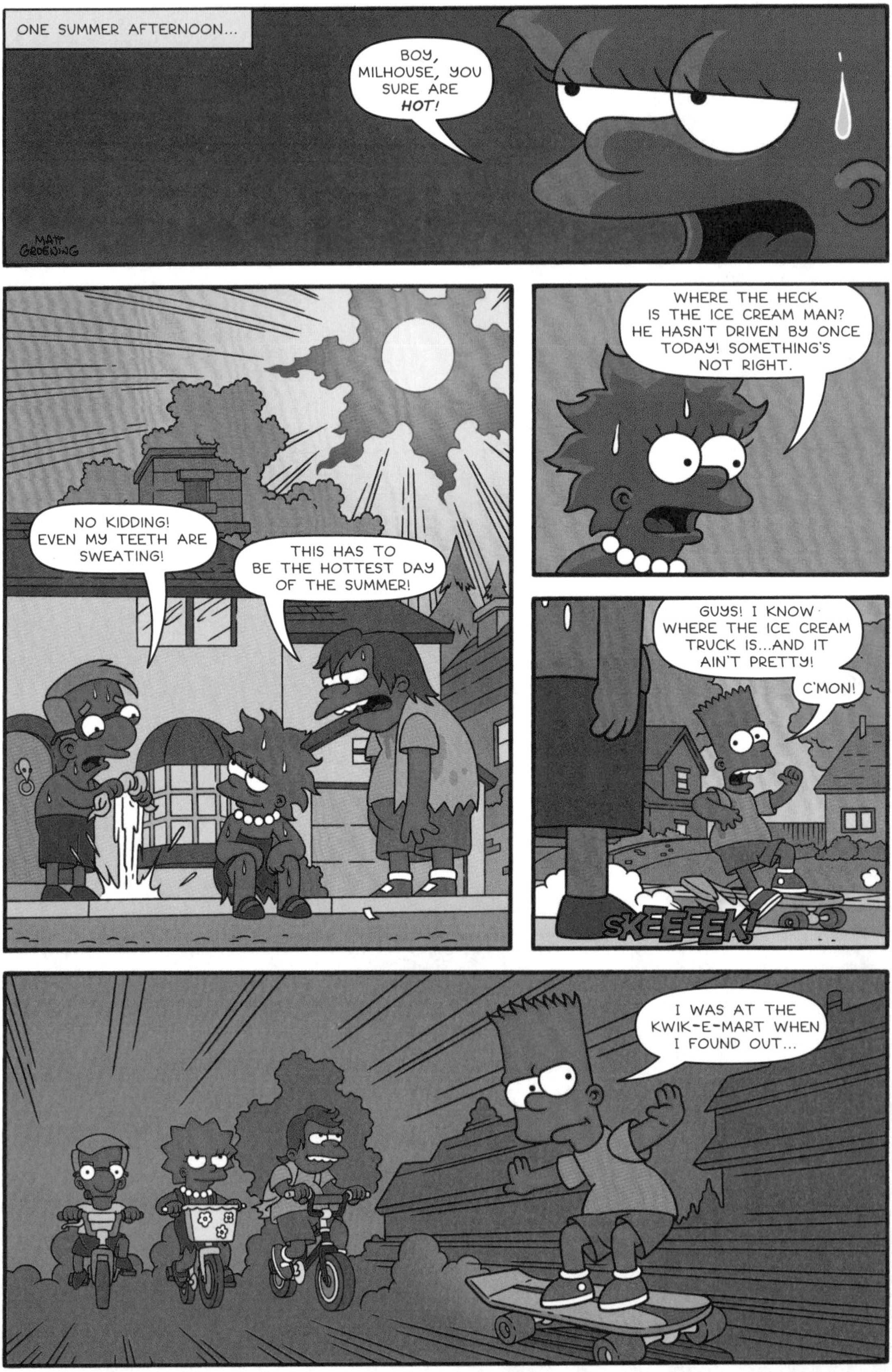
ONE SUMMER AFTERNOON...
BOY, MILHOUSE, YOU SURE ARE *HOT*!
MATT GROENING
NO KIDDING! EVEN MY TEETH ARE SWEATING!
THIS HAS TO BE THE HOTTEST DAY OF THE SUMMER!
WHERE THE HECK IS THE ICE CREAM MAN? HE HASN'T DRIVEN BY ONCE TODAY! SOMETHING'S NOT RIGHT.
GUYS! I KNOW WHERE THE ICE CREAM TRUCK IS...AND IT AIN'T PRETTY!
C'MON!
SKEEEEK!
I WAS AT THE KWIK-E-MART WHEN I FOUND OUT...

ERIC ROGERS SCRIPT | ***JAMES LLOYD*** PENCILS | ***MIKE ROTE*** INKS | ***RICK REESE*** COLORS | ***KAREN BATES*** LETTERS | ***BILL MORRISON*** EDITOR

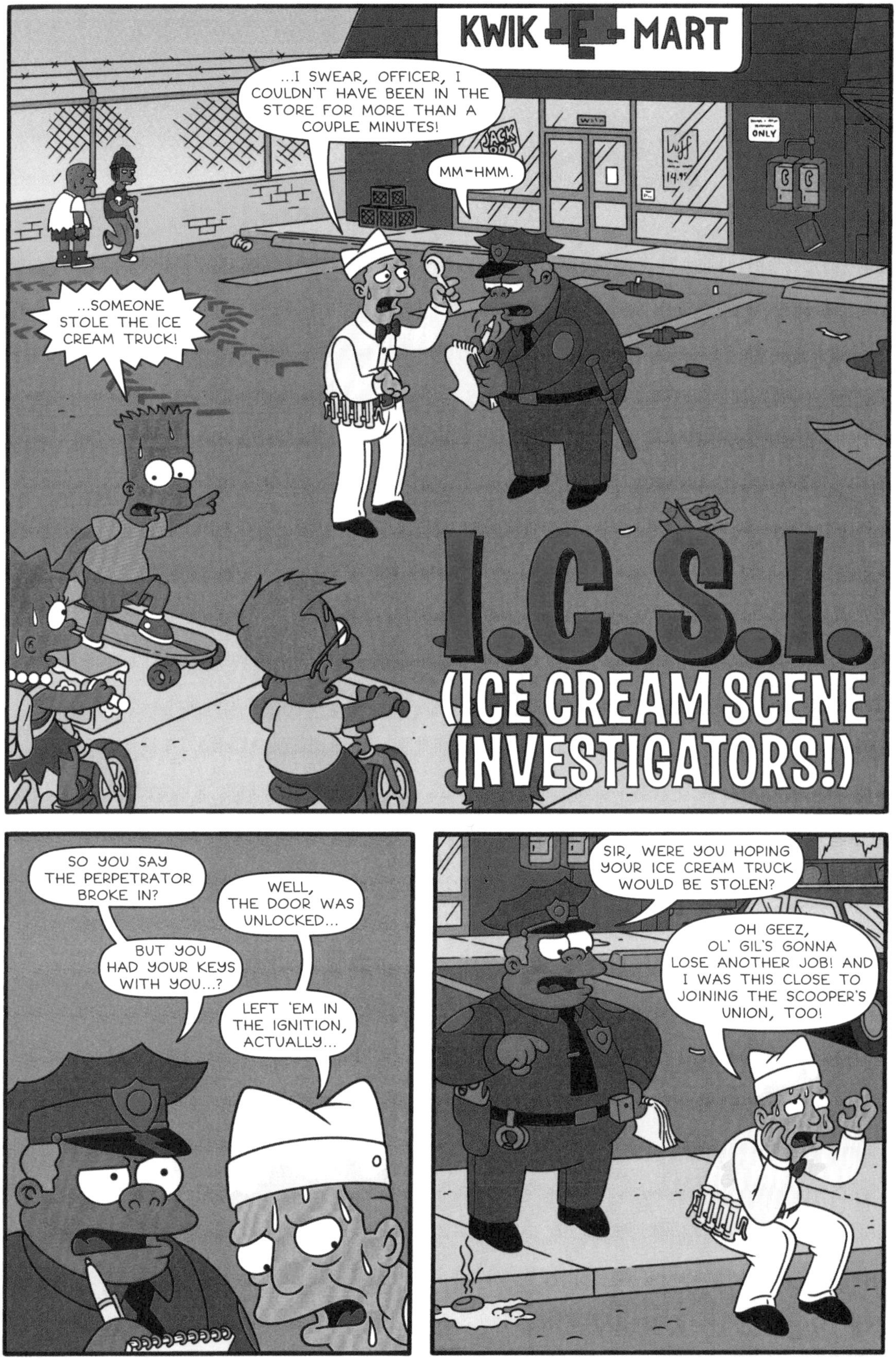
KWIK-E-MART
...I SWEAR, OFFICER, I COULDN'T HAVE BEEN IN THE STORE FOR MORE THAN A COUPLE MINUTES!
MM-HMM.
...SOMEONE STOLE THE ICE CREAM TRUCK!
I.C.S.I.
(ICE CREAM SCENE INVESTIGATORS!)
SO YOU SAY THE PERPETRATOR BROKE IN?
WELL, THE DOOR WAS UNLOCKED...
BUT YOU HAD YOUR KEYS WITH YOU...?
LEFT 'EM IN THE IGNITION, ACTUALLY...
SIR, WERE YOU HOPING YOUR ICE CREAM TRUCK WOULD BE STOLEN?
OH GEEZ, OL' GIL'S GONNA LOSE ANOTHER JOB! AND I WAS THIS CLOSE TO JOINING THE SCOOPER'S UNION, TOO!

ERIC ROGERS SCRIPT · *JAMES LLOYD* PENCILS · *MIKE ROTE* INKS · *RICK REESE* COLORS · *KAREN BATES* LETTERS · *BILL MORRISON* EDITOR

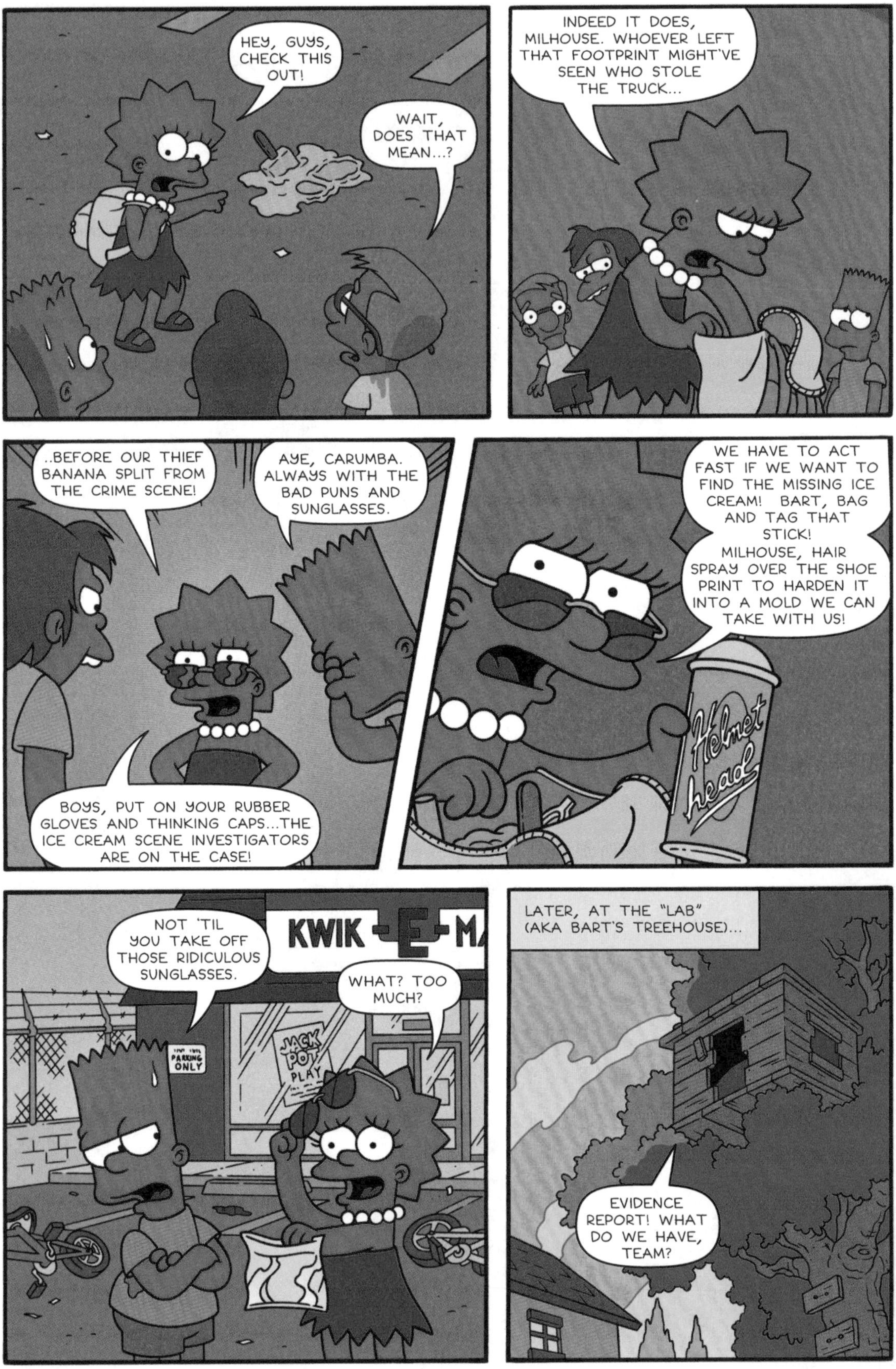
HEY, GUYS, CHECK THIS OUT!
WAIT, DOES THAT MEAN...?
INDEED IT DOES, MILHOUSE. WHOEVER LEFT THAT FOOTPRINT MIGHT'VE SEEN WHO STOLE THE TRUCK...
..BEFORE OUR THIEF BANANA SPLIT FROM THE CRIME SCENE!
AYE, CARUMBA. ALWAYS WITH THE BAD PUNS AND SUNGLASSES.
BOYS, PUT ON YOUR RUBBER GLOVES AND THINKING CAPS...THE ICE CREAM SCENE INVESTIGATORS ARE ON THE CASE!
WE HAVE TO ACT FAST IF WE WANT TO FIND THE MISSING ICE CREAM! BART, BAG AND TAG THAT STICK!
MILHOUSE, HAIR SPRAY OVER THE SHOE PRINT TO HARDEN IT INTO A MOLD WE CAN TAKE WITH US!
Helmet head
NOT 'TIL YOU TAKE OFF THOSE RIDICULOUS SUNGLASSES.
KWIK-E-MA
WHAT? TOO MUCH?
PARKING ONLY
JACK POT PLAY
LATER, AT THE "LAB" (AKA BART'S TREEHOUSE)...
EVIDENCE REPORT! WHAT DO WE HAVE, TEAM?

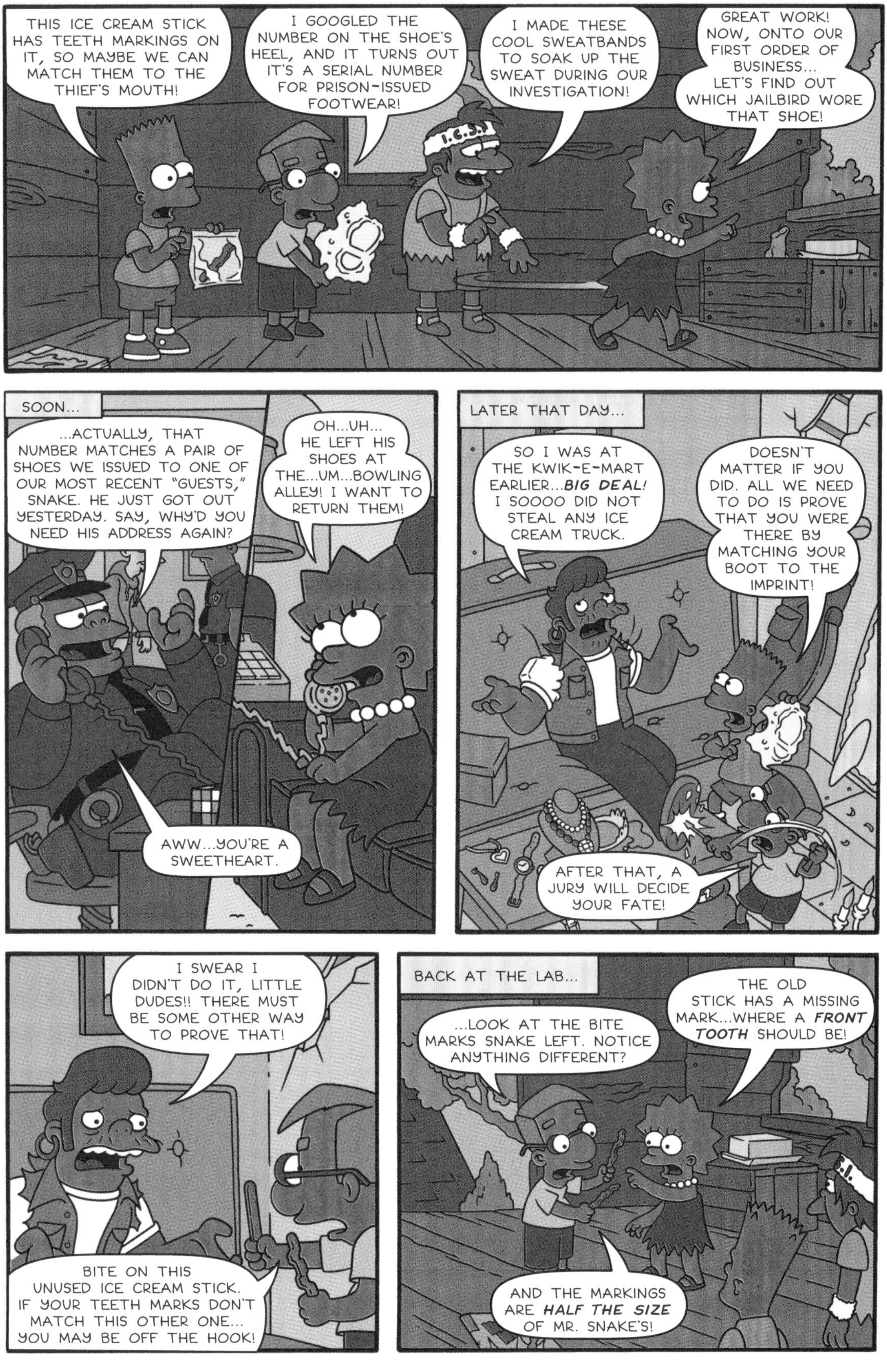
THIS ICE CREAM STICK HAS TEETH MARKINGS ON IT, SO MAYBE WE CAN MATCH THEM TO THE THIEF'S MOUTH!
I GOOGLED THE NUMBER ON THE SHOE'S HEEL, AND IT TURNS OUT IT'S A SERIAL NUMBER FOR PRISON-ISSUED FOOTWEAR!
I MADE THESE COOL SWEATBANDS TO SOAK UP THE SWEAT DURING OUR INVESTIGATION!
GREAT WORK! NOW, ONTO OUR FIRST ORDER OF BUSINESS... LET'S FIND OUT WHICH JAILBIRD WORE THAT SHOE!
SOON...
...ACTUALLY, THAT NUMBER MATCHES A PAIR OF SHOES WE ISSUED TO ONE OF OUR MOST RECENT "GUESTS," SNAKE. HE JUST GOT OUT YESTERDAY. SAY, WHY'D YOU NEED HIS ADDRESS AGAIN?
OH...UH... HE LEFT HIS SHOES AT THE...UM...BOWLING ALLEY! I WANT TO RETURN THEM!
AWW...YOU'RE A SWEETHEART.
LATER THAT DAY...
SO I WAS AT THE KWIK-E-MART EARLIER...**BIG DEAL!** I SOOOO DID NOT STEAL ANY ICE CREAM TRUCK.
DOESN'T MATTER IF YOU DID. ALL WE NEED TO DO IS PROVE THAT YOU WERE THERE BY MATCHING YOUR BOOT TO THE IMPRINT!
AFTER THAT, A JURY WILL DECIDE YOUR FATE!
I SWEAR I DIDN'T DO IT, LITTLE DUDES!! THERE MUST BE SOME OTHER WAY TO PROVE THAT!
BITE ON THIS UNUSED ICE CREAM STICK. IF YOUR TEETH MARKS DON'T MATCH THIS OTHER ONE... YOU MAY BE OFF THE HOOK!
BACK AT THE LAB...
...LOOK AT THE BITE MARKS SNAKE LEFT. NOTICE ANYTHING DIFFERENT?
THE OLD STICK HAS A MISSING MARK...WHERE A **FRONT TOOTH** SHOULD BE!
AND THE MARKINGS ARE **HALF THE SIZE** OF MR. SNAKE'S!

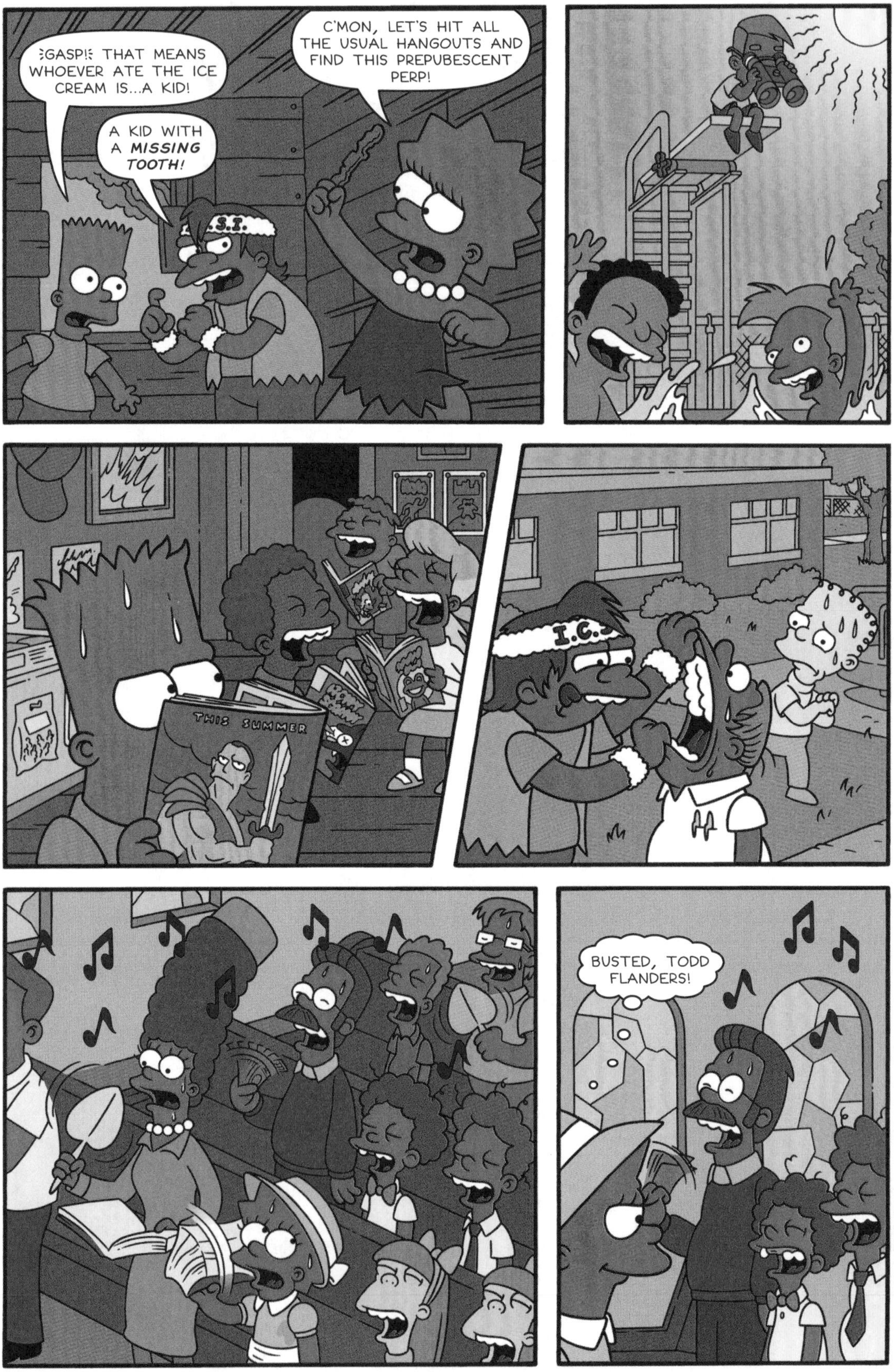

¦GASP!¦ THAT MEANS WHOEVER ATE THE ICE CREAM IS...A KID!
A KID WITH A *MISSING TOOTH!*
C'MON, LET'S HIT ALL THE USUAL HANGOUTS AND FIND THIS PREPUBESCENT PERP!
S.I.
THIS SUMMER
I.C.
BUSTED, TODD FLANDERS!

AFTER CHURCH...

OHH, TODD... I WAS WONDERING IF WE COULD TALK ALONE FOR A MINUTE?

UMM... OKAY.

AGGH! DON'T KISS ME! I'M NOT READY FOR THE BIRDS AND BEES!

ONLY IF YOU TELL ME WHO GAVE YOU THIS ICE CREAM EARLIER TODAY AT THE KWIK-E-MART!

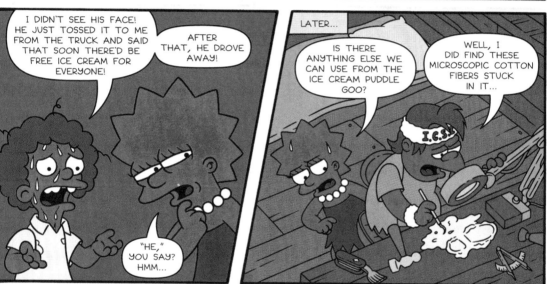

I DIDN'T SEE HIS FACE! HE JUST TOSSED IT TO ME FROM THE TRUCK AND SAID THAT SOON THERE'D BE FREE ICE CREAM FOR EVERYONE!

AFTER THAT, HE DROVE AWAY!

"HE," YOU SAY? HMM...

LATER...

IS THERE ANYTHING ELSE WE CAN USE FROM THE ICE CREAM PUDDLE GOO?

WELL, I DID FIND THESE MICROSCOPIC COTTON FIBERS STUCK IN IT...

THE SAME KIND OF FIBERS USED TO MAKE LAB COATS!

"LAB COATS," YOU SAY? HMM...

SOON...

LAB COATS, CASTLE MOATS & PARADE FLOATS

FORMERLY 'PARTY HATS, COOL TATS & BATHROOM MATS'

...WE SELL HUNDREDS OF LAB COATS A MONTH...

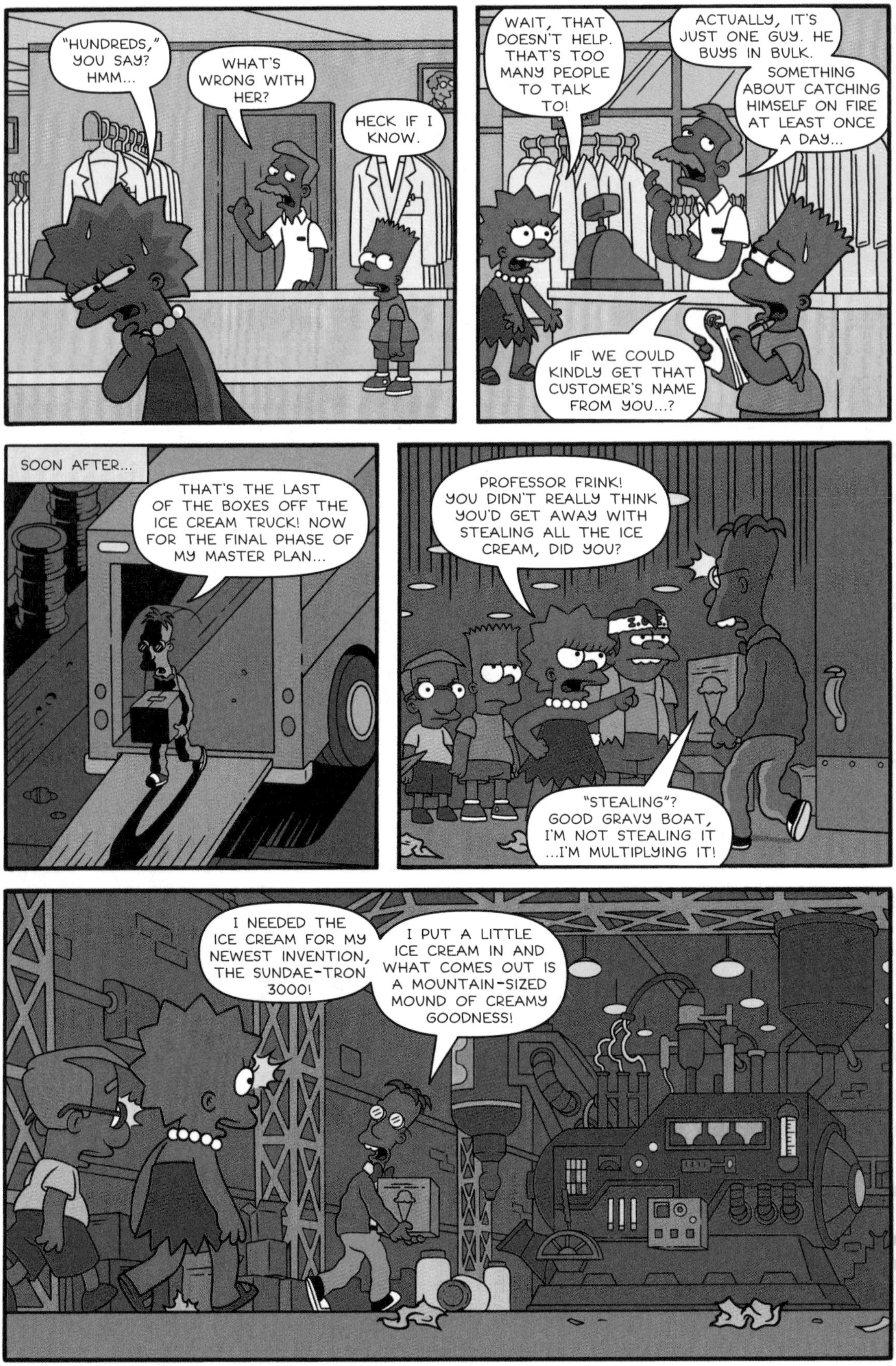
"HUNDREDS," YOU SAY? HMM...
WHAT'S WRONG WITH HER?
HECK IF I KNOW.
WAIT, THAT DOESN'T HELP. THAT'S TOO MANY PEOPLE TO TALK TO!
ACTUALLY, IT'S JUST ONE GUY. HE BUYS IN BULK.
SOMETHING ABOUT CATCHING HIMSELF ON FIRE AT LEAST ONCE A DAY...
IF WE COULD KINDLY GET THAT CUSTOMER'S NAME FROM YOU...?
SOON AFTER...
THAT'S THE LAST OF THE BOXES OFF THE ICE CREAM TRUCK! NOW FOR THE FINAL PHASE OF MY MASTER PLAN...
PROFESSOR FRINK! YOU DIDN'T REALLY THINK YOU'D GET AWAY WITH STEALING ALL THE ICE CREAM, DID YOU?
"STEALING"? GOOD GRAVY BOAT, I'M NOT STEALING IT ...I'M MULTIPLYING IT!
I NEEDED THE ICE CREAM FOR MY NEWEST INVENTION, THE SUNDAE-TRON 3000!
I PUT A LITTLE ICE CREAM IN AND WHAT COMES OUT IS A MOUNTAIN-SIZED MOUND OF CREAMY GOODNESS!

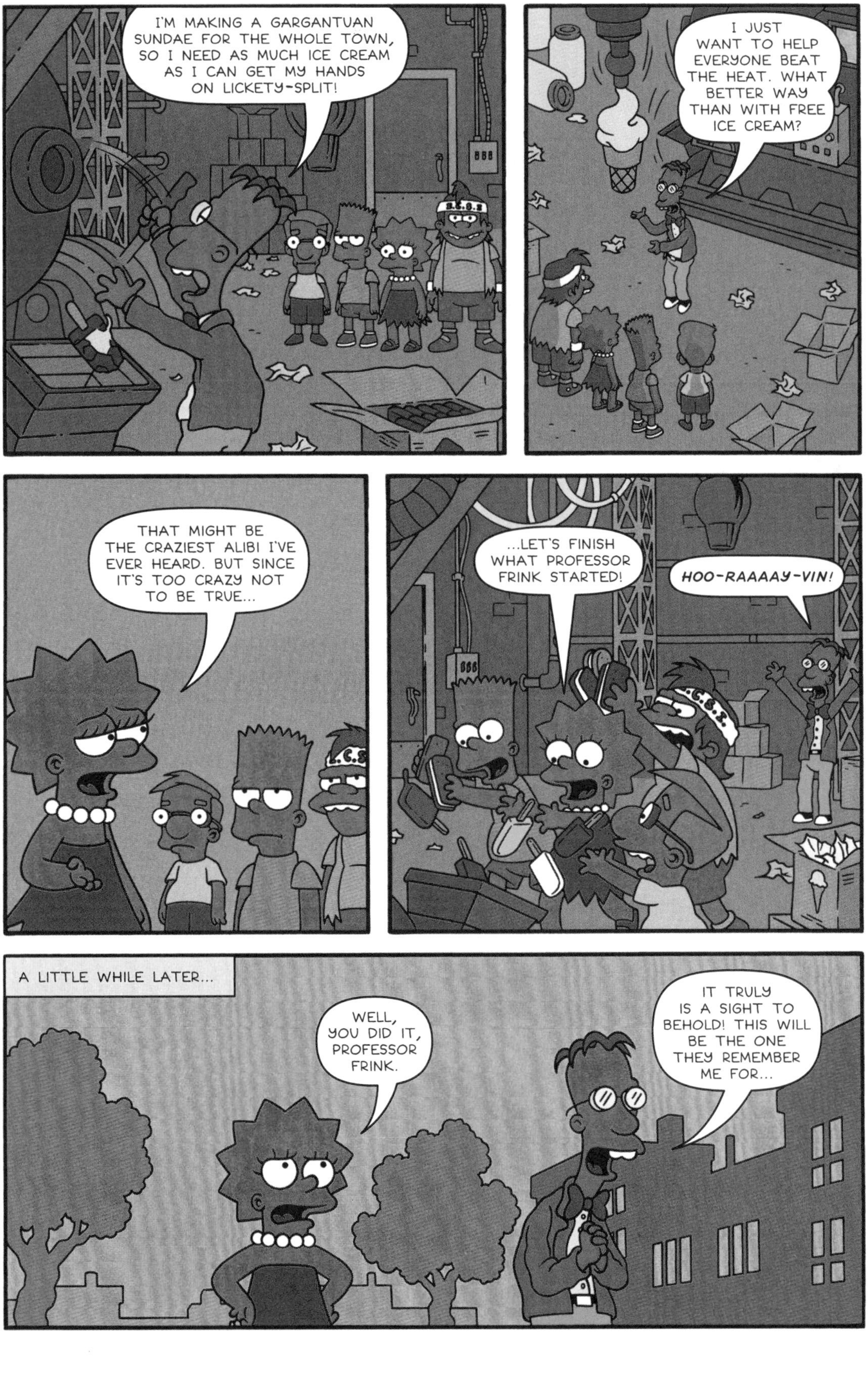
I'M MAKING A GARGANTUAN SUNDAE FOR THE WHOLE TOWN, SO I NEED AS MUCH ICE CREAM AS I CAN GET MY HANDS ON LICKETY-SPLIT!
I JUST WANT TO HELP EVERYONE BEAT THE HEAT. WHAT BETTER WAY THAN WITH FREE ICE CREAM?
THAT MIGHT BE THE CRAZIEST ALIBI I'VE EVER HEARD. BUT SINCE IT'S TOO CRAZY NOT TO BE TRUE...
...LET'S FINISH WHAT PROFESSOR FRINK STARTED!
HOO-RAAAAY-VIN!
A LITTLE WHILE LATER...
WELL, YOU DID IT, PROFESSOR FRINK.
IT TRULY IS A SIGHT TO BEHOLD! THIS WILL BE THE ONE THEY REMEMBER ME FOR...

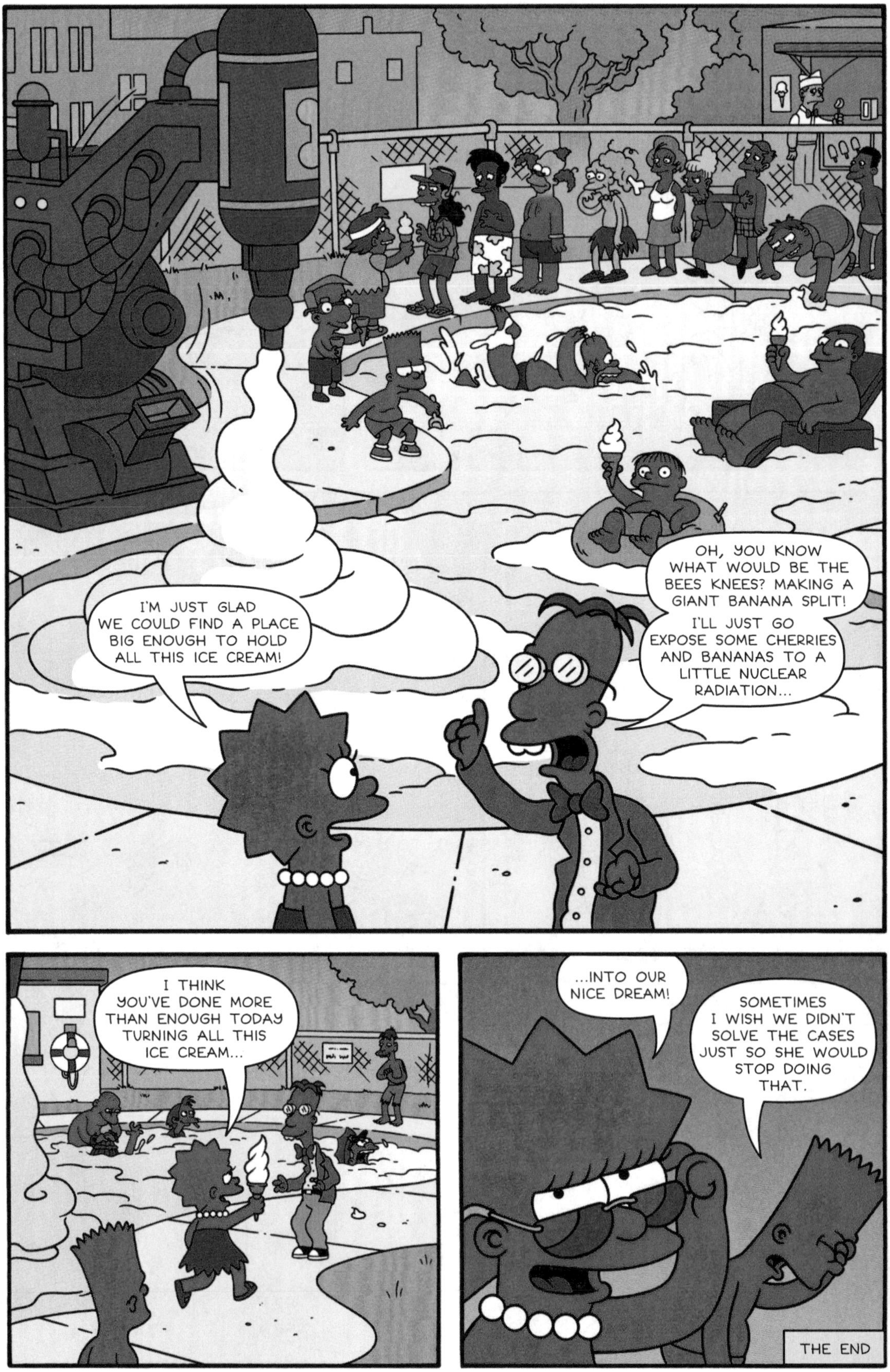
I'M JUST GLAD WE COULD FIND A PLACE BIG ENOUGH TO HOLD ALL THIS ICE CREAM!
OH, YOU KNOW WHAT WOULD BE THE BEES KNEES? MAKING A GIANT BANANA SPLIT!
I'LL JUST GO EXPOSE SOME CHERRIES AND BANANAS TO A LITTLE NUCLEAR RADIATION...
I THINK YOU'VE DONE MORE THAN ENOUGH TODAY TURNING ALL THIS ICE CREAM...
...INTO OUR NICE DREAM!
SOMETIMES I WISH WE DIDN'T SOLVE THE CASES JUST SO SHE WOULD STOP DOING THAT.
THE END

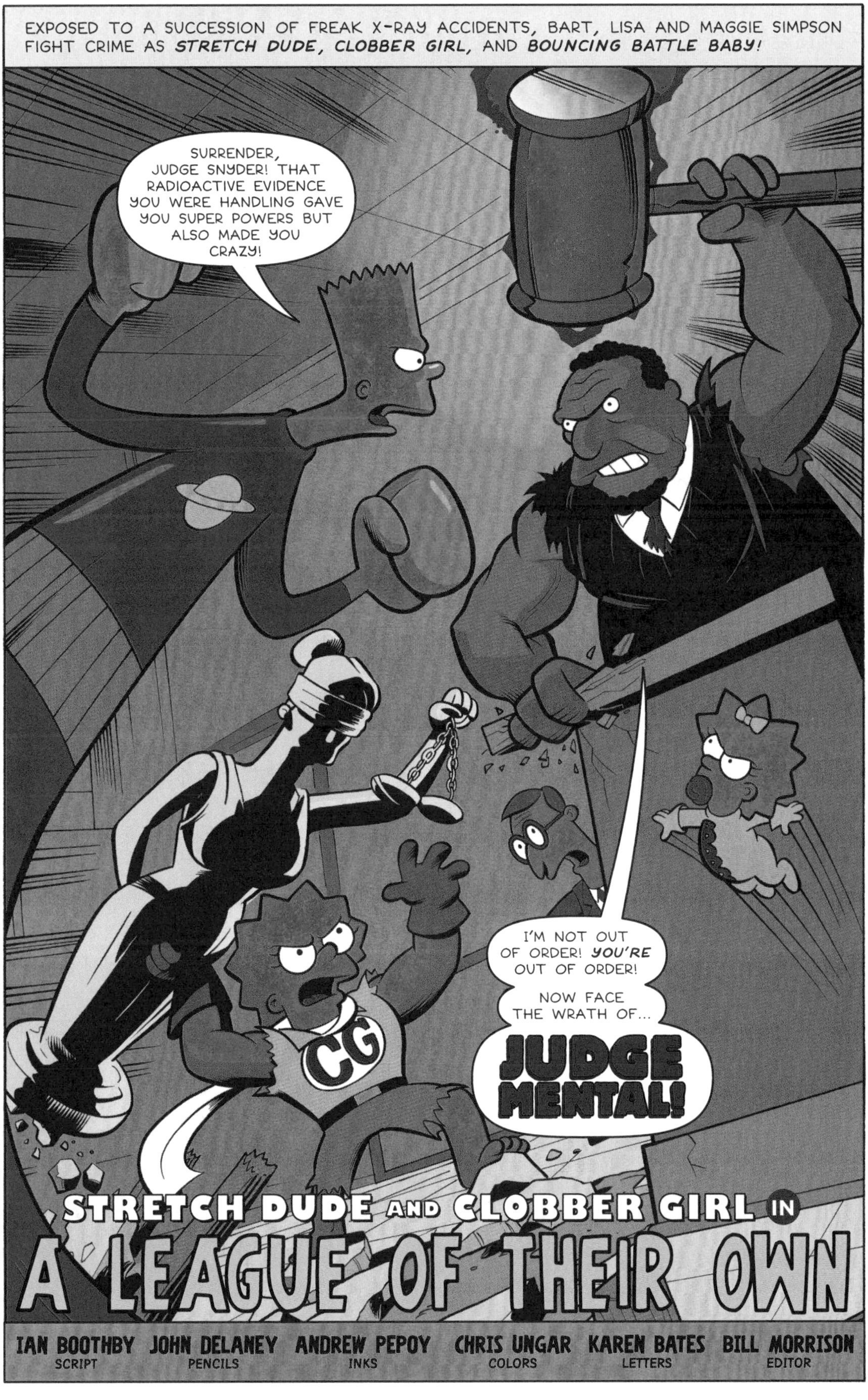

EXPOSED TO A SUCCESSION OF FREAK X-RAY ACCIDENTS, BART, LISA AND MAGGIE SIMPSON FIGHT CRIME AS STRETCH DUDE, CLOBBER GIRL, AND BOUNCING BATTLE BABY!
SURRENDER, JUDGE SNYDER! THAT RADIOACTIVE EVIDENCE YOU WERE HANDLING GAVE YOU SUPER POWERS BUT ALSO MADE YOU CRAZY!
I'M NOT OUT OF ORDER! YOU'RE OUT OF ORDER!
NOW FACE THE WRATH OF...
JUDGE MENTAL!
STRETCH DUDE AND CLOBBER GIRL IN
A LEAGUE OF THEIR OWN
IAN BOOTHBY SCRIPT
JOHN DELANEY PENCILS
ANDREW PEPOY INKS
CHRIS UNGAR COLORS
KAREN BATES LETTERS
BILL MORRISON EDITOR

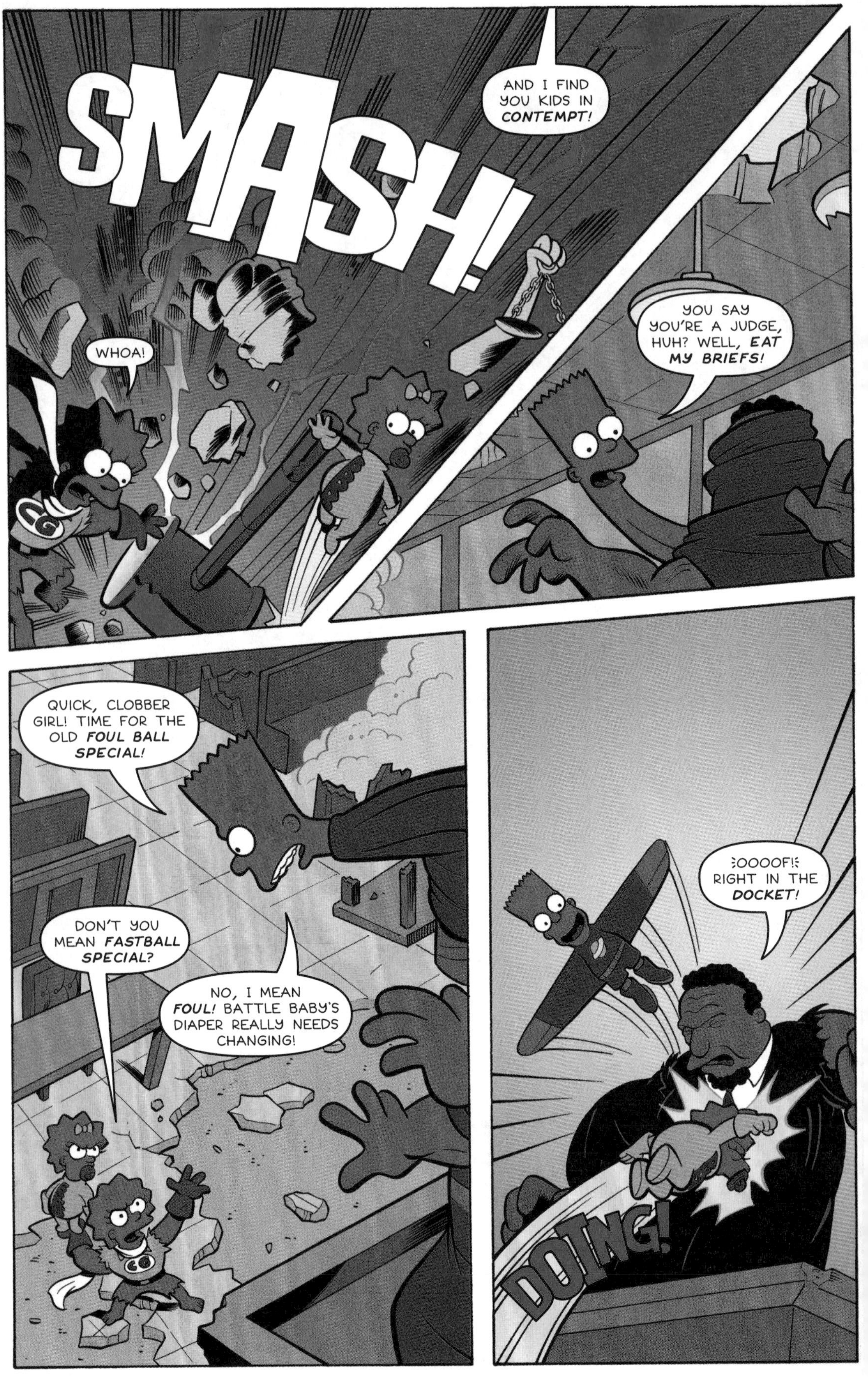
SMASH!
AND I FIND YOU KIDS IN *CONTEMPT*!
WHOA!
YOU SAY YOU'RE A JUDGE, HUH? WELL, **EAT MY BRIEFS!**
QUICK, CLOBBER GIRL! TIME FOR THE OLD **FOUL BALL SPECIAL!**
DON'T YOU MEAN **FASTBALL SPECIAL?**
NO, I MEAN **FOUL!** BATTLE BABY'S DIAPER REALLY NEEDS CHANGING!
OOOOF! RIGHT IN THE *DOCKET*!
DOING!

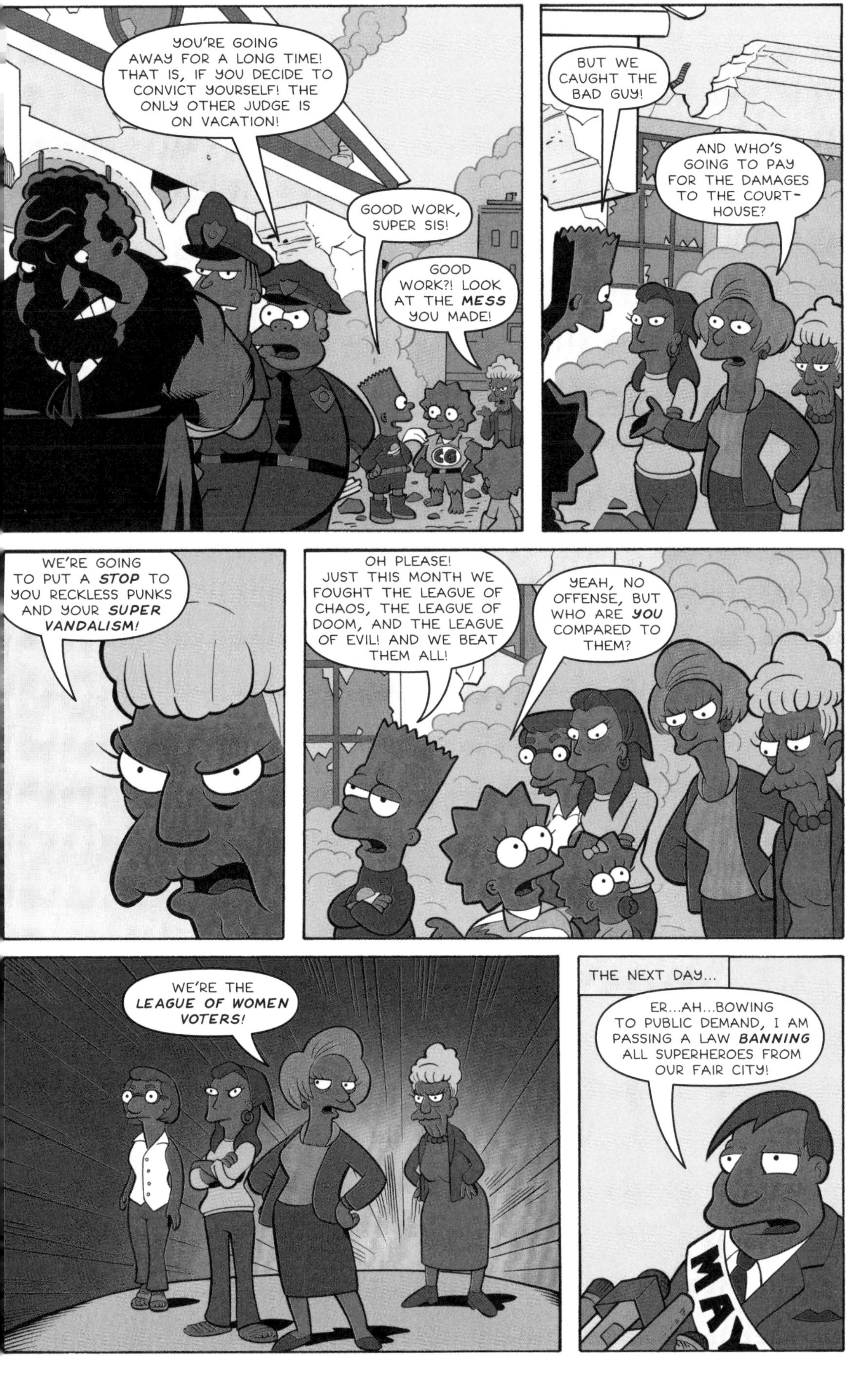
YOU'RE GOING AWAY FOR A LONG TIME! THAT IS, IF YOU DECIDE TO CONVICT YOURSELF! THE ONLY OTHER JUDGE IS ON VACATION!
GOOD WORK, SUPER SIS!
GOOD WORK?! LOOK AT THE MESS YOU MADE!
BUT WE CAUGHT THE BAD GUY!
AND WHO'S GOING TO PAY FOR THE DAMAGES TO THE COURT-HOUSE?
WE'RE GOING TO PUT A STOP TO YOU RECKLESS PUNKS AND YOUR SUPER VANDALISM!
OH PLEASE! JUST THIS MONTH WE FOUGHT THE LEAGUE OF CHAOS, THE LEAGUE OF DOOM, AND THE LEAGUE OF EVIL! AND WE BEAT THEM ALL!
YEAH, NO OFFENSE, BUT WHO ARE YOU COMPARED TO THEM?
WE'RE THE LEAGUE OF WOMEN VOTERS!
THE NEXT DAY...
ER...AH...BOWING TO PUBLIC DEMAND, I AM PASSING A LAW BANNING ALL SUPERHEROES FROM OUR FAIR CITY!

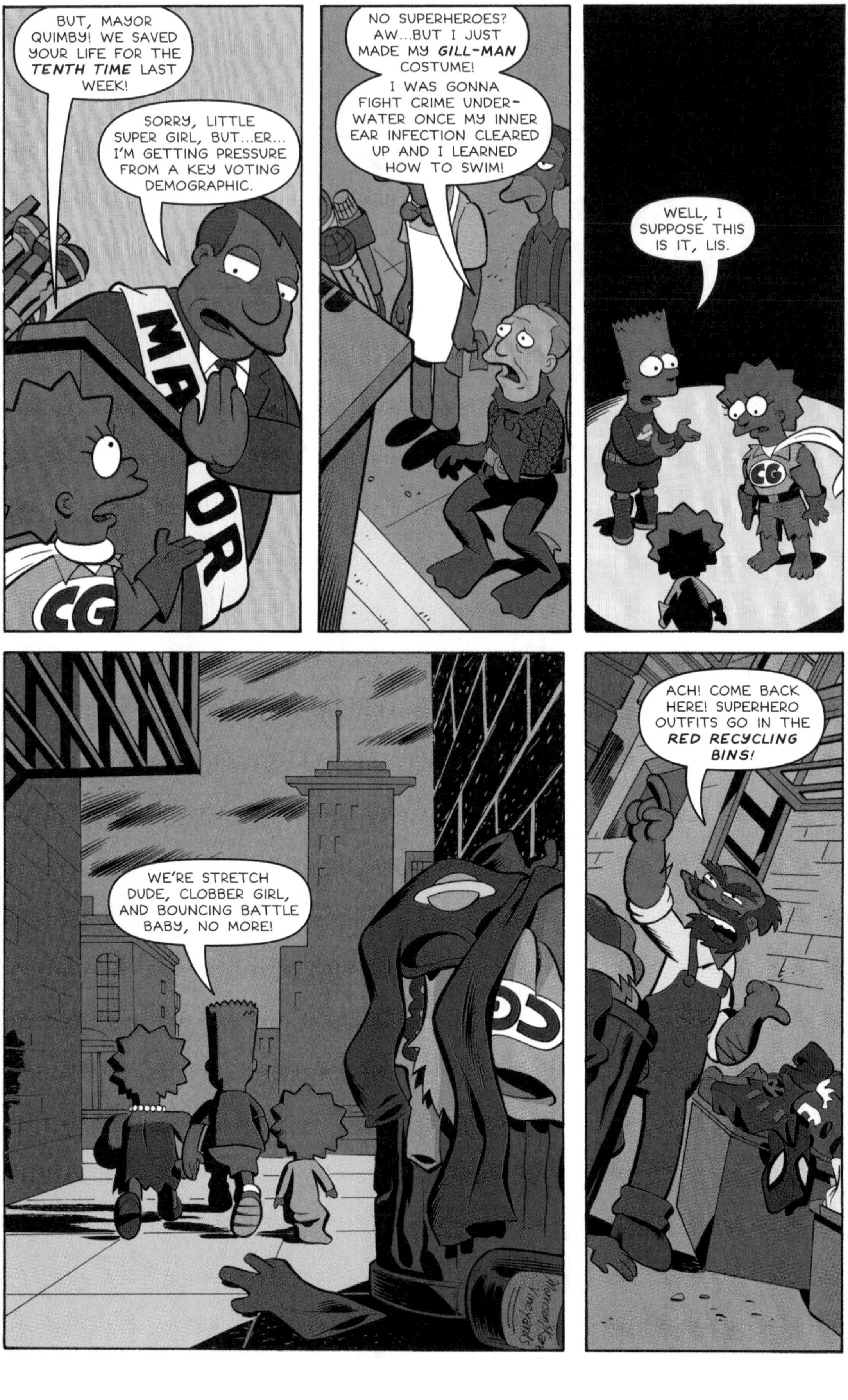
BUT, MAYOR QUIMBY! WE SAVED YOUR LIFE FOR THE *TENTH TIME* LAST WEEK!
SORRY, LITTLE SUPER GIRL, BUT...ER... I'M GETTING PRESSURE FROM A KEY VOTING DEMOGRAPHIC.
MAYOR
NO SUPERHEROES? AW...BUT I JUST MADE MY *GILL-MAN* COSTUME!
I WAS GONNA FIGHT CRIME UNDER-WATER ONCE MY INNER EAR INFECTION CLEARED UP AND I LEARNED HOW TO SWIM!
WELL, I SUPPOSE THIS IS IT, LIS.
CG
WE'RE STRETCH DUDE, CLOBBER GIRL, AND BOUNCING BATTLE BABY, NO MORE!
ACH! COME BACK HERE! SUPERHERO OUTFITS GO IN THE *RED RECYCLING BINS!*

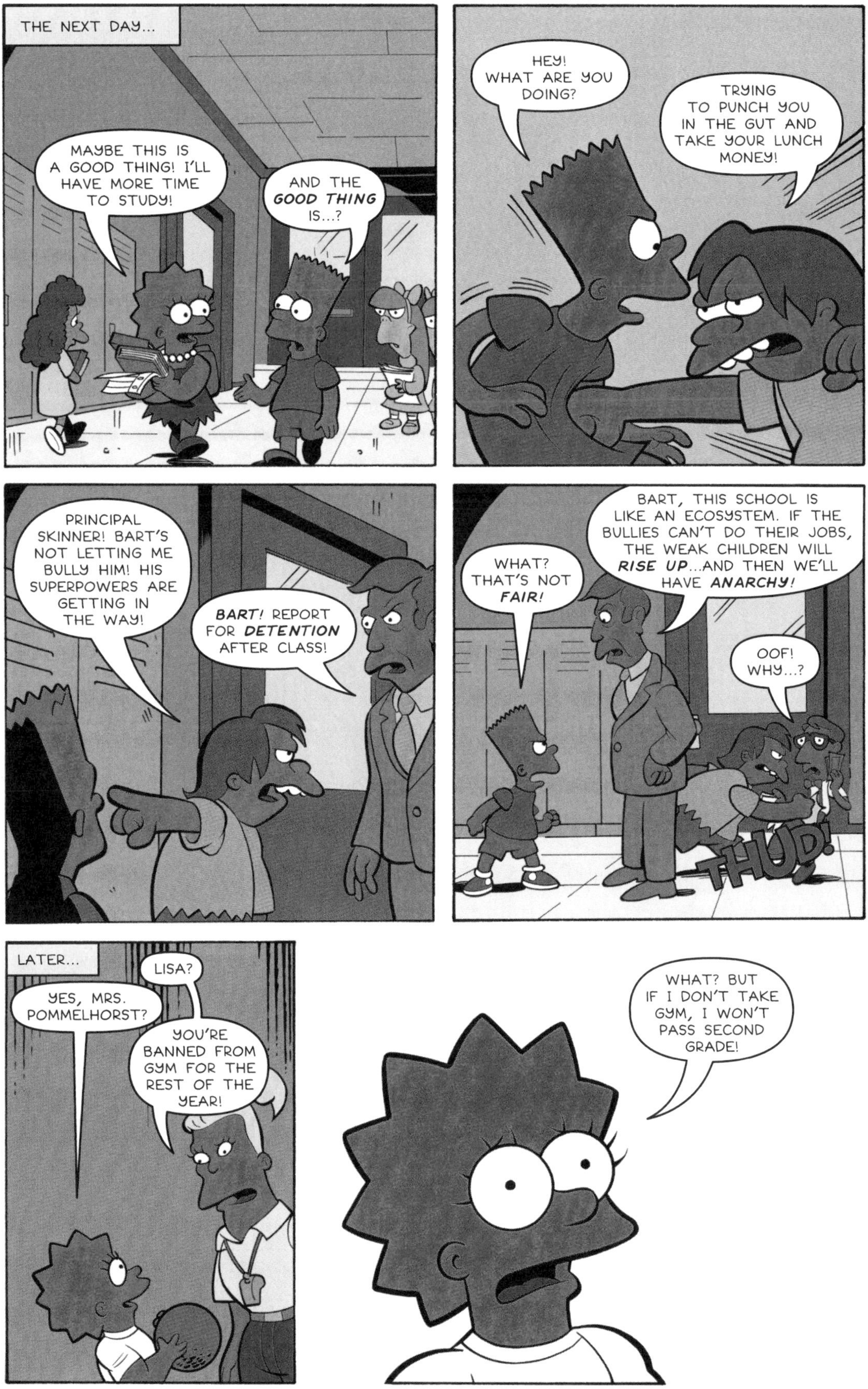
THE NEXT DAY...
MAYBE THIS IS A GOOD THING! I'LL HAVE MORE TIME TO STUDY!
AND THE GOOD THING IS...?
HEY! WHAT ARE YOU DOING?
TRYING TO PUNCH YOU IN THE GUT AND TAKE YOUR LUNCH MONEY!
PRINCIPAL SKINNER! BART'S NOT LETTING ME BULLY HIM! HIS SUPERPOWERS ARE GETTING IN THE WAY!
BART! REPORT FOR DETENTION AFTER CLASS!
WHAT? THAT'S NOT FAIR!
BART, THIS SCHOOL IS LIKE AN ECOSYSTEM. IF THE BULLIES CAN'T DO THEIR JOBS, THE WEAK CHILDREN WILL RISE UP...AND THEN WE'LL HAVE ANARCHY!
OOF! WHY...?
THUD!
LATER...
LISA?
YES, MRS. POMMELHORST?
YOU'RE BANNED FROM GYM FOR THE REST OF THE YEAR!
WHAT? BUT IF I DON'T TAKE GYM, I WON'T PASS SECOND GRADE!

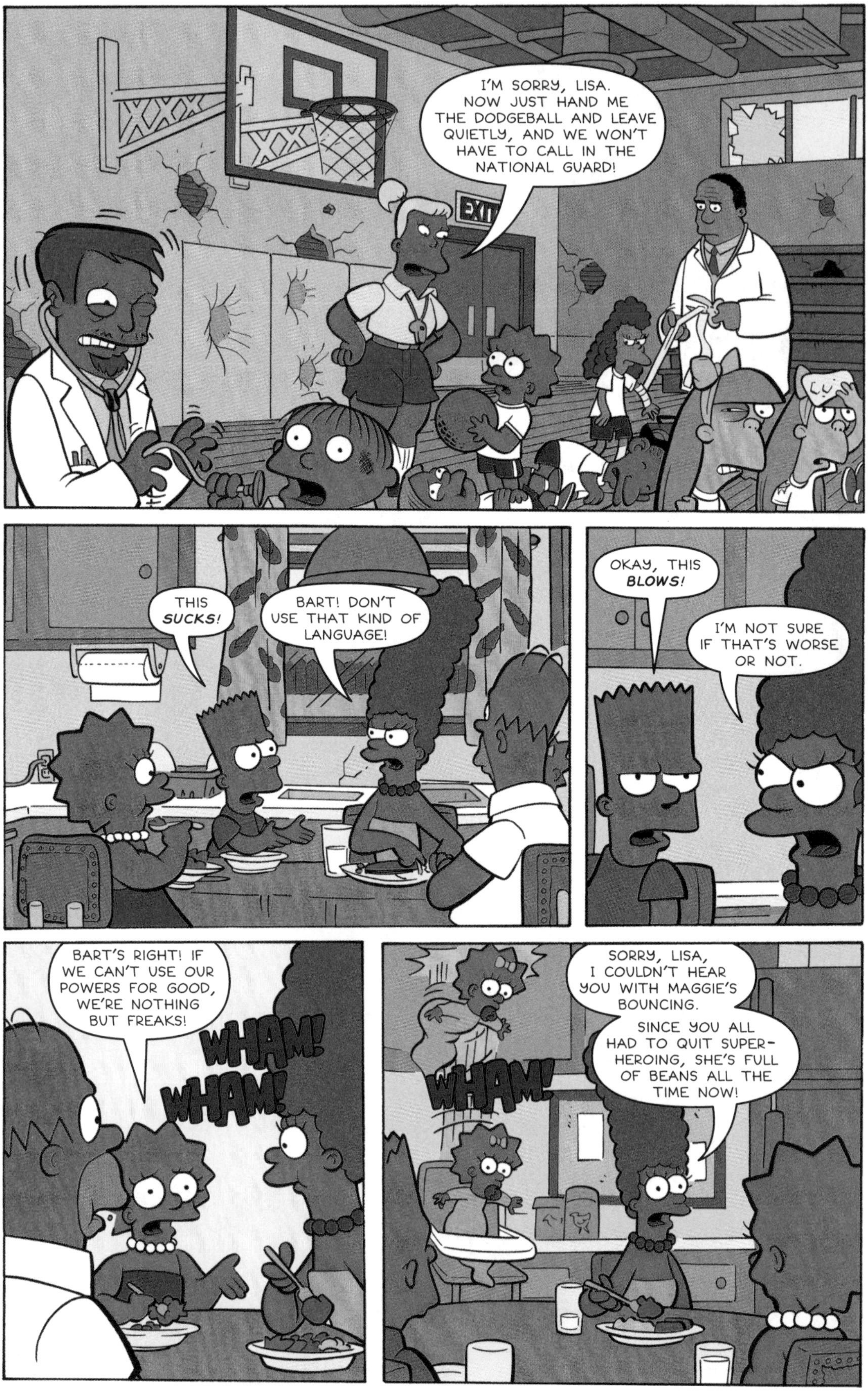

I'M SORRY, LISA. NOW JUST HAND ME THE DODGEBALL AND LEAVE QUIETLY, AND WE WON'T HAVE TO CALL IN THE NATIONAL GUARD!
EXIT
THIS SUCKS!
BART! DON'T USE THAT KIND OF LANGUAGE!
OKAY, THIS BLOWS!
I'M NOT SURE IF THAT'S WORSE OR NOT.
BART'S RIGHT! IF WE CAN'T USE OUR POWERS FOR GOOD, WE'RE NOTHING BUT FREAKS!
WHAM!
WHAM!
WHAM!
SORRY, LISA, I COULDN'T HEAR YOU WITH MAGGIE'S BOUNCING.
SINCE YOU ALL HAD TO QUIT SUPER-HEROING, SHE'S FULL OF BEANS ALL THE TIME NOW!

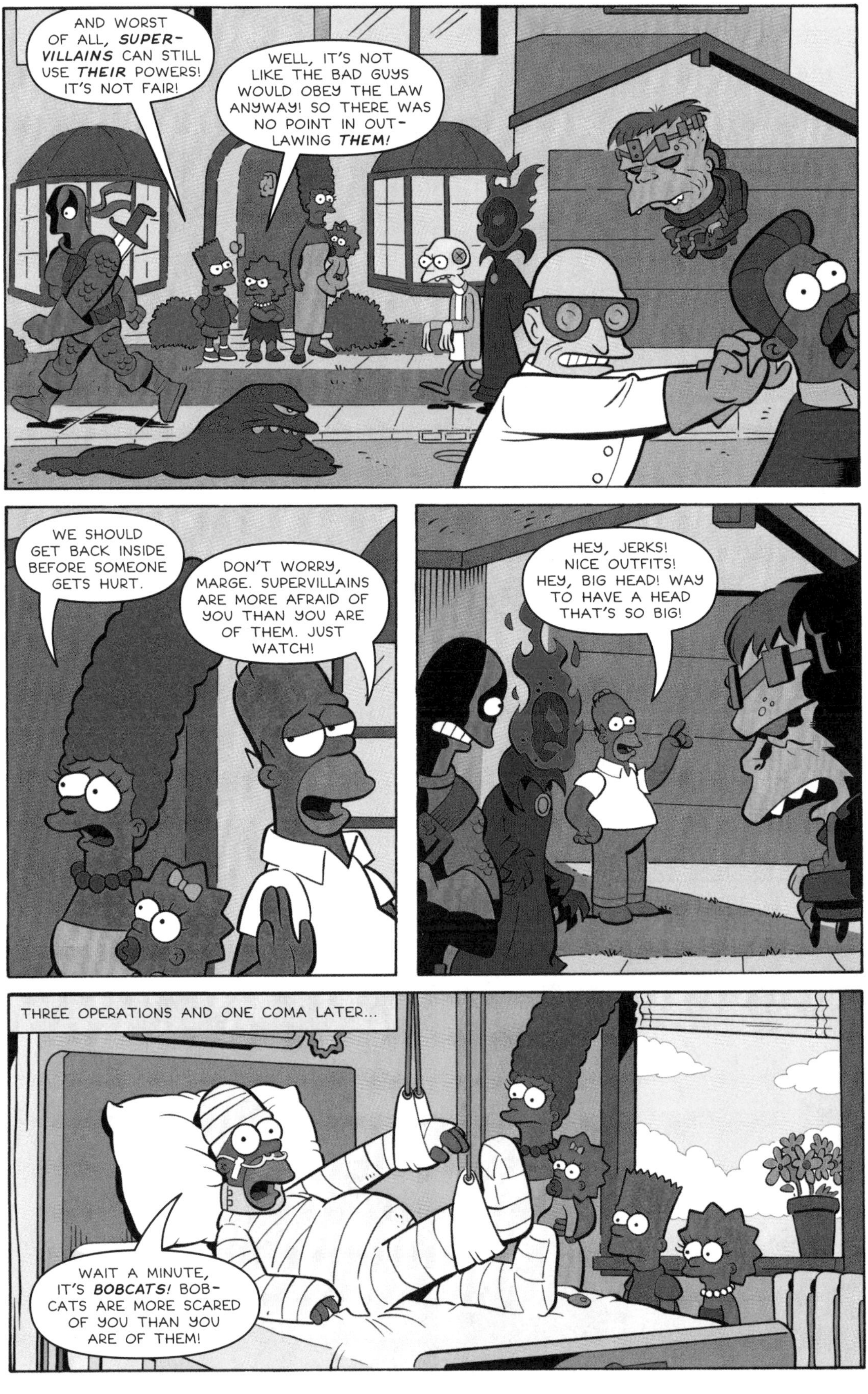
AND WORST OF ALL, **SUPER-VILLAINS** CAN STILL USE **THEIR** POWERS! IT'S NOT FAIR!
WELL, IT'S NOT LIKE THE BAD GUYS WOULD OBEY THE LAW ANYWAY! SO THERE WAS NO POINT IN OUT-LAWING **THEM!**
WE SHOULD GET BACK INSIDE BEFORE SOMEONE GETS HURT.
DON'T WORRY, MARGE. SUPERVILLAINS ARE MORE AFRAID OF YOU THAN YOU ARE OF THEM. JUST WATCH!
HEY, JERKS! NICE OUTFITS! HEY, BIG HEAD! WAY TO HAVE A HEAD THAT'S SO BIG!
THREE OPERATIONS AND ONE COMA LATER...
WAIT A MINUTE, IT'S **BOBCATS!** BOB-CATS ARE MORE SCARED OF YOU THAN YOU ARE OF THEM!

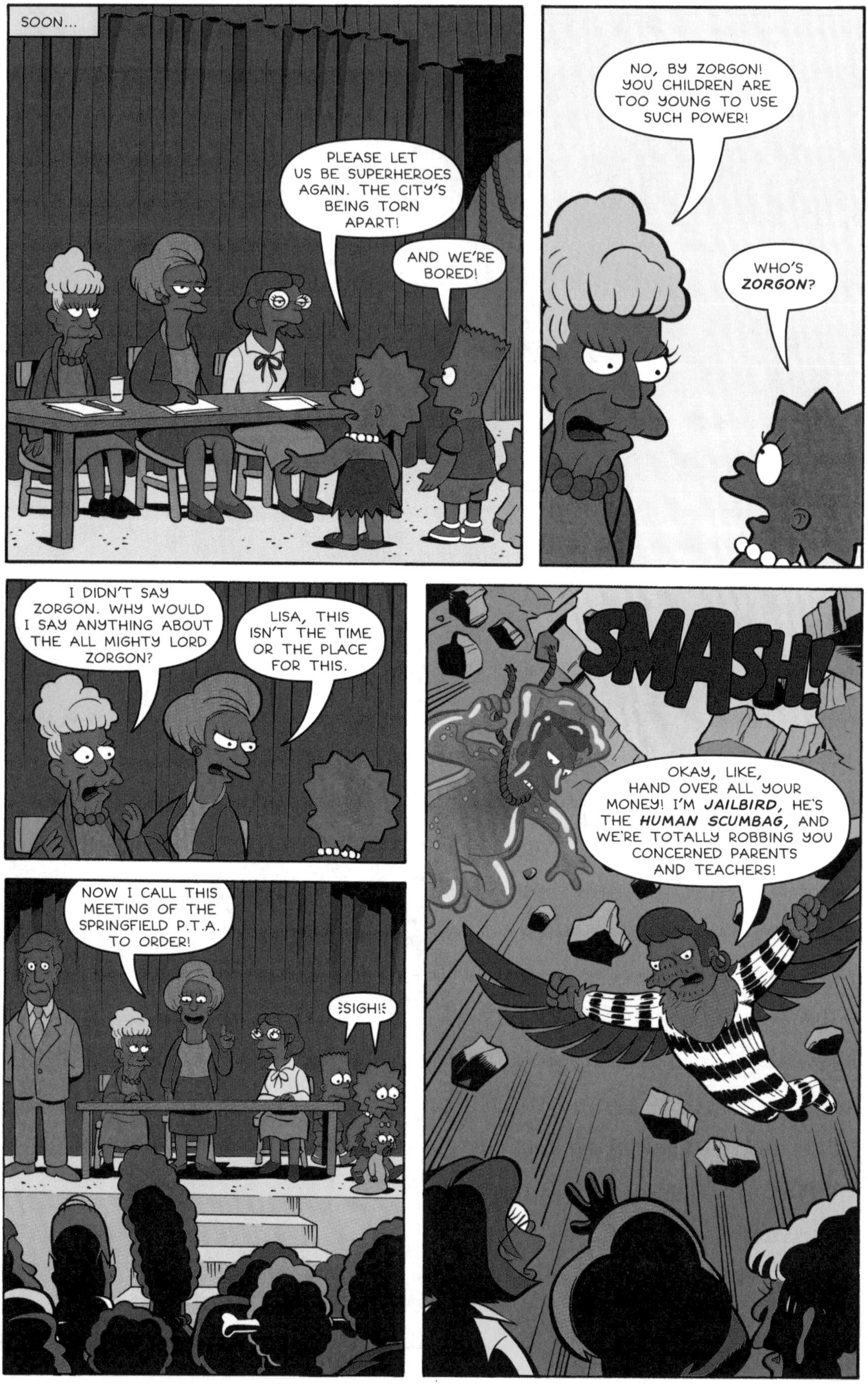
SOON...
PLEASE LET US BE SUPERHEROES AGAIN. THE CITY'S BEING TORN APART!
AND WE'RE BORED!
NO, BY ZORGON! YOU CHILDREN ARE TOO YOUNG TO USE SUCH POWER!
WHO'S ZORGON?
I DIDN'T SAY ZORGON. WHY WOULD I SAY ANYTHING ABOUT THE ALL MIGHTY LORD ZORGON?
LISA, THIS ISN'T THE TIME OR THE PLACE FOR THIS.
NOW I CALL THIS MEETING OF THE SPRINGFIELD P.T.A. TO ORDER!
SIGH!
SMASH!
OKAY, LIKE, HAND OVER ALL YOUR MONEY! I'M JAILBIRD, HE'S THE HUMAN SCUMBAG, AND WE'RE TOTALLY ROBBING YOU CONCERNED PARENTS AND TEACHERS!

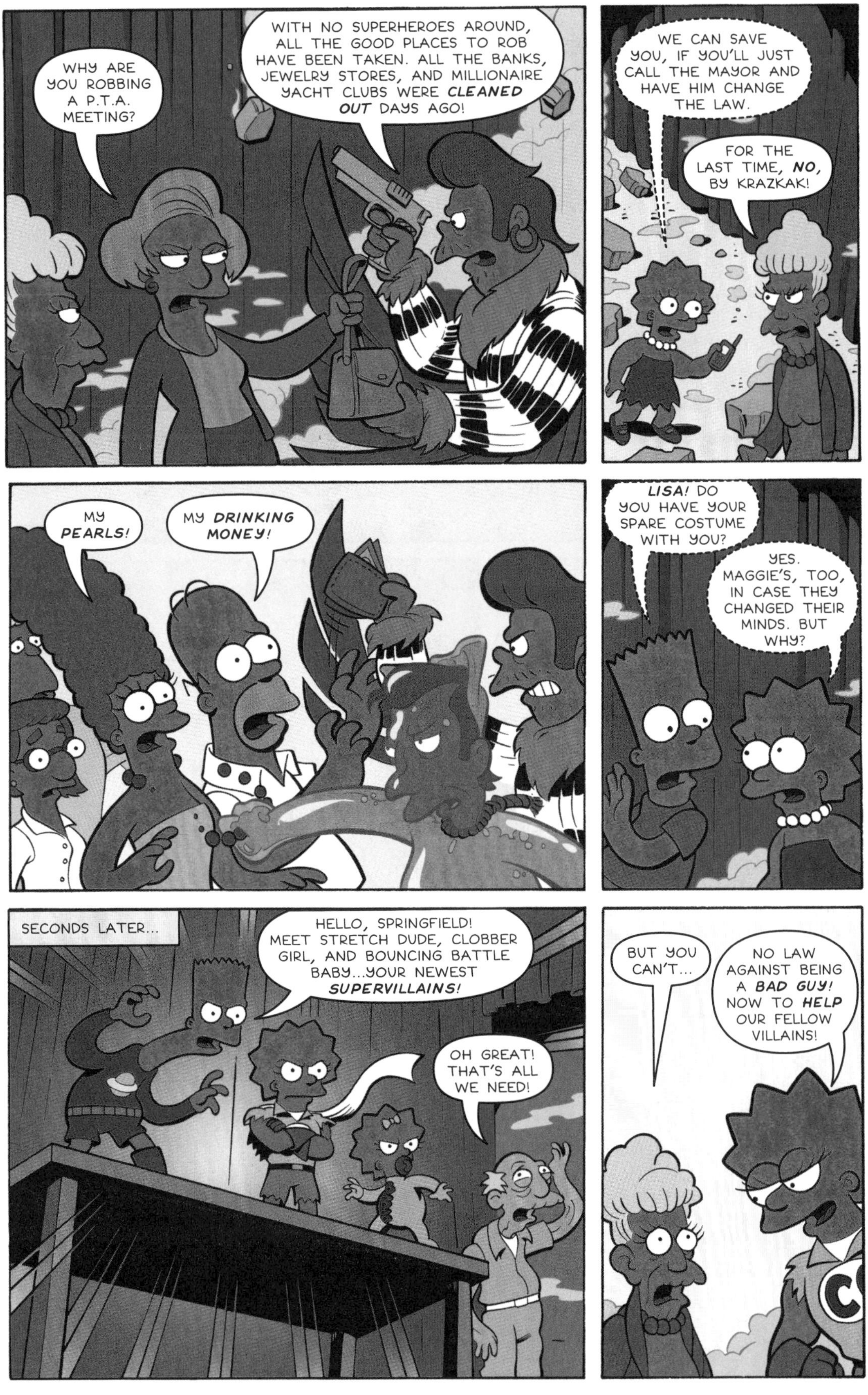

WHY ARE YOU ROBBING A P.T.A. MEETING?
WITH NO SUPERHEROES AROUND, ALL THE GOOD PLACES TO ROB HAVE BEEN TAKEN. ALL THE BANKS, JEWELRY STORES, AND MILLIONAIRE YACHT CLUBS WERE CLEANED OUT DAYS AGO!
WE CAN SAVE YOU, IF YOU'LL JUST CALL THE MAYOR AND HAVE HIM CHANGE THE LAW.
FOR THE LAST TIME, NO, BY KRAZKAK!
MY PEARLS!
MY DRINKING MONEY!
LISA! DO YOU HAVE YOUR SPARE COSTUME WITH YOU?
YES. MAGGIE'S, TOO, IN CASE THEY CHANGED THEIR MINDS. BUT WHY?
SECONDS LATER...
HELLO, SPRINGFIELD! MEET STRETCH DUDE, CLOBBER GIRL, AND BOUNCING BATTLE BABY...YOUR NEWEST SUPERVILLAINS!
OH GREAT! THAT'S ALL WE NEED!
BUT YOU CAN'T...
NO LAW AGAINST BEING A BAD GUY! NOW TO HELP OUR FELLOW VILLAINS!

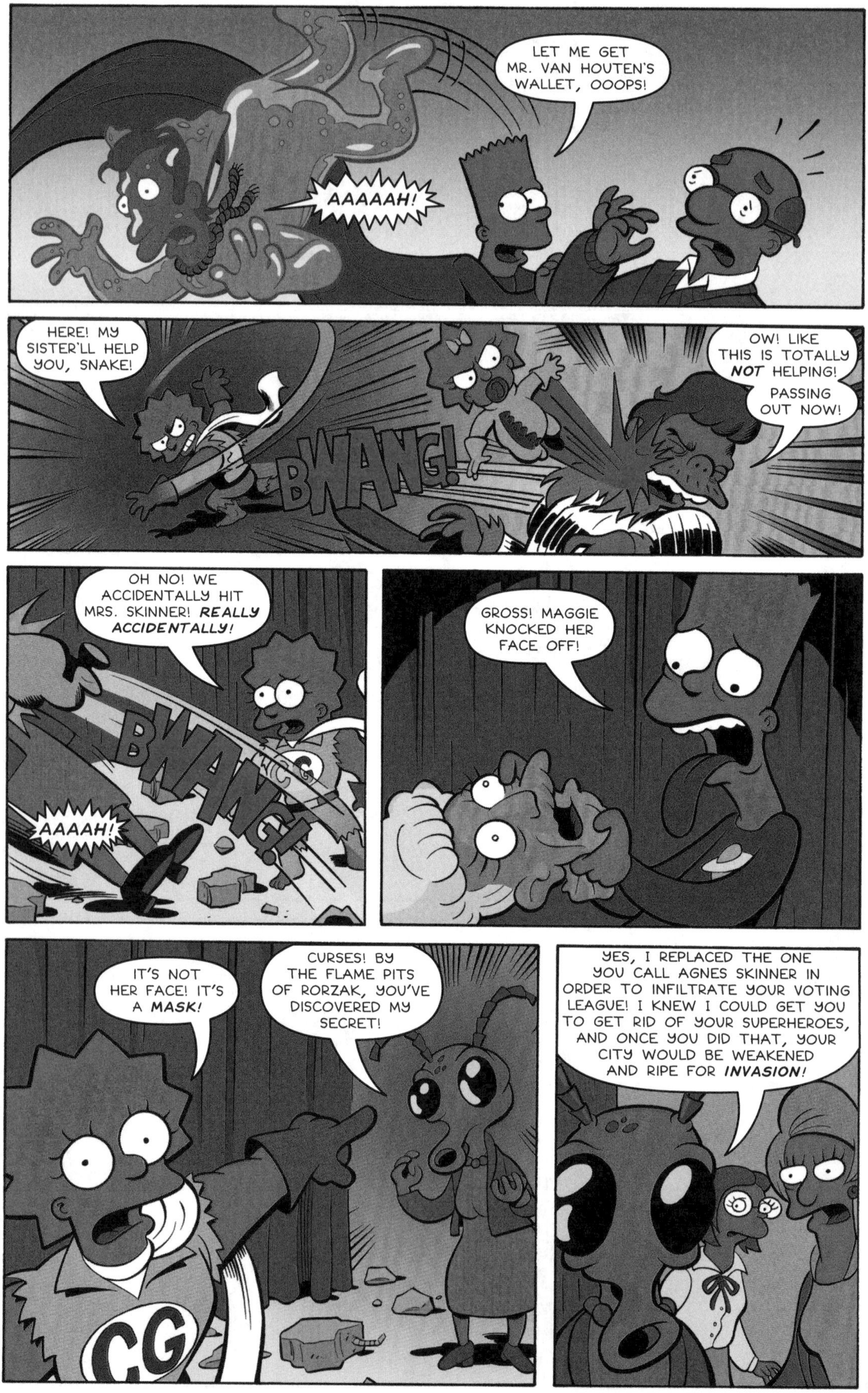

LET ME GET MR. VAN HOUTEN'S WALLET, OOOPS!
AAAAAH!
HERE! MY SISTER'LL HELP YOU, SNAKE!
BWANG!
OW! LIKE THIS IS TOTALLY **NOT** HELPING!
PASSING OUT NOW!
OH NO! WE ACCIDENTALLY HIT MRS. SKINNER! ***REALLY ACCIDENTALLY!***
BWANG!
AAAAH!
GROSS! MAGGIE KNOCKED HER FACE OFF!
IT'S NOT HER FACE! IT'S A ***MASK!***
CURSES! BY THE FLAME PITS OF RORZAK, YOU'VE DISCOVERED MY SECRET!
CG
YES, I REPLACED THE ONE YOU CALL AGNES SKINNER IN ORDER TO INFILTRATE YOUR VOTING LEAGUE! I KNEW I COULD GET YOU TO GET RID OF YOUR SUPERHEROES, AND ONCE YOU DID THAT, YOUR CITY WOULD BE WEAKENED AND RIPE FOR ***INVASION!***

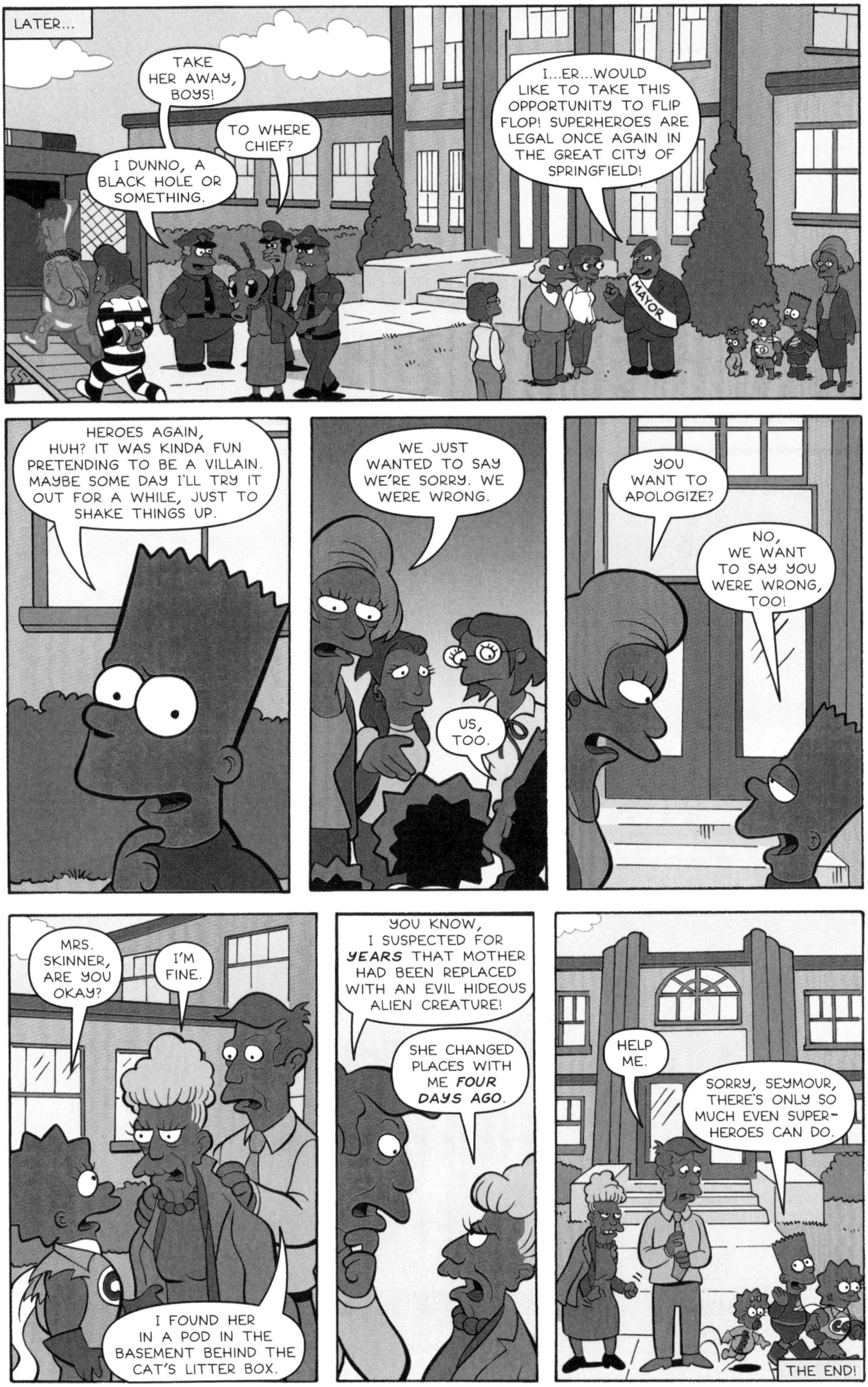
LATER...
TAKE HER AWAY, BOYS!
TO WHERE CHIEF?
I DUNNO, A BLACK HOLE OR SOMETHING.
I...ER...WOULD LIKE TO TAKE THIS OPPORTUNITY TO FLIP FLOP! SUPERHEROES ARE LEGAL ONCE AGAIN IN THE GREAT CITY OF SPRINGFIELD!
MAYOR
HEROES AGAIN, HUH? IT WAS KINDA FUN PRETENDING TO BE A VILLAIN. MAYBE SOME DAY I'LL TRY IT OUT FOR A WHILE, JUST TO SHAKE THINGS UP.
WE JUST WANTED TO SAY WE'RE SORRY. WE WERE WRONG.
US, TOO.
YOU WANT TO APOLOGIZE?
NO, WE WANT TO SAY YOU WERE WRONG, TOO!
MRS. SKINNER, ARE YOU OKAY?
I'M FINE.
I FOUND HER IN A POD IN THE BASEMENT BEHIND THE CAT'S LITTER BOX.
YOU KNOW, I SUSPECTED FOR **YEARS** THAT MOTHER HAD BEEN REPLACED WITH AN EVIL HIDEOUS ALIEN CREATURE!
SHE CHANGED PLACES WITH ME **FOUR DAYS AGO**.
HELP ME.
SORRY, SEYMOUR, THERE'S ONLY SO MUCH EVEN SUPER-HEROES CAN DO.
THE END!

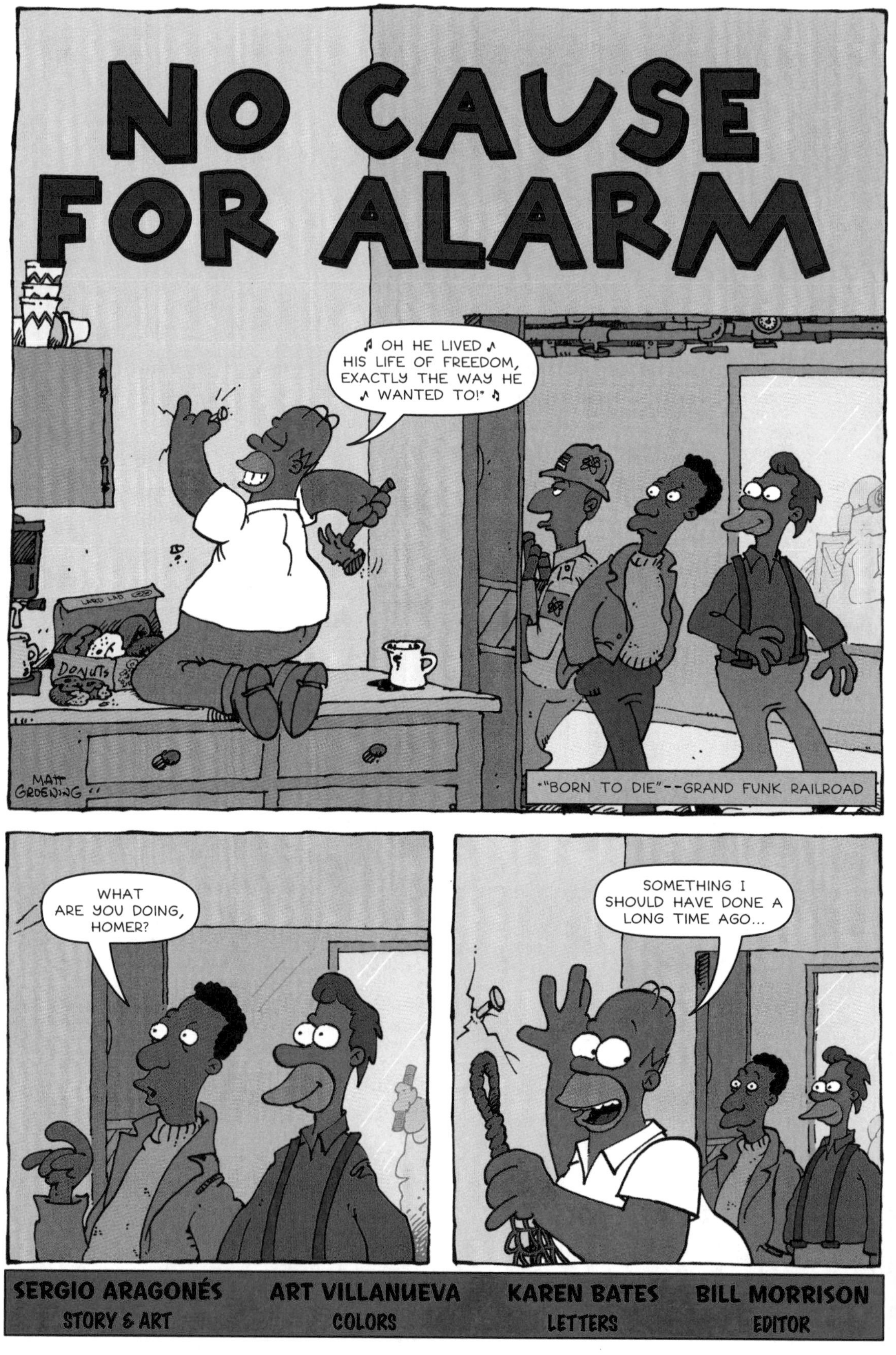
NO CAUSE FOR ALARM
♪ OH HE LIVED ♪ HIS LIFE OF FREEDOM, EXACTLY THE WAY HE ♪ WANTED TO!* ♪
MATT GROENING
*"BORN TO DIE"--GRAND FUNK RAILROAD
WHAT ARE YOU DOING, HOMER?
SOMETHING I SHOULD HAVE DONE A LONG TIME AGO...

SERGIO ARAGONÉS STORY & ART · **ART VILLANUEVA** COLORS · **KAREN BATES** LETTERS · **BILL MORRISON** EDITOR

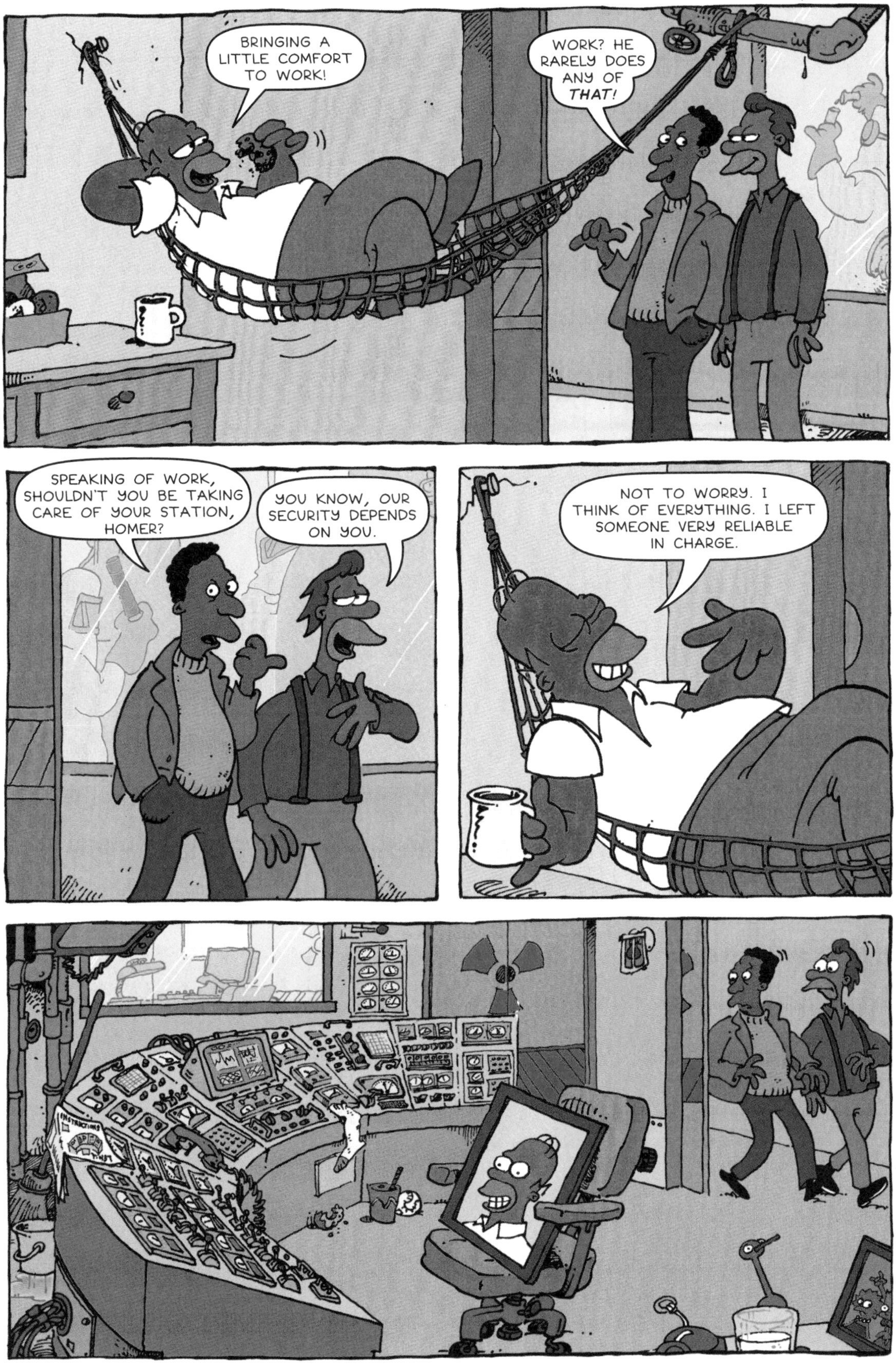
BRINGING A LITTLE COMFORT TO WORK!
WORK? HE RARELY DOES ANY OF *THAT!*
SPEAKING OF WORK, SHOULDN'T YOU BE TAKING CARE OF YOUR STATION, HOMER?
YOU KNOW, OUR SECURITY DEPENDS ON YOU.
NOT TO WORRY. I THINK OF EVERYTHING. I LEFT SOMEONE VERY RELIABLE IN CHARGE.

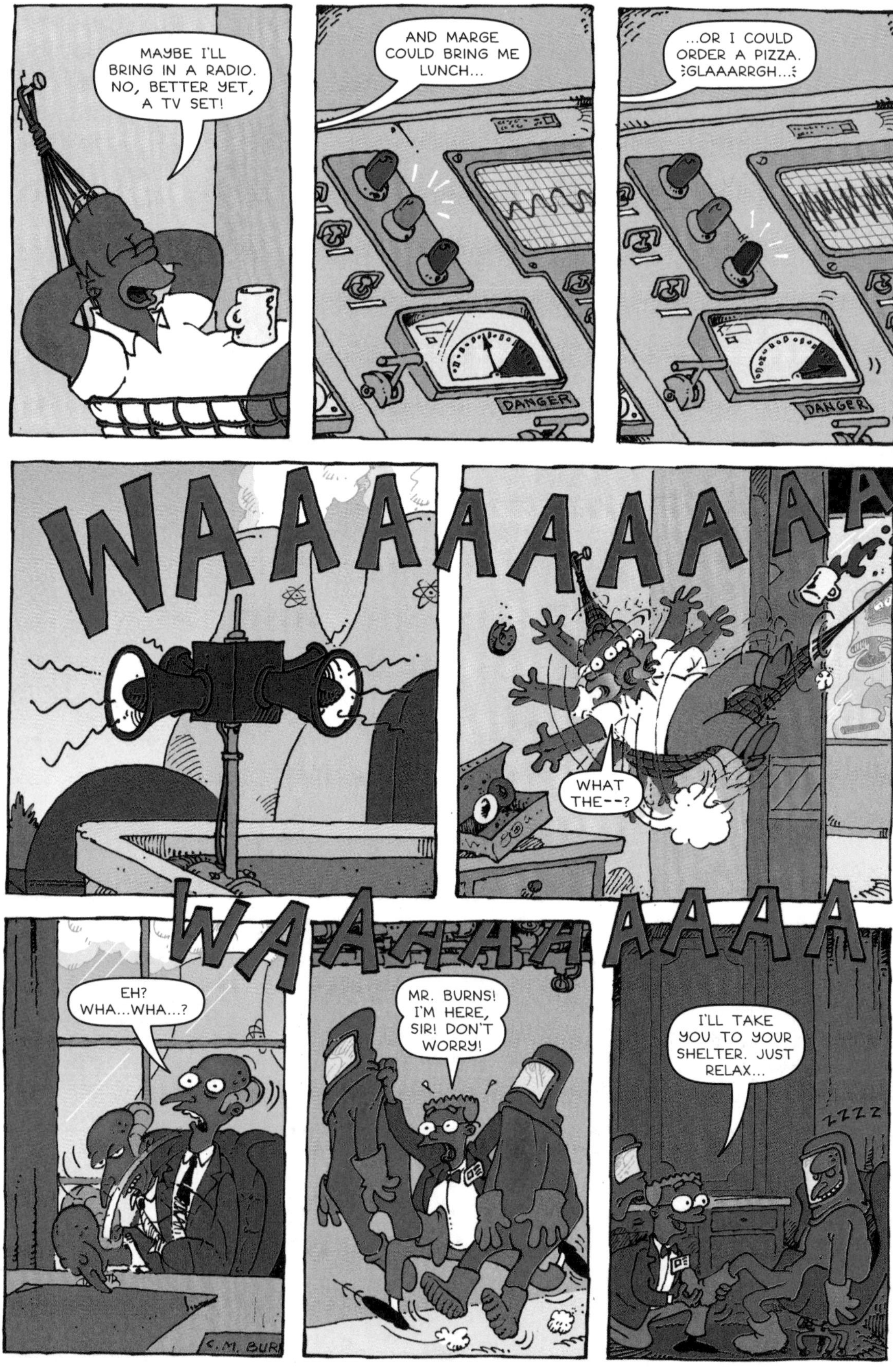
MAYBE I'LL BRING IN A RADIO. NO, BETTER YET, A TV SET!
AND MARGE COULD BRING ME LUNCH...
DANGER
...OR I COULD ORDER A PIZZA. GLAAARRGH...
DANGER
WAAAAAAAAA
WHAT THE--?
WAAAAAAAAA
EH? WHA...WHA...?
C.M. BUR
MR. BURNS! I'M HERE, SIR! DON'T WORRY!
I'LL TAKE YOU TO YOUR SHELTER. JUST RELAX...
ZZZZ

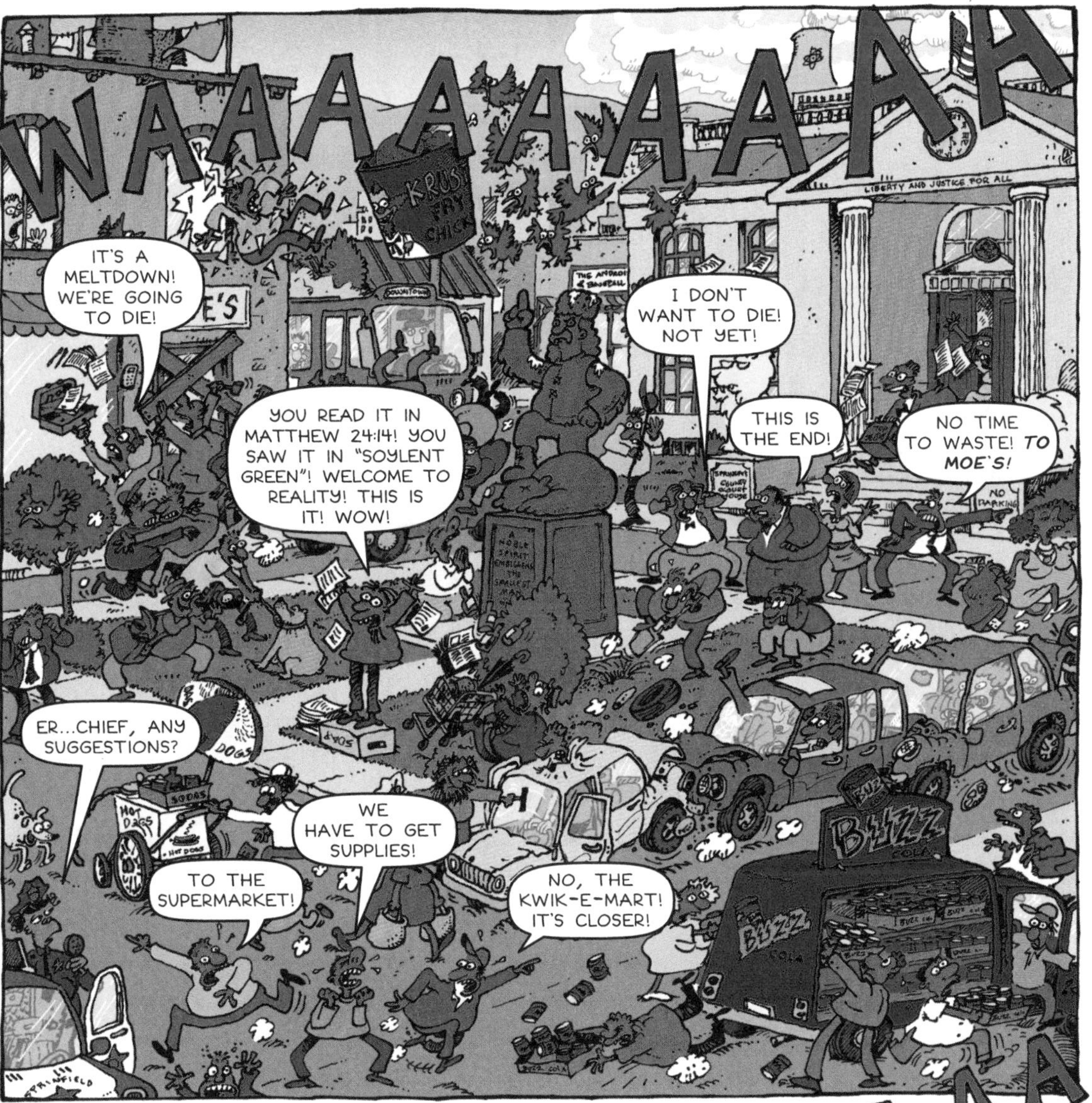
WAAAAAAAAA
IT'S A MELTDOWN! WE'RE GOING TO DIE!
YOU READ IT IN MATTHEW 24:14! YOU SAW IT IN "SOYLENT GREEN"! WELCOME TO REALITY! THIS IS IT! WOW!
I DON'T WANT TO DIE! NOT YET!
THIS IS THE END!
NO TIME TO WASTE! **TO MOE'S!**
ER...CHIEF, ANY SUGGESTIONS?
WE HAVE TO GET SUPPLIES!
TO THE SUPERMARKET!
NO, THE KWIK-E-MART! IT'S CLOSER!
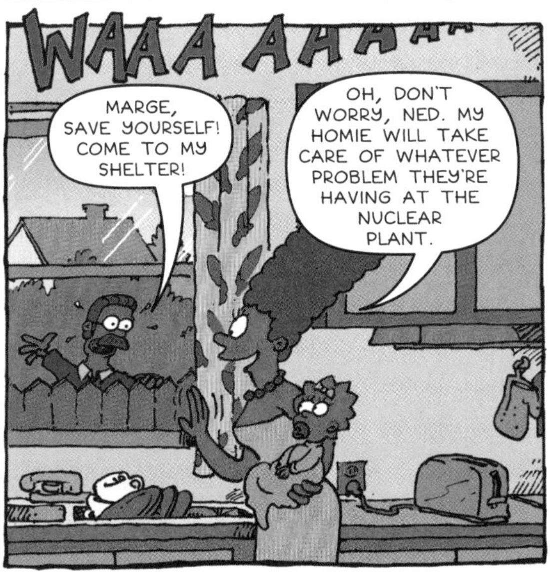
WAAA AAAAA
MARGE, SAVE YOURSELF! COME TO MY SHELTER!
OH, DON'T WORRY, NED. MY HOMIE WILL TAKE CARE OF WHATEVER PROBLEM THEY'RE HAVING AT THE NUCLEAR PLANT.
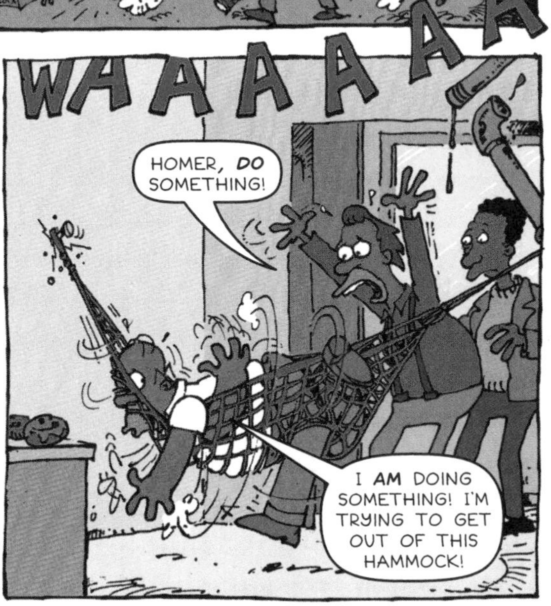
WAAAAAA
HOMER, **DO** SOMETHING!
I **AM** DOING SOMETHING! I'M TRYING TO GET OUT OF THIS HAMMOCK!

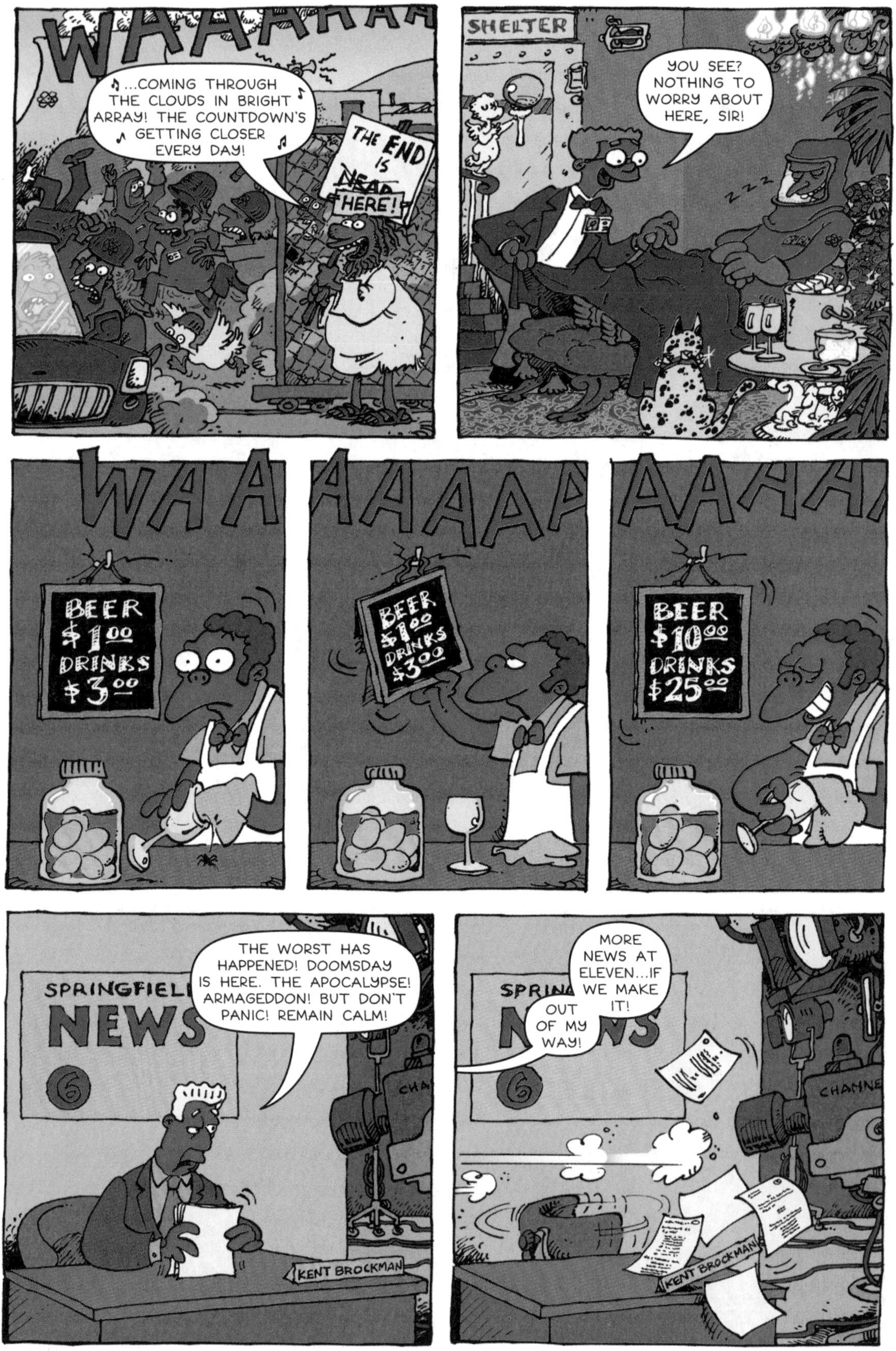
WAAAAAAA
♪ ...COMING THROUGH THE CLOUDS IN BRIGHT ARRAY! THE COUNTDOWN'S GETTING CLOSER EVERY DAY! ♪
THE END IS NEAR HERE!
SHELTER
YOU SEE? NOTHING TO WORRY ABOUT HERE, SIR!
Z Z Z
WAAAAAAAAAA
BEER $1.00 DRINKS $3.00
BEER $1.00 DRINKS $3.00
BEER $10.00 DRINKS $25.00
SPRINGFIELD NEWS 6
THE WORST HAS HAPPENED! DOOMSDAY IS HERE. THE APOCALYPSE! ARMAGEDDON! BUT DON'T PANIC! REMAIN CALM!
KENT BROCKMAN
MORE NEWS AT ELEVEN...IF WE MAKE IT!
OUT OF MY WAY!
KENT BROCKMAN

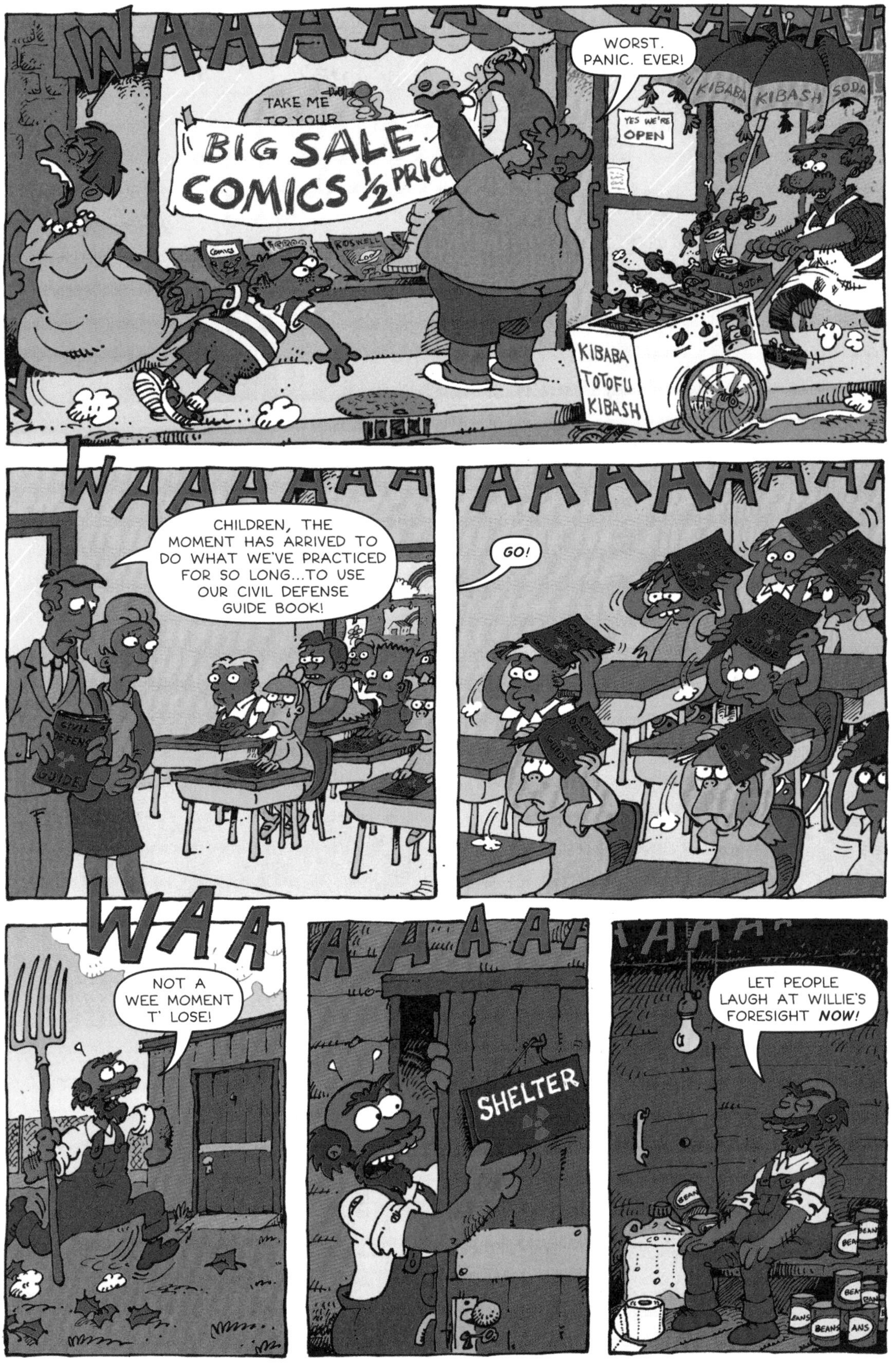
WAAAAA
TAKE ME TO YOUR
BIG SALE COMICS 1/2 PRIC
COMICS
ROSWELL
WORST. PANIC. EVER!
YES WE'RE OPEN
KIBABA
KIBASH
SODA
KIBABA TOTOFU KIBASH
WAAAA
CHILDREN, THE MOMENT HAS ARRIVED TO DO WHAT WE'VE PRACTICED FOR SO LONG...TO USE OUR CIVIL DEFENSE GUIDE BOOK!
CIVIL DEFENSE GUIDE
GO!
WAA
NOT A WEE MOMENT T' LOSE!
SHELTER
LET PEOPLE LAUGH AT WILLIE'S FORESIGHT *NOW!*
BEANS

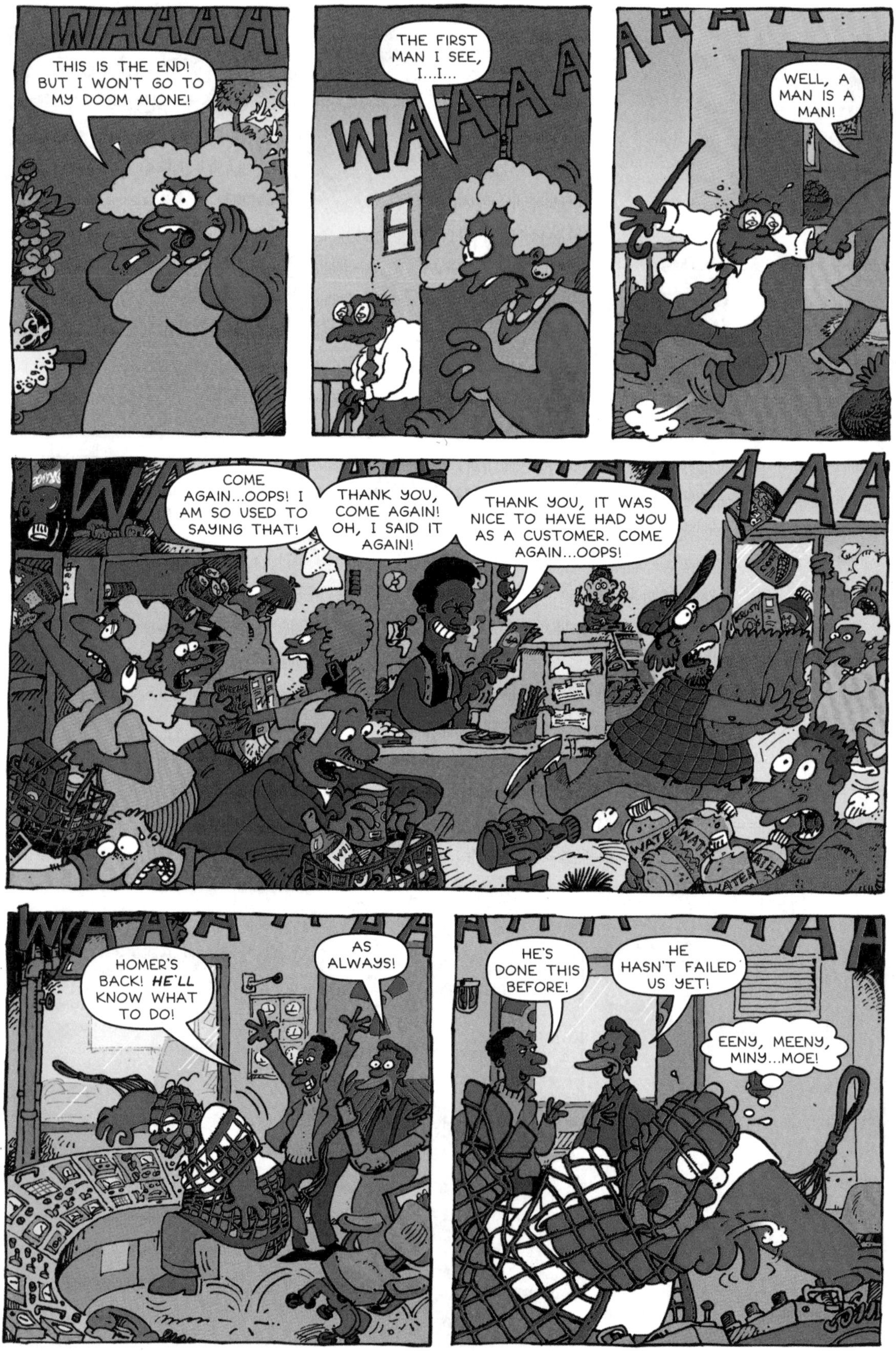
WAAAA
THIS IS THE END! BUT I WON'T GO TO MY DOOM ALONE!
THE FIRST MAN I SEE, I...I...
WAAAA
WAAAA
WELL, A MAN IS A MAN!
COME AGAIN...OOPS! I AM SO USED TO SAYING THAT!
THANK YOU, COME AGAIN! OH, I SAID IT AGAIN!
THANK YOU, IT WAS NICE TO HAVE HAD YOU AS A CUSTOMER. COME AGAIN...OOPS!
HOMER'S BACK! ***HE'LL*** KNOW WHAT TO DO!
AS ALWAYS!
HE'S DONE THIS BEFORE!
HE HASN'T FAILED US YET!
EENY, MEENY, MINY...MOE!

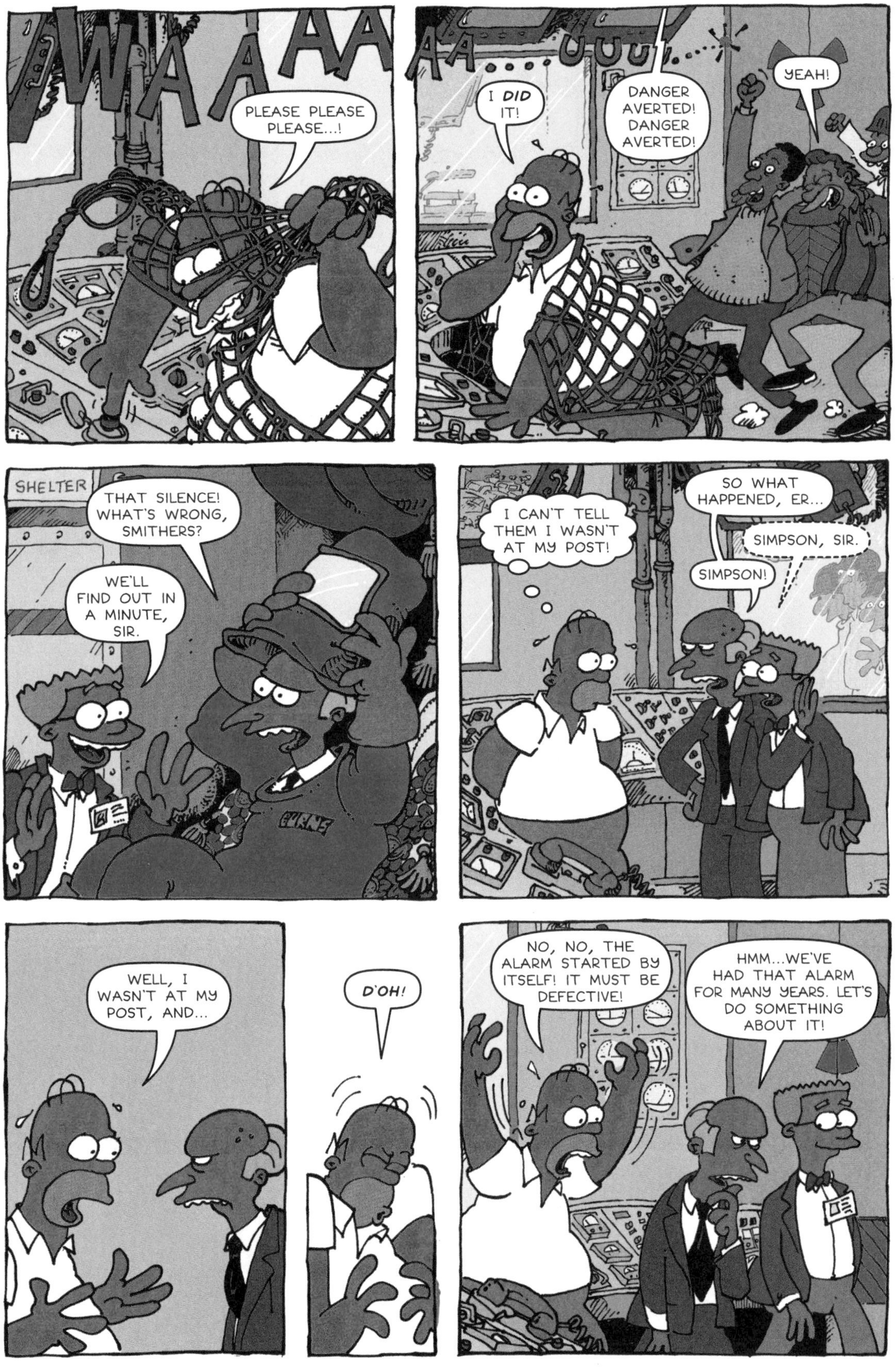
WHAAAAA
PLEASE PLEASE PLEASE...!
AAUUUU
I DID IT!
DANGER AVERTED! DANGER AVERTED!
YEAH!
SHELTER
THAT SILENCE! WHAT'S WRONG, SMITHERS?
WE'LL FIND OUT IN A MINUTE, SIR.
I CAN'T TELL THEM I WASN'T AT MY POST!
SO WHAT HAPPENED, ER...
SIMPSON, SIR.
SIMPSON!
WELL, I WASN'T AT MY POST, AND...
D'OH!
NO, NO, THE ALARM STARTED BY ITSELF! IT MUST BE DEFECTIVE!
HMM...WE'VE HAD THAT ALARM FOR MANY YEARS. LET'S DO SOMETHING ABOUT IT!

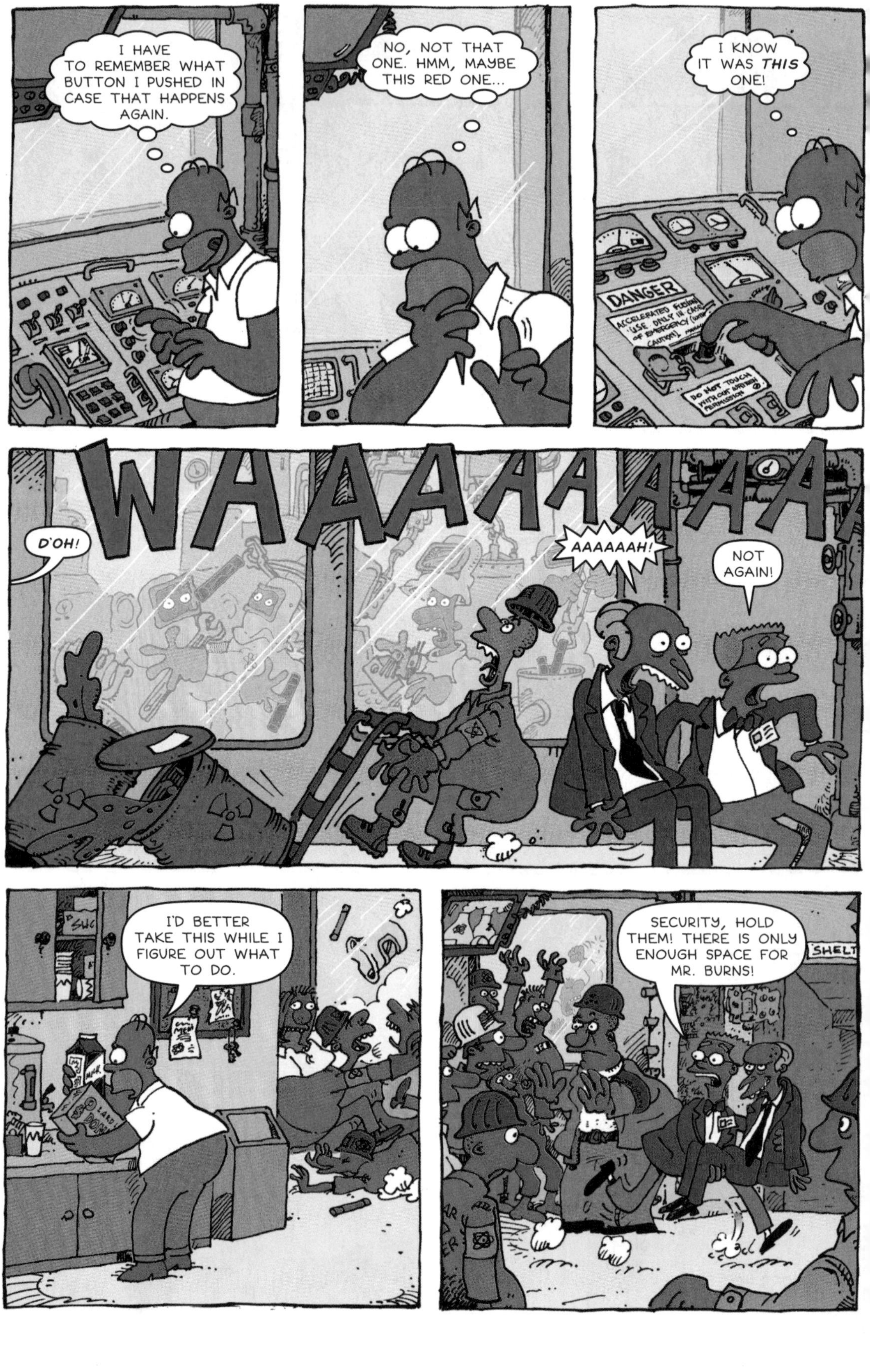
I HAVE TO REMEMBER WHAT BUTTON I PUSHED IN CASE THAT HAPPENS AGAIN.
NO, NOT THAT ONE. HMM, MAYBE THIS RED ONE...
I KNOW IT WAS THIS ONE!
DANGER
WAAAAAAAA
D'OH!
AAAAAAH!
NOT AGAIN!
I'D BETTER TAKE THIS WHILE I FIGURE OUT WHAT TO DO.
SECURITY, HOLD THEM! THERE IS ONLY ENOUGH SPACE FOR MR. BURNS!

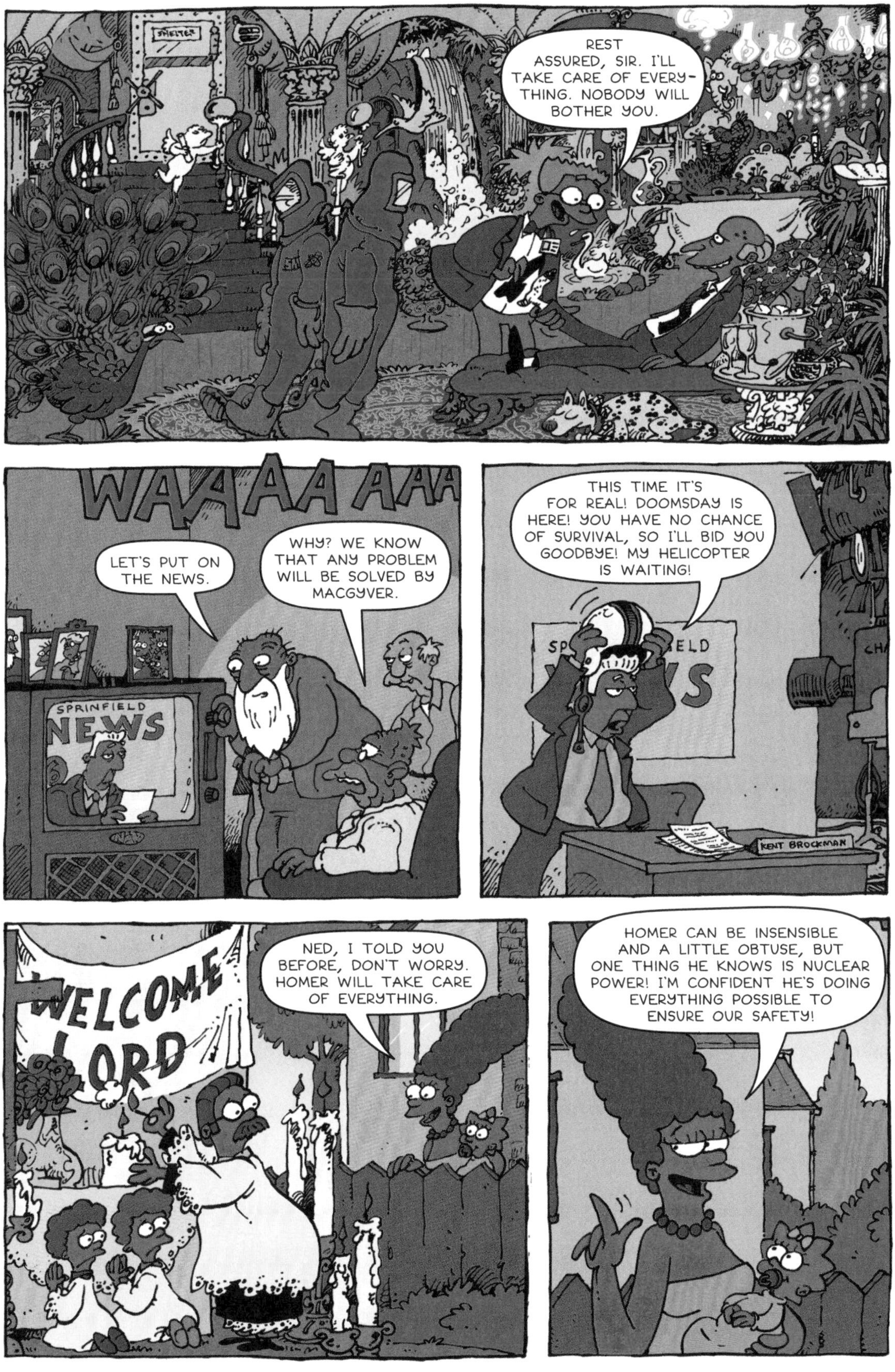
SHELTER
REST ASSURED, SIR. I'LL TAKE CARE OF EVERYTHING. NOBODY WILL BOTHER YOU.
WAAAA AAA
LET'S PUT ON THE NEWS.
WHY? WE KNOW THAT ANY PROBLEM WILL BE SOLVED BY MACGYVER.
SPRINFIELD NEWS
THIS TIME IT'S FOR REAL! DOOMSDAY IS HERE! YOU HAVE NO CHANCE OF SURVIVAL, SO I'LL BID YOU GOODBYE! MY HELICOPTER IS WAITING!
KENT BROCKMAN
WELCOME LORD
NED, I TOLD YOU BEFORE, DON'T WORRY. HOMER WILL TAKE CARE OF EVERYTHING.
HOMER CAN BE INSENSIBLE AND A LITTLE OBTUSE, BUT ONE THING HE KNOWS IS NUCLEAR POWER! I'M CONFIDENT HE'S DOING EVERYTHING POSSIBLE TO ENSURE OUR SAFETY!

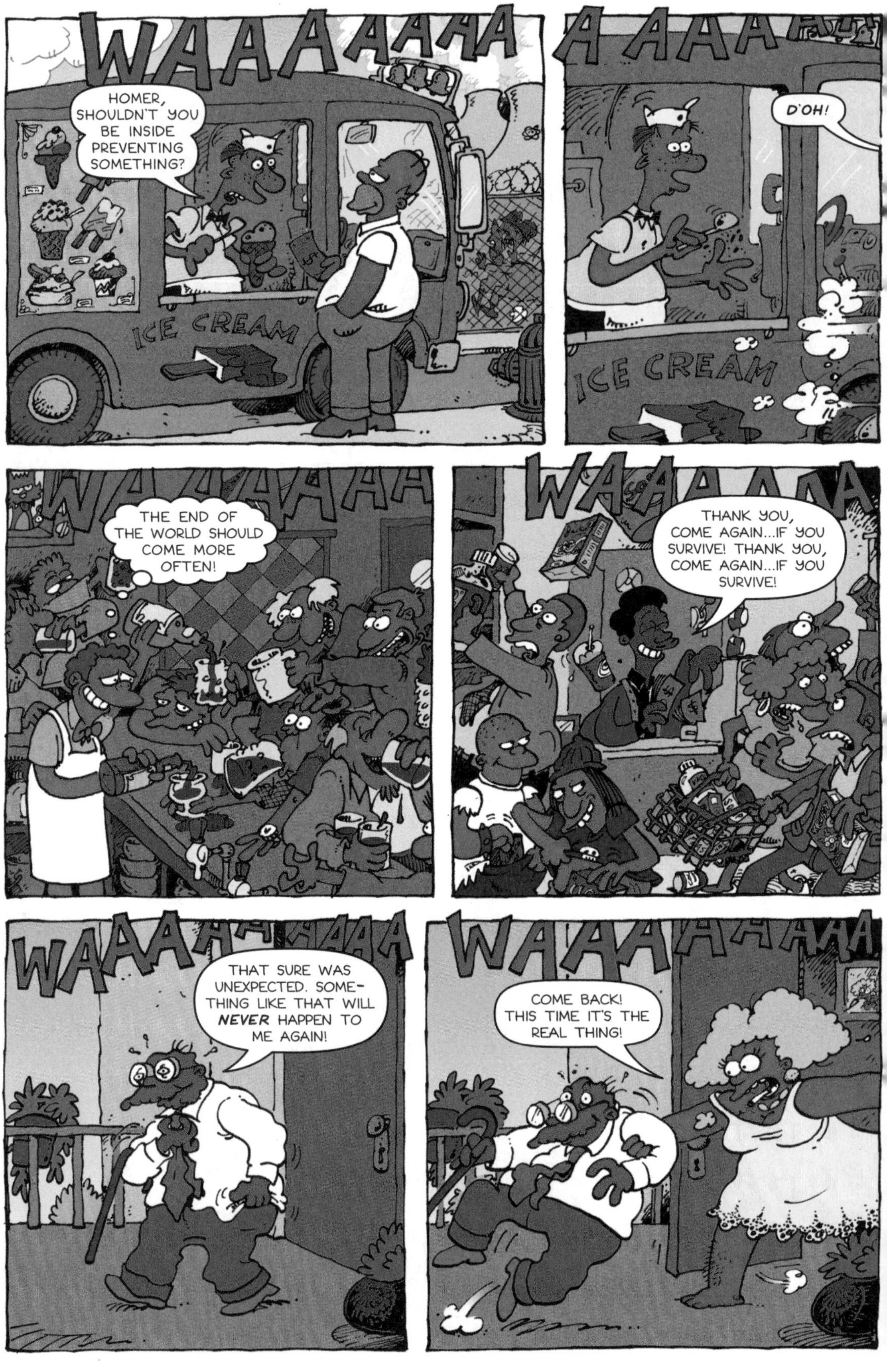
WAAAAAAA
HOMER, SHOULDN'T YOU BE INSIDE PREVENTING SOMETHING?
ICE CREAM
A AAAA
D'OH!
ICE CREAM
WAAAAAAA
THE END OF THE WORLD SHOULD COME MORE OFTEN!
WAAAAAA
THANK YOU, COME AGAIN...IF YOU SURVIVE! THANK YOU, COME AGAIN...IF YOU SURVIVE!
WAAAAAAAA
THAT SURE WAS UNEXPECTED. SOMETHING LIKE THAT WILL **NEVER** HAPPEN TO ME AGAIN!
WAAAAAAAA
COME BACK! THIS TIME IT'S THE REAL THING!

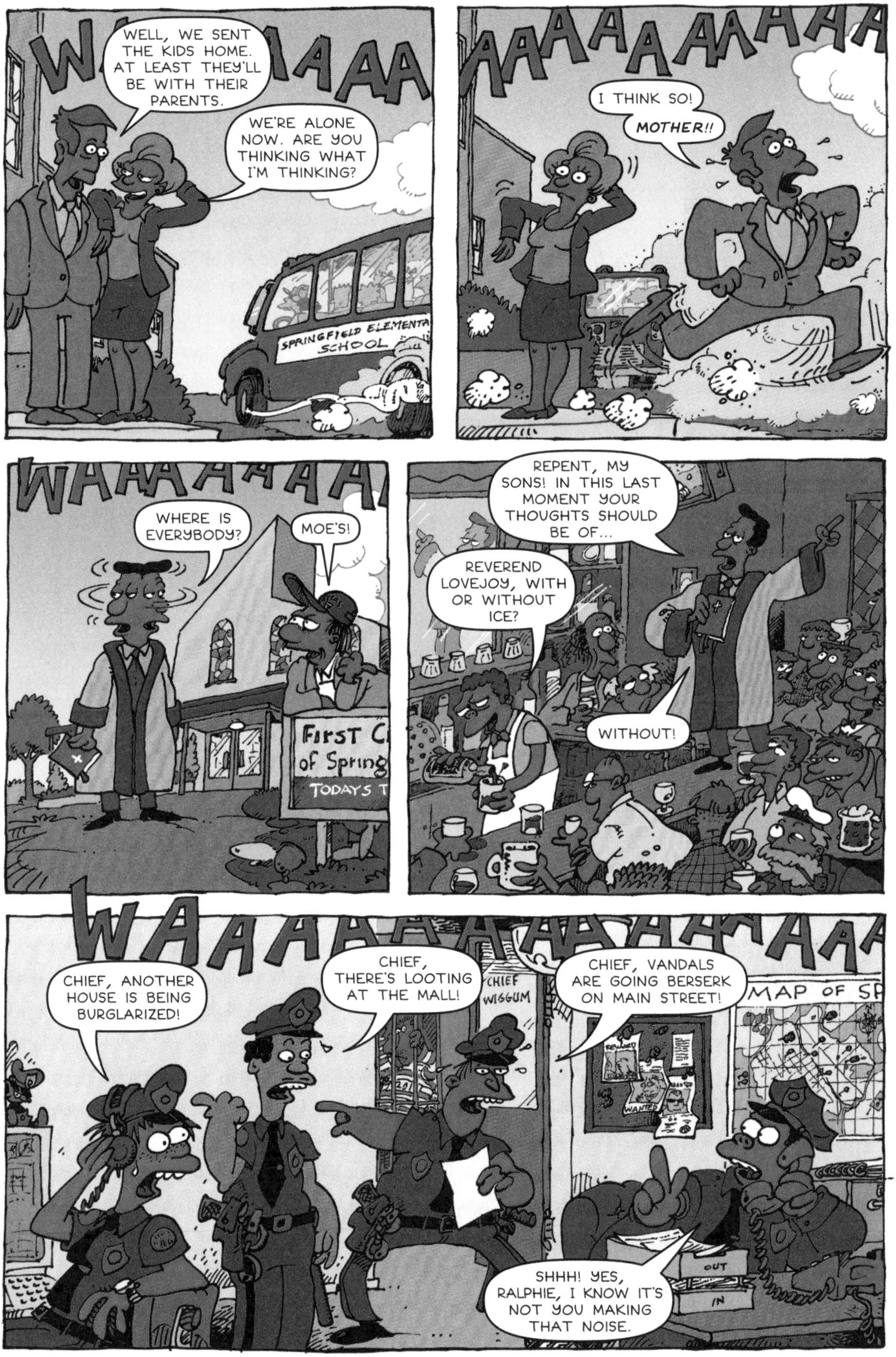
WAAAAA
WELL, WE SENT THE KIDS HOME. AT LEAST THEY'LL BE WITH THEIR PARENTS.
WE'RE ALONE NOW. ARE YOU THINKING WHAT I'M THINKING?
SPRINGFIELD ELEMENTA SCHOOL
AAAAAAAAAA
I THINK SO!
MOTHER!!
WAAAAAAAA
WHERE IS EVERYBODY?
MOE'S!
First C of Spring
TODAYS T
REPENT, MY SONS! IN THIS LAST MOMENT YOUR THOUGHTS SHOULD BE OF...
REVEREND LOVEJOY, WITH OR WITHOUT ICE?
WITHOUT!
WAAAAAAAAAAAAAAA
CHIEF, ANOTHER HOUSE IS BEING BURGLARIZED!
CHIEF, THERE'S LOOTING AT THE MALL!
CHIEF WIGGUM
CHIEF, VANDALS ARE GOING BERSERK ON MAIN STREET!
MAP OF SP
WANTED
OUT
IN
SHHH! YES, RALPHIE, I KNOW IT'S NOT YOU MAKING THAT NOISE.

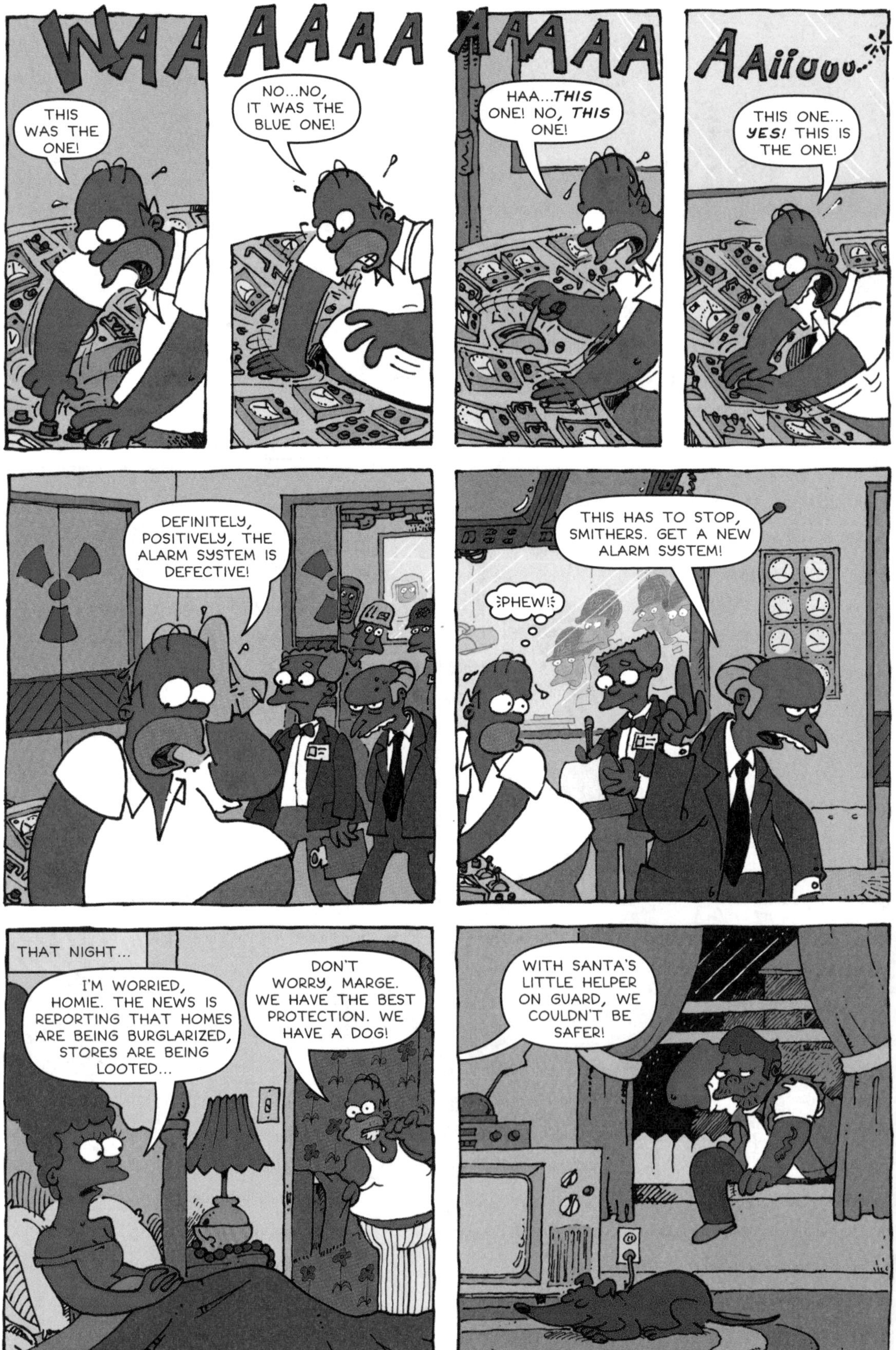
WAAAAAAAAAAAAAiiuuu...
THIS WAS THE ONE!
NO...NO, IT WAS THE BLUE ONE!
HAA...THIS ONE! NO, THIS ONE!
THIS ONE... YES! THIS IS THE ONE!
DEFINITELY, POSITIVELY, THE ALARM SYSTEM IS DEFECTIVE!
PHEW!
THIS HAS TO STOP, SMITHERS. GET A NEW ALARM SYSTEM!
THAT NIGHT...
I'M WORRIED, HOMIE. THE NEWS IS REPORTING THAT HOMES ARE BEING BURGLARIZED, STORES ARE BEING LOOTED...
DON'T WORRY, MARGE. WE HAVE THE BEST PROTECTION. WE HAVE A DOG!
WITH SANTA'S LITTLE HELPER ON GUARD, WE COULDN'T BE SAFER!

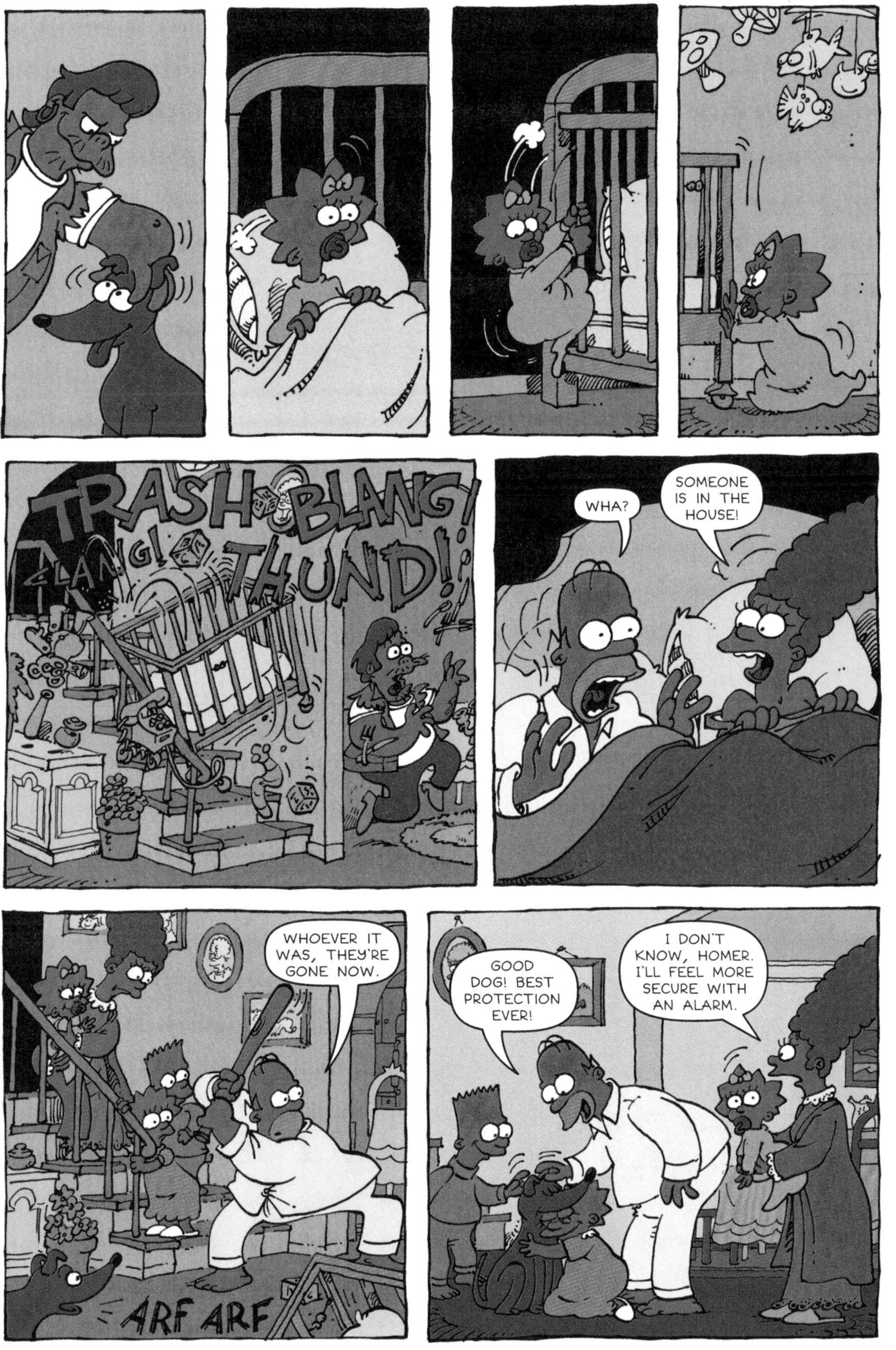
TRASH
BLANG!
CLANG!
THUND!
WHA?
SOMEONE IS IN THE HOUSE!
WHOEVER IT WAS, THEY'RE GONE NOW.
ARF ARF
GOOD DOG! BEST PROTECTION EVER!
I DON'T KNOW, HOMER. I'LL FEEL MORE SECURE WITH AN ALARM.

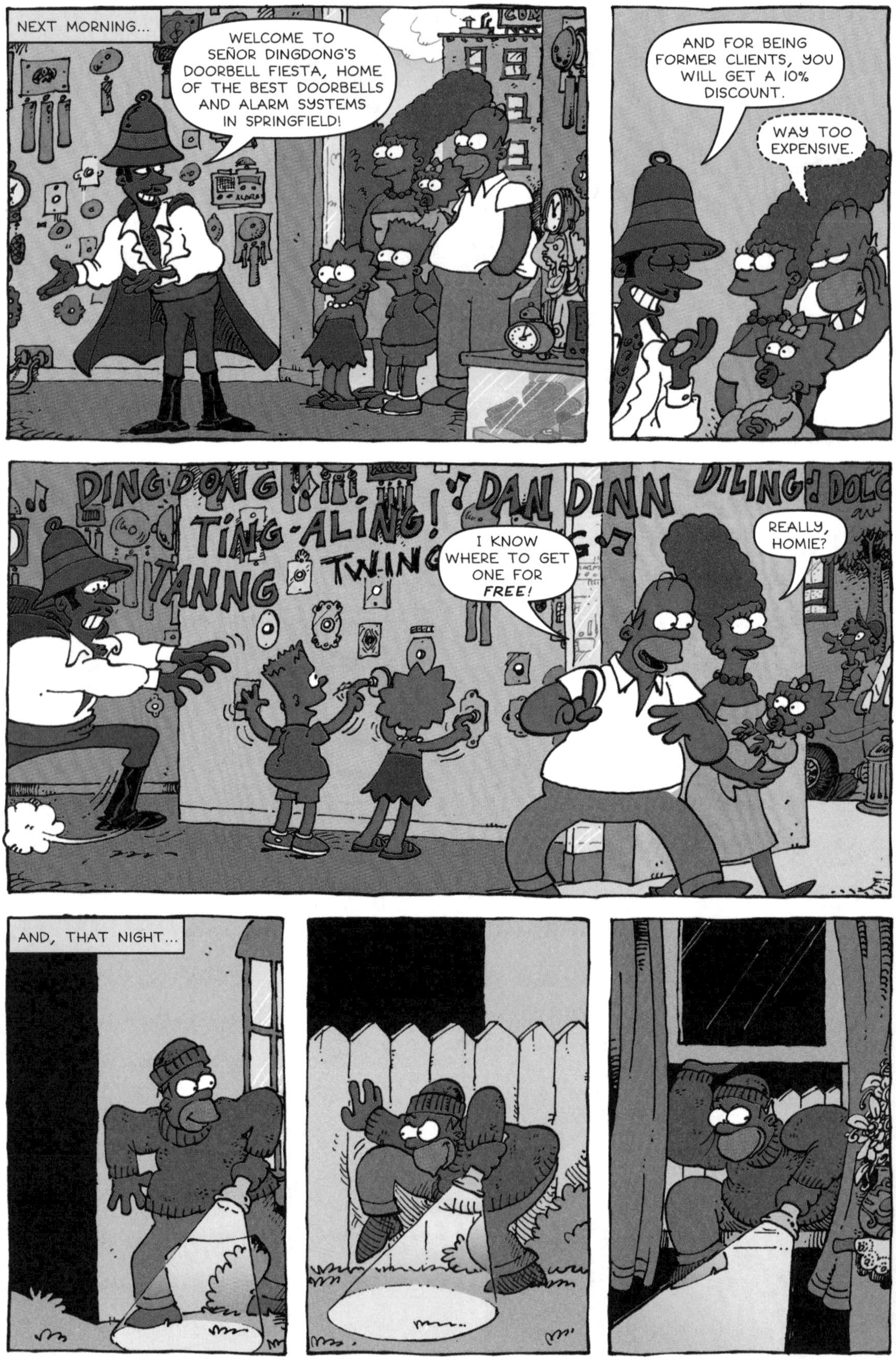
NEXT MORNING...
WELCOME TO SEÑOR DINGDONG'S DOORBELL FIESTA, HOME OF THE BEST DOORBELLS AND ALARM SYSTEMS IN SPRINGFIELD!
AND FOR BEING FORMER CLIENTS, YOU WILL GET A 10% DISCOUNT.
WAY TOO EXPENSIVE.
DING DONG
TING-ALING!
DAN DINN
DILING
TANNG
TWING
I KNOW WHERE TO GET ONE FOR FREE!
REALLY, HOMIE?
AND, THAT NIGHT...

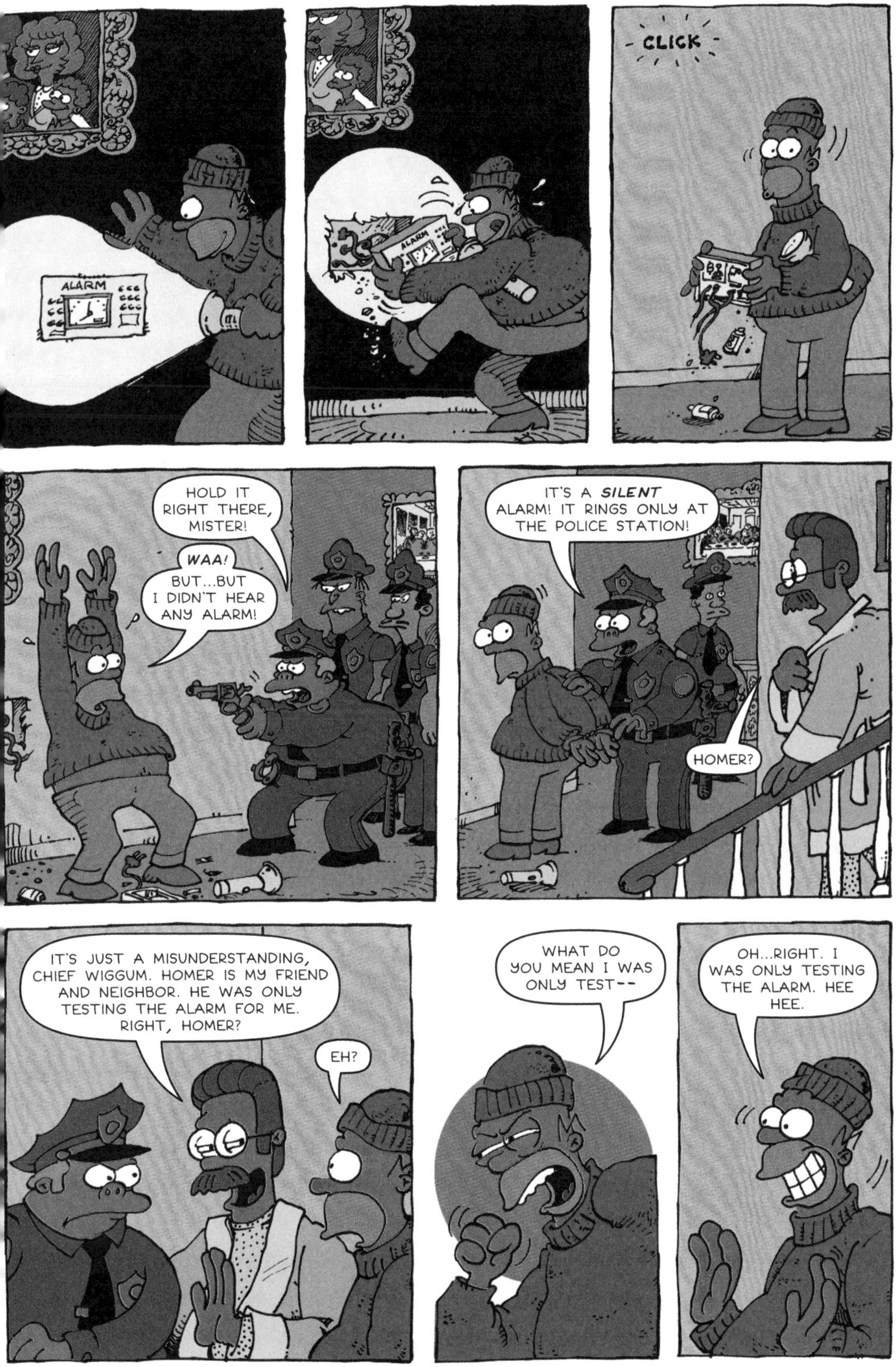
ALARM
ALARM
CLICK
HOLD IT RIGHT THERE, MISTER!
WAA! BUT...BUT I DIDN'T HEAR ANY ALARM!
IT'S A SILENT ALARM! IT RINGS ONLY AT THE POLICE STATION!
HOMER?
IT'S JUST A MISUNDERSTANDING, CHIEF WIGGUM. HOMER IS MY FRIEND AND NEIGHBOR. HE WAS ONLY TESTING THE ALARM FOR ME. RIGHT, HOMER?
EH?
WHAT DO YOU MEAN I WAS ONLY TEST--
OH...RIGHT. I WAS ONLY TESTING THE ALARM. HEE HEE.

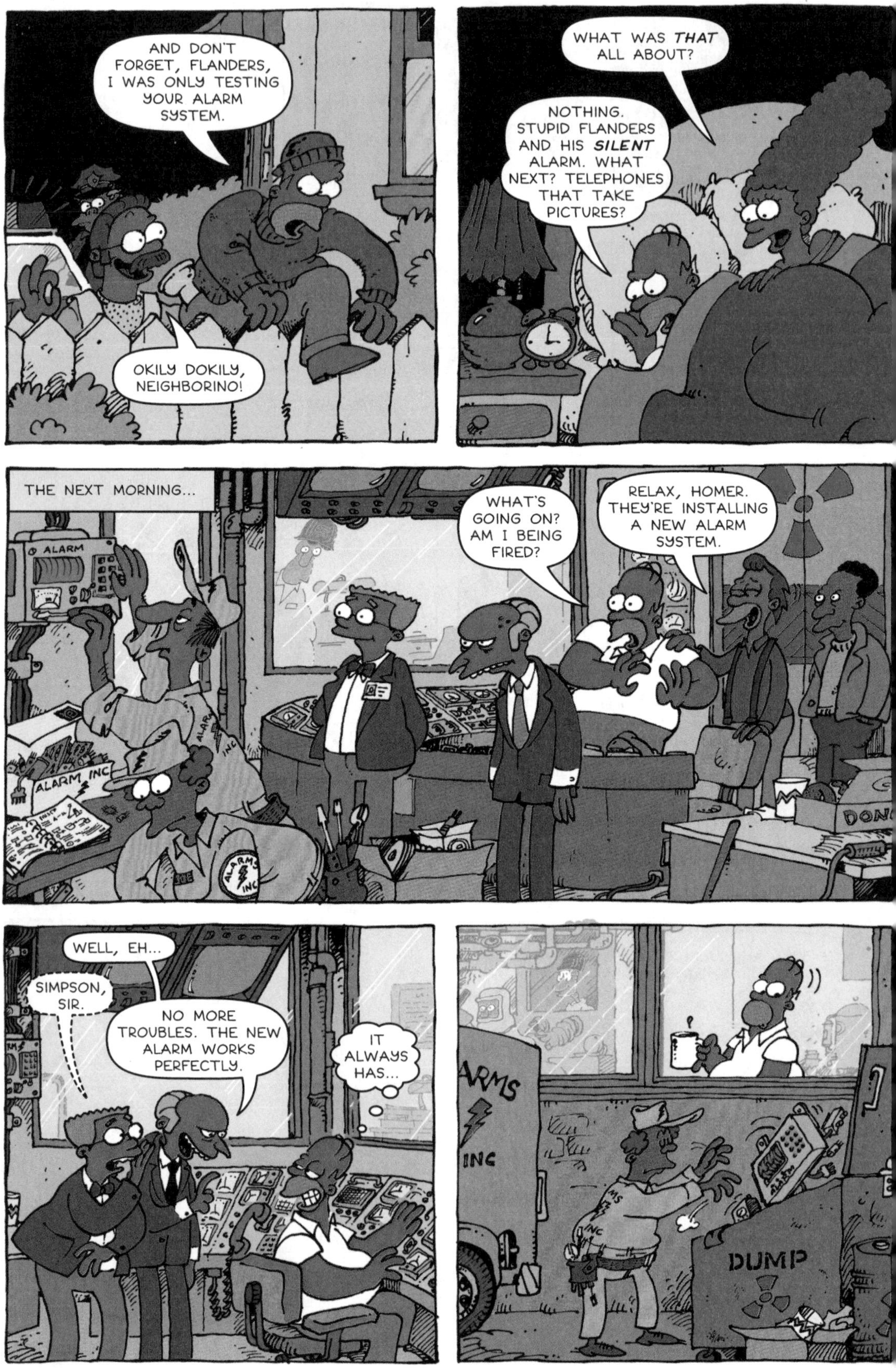
AND DON'T FORGET, FLANDERS, I WAS ONLY TESTING YOUR ALARM SYSTEM.
OKILY DOKILY, NEIGHBORINO!
WHAT WAS *THAT* ALL ABOUT?
NOTHING. STUPID FLANDERS AND HIS *SILENT* ALARM. WHAT NEXT? TELEPHONES THAT TAKE PICTURES?
THE NEXT MORNING...
ALARM
ALARM INC
WHAT'S GOING ON? AM I BEING FIRED?
RELAX, HOMER. THEY'RE INSTALLING A NEW ALARM SYSTEM.
WELL, EH...
SIMPSON, SIR.
NO MORE TROUBLES. THE NEW ALARM WORKS PERFECTLY.
IT ALWAYS HAS...
INC
DUMP

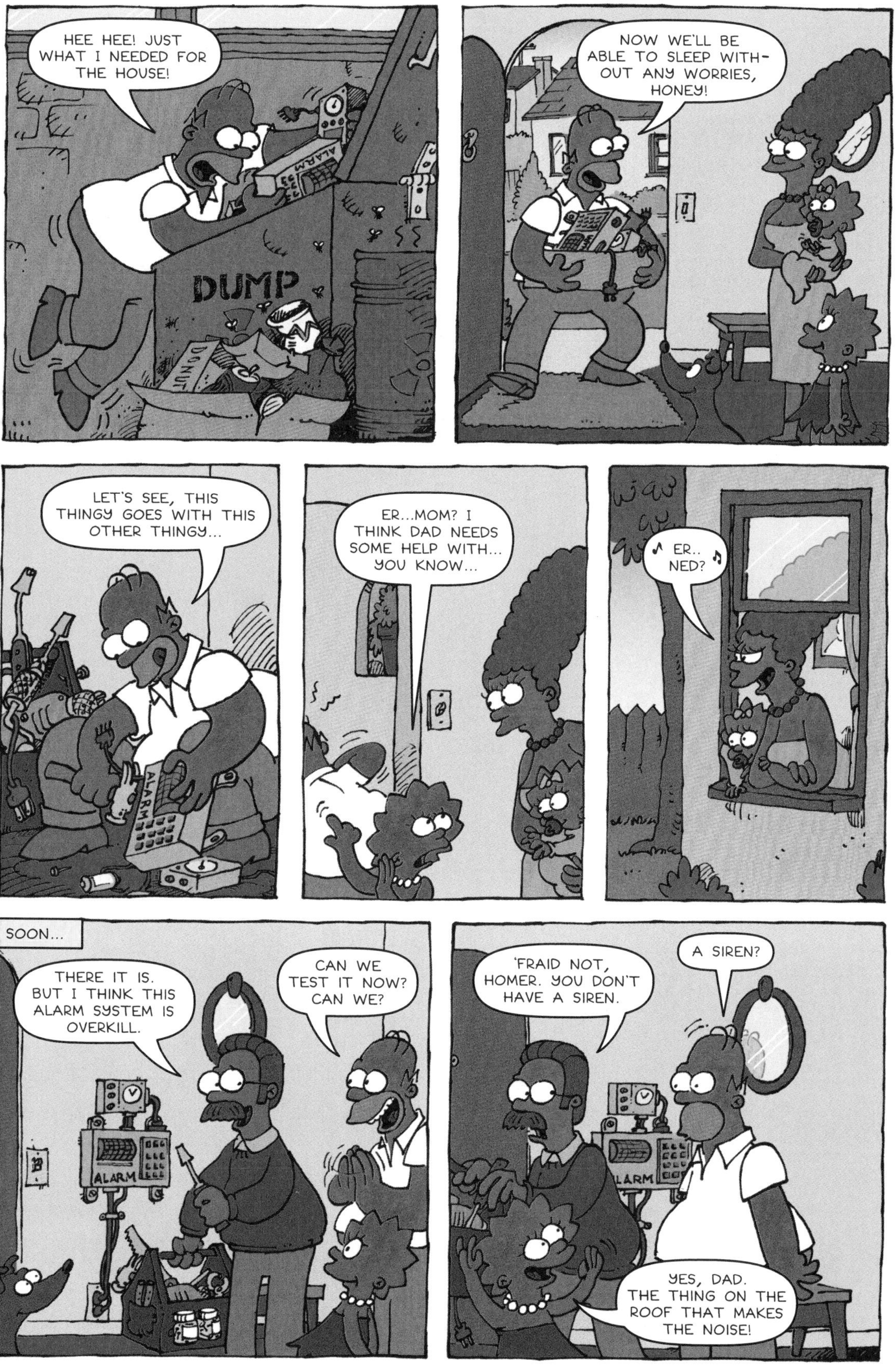
HEE HEE! JUST WHAT I NEEDED FOR THE HOUSE!
ALARM
DUMP
DONUT
NOW WE'LL BE ABLE TO SLEEP WITH-OUT ANY WORRIES, HONEY!
LET'S SEE, THIS THINGY GOES WITH THIS OTHER THINGY...
ALARM
ER...MOM? I THINK DAD NEEDS SOME HELP WITH... YOU KNOW...
♪ ER.. NED? ♪
SOON...
THERE IT IS. BUT I THINK THIS ALARM SYSTEM IS OVERKILL.
CAN WE TEST IT NOW? CAN WE?
ALARM
'FRAID NOT, HOMER. YOU DON'T HAVE A SIREN.
A SIREN?
ALARM
YES, DAD. THE THING ON THE ROOF THAT MAKES THE NOISE!

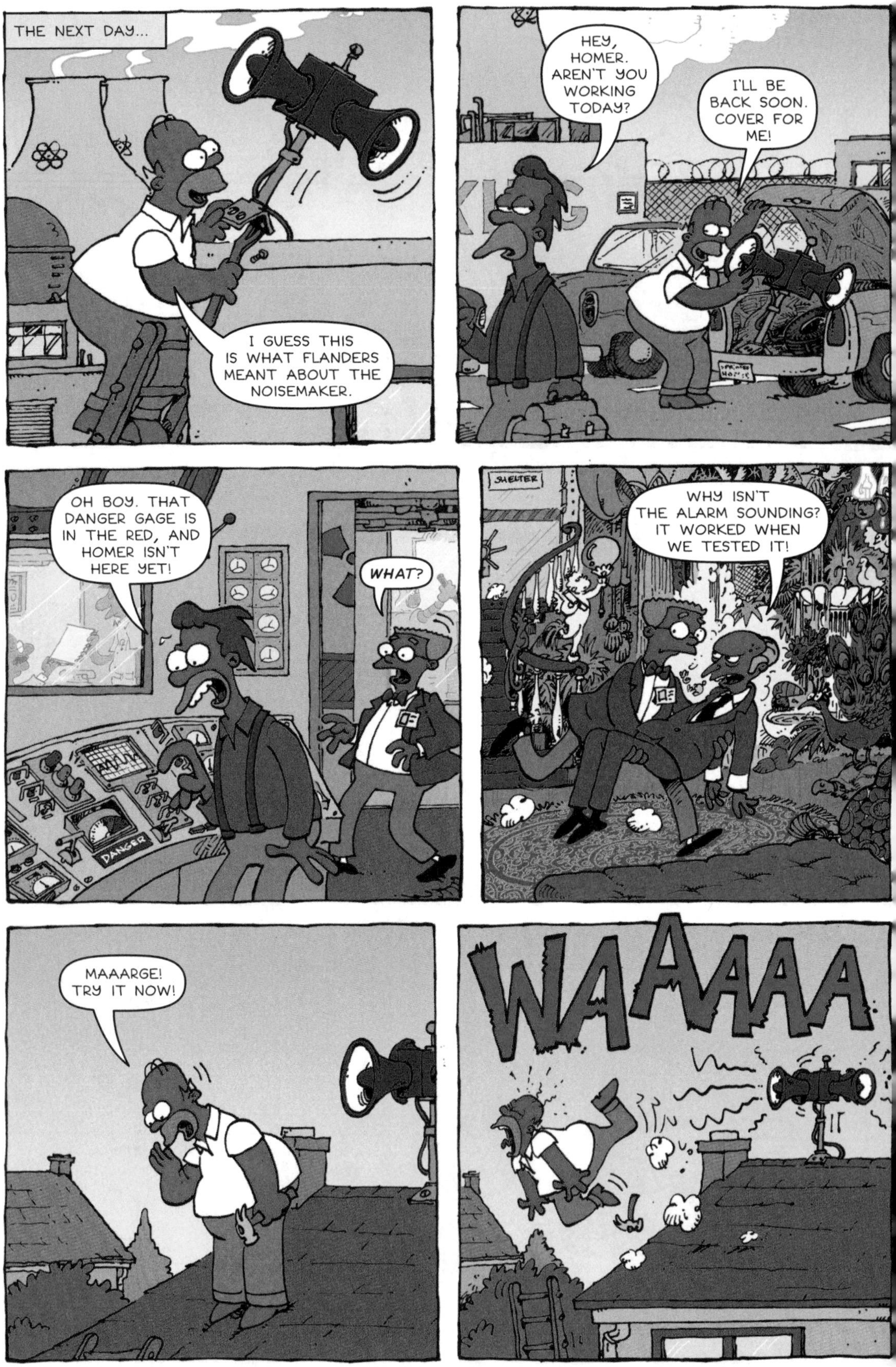
THE NEXT DAY...
I GUESS THIS IS WHAT FLANDERS MEANT ABOUT THE NOISEMAKER.
HEY, HOMER. AREN'T YOU WORKING TODAY?
I'LL BE BACK SOON. COVER FOR ME!
OH BOY. THAT DANGER GAGE IS IN THE RED, AND HOMER ISN'T HERE YET!
WHAT?
DANGER
SHELTER
WHY ISN'T THE ALARM SOUNDING? IT WORKED WHEN WE TESTED IT!
MAAARGE! TRY IT NOW!
WAAAAA

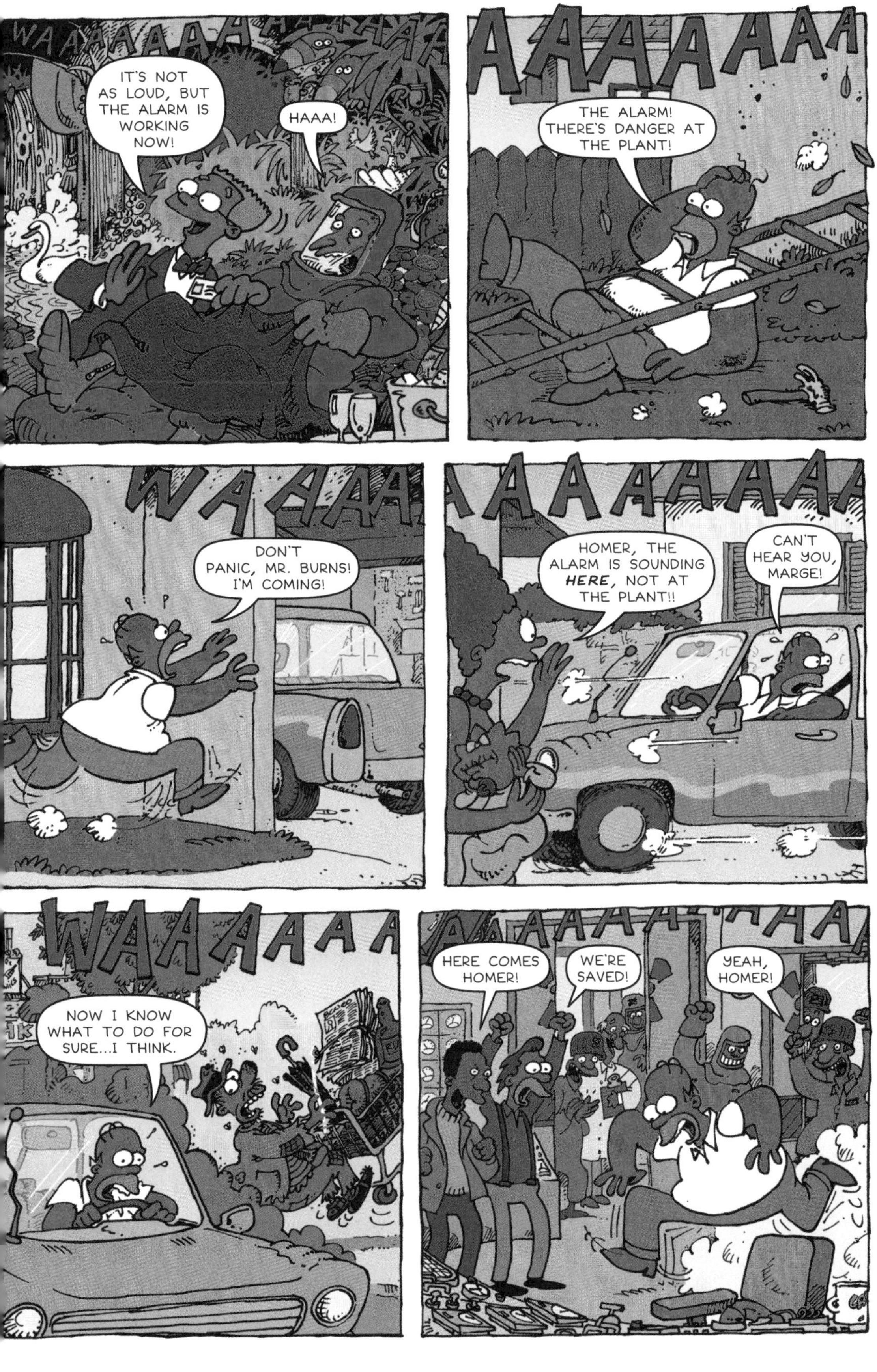
IT'S NOT AS LOUD, BUT THE ALARM IS WORKING NOW!
HAAA!
THE ALARM! THERE'S DANGER AT THE PLANT!
DON'T PANIC, MR. BURNS! I'M COMING!
HOMER, THE ALARM IS SOUNDING *HERE*, NOT AT THE PLANT!!
CAN'T HEAR YOU, MARGE!
NOW I KNOW WHAT TO DO FOR SURE...I THINK.
HERE COMES HOMER!
WE'RE SAVED!
YEAH, HOMER!

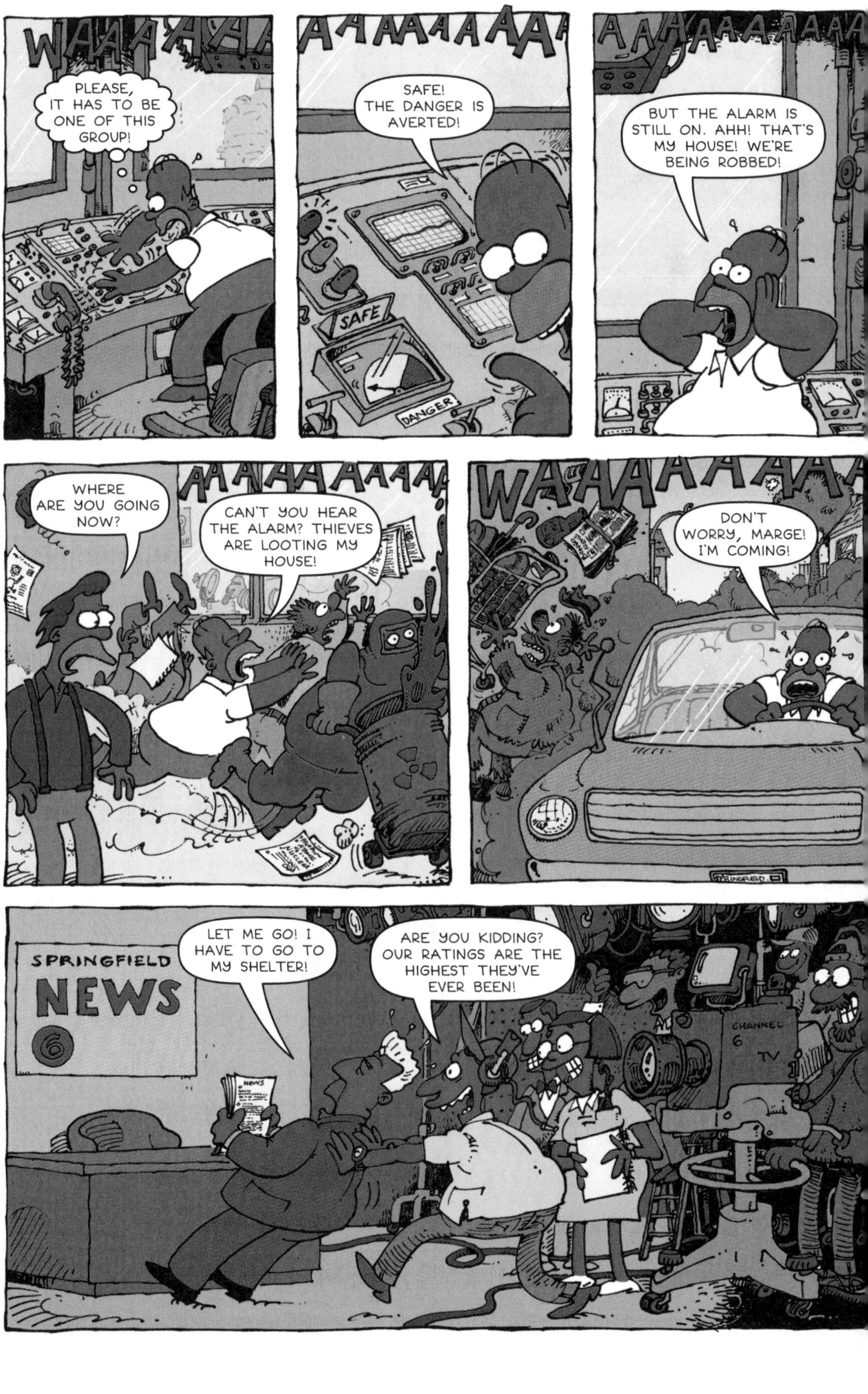

PLEASE, IT HAS TO BE ONE OF THIS GROUP!
SAFE! THE DANGER IS AVERTED!
SAFE
DANGER
BUT THE ALARM IS STILL ON. AHH! THAT'S MY HOUSE! WE'RE BEING ROBBED!
WHERE ARE YOU GOING NOW?
CAN'T YOU HEAR THE ALARM? THIEVES ARE LOOTING MY HOUSE!
DON'T WORRY, MARGE! I'M COMING!
SPRINGFIELD
SPRINGFIELD NEWS 6
LET ME GO! I HAVE TO GO TO MY SHELTER!
ARE YOU KIDDING? OUR RATINGS ARE THE HIGHEST THEY'VE EVER BEEN!
NEWS
CHANNEL 6 TV

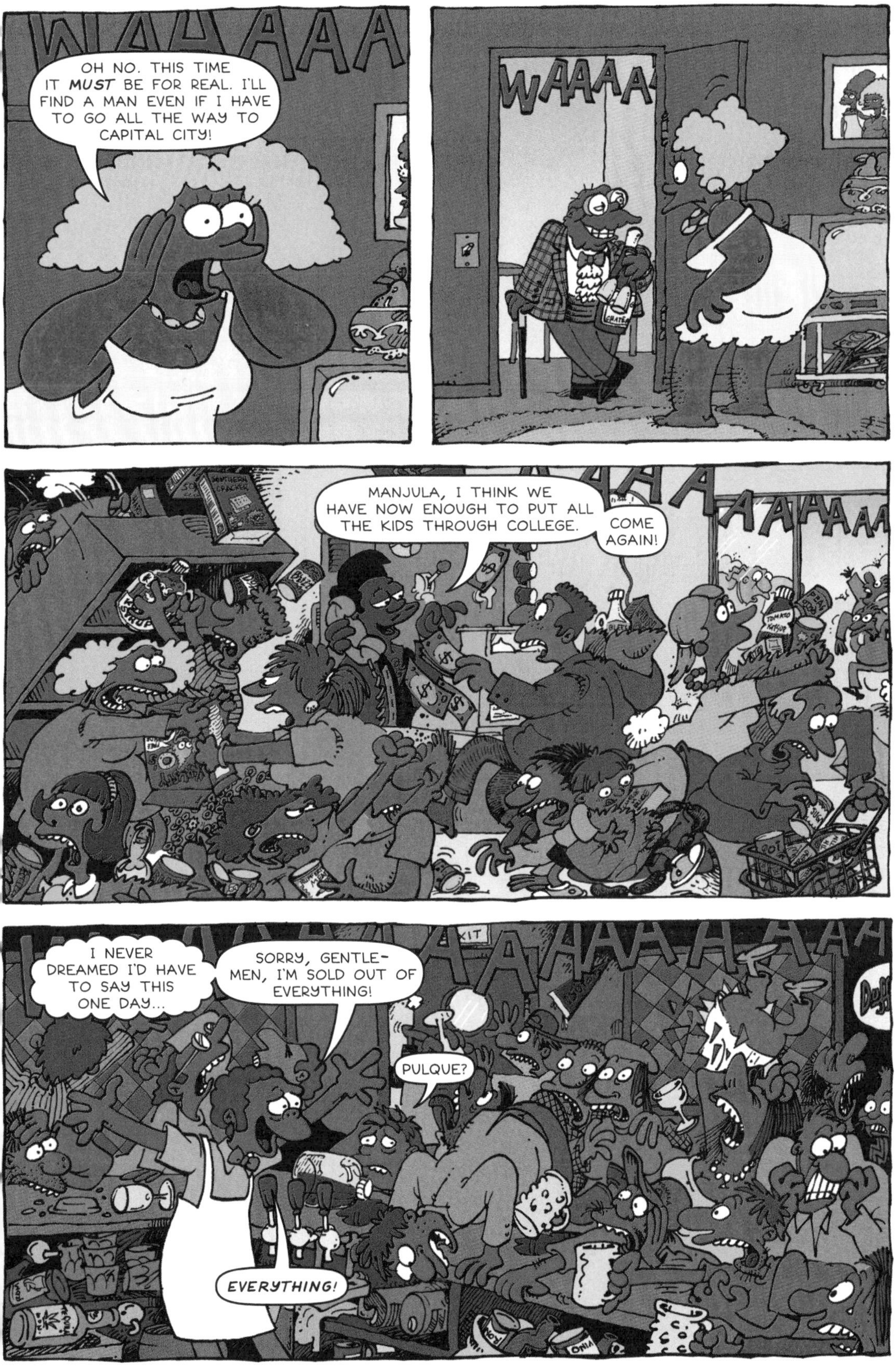
OH NO. THIS TIME IT *MUST* BE FOR REAL. I'LL FIND A MAN EVEN IF I HAVE TO GO ALL THE WAY TO CAPITAL CITY!
WAAAA
MANJULA, I THINK WE HAVE NOW ENOUGH TO PUT ALL THE KIDS THROUGH COLLEGE.
COME AGAIN!
I NEVER DREAMED I'D HAVE TO SAY THIS ONE DAY...
SORRY, GENTLE-MEN, I'M SOLD OUT OF EVERYTHING!
PULQUE?
EVERYTHING!

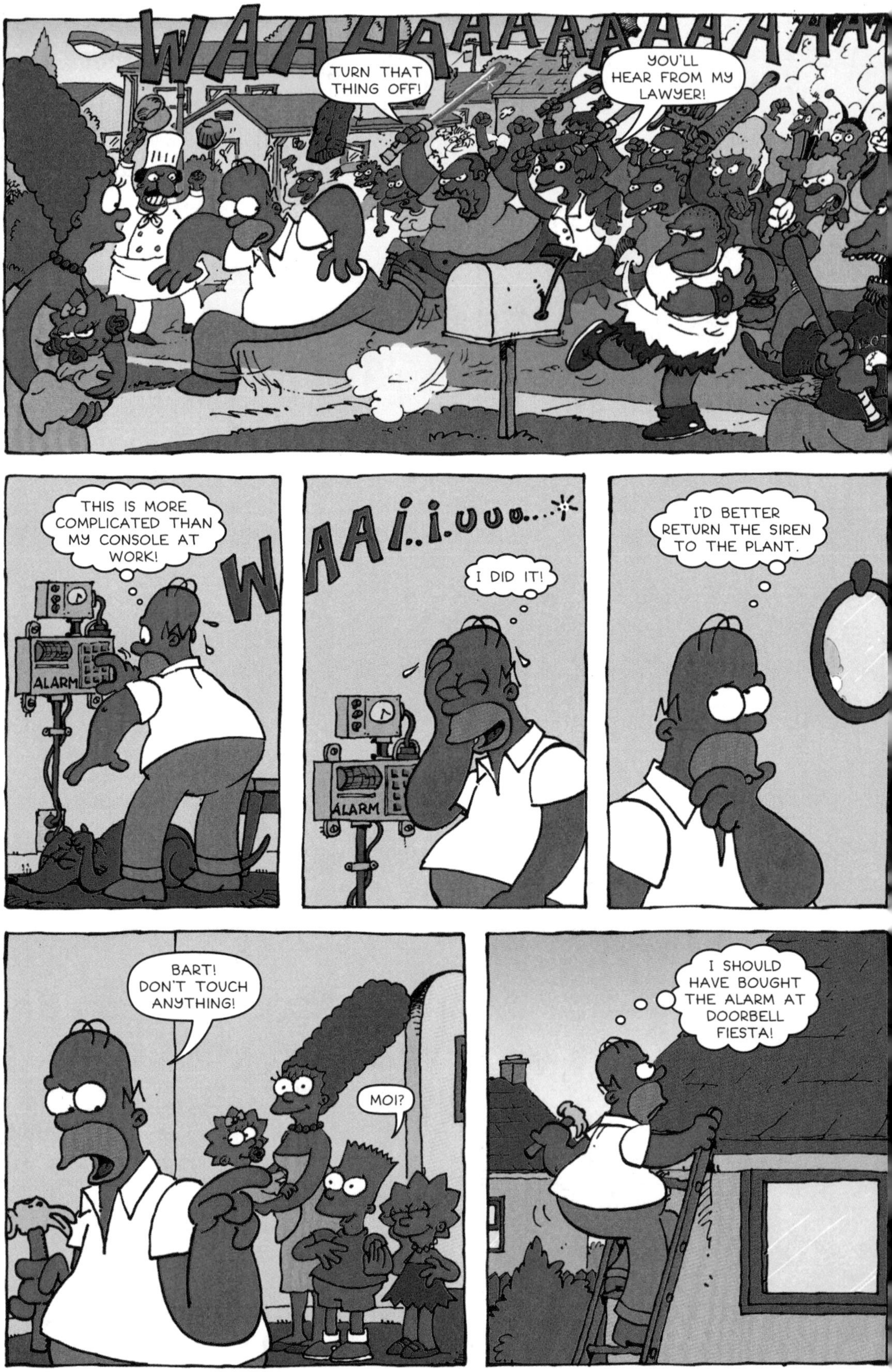
WAAAAAAAAAAAAA
TURN THAT THING OFF!
YOU'LL HEAR FROM MY LAWYER!
THIS IS MORE COMPLICATED THAN MY CONSOLE AT WORK!
W
WAAi..i..uuu...
I DID IT!
I'D BETTER RETURN THE SIREN TO THE PLANT.
ALARM
BART! DON'T TOUCH ANYTHING!
MOI?
I SHOULD HAVE BOUGHT THE ALARM AT DOORBELL FIESTA!

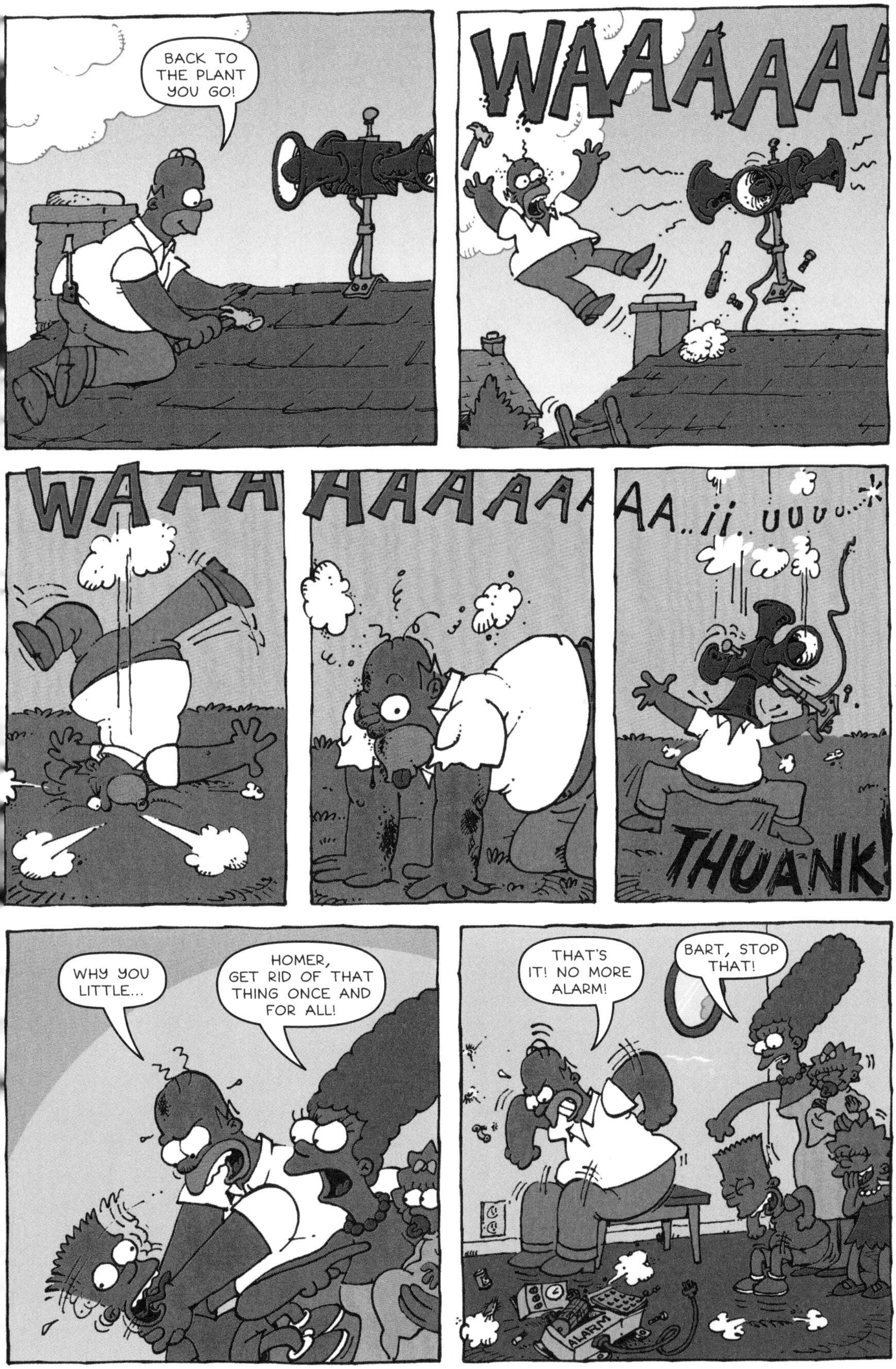
BACK TO THE PLANT YOU GO!
WAAAAAA
WAAA
AAAAAA
AA..ii..uuuu..
THUANK!
WHY YOU LITTLE...
HOMER, GET RID OF THAT THING ONCE AND FOR ALL!
THAT'S IT! NO MORE ALARM!
BART, STOP THAT!
ALARM

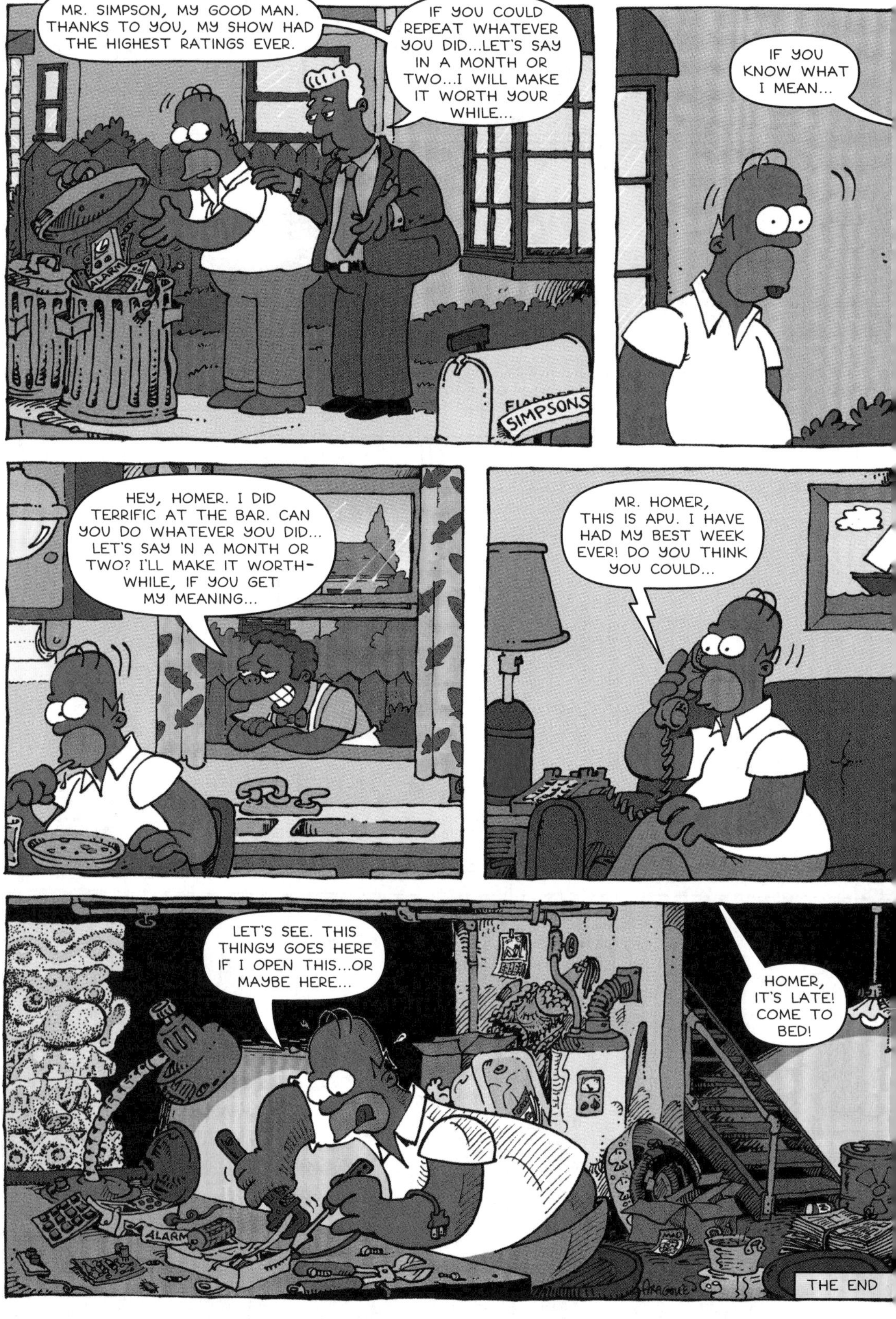
MR. SIMPSON, MY GOOD MAN. THANKS TO YOU, MY SHOW HAD THE HIGHEST RATINGS EVER.
IF YOU COULD REPEAT WHATEVER YOU DID...LET'S SAY IN A MONTH OR TWO...I WILL MAKE IT WORTH YOUR WHILE...
SIMPSONS
IF YOU KNOW WHAT I MEAN...
HEY, HOMER. I DID TERRIFIC AT THE BAR. CAN YOU DO WHATEVER YOU DID... LET'S SAY IN A MONTH OR TWO? I'LL MAKE IT WORTH-WHILE, IF YOU GET MY MEANING...
MR. HOMER, THIS IS APU. I HAVE HAD MY BEST WEEK EVER! DO YOU THINK YOU COULD...
LET'S SEE. THIS THINGY GOES HERE IF I OPEN THIS...OR MAYBE HERE...
HOMER, IT'S LATE! COME TO BED!
ALARM
THE END

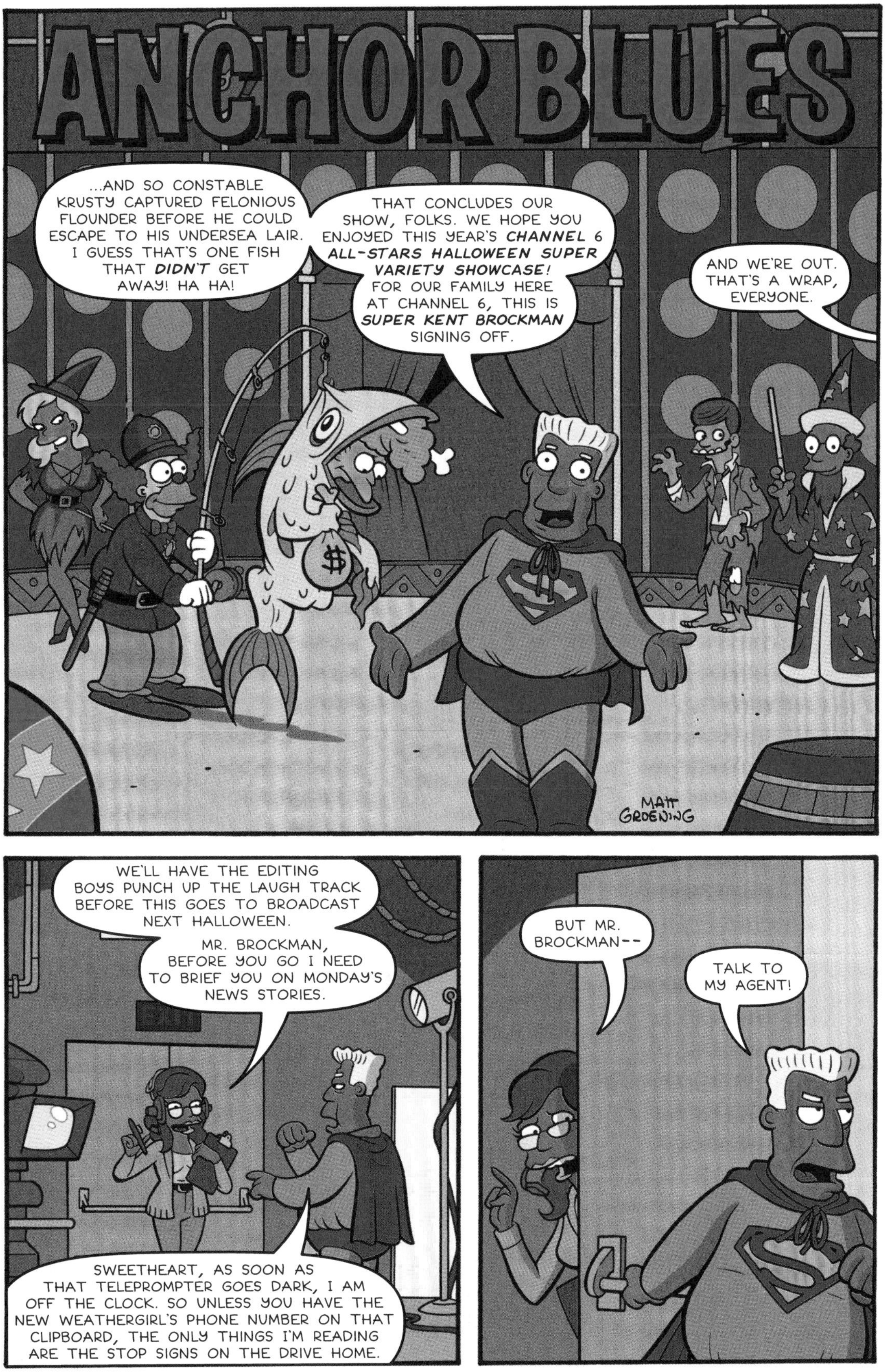
ANCHOR BLUES
...AND SO CONSTABLE KRUSTY CAPTURED FELONIOUS FLOUNDER BEFORE HE COULD ESCAPE TO HIS UNDERSEA LAIR. I GUESS THAT'S ONE FISH THAT *DIDN'T* GET AWAY! HA HA!
THAT CONCLUDES OUR SHOW, FOLKS. WE HOPE YOU ENJOYED THIS YEAR'S ***CHANNEL 6 ALL-STARS HALLOWEEN SUPER VARIETY SHOWCASE!*** FOR OUR FAMILY HERE AT CHANNEL 6, THIS IS ***SUPER KENT BROCKMAN*** SIGNING OFF.
AND WE'RE OUT. THAT'S A WRAP, EVERYONE.
MATT GROENING
WE'LL HAVE THE EDITING BOYS PUNCH UP THE LAUGH TRACK BEFORE THIS GOES TO BROADCAST NEXT HALLOWEEN.
MR. BROCKMAN, BEFORE YOU GO I NEED TO BRIEF YOU ON MONDAY'S NEWS STORIES.
SWEETHEART, AS SOON AS THAT TELEPROMPTER GOES DARK, I AM OFF THE CLOCK. SO UNLESS YOU HAVE THE NEW WEATHERGIRL'S PHONE NUMBER ON THAT CLIPBOARD, THE ONLY THINGS I'M READING ARE THE STOP SIGNS ON THE DRIVE HOME.
BUT MR. BROCKMAN--
TALK TO MY AGENT!

TONY DIGEROLAMO & NATHAN KANE STORY

JAMES LLOYD PENCILS

ANDREW PEPOY INKS

NATHAN HAMILL COLORS

KAREN BATES LETTERS

BILL MORRISON EDITOR

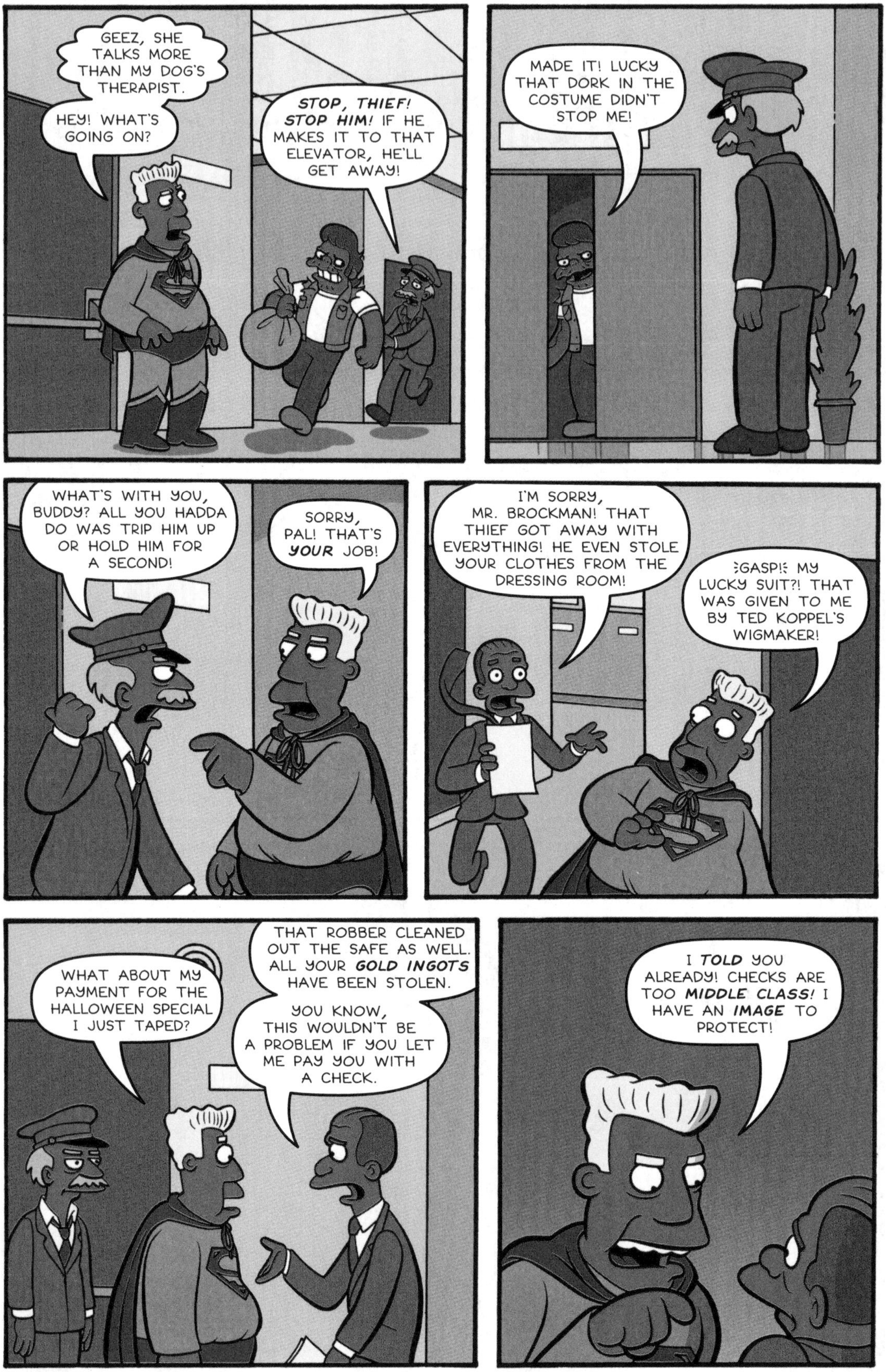
GEEZ, SHE TALKS MORE THAN MY DOG'S THERAPIST.
HEY! WHAT'S GOING ON?
STOP, THIEF! STOP HIM! IF HE MAKES IT TO THAT ELEVATOR, HE'LL GET AWAY!
MADE IT! LUCKY THAT DORK IN THE COSTUME DIDN'T STOP ME!
WHAT'S WITH YOU, BUDDY? ALL YOU HADDA DO WAS TRIP HIM UP OR HOLD HIM FOR A SECOND!
SORRY, PAL! THAT'S YOUR JOB!
I'M SORRY, MR. BROCKMAN! THAT THIEF GOT AWAY WITH EVERYTHING! HE EVEN STOLE YOUR CLOTHES FROM THE DRESSING ROOM!
GASP! MY LUCKY SUIT?! THAT WAS GIVEN TO ME BY TED KOPPEL'S WIGMAKER!
WHAT ABOUT MY PAYMENT FOR THE HALLOWEEN SPECIAL I JUST TAPED?
THAT ROBBER CLEANED OUT THE SAFE AS WELL. ALL YOUR GOLD INGOTS HAVE BEEN STOLEN.
YOU KNOW, THIS WOULDN'T BE A PROBLEM IF YOU LET ME PAY YOU WITH A CHECK.
I TOLD YOU ALREADY! CHECKS ARE TOO MIDDLE CLASS! I HAVE AN IMAGE TO PROTECT!

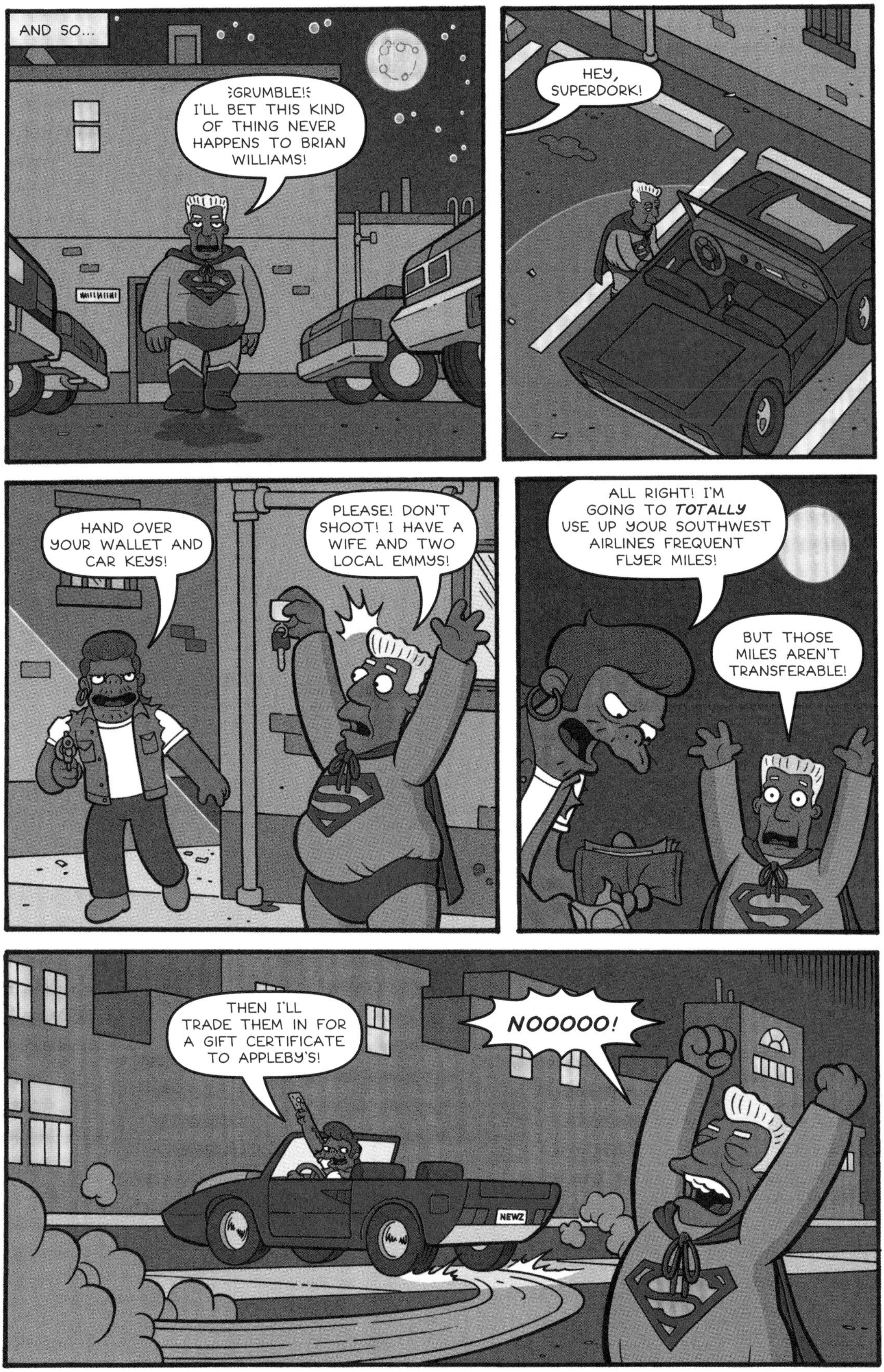
AND SO...
≷GRUMBLE!≶ I'LL BET THIS KIND OF THING NEVER HAPPENS TO BRIAN WILLIAMS!
HEY, SUPERDORK!
HAND OVER YOUR WALLET AND CAR KEYS!
PLEASE! DON'T SHOOT! I HAVE A WIFE AND TWO LOCAL EMMYS!
ALL RIGHT! I'M GOING TO *TOTALLY* USE UP YOUR SOUTHWEST AIRLINES FREQUENT FLYER MILES!
BUT THOSE MILES AREN'T TRANSFERABLE!
THEN I'LL TRADE THEM IN FOR A GIFT CERTIFICATE TO APPLEBY'S!
NOOOOO!
NEWZ

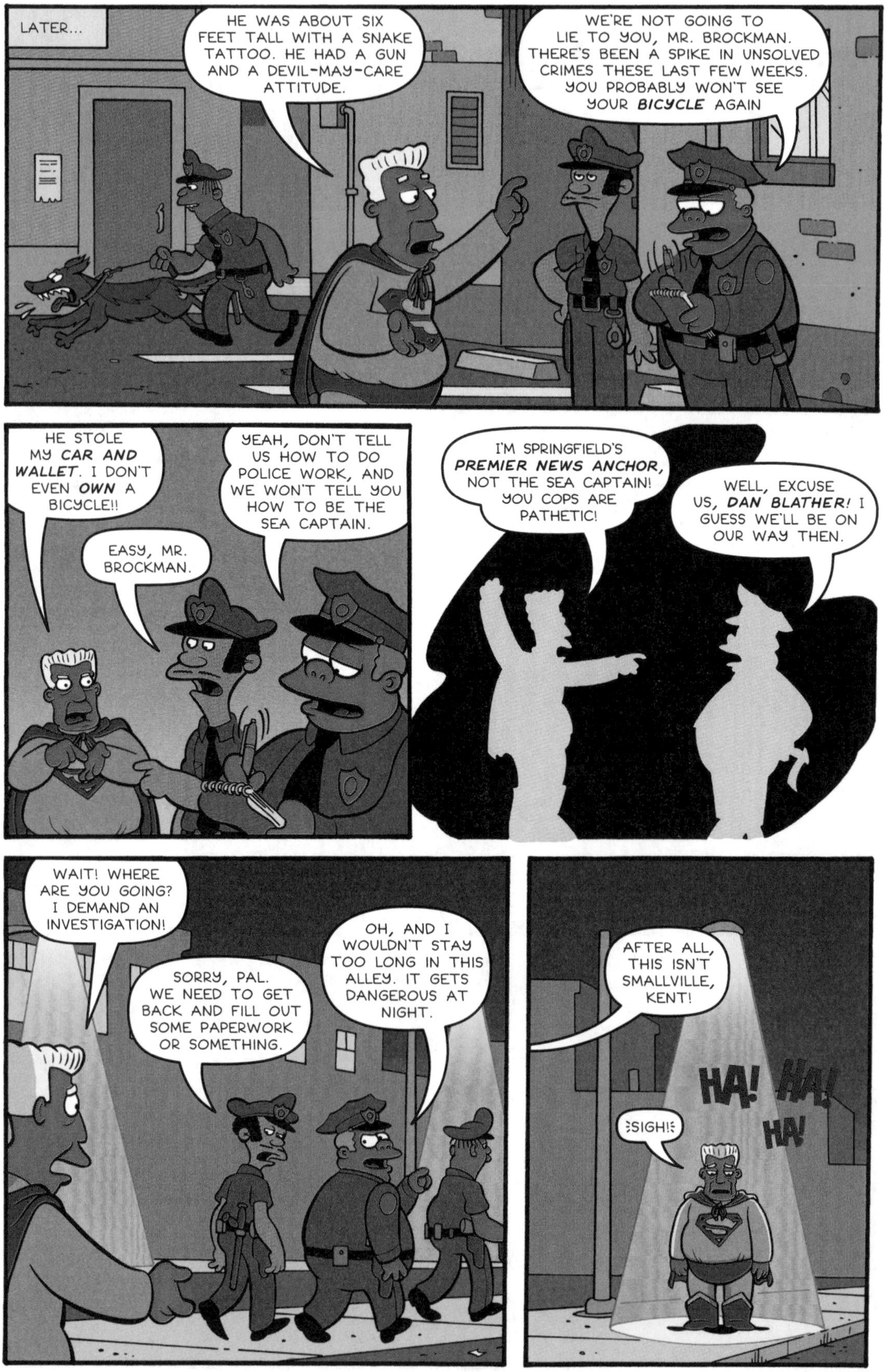
LATER...
HE WAS ABOUT SIX FEET TALL WITH A SNAKE TATTOO. HE HAD A GUN AND A DEVIL-MAY-CARE ATTITUDE.
WE'RE NOT GOING TO LIE TO YOU, MR. BROCKMAN. THERE'S BEEN A SPIKE IN UNSOLVED CRIMES THESE LAST FEW WEEKS. YOU PROBABLY WON'T SEE YOUR BICYCLE AGAIN
HE STOLE MY CAR AND WALLET. I DON'T EVEN OWN A BICYCLE!!
YEAH, DON'T TELL US HOW TO DO POLICE WORK, AND WE WON'T TELL YOU HOW TO BE THE SEA CAPTAIN.
EASY, MR. BROCKMAN.
I'M SPRINGFIELD'S PREMIER NEWS ANCHOR, NOT THE SEA CAPTAIN! YOU COPS ARE PATHETIC!
WELL, EXCUSE US, DAN BLATHER! I GUESS WE'LL BE ON OUR WAY THEN.
WAIT! WHERE ARE YOU GOING? I DEMAND AN INVESTIGATION!
SORRY, PAL. WE NEED TO GET BACK AND FILL OUT SOME PAPERWORK OR SOMETHING.
OH, AND I WOULDN'T STAY TOO LONG IN THIS ALLEY. IT GETS DANGEROUS AT NIGHT.
AFTER ALL, THIS ISN'T SMALLVILLE, KENT!
HA! HA! HA!
SIGH!

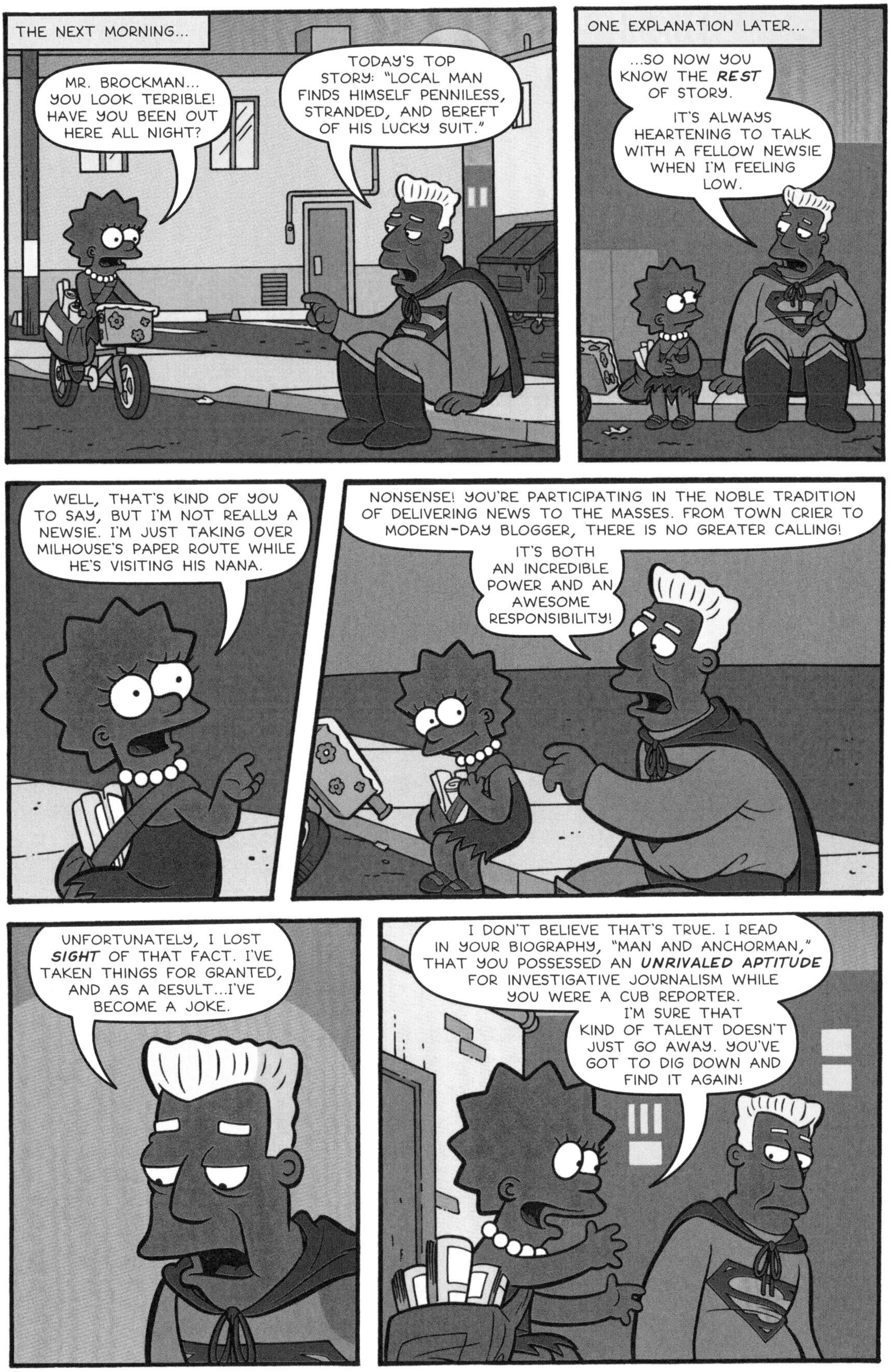
THE NEXT MORNING...
MR. BROCKMAN... YOU LOOK TERRIBLE! HAVE YOU BEEN OUT HERE ALL NIGHT?
TODAY'S TOP STORY: "LOCAL MAN FINDS HIMSELF PENNILESS, STRANDED, AND BEREFT OF HIS LUCKY SUIT."
ONE EXPLANATION LATER...
...SO NOW YOU KNOW THE *REST* OF STORY.
IT'S ALWAYS HEARTENING TO TALK WITH A FELLOW NEWSIE WHEN I'M FEELING LOW.
WELL, THAT'S KIND OF YOU TO SAY, BUT I'M NOT REALLY A NEWSIE. I'M JUST TAKING OVER MILHOUSE'S PAPER ROUTE WHILE HE'S VISITING HIS NANA.
NONSENSE! YOU'RE PARTICIPATING IN THE NOBLE TRADITION OF DELIVERING NEWS TO THE MASSES. FROM TOWN CRIER TO MODERN-DAY BLOGGER, THERE IS NO GREATER CALLING!
IT'S BOTH AN INCREDIBLE POWER AND AN AWESOME RESPONSIBILITY!
UNFORTUNATELY, I LOST *SIGHT* OF THAT FACT. I'VE TAKEN THINGS FOR GRANTED, AND AS A RESULT...I'VE BECOME A JOKE.
I DON'T BELIEVE THAT'S TRUE. I READ IN YOUR BIOGRAPHY, "MAN AND ANCHORMAN," THAT YOU POSSESSED AN ***UNRIVALED APTITUDE*** FOR INVESTIGATIVE JOURNALISM WHILE YOU WERE A CUB REPORTER.
I'M SURE THAT KIND OF TALENT DOESN'T JUST GO AWAY. YOU'VE GOT TO DIG DOWN AND FIND IT AGAIN!

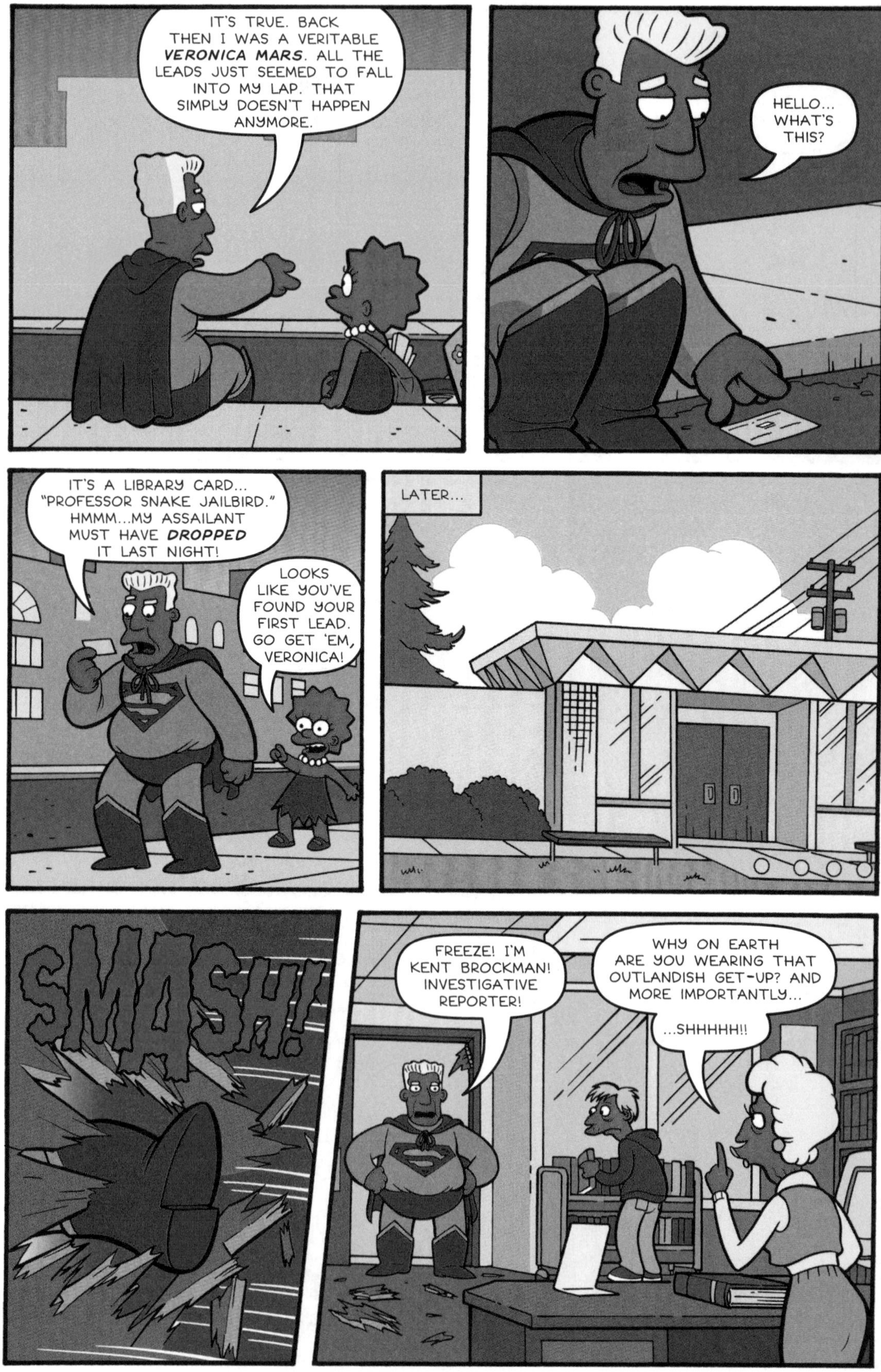
IT'S TRUE. BACK THEN I WAS A VERITABLE **VERONICA MARS**. ALL THE LEADS JUST SEEMED TO FALL INTO MY LAP. THAT SIMPLY DOESN'T HAPPEN ANYMORE.
HELLO... WHAT'S THIS?
IT'S A LIBRARY CARD... "PROFESSOR SNAKE JAILBIRD." HMMM...MY ASSAILANT MUST HAVE **DROPPED** IT LAST NIGHT!
LOOKS LIKE YOU'VE FOUND YOUR FIRST LEAD. GO GET 'EM, VERONICA!
LATER...
SMASH!!
FREEZE! I'M KENT BROCKMAN! INVESTIGATIVE REPORTER!
WHY ON EARTH ARE YOU WEARING THAT OUTLANDISH GET-UP? AND MORE IMPORTANTLY...
...SHHHHH!!

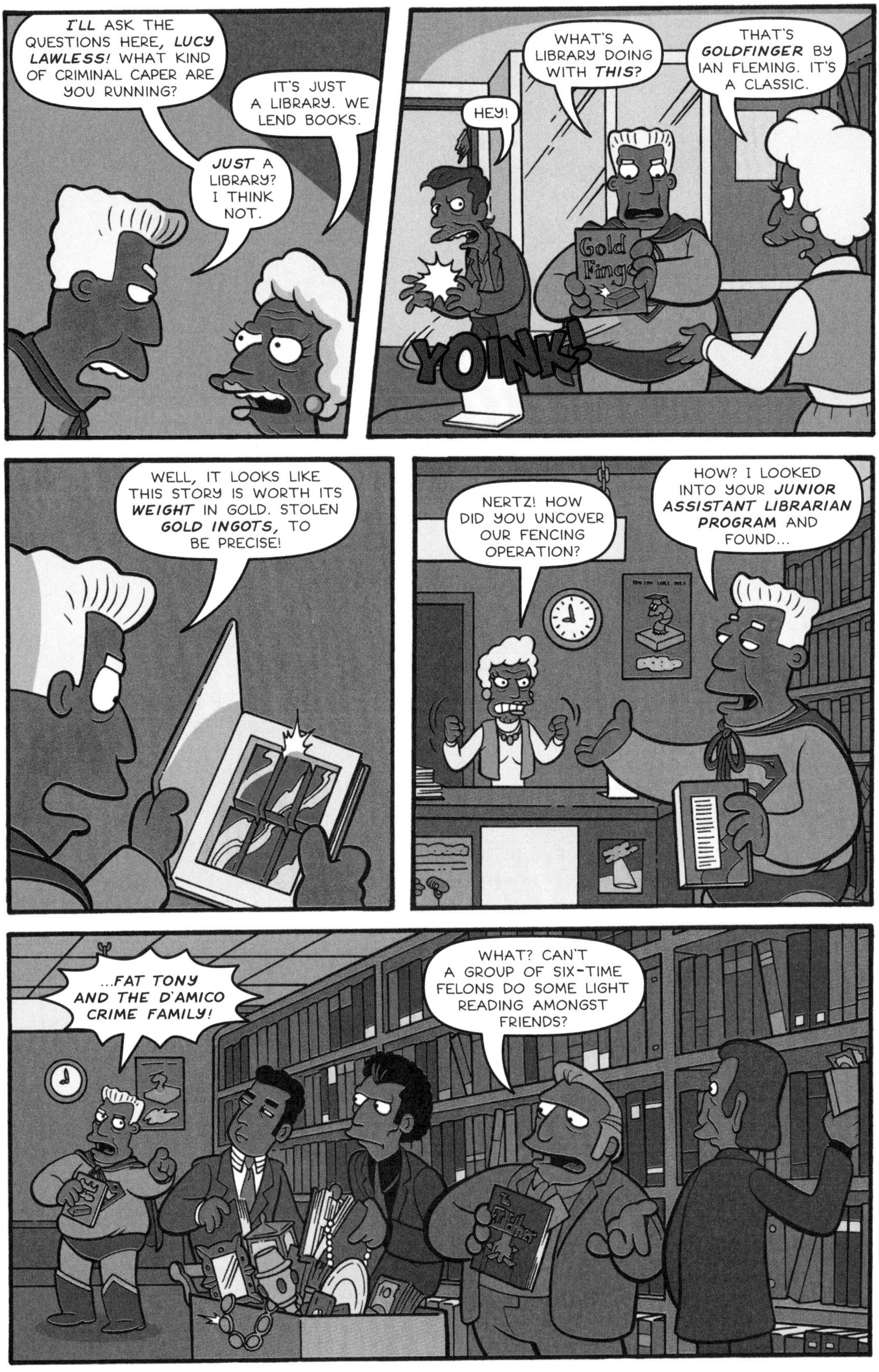
I'LL ASK THE QUESTIONS HERE, LUCY LAWLESS! WHAT KIND OF CRIMINAL CAPER ARE YOU RUNNING?
IT'S JUST A LIBRARY. WE LEND BOOKS.
JUST A LIBRARY? I THINK NOT.
WHAT'S A LIBRARY DOING WITH THIS?
THAT'S GOLDFINGER BY IAN FLEMING. IT'S A CLASSIC.
HEY!
Gold Finge
YOINK!
WELL, IT LOOKS LIKE THIS STORY IS WORTH ITS WEIGHT IN GOLD. STOLEN GOLD INGOTS, TO BE PRECISE!
NERTZ! HOW DID YOU UNCOVER OUR FENCING OPERATION?
HOW? I LOOKED INTO YOUR JUNIOR ASSISTANT LIBRARIAN PROGRAM AND FOUND...
...FAT TONY AND THE D'AMICO CRIME FAMILY!
WHAT? CAN'T A GROUP OF SIX-TIME FELONS DO SOME LIGHT READING AMONGST FRIENDS?

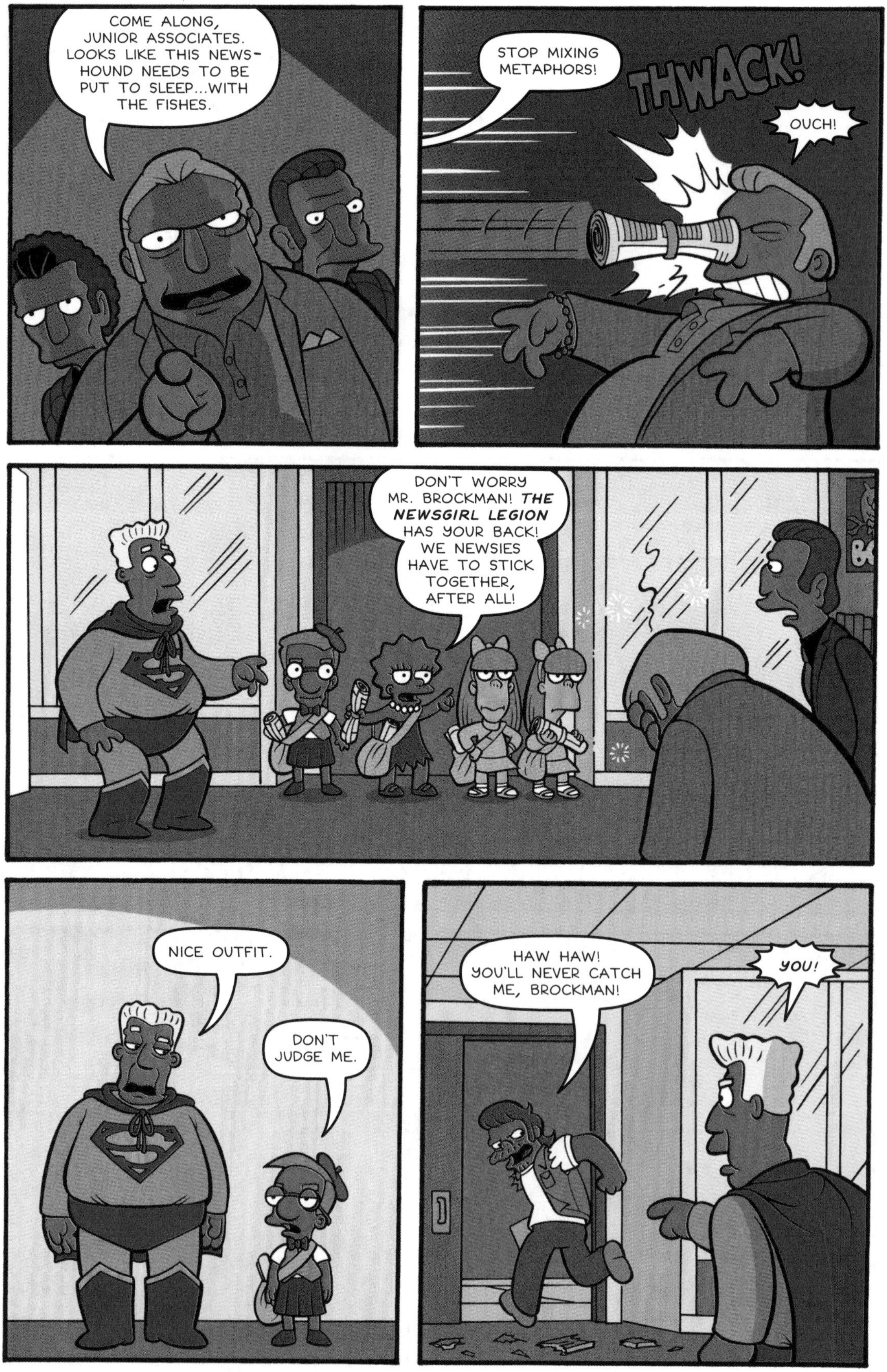
COME ALONG, JUNIOR ASSOCIATES. LOOKS LIKE THIS NEWS-HOUND NEEDS TO BE PUT TO SLEEP...WITH THE FISHES.
STOP MIXING METAPHORS!
THWACK!
OUCH!
DON'T WORRY MR. BROCKMAN! THE NEWSGIRL LEGION HAS YOUR BACK! WE NEWSIES HAVE TO STICK TOGETHER, AFTER ALL!
NICE OUTFIT.
DON'T JUDGE ME.
HAW HAW! YOU'LL NEVER CATCH ME, BROCKMAN!
YOU!

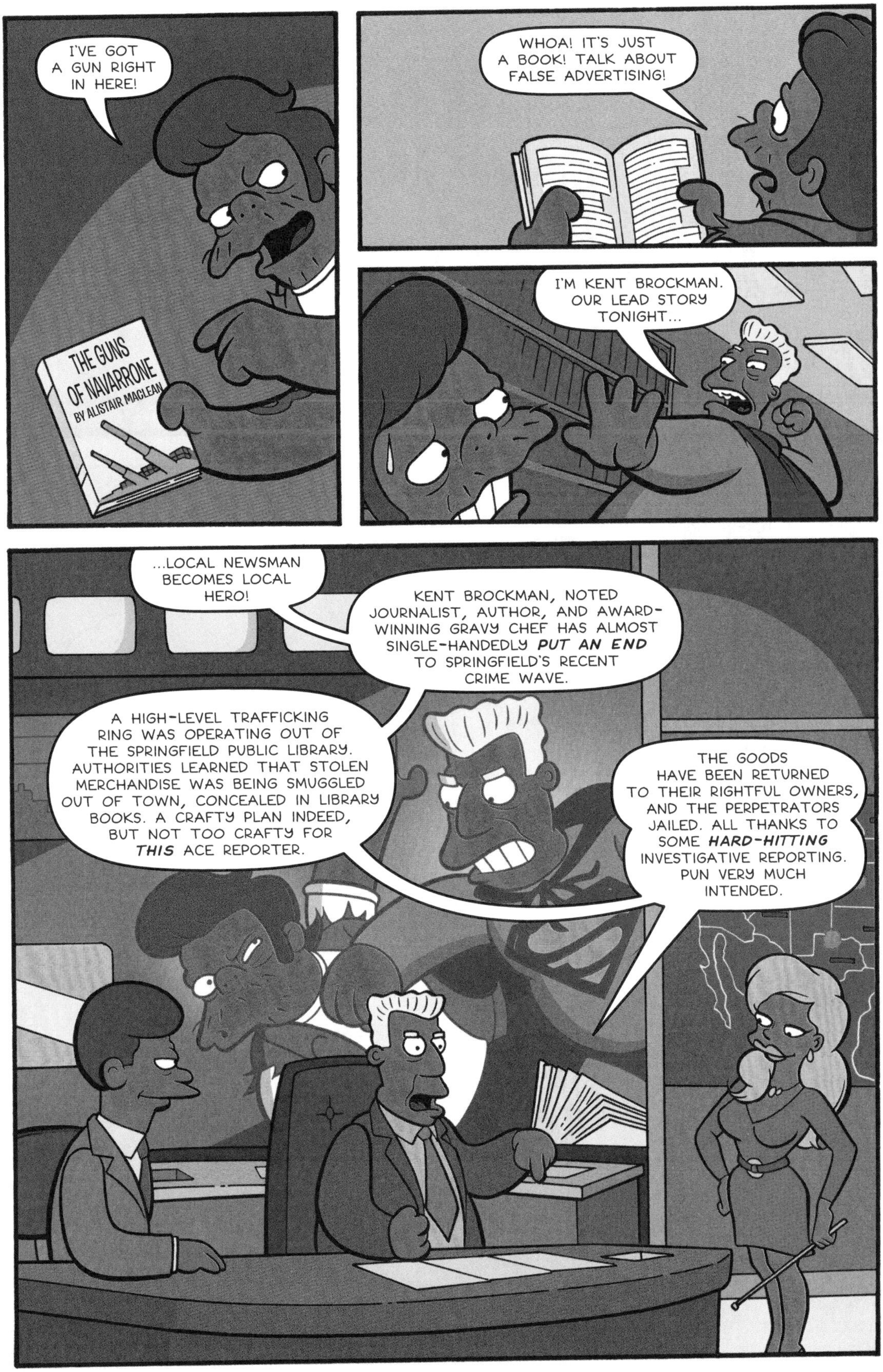
I'VE GOT A GUN RIGHT IN HERE!
THE GUNS OF NAVARRONE
BY ALISTAIR MACLEAN
WHOA! IT'S JUST A BOOK! TALK ABOUT FALSE ADVERTISING!
I'M KENT BROCKMAN. OUR LEAD STORY TONIGHT...
...LOCAL NEWSMAN BECOMES LOCAL HERO!
KENT BROCKMAN, NOTED JOURNALIST, AUTHOR, AND AWARD-WINNING GRAVY CHEF HAS ALMOST SINGLE-HANDEDLY PUT AN END TO SPRINGFIELD'S RECENT CRIME WAVE.
A HIGH-LEVEL TRAFFICKING RING WAS OPERATING OUT OF THE SPRINGFIELD PUBLIC LIBRARY. AUTHORITIES LEARNED THAT STOLEN MERCHANDISE WAS BEING SMUGGLED OUT OF TOWN, CONCEALED IN LIBRARY BOOKS. A CRAFTY PLAN INDEED, BUT NOT TOO CRAFTY FOR THIS ACE REPORTER.
THE GOODS HAVE BEEN RETURNED TO THEIR RIGHTFUL OWNERS, AND THE PERPETRATORS JAILED. ALL THANKS TO SOME HARD-HITTING INVESTIGATIVE REPORTING. PUN VERY MUCH INTENDED.

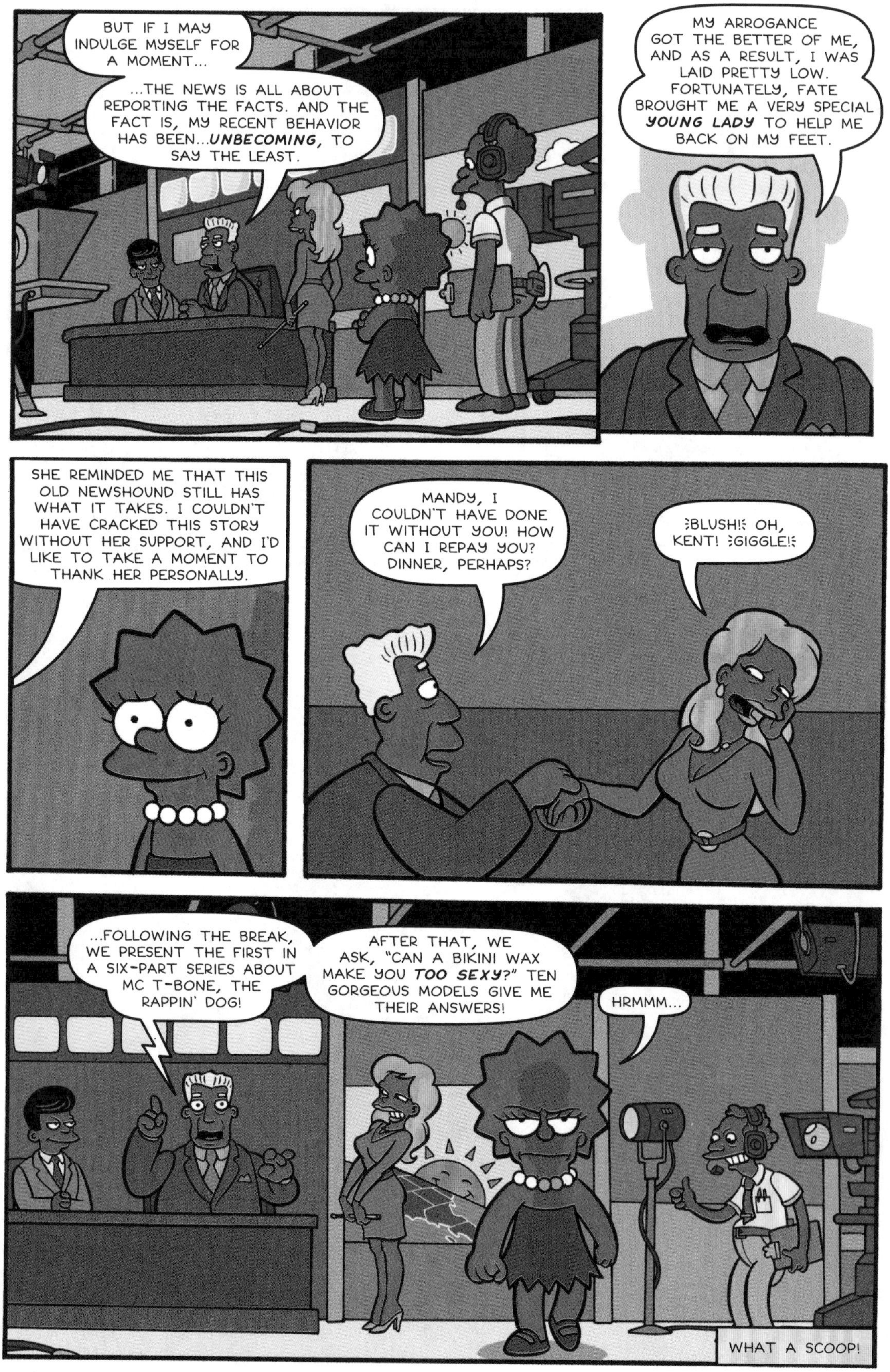
BUT IF I MAY INDULGE MYSELF FOR A MOMENT...
...THE NEWS IS ALL ABOUT REPORTING THE FACTS. AND THE FACT IS, MY RECENT BEHAVIOR HAS BEEN...UNBECOMING, TO SAY THE LEAST.
MY ARROGANCE GOT THE BETTER OF ME, AND AS A RESULT, I WAS LAID PRETTY LOW. FORTUNATELY, FATE BROUGHT ME A VERY SPECIAL YOUNG LADY TO HELP ME BACK ON MY FEET.
SHE REMINDED ME THAT THIS OLD NEWSHOUND STILL HAS WHAT IT TAKES. I COULDN'T HAVE CRACKED THIS STORY WITHOUT HER SUPPORT, AND I'D LIKE TO TAKE A MOMENT TO THANK HER PERSONALLY.
MANDY, I COULDN'T HAVE DONE IT WITHOUT YOU! HOW CAN I REPAY YOU? DINNER, PERHAPS?
BLUSH! OH, KENT! GIGGLE!
...FOLLOWING THE BREAK, WE PRESENT THE FIRST IN A SIX-PART SERIES ABOUT MC T-BONE, THE RAPPIN' DOG!
AFTER THAT, WE ASK, "CAN A BIKINI WAX MAKE YOU TOO SEXY?" TEN GORGEOUS MODELS GIVE ME THEIR ANSWERS!
HRMMM...
WHAT A SCOOP!

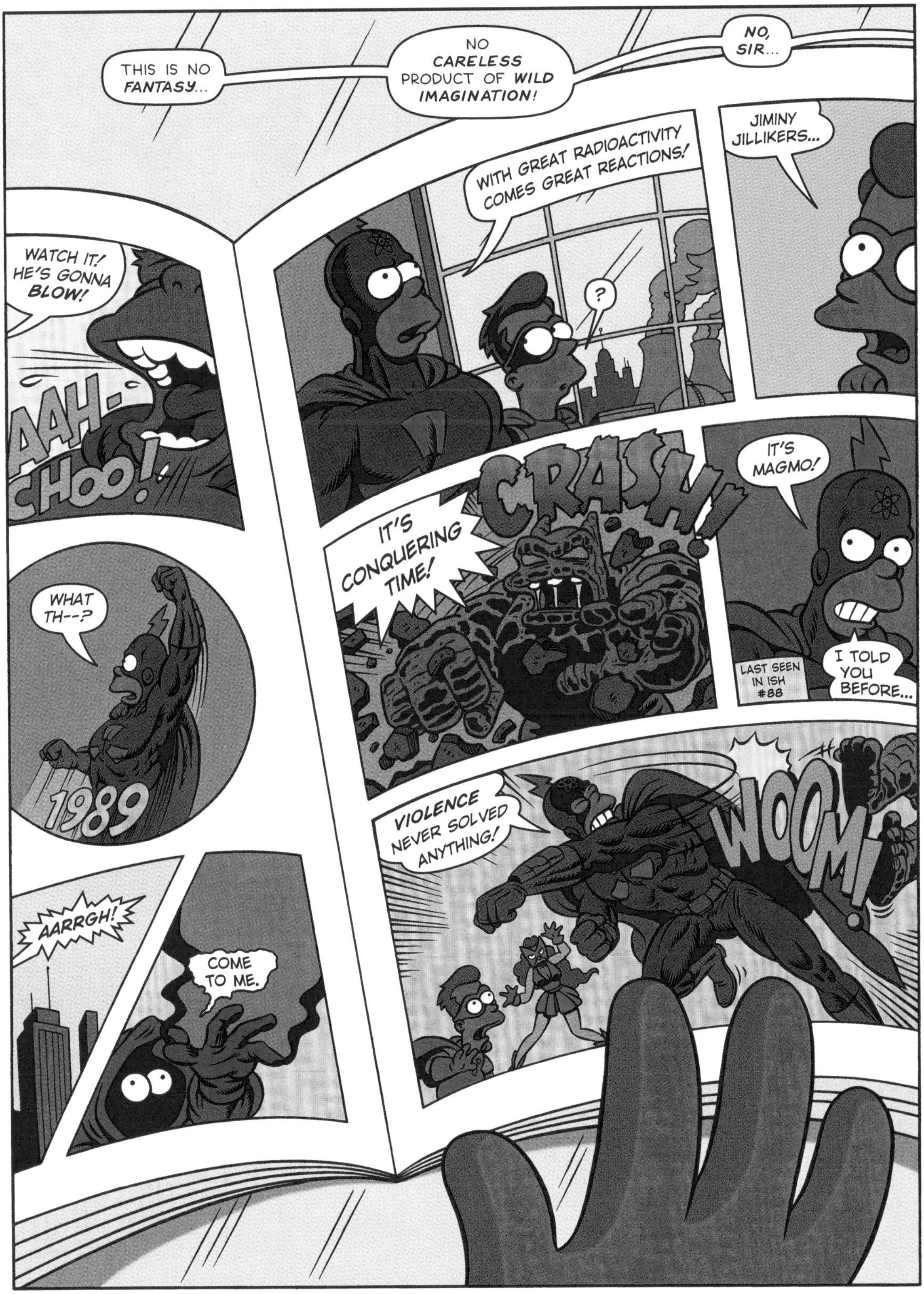
THIS IS NO FANTASY...
NO CARELESS PRODUCT OF WILD IMAGINATION!
NO, SIR...
WATCH IT! HE'S GONNA BLOW!
AAH-CHOO!
WITH GREAT RADIOACTIVITY COMES GREAT REACTIONS!
?
JIMINY JILLIKERS...
WHAT TH--?
1989
IT'S CONQUERING TIME!
CRASH!
IT'S MAGMO!
LAST SEEN IN ISH #88
I TOLD YOU BEFORE...
VIOLENCE NEVER SOLVED ANYTHING!
WOOM!
AARRGH!
COME TO ME.

A MATT GROENING PRODUCTION, BROUGHT TO YOU BY:

SCRIPT	1963 SEQUENCE	COMIC SHOP SEQUENCE	LETTERS
BATTON LASH	PENCILS: HILARY BARTA INKS: BOB SMITH COLORS: NATHAN KANE	PENCILS: BILL MORRISON INKS: STEVE STEERE, JR. COLORS: CHRIS UNGAR	CHRIS UNGAR

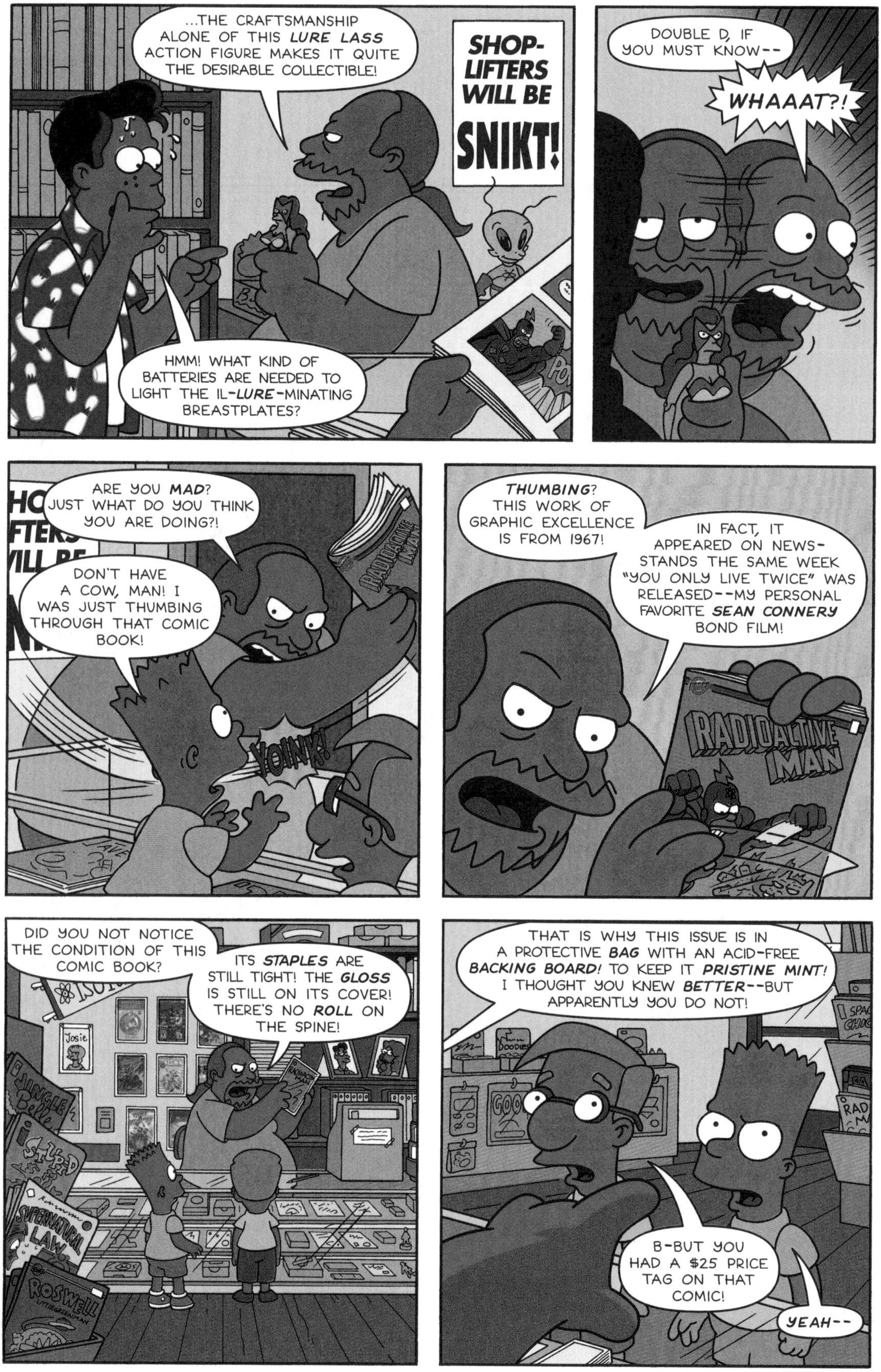
...THE CRAFTSMANSHIP ALONE OF THIS LURE LASS ACTION FIGURE MAKES IT QUITE THE DESIRABLE COLLECTIBLE!
SHOP-LIFTERS WILL BE SNIKT!
HMM! WHAT KIND OF BATTERIES ARE NEEDED TO LIGHT THE IL-LURE-MINATING BREASTPLATES?
DOUBLE D, IF YOU MUST KNOW--
WHAAAT?!
ARE YOU MAD? JUST WHAT DO YOU THINK YOU ARE DOING?!
DON'T HAVE A COW, MAN! I WAS JUST THUMBING THROUGH THAT COMIC BOOK!
YOINK!
THUMBING? THIS WORK OF GRAPHIC EXCELLENCE IS FROM 1967!
IN FACT, IT APPEARED ON NEWS-STANDS THE SAME WEEK "YOU ONLY LIVE TWICE" WAS RELEASED--MY PERSONAL FAVORITE SEAN CONNERY BOND FILM!
RADIOACTIVE MAN
DID YOU NOT NOTICE THE CONDITION OF THIS COMIC BOOK?
ITS STAPLES ARE STILL TIGHT! THE GLOSS IS STILL ON ITS COVER! THERE'S NO ROLL ON THE SPINE!
Josie
SUPERNATURAL LAW
ROSWELL
THAT IS WHY THIS ISSUE IS IN A PROTECTIVE BAG WITH AN ACID-FREE BACKING BOARD! TO KEEP IT PRISTINE MINT! I THOUGHT YOU KNEW BETTER--BUT APPARENTLY YOU DO NOT!
B-BUT YOU HAD A $25 PRICE TAG ON THAT COMIC!
YEAH--

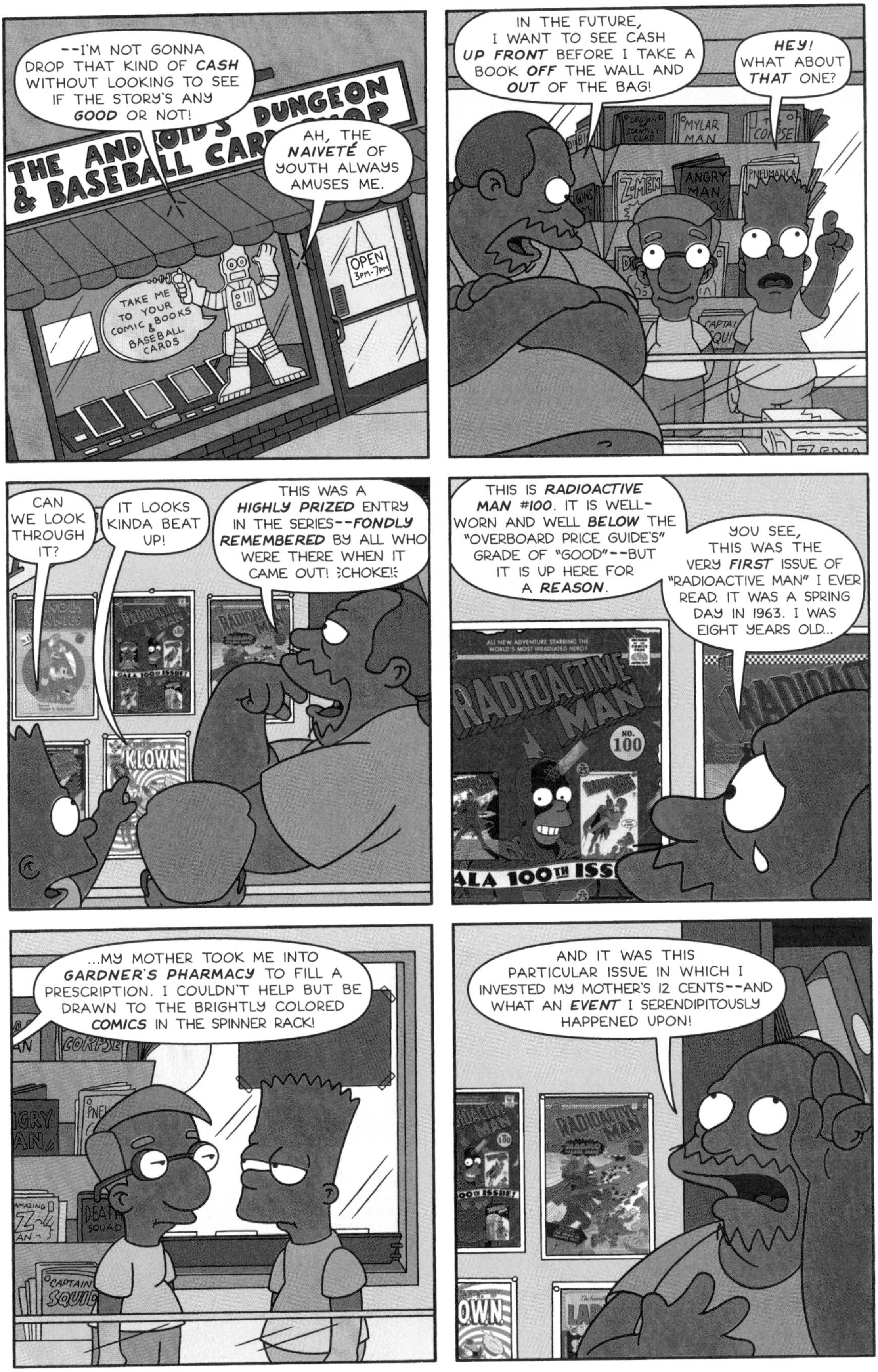
--I'M NOT GONNA DROP THAT KIND OF CASH WITHOUT LOOKING TO SEE IF THE STORY'S ANY GOOD OR NOT!
THE ANDROID'S DUNGEON & BASEBALL CARD SHOP
AH, THE NAIVETÉ OF YOUTH ALWAYS AMUSES ME.
TAKE ME TO YOUR COMIC BOOKS & BASEBALL CARDS
OPEN 3PM-7PM
IN THE FUTURE, I WANT TO SEE CASH UP FRONT BEFORE I TAKE A BOOK OFF THE WALL AND OUT OF THE BAG!
HEY! WHAT ABOUT THAT ONE?
MYLAR MAN
ANGRY MAN
PNEUMATICA
CAN WE LOOK THROUGH IT?
IT LOOKS KINDA BEAT UP!
THIS WAS A HIGHLY PRIZED ENTRY IN THE SERIES--FONDLY REMEMBERED BY ALL WHO WERE THERE WHEN IT CAME OUT! CHOKE!
THIS IS RADIOACTIVE MAN #100. IT IS WELL-WORN AND WELL BELOW THE "OVERBOARD PRICE GUIDE'S" GRADE OF "GOOD"--BUT IT IS UP HERE FOR A REASON.
YOU SEE, THIS WAS THE VERY FIRST ISSUE OF "RADIOACTIVE MAN" I EVER READ. IT WAS A SPRING DAY IN 1963. I WAS EIGHT YEARS OLD...
RADIOACTIVE MAN
NO. 100
...MY MOTHER TOOK ME INTO GARDNER'S PHARMACY TO FILL A PRESCRIPTION. I COULDN'T HELP BUT BE DRAWN TO THE BRIGHTLY COLORED COMICS IN THE SPINNER RACK!
AND IT WAS THIS PARTICULAR ISSUE IN WHICH I INVESTED MY MOTHER'S 12 CENTS--AND WHAT AN EVENT I SERENDIPITOUSLY HAPPENED UPON!

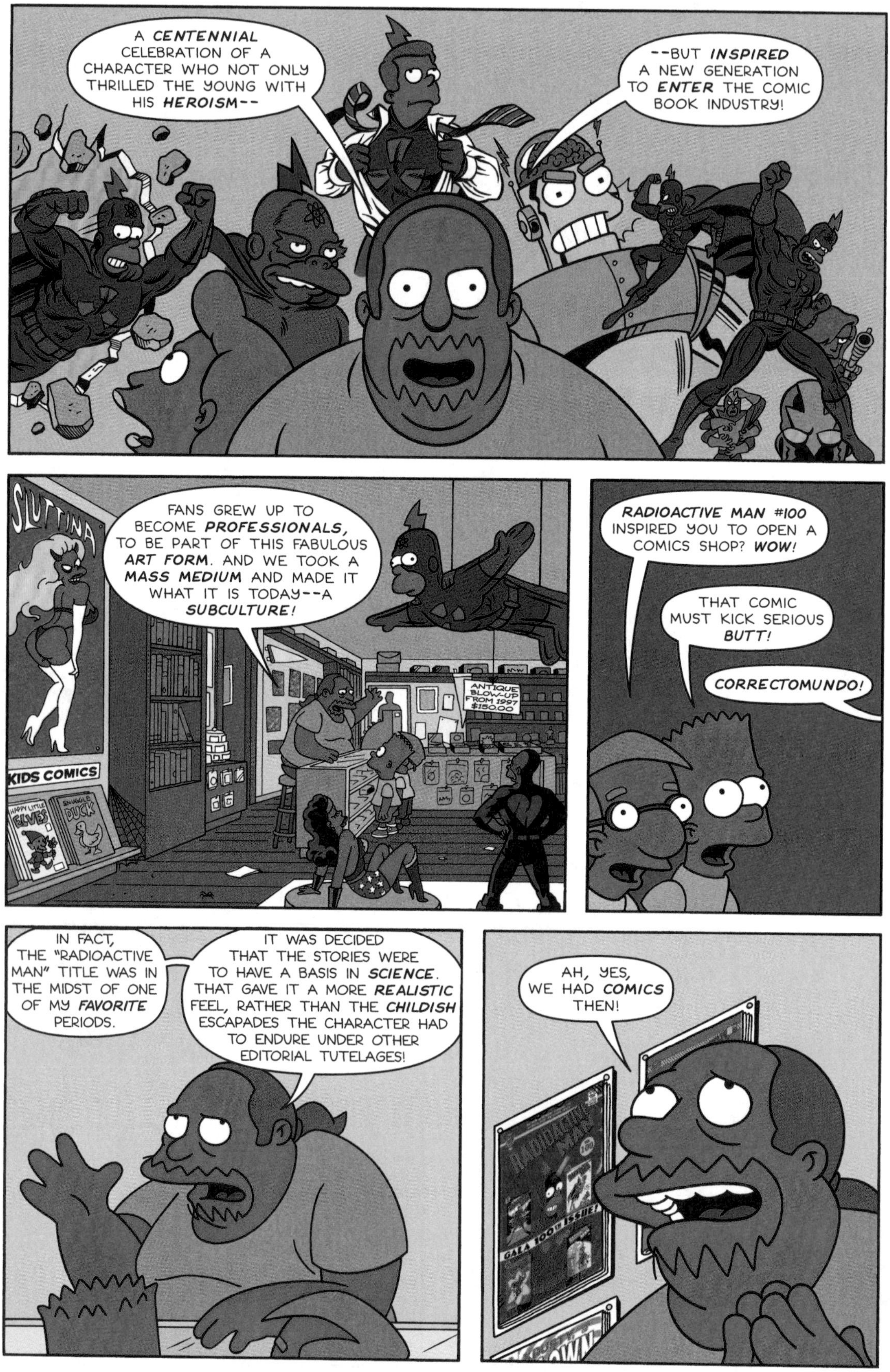

A CENTENNIAL CELEBRATION OF A CHARACTER WHO NOT ONLY THRILLED THE YOUNG WITH HIS HEROISM--
--BUT INSPIRED A NEW GENERATION TO ENTER THE COMIC BOOK INDUSTRY!
SLUTTINA
FANS GREW UP TO BECOME PROFESSIONALS, TO BE PART OF THIS FABULOUS ART FORM. AND WE TOOK A MASS MEDIUM AND MADE IT WHAT IT IS TODAY--A SUBCULTURE!
ANTIQUE BLOW-UP FROM 1997 $150.00
KIDS COMICS
HAPPY LITTLE ELVES
SNUGGLE DUCK
RADIOACTIVE MAN #100 INSPIRED YOU TO OPEN A COMICS SHOP? WOW!
THAT COMIC MUST KICK SERIOUS BUTT!
CORRECTOMUNDO!
IN FACT, THE "RADIOACTIVE MAN" TITLE WAS IN THE MIDST OF ONE OF MY FAVORITE PERIODS.
IT WAS DECIDED THAT THE STORIES WERE TO HAVE A BASIS IN SCIENCE. THAT GAVE IT A MORE REALISTIC FEEL, RATHER THAN THE CHILDISH ESCAPADES THE CHARACTER HAD TO ENDURE UNDER OTHER EDITORIAL TUTELAGES!
AH, YES, WE HAD COMICS THEN!
RADIOACTIVE MAN
GALA 100th ISSUE!

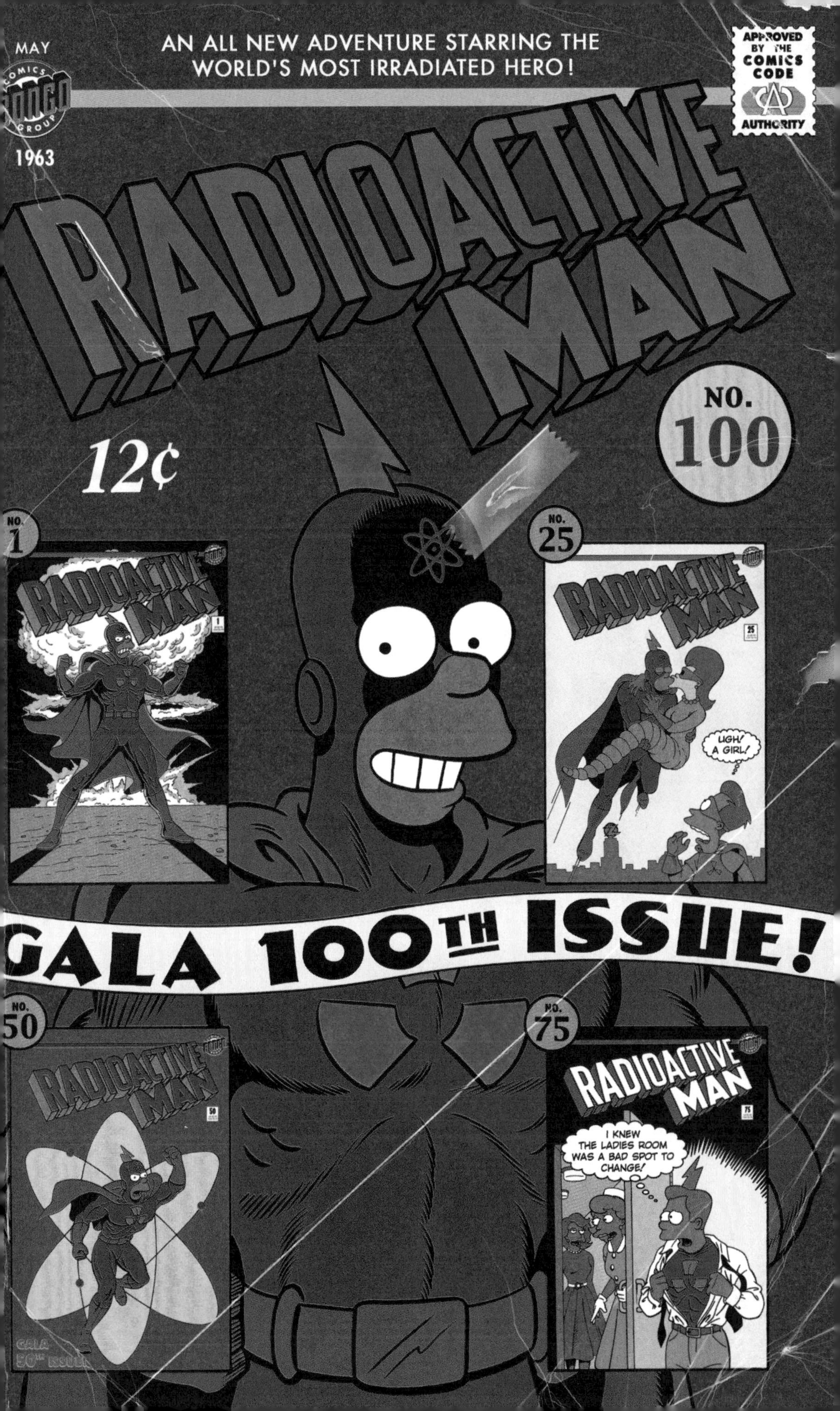
MAY
1963
AN ALL NEW ADVENTURE STARRING THE WORLD'S MOST IRRADIATED HERO!
APPROVED BY THE COMICS CODE AUTHORITY
RADIOACTIVE MAN
NO. 100
12¢
NO. 1
RADIOACTIVE MAN
NO. 25
RADIOACTIVE MAN
UGH! A GIRL!
GALA 100TH ISSUE!
NO. 50
RADIOACTIVE MAN
NO. 75
RADIOACTIVE MAN
I KNEW THE LADIES ROOM WAS A BAD SPOT TO CHANGE!

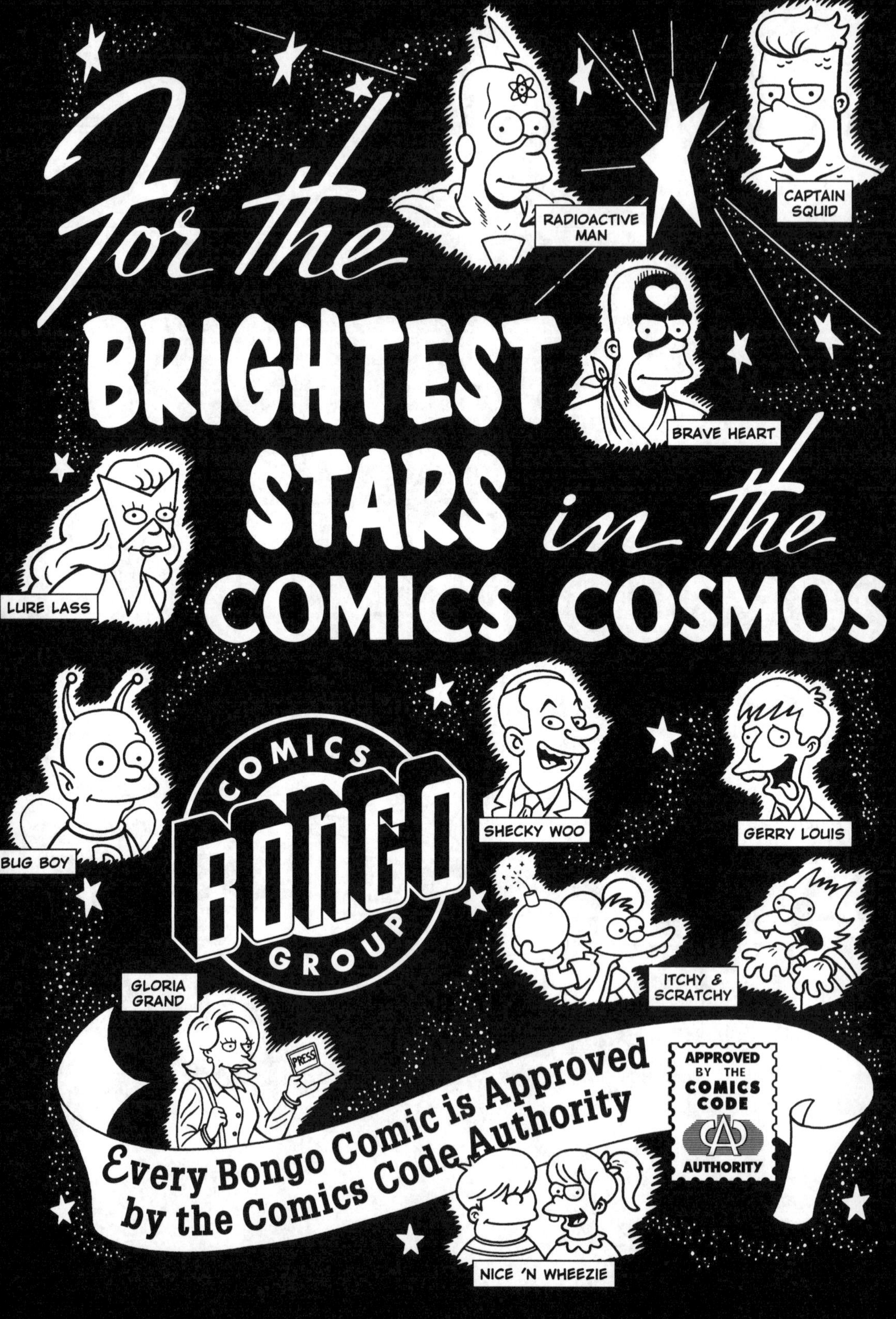

For the
BRIGHTEST
STARS in the
COMICS COSMOS
RADIOACTIVE MAN
CAPTAIN SQUID
BRAVE HEART
LURE LASS
BUG BOY
COMICS
BONGO
GROUP
SHECKY WOO
GERRY LOUIS
ITCHY & SCRATCHY
GLORIA GRAND
PRESS
Every Bongo Comic is Approved
by the Comics Code Authority
APPROVED BY THE COMICS CODE AUTHORITY
NICE 'N WHEEZIE

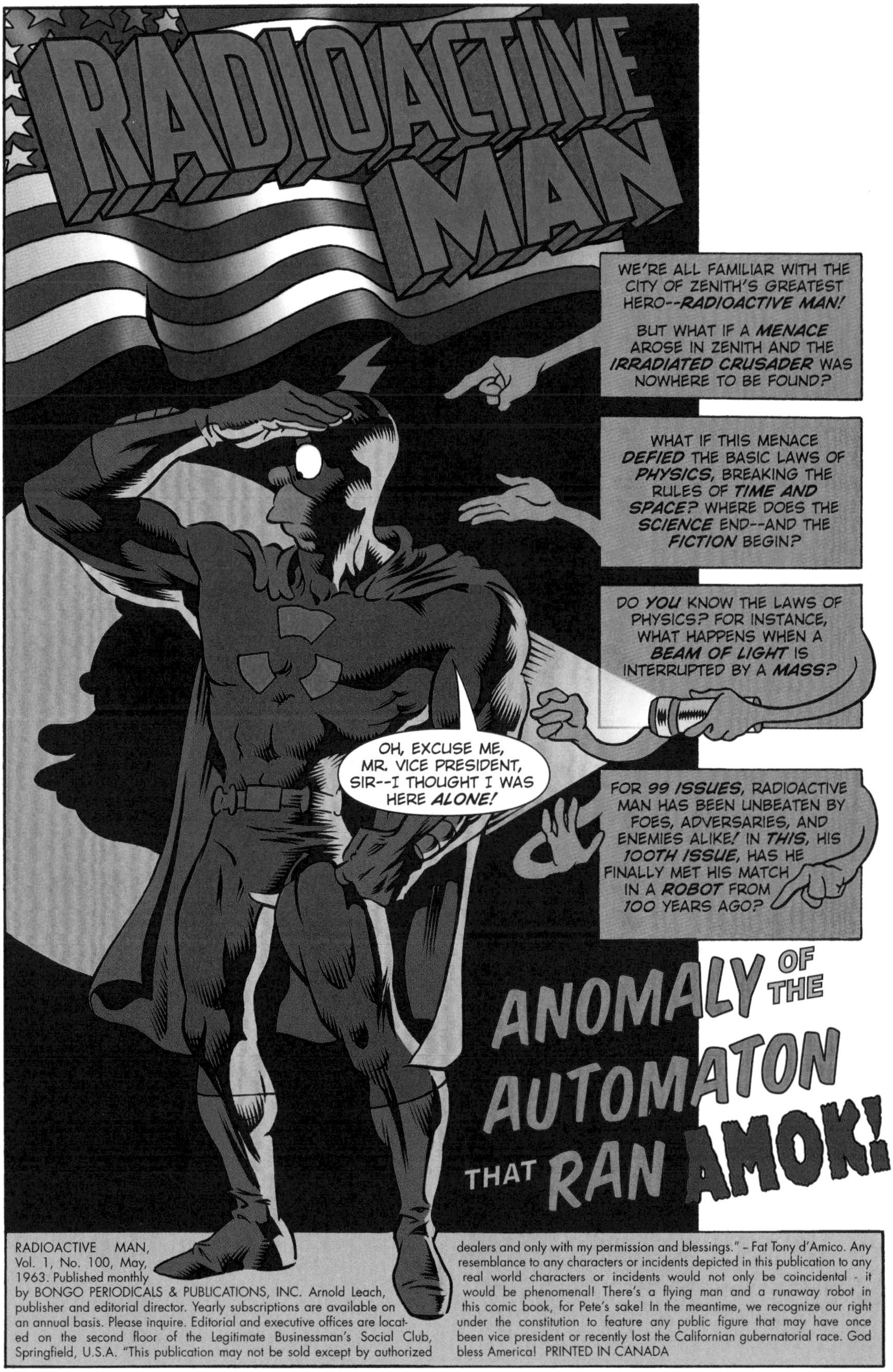
RADIOACTIVE MAN
WE'RE ALL FAMILIAR WITH THE CITY OF ZENITH'S GREATEST HERO--RADIOACTIVE MAN!
BUT WHAT IF A MENACE AROSE IN ZENITH AND THE IRRADIATED CRUSADER WAS NOWHERE TO BE FOUND?
WHAT IF THIS MENACE DEFIED THE BASIC LAWS OF PHYSICS, BREAKING THE RULES OF TIME AND SPACE? WHERE DOES THE SCIENCE END--AND THE FICTION BEGIN?
DO YOU KNOW THE LAWS OF PHYSICS? FOR INSTANCE, WHAT HAPPENS WHEN A BEAM OF LIGHT IS INTERRUPTED BY A MASS?
OH, EXCUSE ME, MR. VICE PRESIDENT, SIR--I THOUGHT I WAS HERE ALONE!
FOR 99 ISSUES, RADIOACTIVE MAN HAS BEEN UNBEATEN BY FOES, ADVERSARIES, AND ENEMIES ALIKE! IN THIS, HIS 100TH ISSUE, HAS HE FINALLY MET HIS MATCH IN A ROBOT FROM 100 YEARS AGO?
ANOMALY OF THE AUTOMATON THAT RAN AMOK!

RADIOACTIVE MAN, Vol. 1, No. 100, May, 1963. Published monthly by BONGO PERIODICALS & PUBLICATIONS, INC. Arnold Leach, publisher and editorial director. Yearly subscriptions are available on an annual basis. Please inquire. Editorial and executive offices are located on the second floor of the Legitimate Businessman's Social Club, Springfield, U.S.A. "This publication may not be sold except by authorized dealers and only with my permission and blessings." – Fat Tony d'Amico. Any resemblance to any characters or incidents depicted in this publication to any real world characters or incidents would not only be coincidental - it would be phenomenal! There's a flying man and a runaway robot in this comic book, for Pete's sake! In the meantime, we recognize our right under the constitution to feature any public figure that may have once been vice president or recently lost the Californian gubernatorial race. God bless America! PRINTED IN CANADA

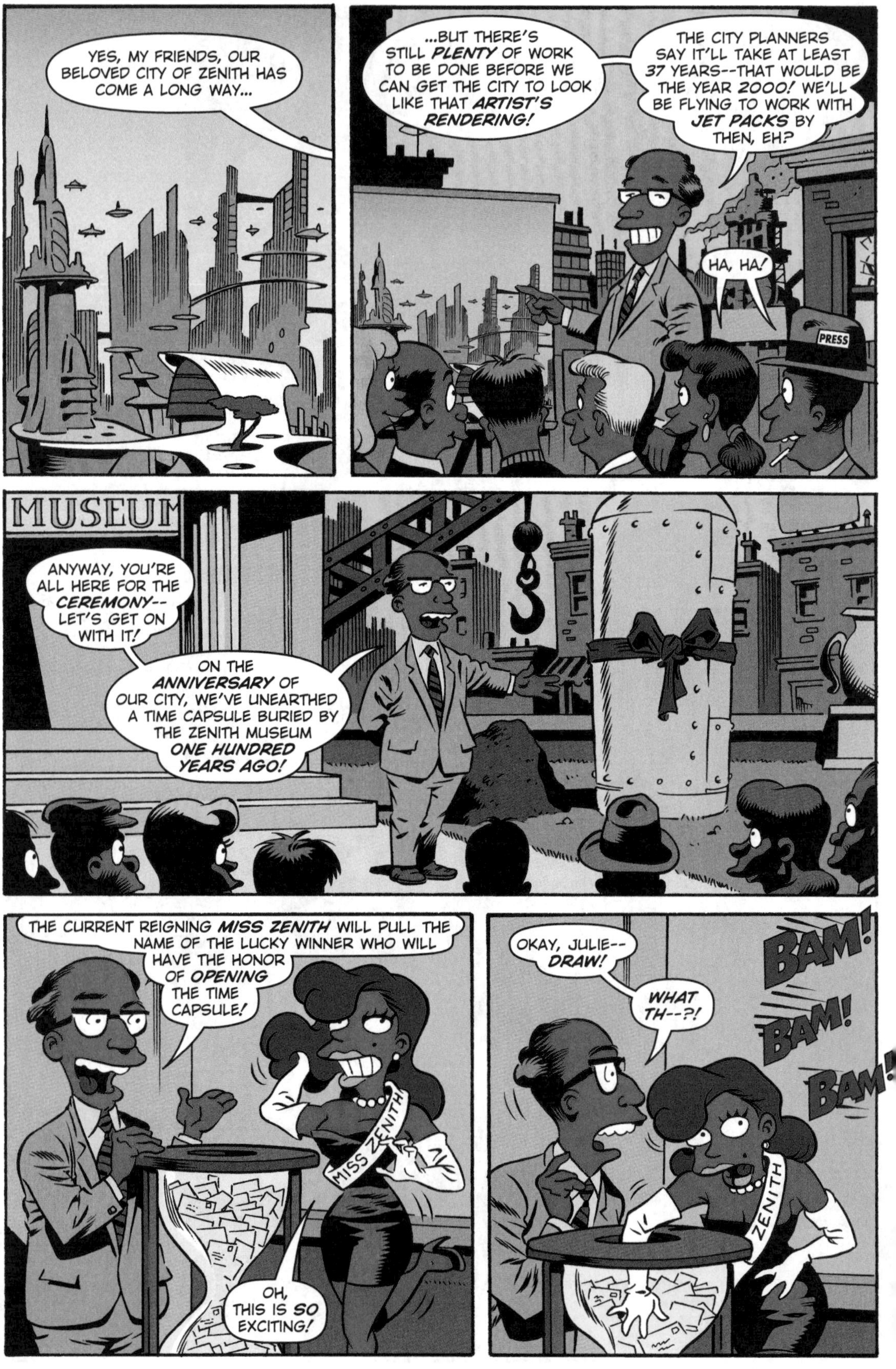
YES, MY FRIENDS, OUR BELOVED CITY OF ZENITH HAS COME A LONG WAY...
...BUT THERE'S STILL PLENTY OF WORK TO BE DONE BEFORE WE CAN GET THE CITY TO LOOK LIKE THAT ARTIST'S RENDERING!
THE CITY PLANNERS SAY IT'LL TAKE AT LEAST 37 YEARS--THAT WOULD BE THE YEAR 2000! WE'LL BE FLYING TO WORK WITH JET PACKS BY THEN, EH?
HA, HA!
PRESS
MUSEUM
ANYWAY, YOU'RE ALL HERE FOR THE CEREMONY-- LET'S GET ON WITH IT!
ON THE ANNIVERSARY OF OUR CITY, WE'VE UNEARTHED A TIME CAPSULE BURIED BY THE ZENITH MUSEUM ONE HUNDRED YEARS AGO!
THE CURRENT REIGNING MISS ZENITH WILL PULL THE NAME OF THE LUCKY WINNER WHO WILL HAVE THE HONOR OF OPENING THE TIME CAPSULE!
MISS ZENITH
OH, THIS IS SO EXCITING!
OKAY, JULIE-- DRAW!
WHAT TH--?!
BAM!
BAM!
BAM!
ZENITH

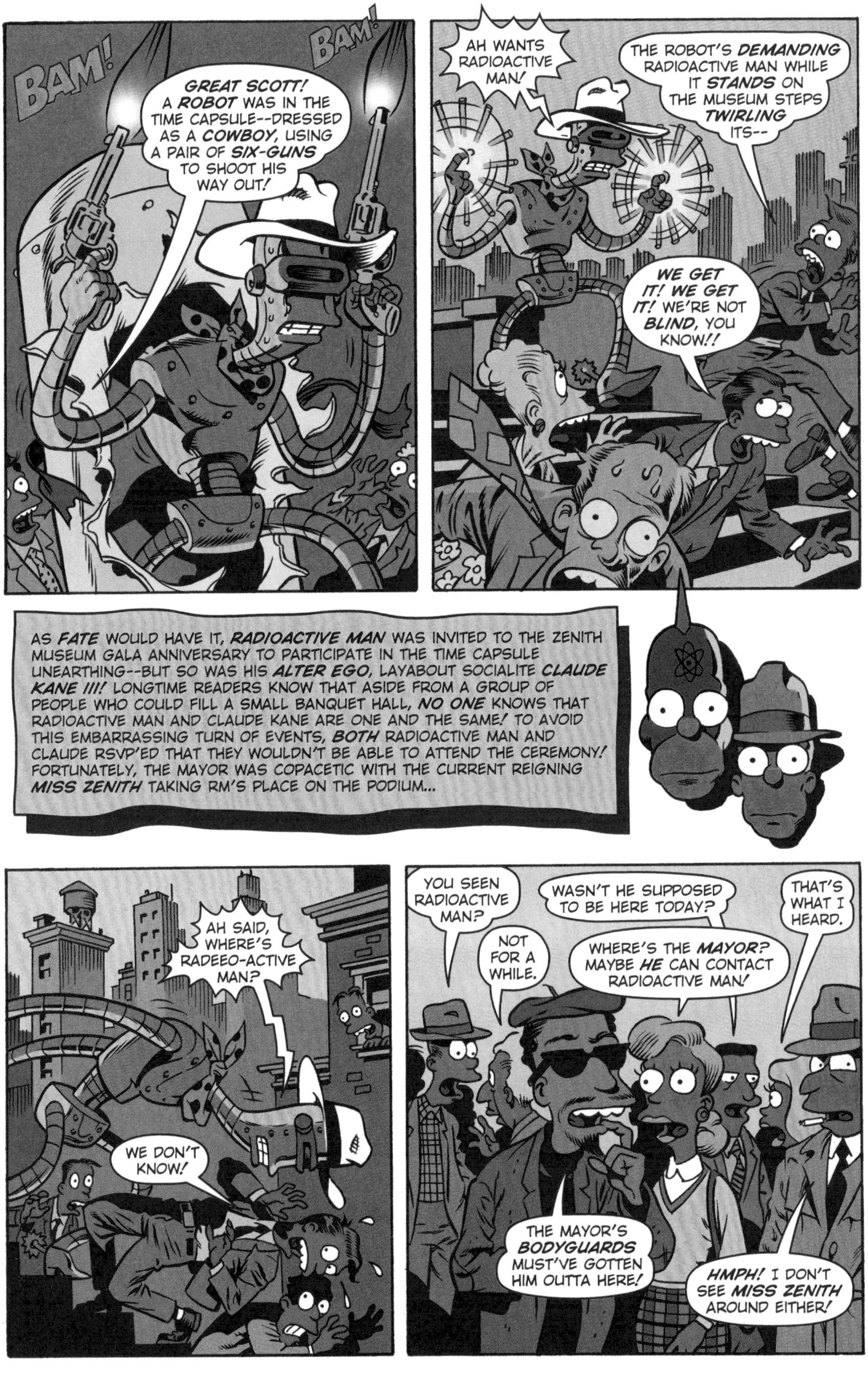
BAM!
BAM!
GREAT SCOTT! A ROBOT WAS IN THE TIME CAPSULE--DRESSED AS A COWBOY, USING A PAIR OF SIX-GUNS TO SHOOT HIS WAY OUT!
AH WANTS RADIOACTIVE MAN!
THE ROBOT'S DEMANDING RADIOACTIVE MAN WHILE IT STANDS ON THE MUSEUM STEPS TWIRLING ITS--
WE GET IT! WE GET IT! WE'RE NOT BLIND, YOU KNOW!!
AS FATE WOULD HAVE IT, RADIOACTIVE MAN WAS INVITED TO THE ZENITH MUSEUM GALA ANNIVERSARY TO PARTICIPATE IN THE TIME CAPSULE UNEARTHING--BUT SO WAS HIS ALTER EGO, LAYABOUT SOCIALITE CLAUDE KANE III! LONGTIME READERS KNOW THAT ASIDE FROM A GROUP OF PEOPLE WHO COULD FILL A SMALL BANQUET HALL, NO ONE KNOWS THAT RADIOACTIVE MAN AND CLAUDE KANE ARE ONE AND THE SAME! TO AVOID THIS EMBARRASSING TURN OF EVENTS, BOTH RADIOACTIVE MAN AND CLAUDE RSVP'ED THAT THEY WOULDN'T BE ABLE TO ATTEND THE CEREMONY! FORTUNATELY, THE MAYOR WAS COPACETIC WITH THE CURRENT REIGNING MISS ZENITH TAKING RM'S PLACE ON THE PODIUM...
AH SAID, WHERE'S RADEEO-ACTIVE MAN?
WE DON'T KNOW!
YOU SEEN RADIOACTIVE MAN?
NOT FOR A WHILE.
WASN'T HE SUPPOSED TO BE HERE TODAY?
WHERE'S THE MAYOR? MAYBE HE CAN CONTACT RADIOACTIVE MAN!
THAT'S WHAT I HEARD.
THE MAYOR'S BODYGUARDS MUST'VE GOTTEN HIM OUTTA HERE!
HMPH! I DON'T SEE MISS ZENITH AROUND EITHER!

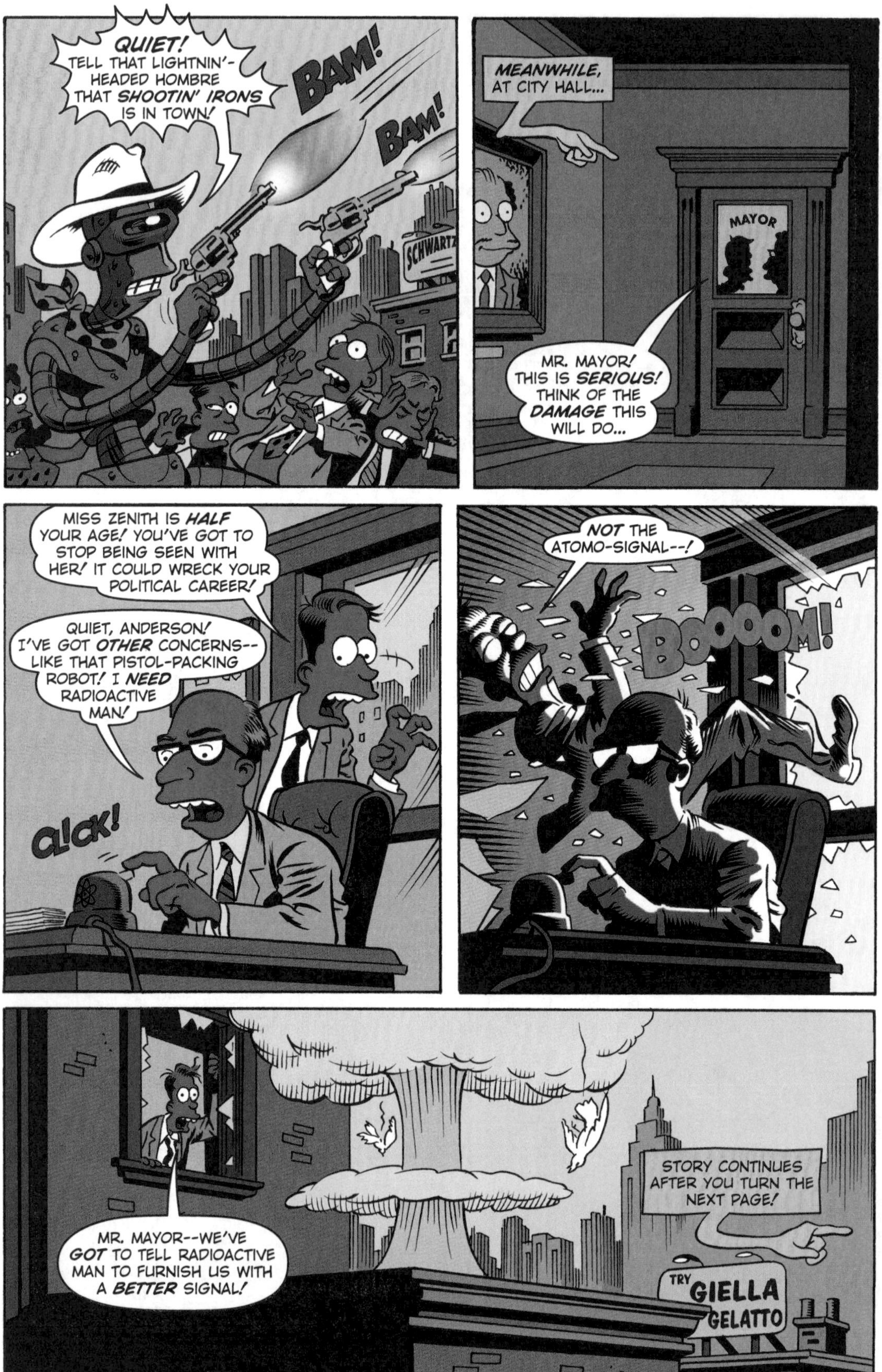
QUIET! TELL THAT LIGHTNIN'-HEADED HOMBRE THAT SHOOTIN' IRONS IS IN TOWN!
BAM!
BAM!
SCHWARTZ
MEANWHILE, AT CITY HALL...
MAYOR
MR. MAYOR! THIS IS SERIOUS! THINK OF THE DAMAGE THIS WILL DO...
MISS ZENITH IS HALF YOUR AGE! YOU'VE GOT TO STOP BEING SEEN WITH HER! IT COULD WRECK YOUR POLITICAL CAREER!
QUIET, ANDERSON! I'VE GOT OTHER CONCERNS--LIKE THAT PISTOL-PACKING ROBOT! I NEED RADIOACTIVE MAN!
CLICK!
NOT THE ATOMO-SIGNAL--!
BOOOOM!
MR. MAYOR--WE'VE GOT TO TELL RADIOACTIVE MAN TO FURNISH US WITH A BETTER SIGNAL!
STORY CONTINUES AFTER YOU TURN THE NEXT PAGE!
TRY GIELLA GELATTO

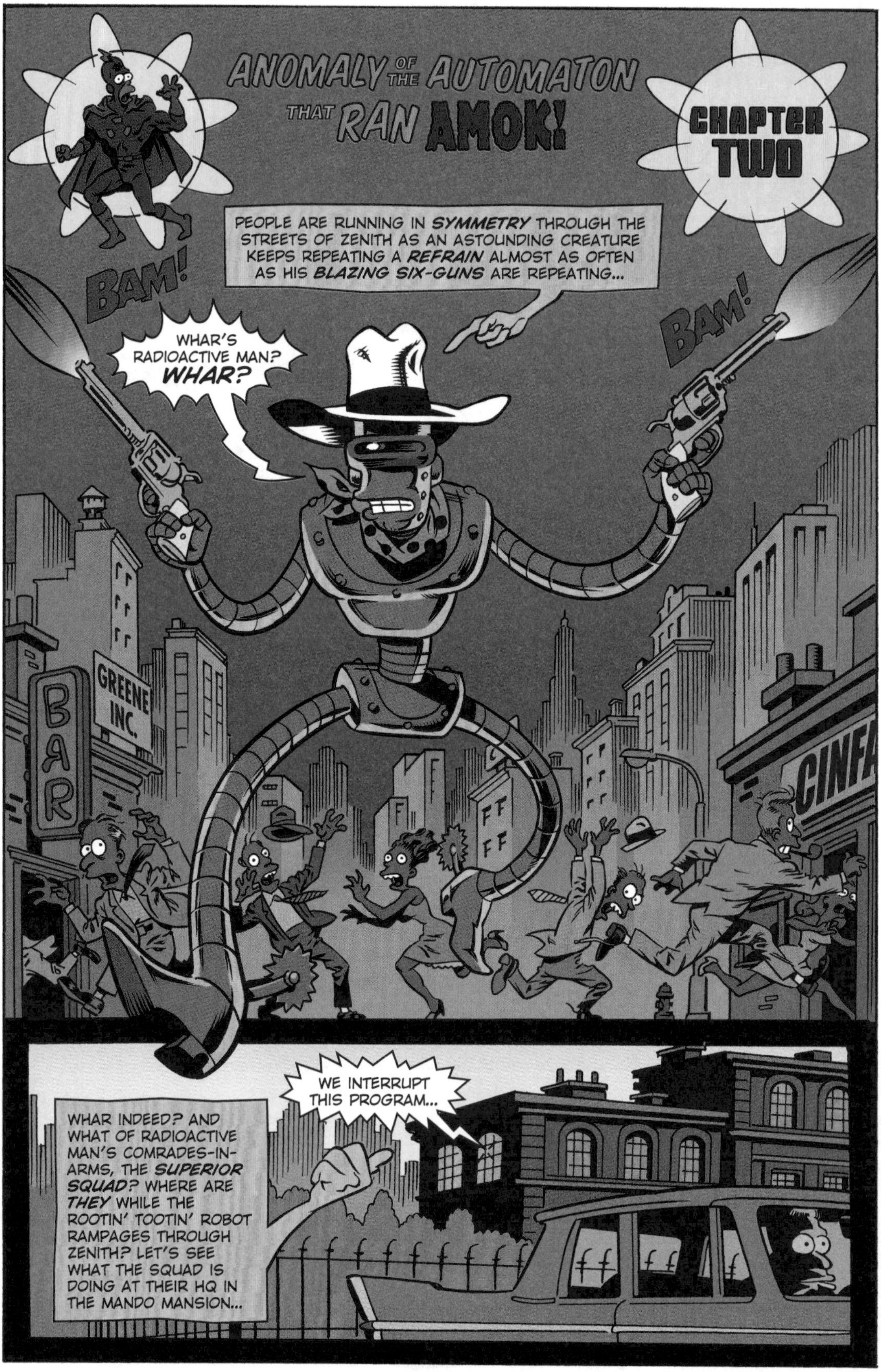
ANOMALY OF THE AUTOMATON THAT RAN AMOK!
CHAPTER TWO
PEOPLE ARE RUNNING IN SYMMETRY THROUGH THE STREETS OF ZENITH AS AN ASTOUNDING CREATURE KEEPS REPEATING A REFRAIN ALMOST AS OFTEN AS HIS BLAZING SIX-GUNS ARE REPEATING...
BAM!
BAM!
WHAR'S RADIOACTIVE MAN? WHAR?
BAR
GREENE INC.
CINFA
WHAR INDEED? AND WHAT OF RADIOACTIVE MAN'S COMRADES-IN-ARMS, THE SUPERIOR SQUAD? WHERE ARE THEY WHILE THE ROOTIN' TOOTIN' ROBOT RAMPAGES THROUGH ZENITH? LET'S SEE WHAT THE SQUAD IS DOING AT THEIR HQ IN THE MANDO MANSION...
WE INTERRUPT THIS PROGRAM...

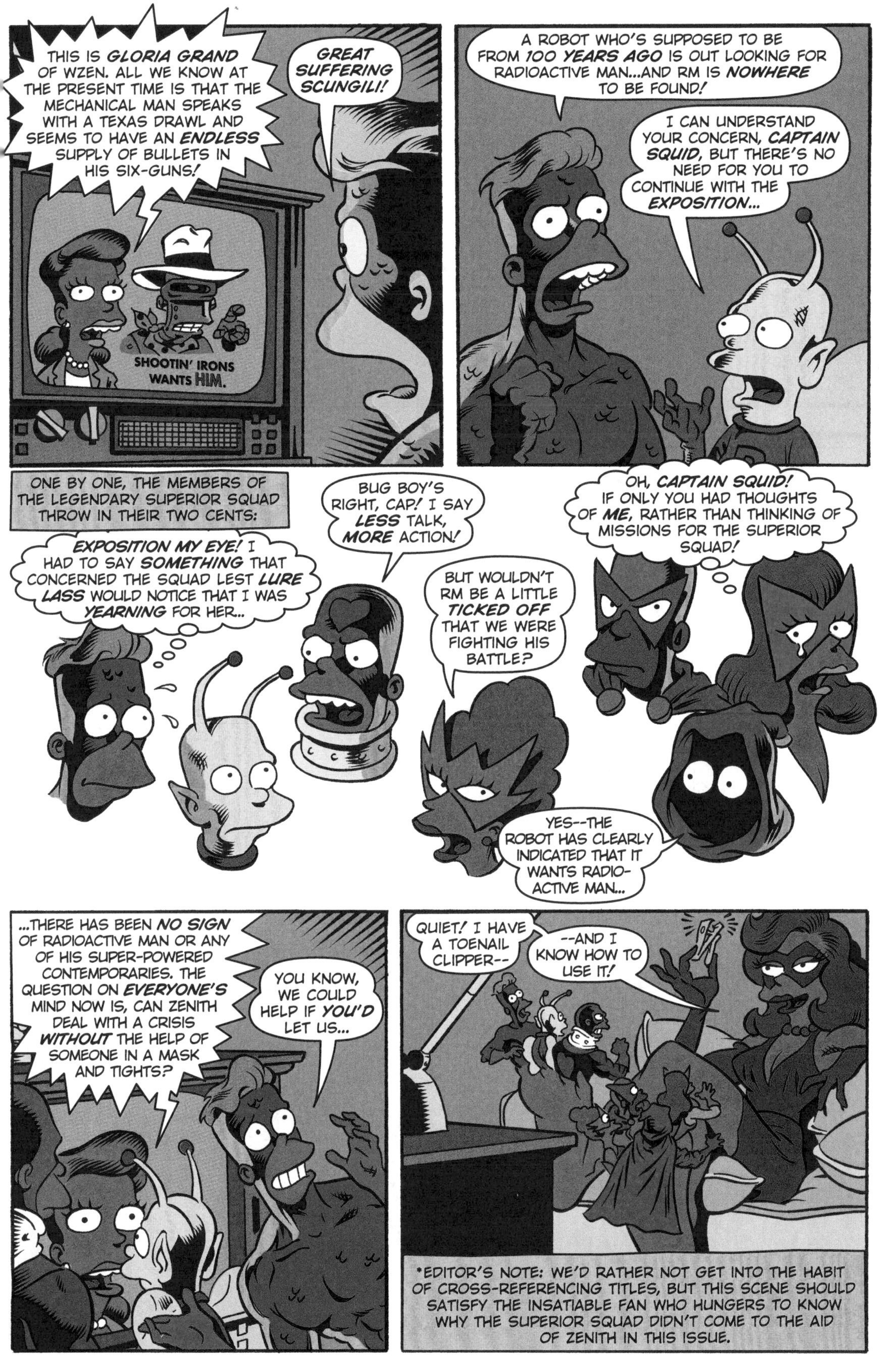
THIS IS GLORIA GRAND OF WZEN. ALL WE KNOW AT THE PRESENT TIME IS THAT THE MECHANICAL MAN SPEAKS WITH A TEXAS DRAWL AND SEEMS TO HAVE AN ENDLESS SUPPLY OF BULLETS IN HIS SIX-GUNS!
SHOOTIN' IRONS WANTS HIM.
GREAT SUFFERING SCUNGILI!
A ROBOT WHO'S SUPPOSED TO BE FROM 100 YEARS AGO IS OUT LOOKING FOR RADIOACTIVE MAN...AND RM IS NOWHERE TO BE FOUND!
I CAN UNDERSTAND YOUR CONCERN, CAPTAIN SQUID, BUT THERE'S NO NEED FOR YOU TO CONTINUE WITH THE EXPOSITION...
ONE BY ONE, THE MEMBERS OF THE LEGENDARY SUPERIOR SQUAD THROW IN THEIR TWO CENTS:
EXPOSITION MY EYE! I HAD TO SAY SOMETHING THAT CONCERNED THE SQUAD LEST LURE LASS WOULD NOTICE THAT I WAS YEARNING FOR HER...
BUG BOY'S RIGHT, CAP! I SAY LESS TALK, MORE ACTION!
BUT WOULDN'T RM BE A LITTLE TICKED OFF THAT WE WERE FIGHTING HIS BATTLE?
OH, CAPTAIN SQUID! IF ONLY YOU HAD THOUGHTS OF ME, RATHER THAN THINKING OF MISSIONS FOR THE SUPERIOR SQUAD!
YES--THE ROBOT HAS CLEARLY INDICATED THAT IT WANTS RADIO-ACTIVE MAN...
...THERE HAS BEEN NO SIGN OF RADIOACTIVE MAN OR ANY OF HIS SUPER-POWERED CONTEMPORARIES. THE QUESTION ON EVERYONE'S MIND NOW IS, CAN ZENITH DEAL WITH A CRISIS WITHOUT THE HELP OF SOMEONE IN A MASK AND TIGHTS?
YOU KNOW, WE COULD HELP IF YOU'D LET US...
QUIET! I HAVE A TOENAIL CLIPPER--
--AND I KNOW HOW TO USE IT!
*EDITOR'S NOTE: WE'D RATHER NOT GET INTO THE HABIT OF CROSS-REFERENCING TITLES, BUT THIS SCENE SHOULD SATISFY THE INSATIABLE FAN WHO HUNGERS TO KNOW WHY THE SUPERIOR SQUAD DIDN'T COME TO THE AID OF ZENITH IN THIS ISSUE.

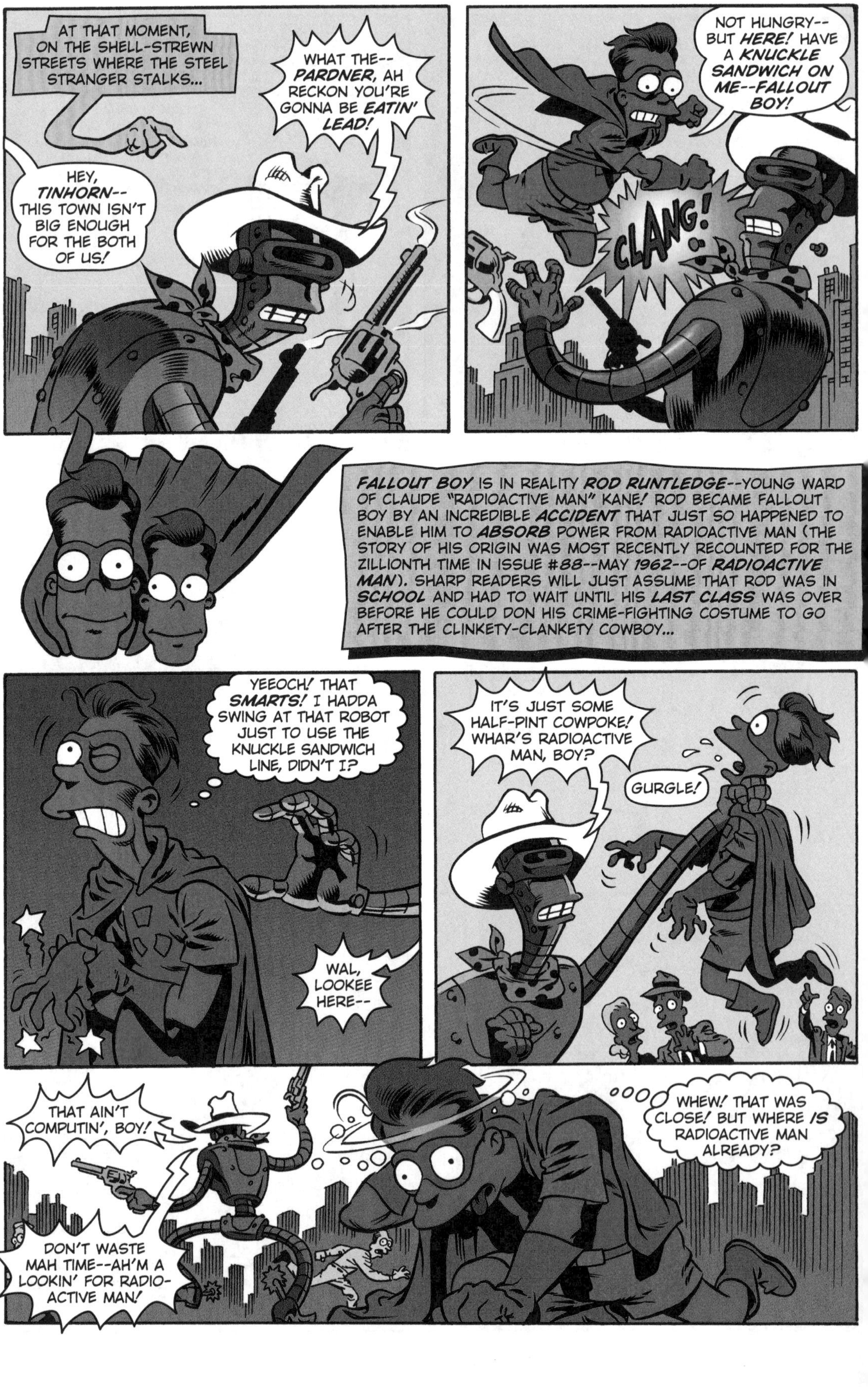
AT THAT MOMENT, ON THE SHELL-STREWN STREETS WHERE THE STEEL STRANGER STALKS...
HEY, TINHORN-- THIS TOWN ISN'T BIG ENOUGH FOR THE BOTH OF US!
WHAT THE-- PARDNER, AH RECKON YOU'RE GONNA BE EATIN' LEAD!
NOT HUNGRY-- BUT HERE! HAVE A KNUCKLE SANDWICH ON ME--FALLOUT BOY!
CLANG!
FALLOUT BOY IS IN REALITY ROD RUNTLEDGE--YOUNG WARD OF CLAUDE "RADIOACTIVE MAN" KANE! ROD BECAME FALLOUT BOY BY AN INCREDIBLE ACCIDENT THAT JUST SO HAPPENED TO ENABLE HIM TO ABSORB POWER FROM RADIOACTIVE MAN (THE STORY OF HIS ORIGIN WAS MOST RECENTLY RECOUNTED FOR THE ZILLIONTH TIME IN ISSUE #88--MAY 1962--OF RADIOACTIVE MAN). SHARP READERS WILL JUST ASSUME THAT ROD WAS IN SCHOOL AND HAD TO WAIT UNTIL HIS LAST CLASS WAS OVER BEFORE HE COULD DON HIS CRIME-FIGHTING COSTUME TO GO AFTER THE CLINKETY-CLANKETY COWBOY...
YEEOCH! THAT SMARTS! I HADDA SWING AT THAT ROBOT JUST TO USE THE KNUCKLE SANDWICH LINE, DIDN'T I?
WAL, LOOKEE HERE--
IT'S JUST SOME HALF-PINT COWPOKE! WHAR'S RADIOACTIVE MAN, BOY?
GURGLE!
THAT AIN'T COMPUTIN', BOY!
DON'T WASTE MAH TIME--AH'M A LOOKIN' FOR RADIO-ACTIVE MAN!
WHEW! THAT WAS CLOSE! BUT WHERE IS RADIOACTIVE MAN ALREADY?

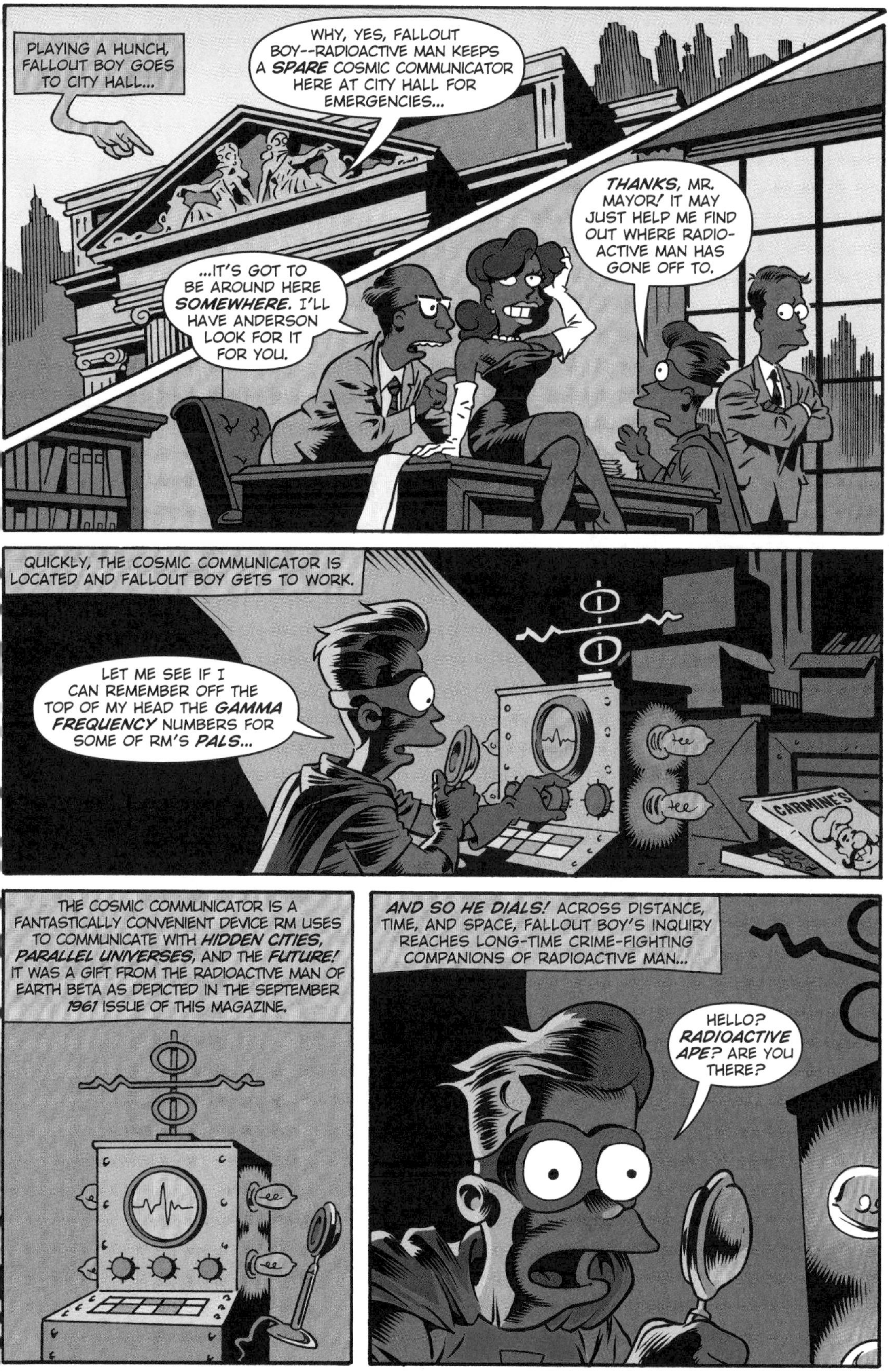
PLAYING A HUNCH, FALLOUT BOY GOES TO CITY HALL...
WHY, YES, FALLOUT BOY--RADIOACTIVE MAN KEEPS A SPARE COSMIC COMMUNICATOR HERE AT CITY HALL FOR EMERGENCIES...
...IT'S GOT TO BE AROUND HERE SOMEWHERE. I'LL HAVE ANDERSON LOOK FOR IT FOR YOU.
THANKS, MR. MAYOR! IT MAY JUST HELP ME FIND OUT WHERE RADIO-ACTIVE MAN HAS GONE OFF TO.
QUICKLY, THE COSMIC COMMUNICATOR IS LOCATED AND FALLOUT BOY GETS TO WORK.
LET ME SEE IF I CAN REMEMBER OFF THE TOP OF MY HEAD THE GAMMA FREQUENCY NUMBERS FOR SOME OF RM'S PALS...
CARMINE'S
THE COSMIC COMMUNICATOR IS A FANTASTICALLY CONVENIENT DEVICE RM USES TO COMMUNICATE WITH HIDDEN CITIES, PARALLEL UNIVERSES, AND THE FUTURE! IT WAS A GIFT FROM THE RADIOACTIVE MAN OF EARTH BETA AS DEPICTED IN THE SEPTEMBER 1961 ISSUE OF THIS MAGAZINE.
AND SO HE DIALS! ACROSS DISTANCE, TIME, AND SPACE, FALLOUT BOY'S INQUIRY REACHES LONG-TIME CRIME-FIGHTING COMPANIONS OF RADIOACTIVE MAN...
HELLO? RADIOACTIVE APE? ARE YOU THERE?

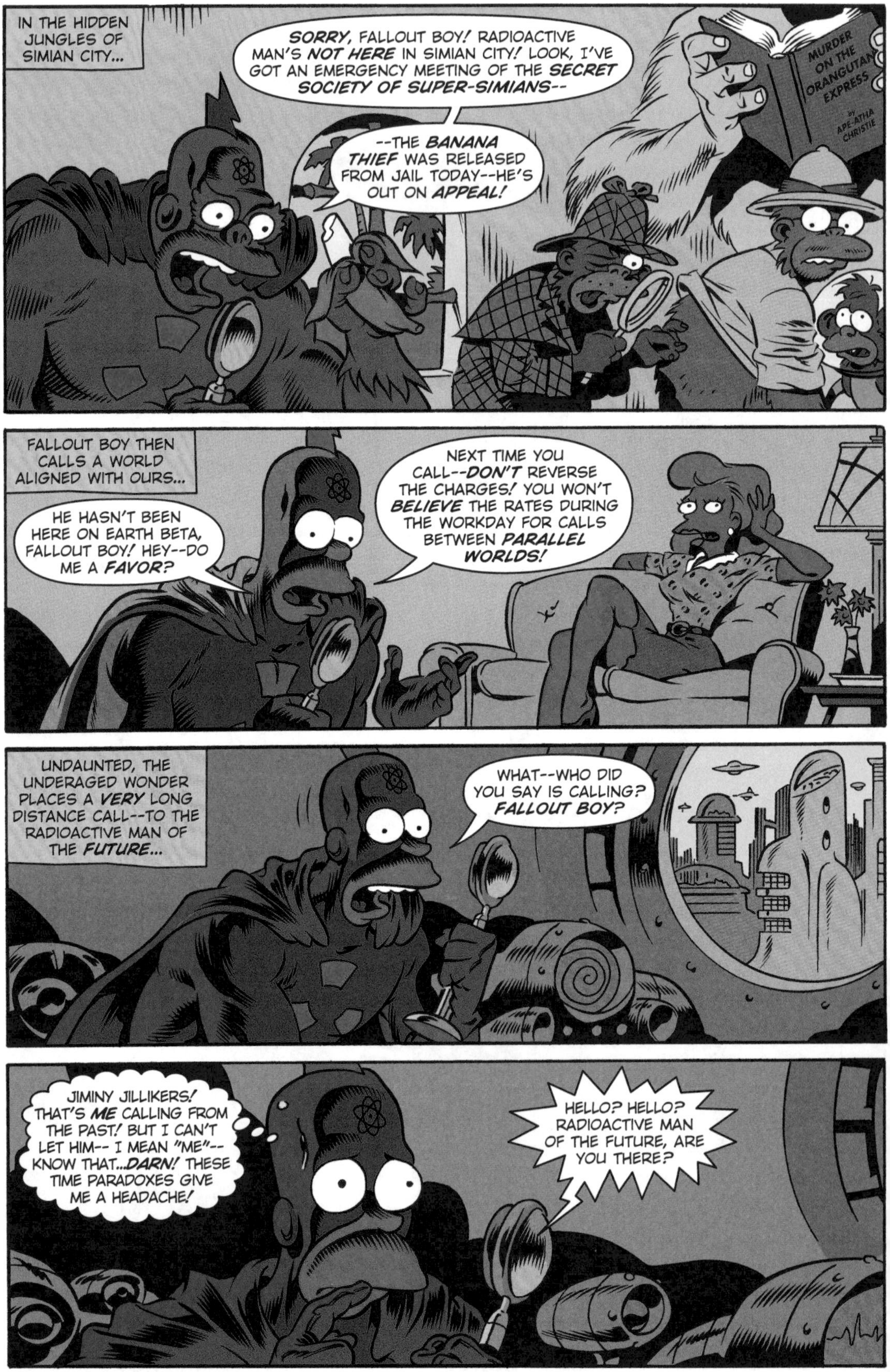
IN THE HIDDEN JUNGLES OF SIMIAN CITY...
SORRY, FALLOUT BOY! RADIOACTIVE MAN'S NOT HERE IN SIMIAN CITY! LOOK, I'VE GOT AN EMERGENCY MEETING OF THE SECRET SOCIETY OF SUPER-SIMIANS--
--THE BANANA THIEF WAS RELEASED FROM JAIL TODAY--HE'S OUT ON APPEAL!
MURDER ON THE ORANGUTAN EXPRESS
BY APE-ATHA CHRISTIE
FALLOUT BOY THEN CALLS A WORLD ALIGNED WITH OURS...
HE HASN'T BEEN HERE ON EARTH BETA, FALLOUT BOY! HEY--DO ME A FAVOR?
NEXT TIME YOU CALL--DON'T REVERSE THE CHARGES! YOU WON'T BELIEVE THE RATES DURING THE WORKDAY FOR CALLS BETWEEN PARALLEL WORLDS!
UNDAUNTED, THE UNDERAGED WONDER PLACES A VERY LONG DISTANCE CALL--TO THE RADIOACTIVE MAN OF THE FUTURE...
WHAT--WHO DID YOU SAY IS CALLING? FALLOUT BOY?
JIMINY JILLIKERS! THAT'S ME CALLING FROM THE PAST! BUT I CAN'T LET HIM-- I MEAN "ME"-- KNOW THAT...DARN! THESE TIME PARADOXES GIVE ME A HEADACHE!
HELLO? HELLO? RADIOACTIVE MAN OF THE FUTURE, ARE YOU THERE?

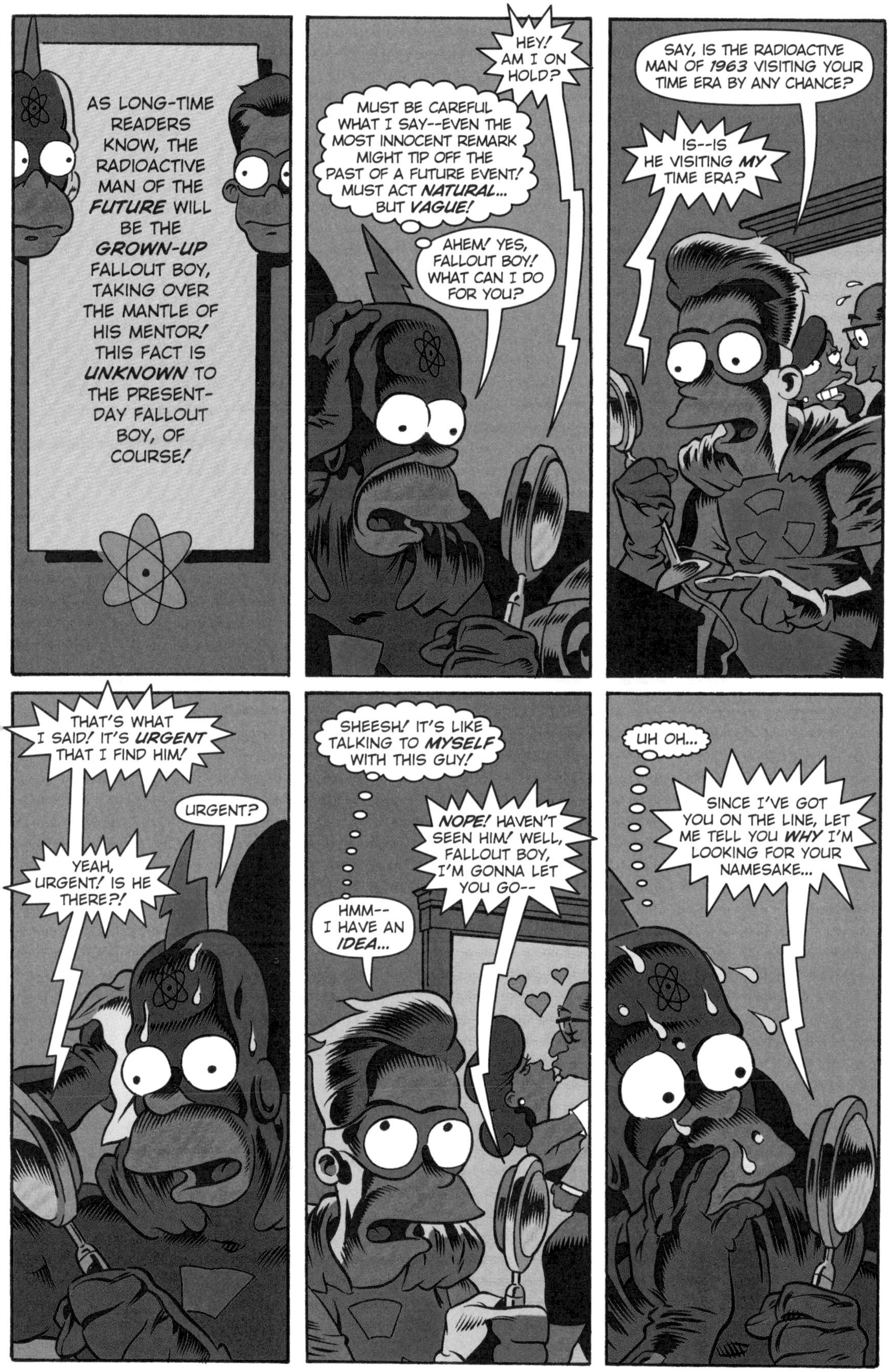
AS LONG-TIME READERS KNOW, THE RADIOACTIVE MAN OF THE FUTURE WILL BE THE GROWN-UP FALLOUT BOY, TAKING OVER THE MANTLE OF HIS MENTOR! THIS FACT IS UNKNOWN TO THE PRESENT-DAY FALLOUT BOY, OF COURSE!
HEY! AM I ON HOLD?
MUST BE CAREFUL WHAT I SAY--EVEN THE MOST INNOCENT REMARK MIGHT TIP OFF THE PAST OF A FUTURE EVENT! MUST ACT NATURAL... BUT VAGUE!
AHEM! YES, FALLOUT BOY! WHAT CAN I DO FOR YOU?
SAY, IS THE RADIOACTIVE MAN OF 1963 VISITING YOUR TIME ERA BY ANY CHANCE?
IS--IS HE VISITING MY TIME ERA?
THAT'S WHAT I SAID! IT'S URGENT THAT I FIND HIM!
URGENT?
YEAH, URGENT! IS HE THERE?!
SHEESH! IT'S LIKE TALKING TO MYSELF WITH THIS GUY!
NOPE! HAVEN'T SEEN HIM! WELL, FALLOUT BOY, I'M GONNA LET YOU GO--
HMM-- I HAVE AN IDEA...
UH OH...
SINCE I'VE GOT YOU ON THE LINE, LET ME TELL YOU WHY I'M LOOKING FOR YOUR NAMESAKE...

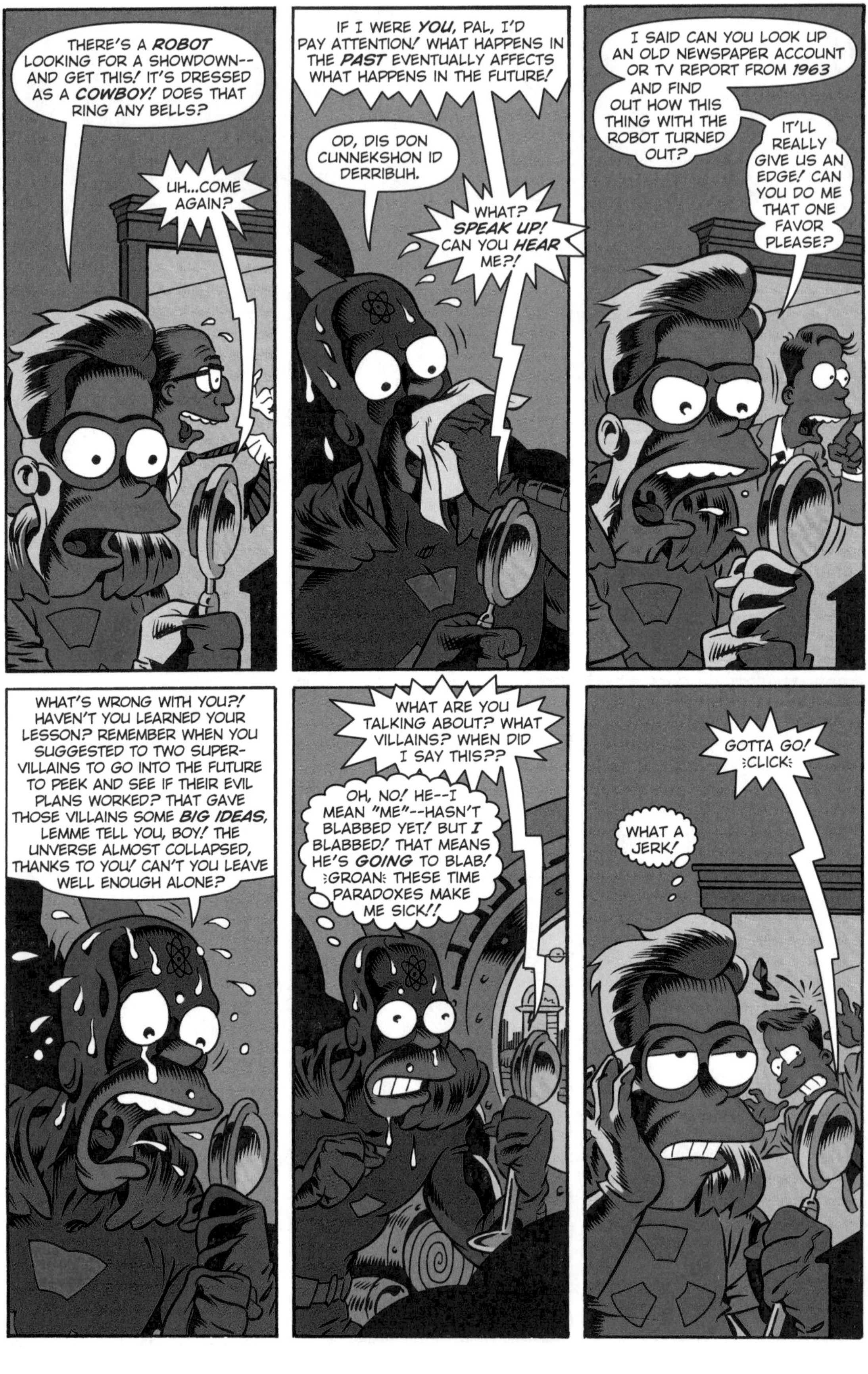
THERE'S A ROBOT LOOKING FOR A SHOWDOWN--AND GET THIS! IT'S DRESSED AS A COWBOY! DOES THAT RING ANY BELLS?
UH...COME AGAIN?
IF I WERE YOU, PAL, I'D PAY ATTENTION! WHAT HAPPENS IN THE PAST EVENTUALLY AFFECTS WHAT HAPPENS IN THE FUTURE!
OD, DIS DON CUNNEKSHON ID DERRIBUH.
WHAT? SPEAK UP! CAN YOU HEAR ME?!
I SAID CAN YOU LOOK UP AN OLD NEWSPAPER ACCOUNT OR TV REPORT FROM 1963
AND FIND OUT HOW THIS THING WITH THE ROBOT TURNED OUT?
IT'LL REALLY GIVE US AN EDGE! CAN YOU DO ME THAT ONE FAVOR PLEASE?
WHAT'S WRONG WITH YOU?! HAVEN'T YOU LEARNED YOUR LESSON? REMEMBER WHEN YOU SUGGESTED TO TWO SUPER-VILLAINS TO GO INTO THE FUTURE TO PEEK AND SEE IF THEIR EVIL PLANS WORKED? THAT GAVE THOSE VILLAINS SOME BIG IDEAS, LEMME TELL YOU, BOY! THE UNVERSE ALMOST COLLAPSED, THANKS TO YOU! CAN'T YOU LEAVE WELL ENOUGH ALONE?
WHAT ARE YOU TALKING ABOUT? WHAT VILLAINS? WHEN DID I SAY THIS??
OH, NO! HE--I MEAN "ME"--HASN'T BLABBED YET! BUT I BLABBED! THAT MEANS HE'S GOING TO BLAB! GROAN THESE TIME PARADOXES MAKE ME SICK!!
GOTTA GO! CLICK
WHAT A JERK!

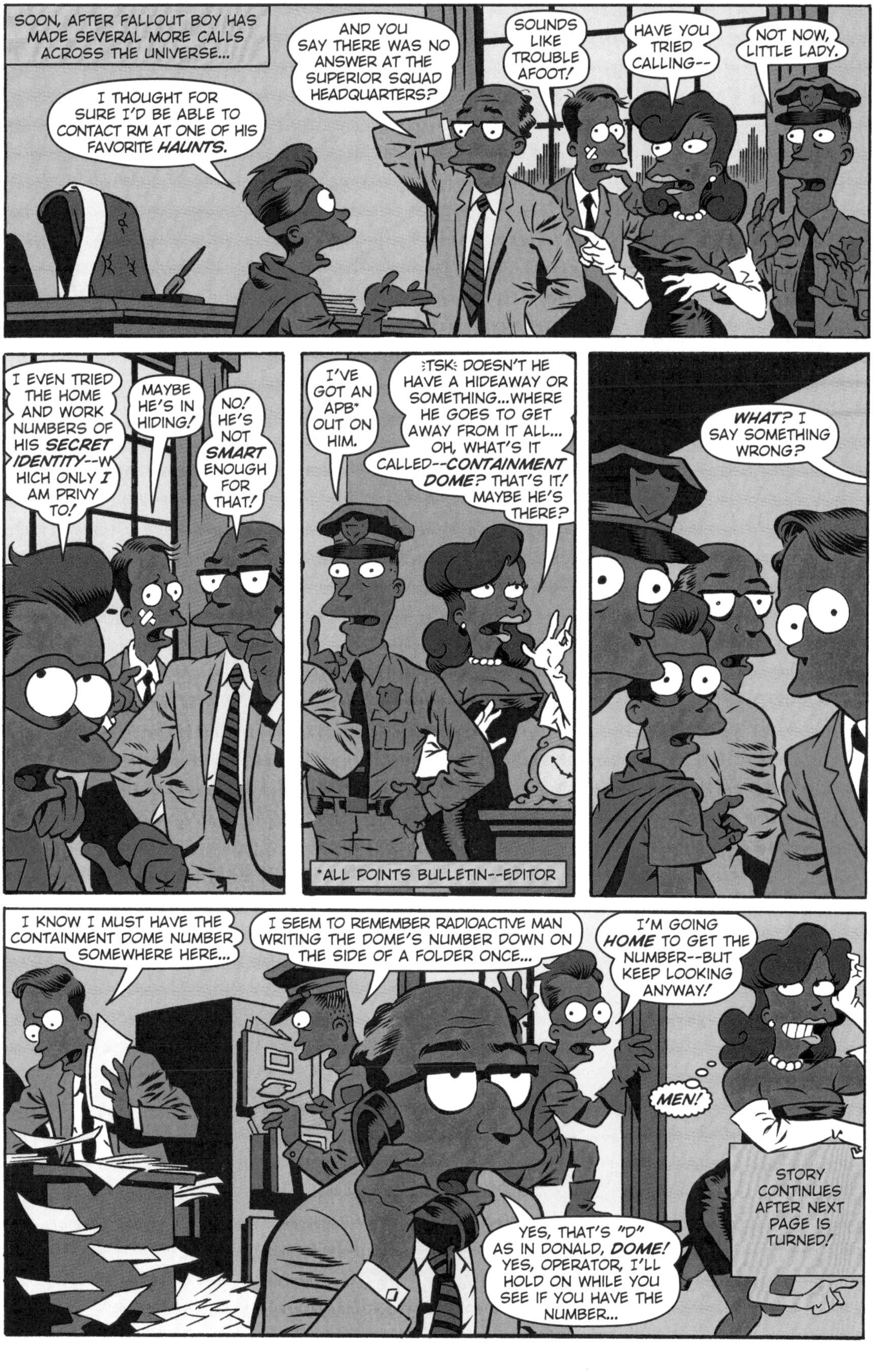
SOON, AFTER FALLOUT BOY HAS MADE SEVERAL MORE CALLS ACROSS THE UNIVERSE...
I THOUGHT FOR SURE I'D BE ABLE TO CONTACT RM AT ONE OF HIS FAVORITE HAUNTS.
AND YOU SAY THERE WAS NO ANSWER AT THE SUPERIOR SQUAD HEADQUARTERS?
SOUNDS LIKE TROUBLE AFOOT!
HAVE YOU TRIED CALLING--
NOT NOW, LITTLE LADY.
I EVEN TRIED THE HOME AND WORK NUMBERS OF HIS SECRET IDENTITY--W HICH ONLY I AM PRIVY TO!
MAYBE HE'S IN HIDING!
NO! HE'S NOT SMART ENOUGH FOR THAT!
I'VE GOT AN APB* OUT ON HIM.
TSK DOESN'T HE HAVE A HIDEAWAY OR SOMETHING...WHERE HE GOES TO GET AWAY FROM IT ALL... OH, WHAT'S IT CALLED--CONTAINMENT DOME? THAT'S IT! MAYBE HE'S THERE?
*ALL POINTS BULLETIN--EDITOR
WHAT? I SAY SOMETHING WRONG?
I KNOW I MUST HAVE THE CONTAINMENT DOME NUMBER SOMEWHERE HERE...
I SEEM TO REMEMBER RADIOACTIVE MAN WRITING THE DOME'S NUMBER DOWN ON THE SIDE OF A FOLDER ONCE...
I'M GOING HOME TO GET THE NUMBER--BUT KEEP LOOKING ANYWAY!
MEN!
YES, THAT'S "D" AS IN DONALD, DOME! YES, OPERATOR, I'LL HOLD ON WHILE YOU SEE IF YOU HAVE THE NUMBER...
STORY CONTINUES AFTER NEXT PAGE IS TURNED!

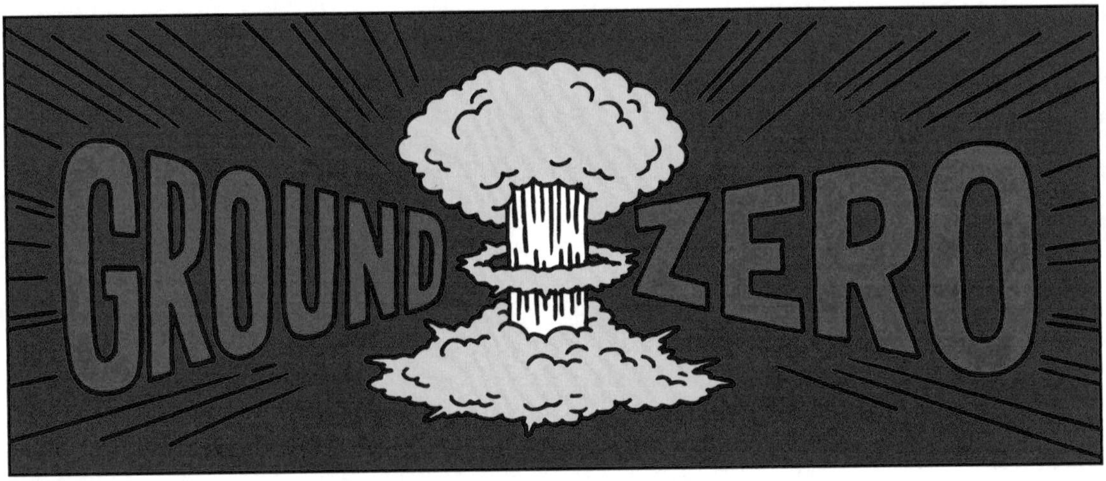
GROUND ZERO

Dear Editor: I suppose "The Red Light, Green Light, One, Two, Three Crimes of Dr. Broome" in *Radioactive Man* #97 had its moments. For *this* Golden Age fan, it was the glimpse at RM's 1940 incarnation--Radio Man--that was the *real* highlight (even though the artist drew him with his tunic button on the right, rather than the left)! I'm a wee bit concerned that your writer is relying too much on RM's plot device of choice--the trans-spatial stairclimber. That thingamajig has been hauled out to resolve the story in issues #57, 62, 69, 91, and now 97 (plus, I believe the stairclimber was what Plasmo was referring to when he told the Superior Squad a secret device helped save them in SS #5). Give it a rest! Also, your artist can't seem to decide whether the stairclimber has 13 steps or 12 steps. Consistency is what the fans want to see--nay, we demand it! Now, does my brutal honesty earn me some of that original art you like to dole out to readers who write the most provocative letters?

Roger Doubt
Johnson, Miss.

(We're always pleased to parry with regular correspondent "Doubting" Roger, but we must again point out that we simply can't write or design our comics just for nit-picking, continuity-obsessed fans! If the general reader feels left out, sales will slip across the board--and eventually there will be no comics, period! Although comics professionals are amused by the adulation and obsessiveness of fans, we think saner heads prevail when we aim our books to a general audience! As for "doling" out the original art--not this time, Roger! You write several letters a month under assumed names to all our titles! Frankly, you're getting on my nerves! How's that for "brutal honesty"? --Editor)

Dear Editor: I love your comic books! Especially the ads—mmm—Tootsie Rolls! Mmm—ice cream bars! Mmm—more candy ads!

Homer J. Simpson (age 5)
Springfield, USA

(Homer's letter offers food for thought--so we're awarding him the art for Chapter One of "The Red Light, Green Light, One, Two, Three Crimes of Dr. Broome." Glad you liked the food ads in #97--but there was also a public service strip about nuclear power plants...What's the matter, Homer? Not interested? --Editor)

Dear Editor: I've never written to *Radioactive Man* before, but I feel that I must. RM is my favorite hero (Brave Heart being a close second). I think the scientific accuracy that's put in the stories elevates it a notch or two above kiddie stuff like Hartley Comics. My schoolmates would always rib me about reading comic books (I'm an undergraduate at Chico State) but when I point out the scientific basis for your stories, they get positively speechless and just stare at me! Let 'em keep their Holden Caulfield--I've got Claude Kane!

Melvin Coznowski
Chico, Calif.

(We were going to award Melvin the art for Chapter Two of "The Red Light, Green Light, One, Two, Three Crimes of Dr. Broome," but our handwriting expert in residence says this letter is really from Roger Doubt! Close, but no cigar, Roger! --Editor)

Dear Editor: May I make a suggestion? You've got to start bringing Radioactive Man into the stories earlier! In #95, #96, and the current issue RM doesn't show up until half the story's over! I hope you make up for the recent lack of RM in your upcoming one hundredth issue and have him in every panel! By the way, I noticed several typos in #97. Someone in the editorial department may need replacing!

Terry Delegeane
Millbrae, CA

(Calm down, Terry! If ye editor didn't know better, he'd think you were after his job! We're sending you the original art for Chapter Two of "The Red Light, Green Light, One, Two, Three Crimes of Dr. Broome," and see if you can figure out what all the blue pencil marks in the margins are supposed to mean! --Editor)

Dear Editor: I notice that you "award" original art from your publication to letter writers. Why don't you just give the artwork back to the *artist?*

Chester J. Lampwick
Los Angeles, Calif.

(It's simply company policy to give the original art to total strangers who write inane letters rather than back to the freelancers who have drawn for us for years. I'm sure you'll agree with our policy when you receive in the mail the original art from RM #97's backup story: "Fallout Boy's Atomic Wedgie!" --Editor)

Send correspondence to Ground Zero, Bongo Periodicals and Publications.

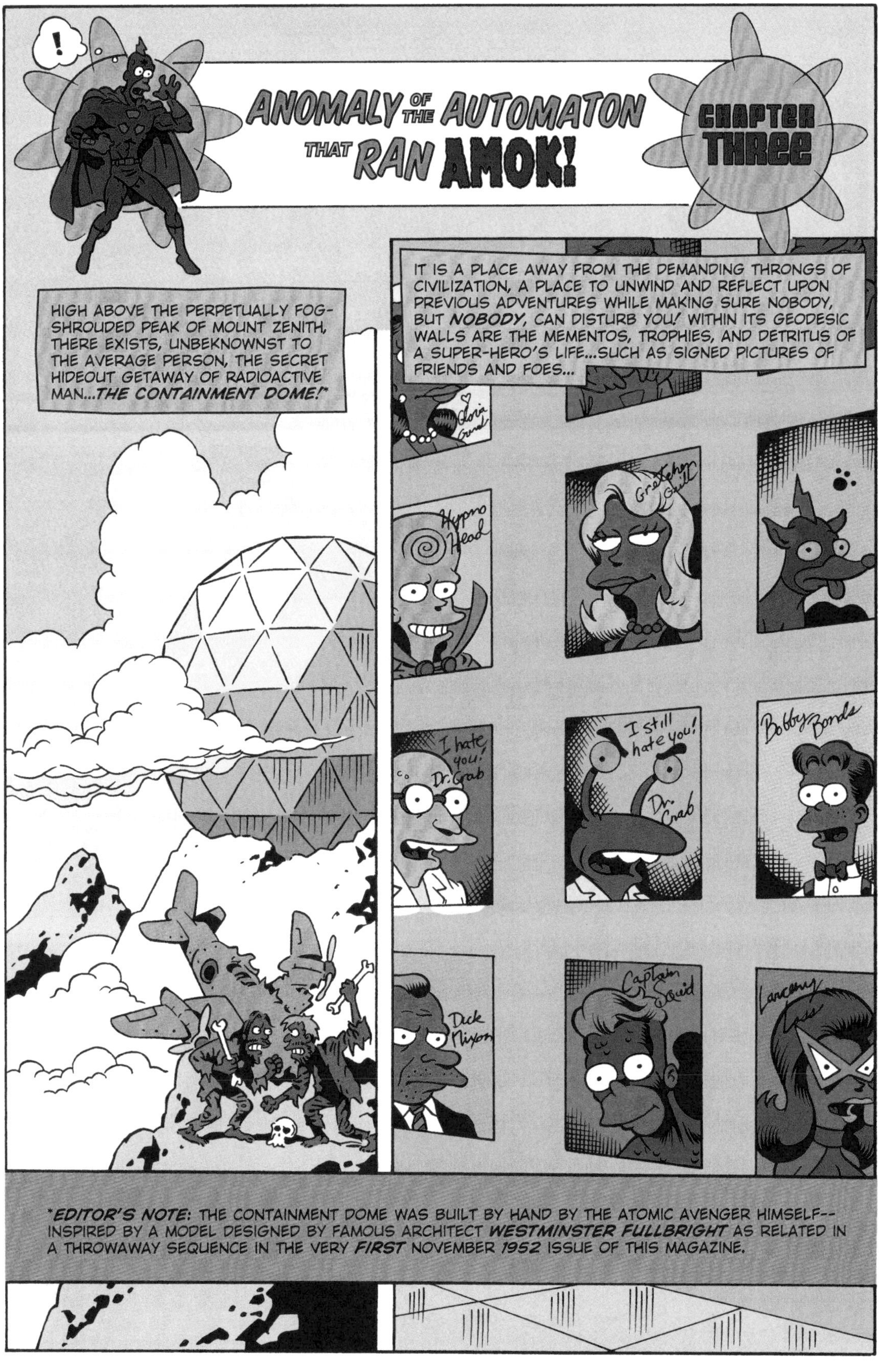
!
ANOMALY OF THE AUTOMATON THAT RAN AMOK!
CHAPTER THREE
HIGH ABOVE THE PERPETUALLY FOG-SHROUDED PEAK OF MOUNT ZENITH, THERE EXISTS, UNBEKNOWNST TO THE AVERAGE PERSON, THE SECRET HIDEOUT GETAWAY OF RADIOACTIVE MAN...*THE CONTAINMENT DOME!**
IT IS A PLACE AWAY FROM THE DEMANDING THRONGS OF CIVILIZATION, A PLACE TO UNWIND AND REFLECT UPON PREVIOUS ADVENTURES WHILE MAKING SURE NOBODY, BUT *NOBODY*, CAN DISTURB YOU! WITHIN ITS GEODESIC WALLS ARE THE MEMENTOS, TROPHIES, AND DETRITUS OF A SUPER-HERO'S LIFE...SUCH AS SIGNED PICTURES OF FRIENDS AND FOES...
Gretchen Guill
Hypno Head
I hate you! Dr. Crab
I still hate you! Dr. Crab
Bobby Bonds
Dick Nixon
Captain Squid
*EDITOR'S NOTE: THE CONTAINMENT DOME WAS BUILT BY HAND BY THE ATOMIC AVENGER HIMSELF--INSPIRED BY A MODEL DESIGNED BY FAMOUS ARCHITECT *WESTMINSTER FULLBRIGHT* AS RELATED IN A THROWAWAY SEQUENCE IN THE VERY *FIRST* NOVEMBER *1952* ISSUE OF THIS MAGAZINE.

AH, THERE'S NOTHING LIKE *RELAXING* AND WATCHING PAST EXPLOITS IN THE *COMFORT* OF ONE'S OWN HOME...

...ALTHOUGH I SHOULD'VE PICKED A *DIFFERENT* ADVENTURE! THIS IS MY RECENT ENCOUNTER WITH *DR. BROOME!* HE MANAGED TO *ELUDE* ME, LEAVING A *LOOSE END* DANGLING THAT I HAVE THE COMPULSIVE NEED TO TIE UP BEFORE I ENTER THIS BATTLE INTO MY *CASEBOOK!**

*EDITOR'S NOTE: THE FULL STORY OF RM'S DUEL WITH DR. BROOME WAS RELATED IN *ISSUE 97* OF RADIOACTIVE MAN!

I SHOULDN'T COMPLAIN--LIFE IS GOOD! I HAVE SO MANY SUCCESSFUL ADVENTURES AND THIS SWELL HOME VIDEO ENTERTAINMENT CENTER! THE AVERAGE AMERICAN WON'T HAVE ACCESS TO ONE OF THESE BABIES UNTIL *AT LEAST* THE 80'S! ⟩CHUCKLE⟨

CLICK

STILL, WITH ALL THE TECHNOLOGICAL ADVANCES THAT HAVE BEEN MADE, I'M *STYMIED* BY MY CONSTANT FAILURE TO FIND A WAY TO REMOVE THE LIGHTNING-SHAPED SHRAPNEL EMBEDDED IN MY HEAD...

AS YOU KNOW, DEAR READER, THIS IS THE ALTER-EGO OF THE CONTAMINATED CRUSADER, *CLAUDE KANE III*...

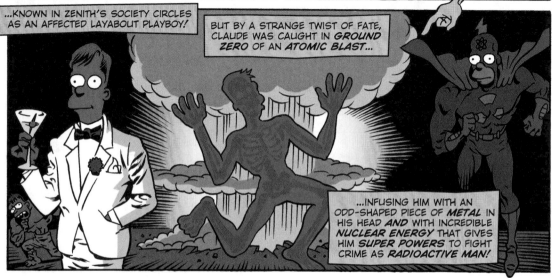

...KNOWN IN ZENITH'S SOCIETY CIRCLES AS AN AFFECTED LAYABOUT PLAYBOY!

BUT BY A STRANGE TWIST OF FATE, CLAUDE WAS CAUGHT IN *GROUND ZERO* OF AN *ATOMIC BLAST*...

...INFUSING HIM WITH AN ODD-SHAPED PIECE OF *METAL* IN HIS HEAD *AND* WITH INCREDIBLE *NUCLEAR ENERGY* THAT GIVES HIM *SUPER POWERS* TO FIGHT CRIME AS *RADIOACTIVE MAN!*

OF COURSE I HAVE TO WEAR A *HAT* WHENEVER I'M IN MIXED COMPANY AS CLAUDE KANE! ASIDE FROM A SMALL LEGION OF SUPER-POWERED BEINGS, INCLUDING MY SIDEKICK AND WARD *FALLOUT BOY*, NO ONE KNOWS THE SECRET OF MY TRUE IDENTITY!

THRLLLL

CLAUDE? IT'S ME-- *FALLOUT BOY!!* WE'VE BEEN LOOKING *ALL OVER* FOR YOU! WHAT DO YOU MEAN, "WHY DIDN'T ANYONE CALL"? NO ONE HAD THE UNLISTED NUMBER OF THE *CONTAINMENT DOME!*

IT'S A GOOD THING YOU LEFT THE NUMBER ON THE FRIDGE! LET ME TELL YOU WHAT'S BEEN GOING ON--AND DO ME A FAVOR? NEXT TIME YOU WANNA TAKE A FEW DAYS OFF, LET *ME* KNOW!

EGGS MILK

QUICKLY, A CRANKY FALLOUT BOY BRIEFS HIS MENTOR...

THE TECHNOLOGY *DIDN'T EXIST* IN 1863 FOR A ROBOT OF THAT SOPHISTICATION TO BE BUILT! AND *I* CERTAINLY WASN'T AROUND IN *1863!*

HMPH! SO MUCH FOR SOME R&R! BUT I CAN'T HELP BUT BE INTRIGUED...A HUNDRED-YEAR-OLD ROBOT GUNNING FOR ME? HOW CAN THAT BE?

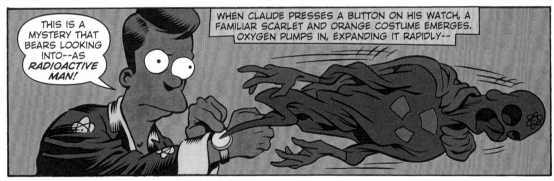

THIS IS A MYSTERY THAT BEARS LOOKING INTO--AS *RADIOACTIVE MAN!*

WHEN CLAUDE PRESSES A BUTTON ON HIS WATCH, A FAMILIAR SCARLET AND ORANGE COSTUME EMERGES. OXYGEN PUMPS IN, EXPANDING IT RAPIDLY--

CRASH!!

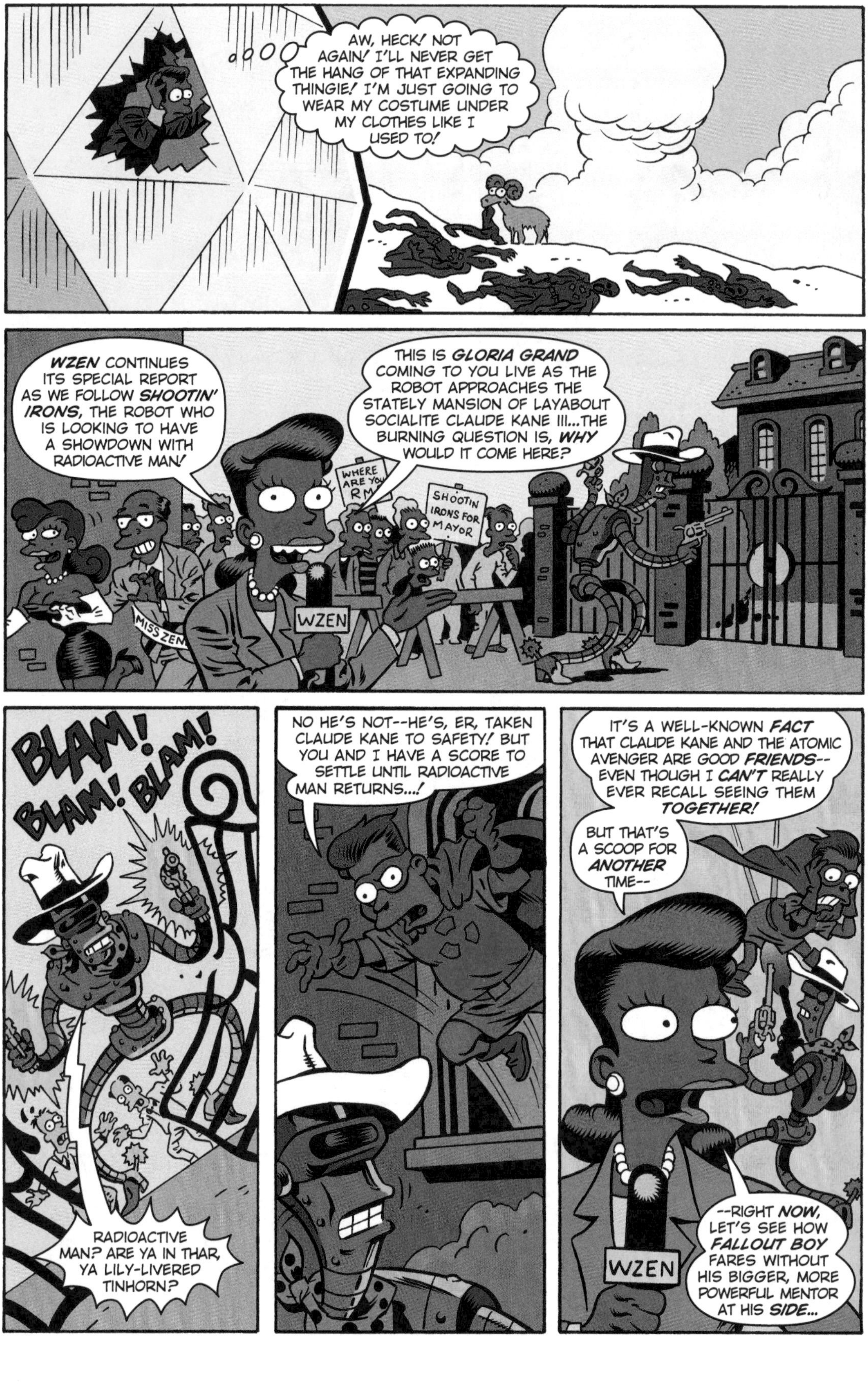
AW, HECK! NOT AGAIN! I'LL NEVER GET THE HANG OF THAT EXPANDING THINGIE! I'M JUST GOING TO WEAR MY COSTUME UNDER MY CLOTHES LIKE I USED TO!
WZEN CONTINUES ITS SPECIAL REPORT AS WE FOLLOW SHOOTIN' IRONS, THE ROBOT WHO IS LOOKING TO HAVE A SHOWDOWN WITH RADIOACTIVE MAN!
THIS IS GLORIA GRAND COMING TO YOU LIVE AS THE ROBOT APPROACHES THE STATELY MANSION OF LAYABOUT SOCIALITE CLAUDE KANE III...THE BURNING QUESTION IS, WHY WOULD IT COME HERE?
WHERE ARE YOU RM
SHOOTIN IRONS FOR MAYOR
MISS ZEN
WZEN
BLAM! BLAM! BLAM!
RADIOACTIVE MAN? ARE YA IN THAR, YA LILY-LIVERED TINHORN?
NO HE'S NOT--HE'S, ER, TAKEN CLAUDE KANE TO SAFETY! BUT YOU AND I HAVE A SCORE TO SETTLE UNTIL RADIOACTIVE MAN RETURNS...!
IT'S A WELL-KNOWN FACT THAT CLAUDE KANE AND THE ATOMIC AVENGER ARE GOOD FRIENDS--EVEN THOUGH I CAN'T REALLY EVER RECALL SEEING THEM TOGETHER!
BUT THAT'S A SCOOP FOR ANOTHER TIME--
--RIGHT NOW, LET'S SEE HOW FALLOUT BOY FARES WITHOUT HIS BIGGER, MORE POWERFUL MENTOR AT HIS SIDE...
WZEN

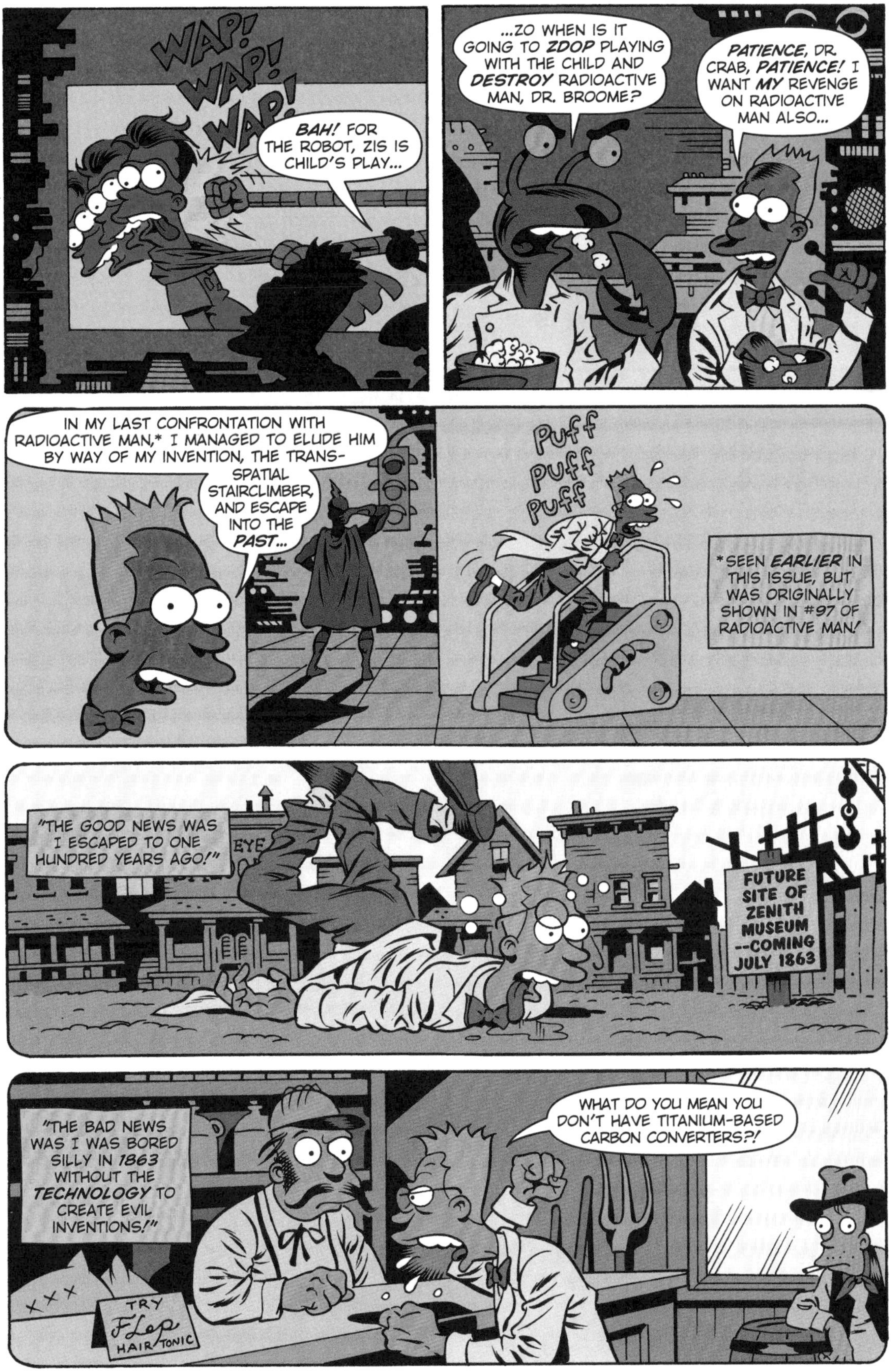
WAP! WAP! WAP!
BAH! FOR THE ROBOT, ZIS IS CHILD'S PLAY...
...ZO WHEN IS IT GOING TO ZDOP PLAYING WITH THE CHILD AND DESTROY RADIOACTIVE MAN, DR. BROOME?
PATIENCE, DR. CRAB, PATIENCE! I WANT MY REVENGE ON RADIOACTIVE MAN ALSO...
IN MY LAST CONFRONTATION WITH RADIOACTIVE MAN,* I MANAGED TO ELUDE HIM BY WAY OF MY INVENTION, THE TRANS-SPATIAL STAIRCLIMBER, AND ESCAPE INTO THE PAST...
Puff puff puff
*SEEN EARLIER IN THIS ISSUE, BUT WAS ORIGINALLY SHOWN IN #97 OF RADIOACTIVE MAN!
"THE GOOD NEWS WAS I ESCAPED TO ONE HUNDRED YEARS AGO!"
FUTURE SITE OF ZENITH MUSEUM --COMING JULY 1863
"THE BAD NEWS WAS I WAS BORED SILLY IN 1863 WITHOUT THE TECHNOLOGY TO CREATE EVIL INVENTIONS!"
WHAT DO YOU MEAN YOU DON'T HAVE TITANIUM-BASED CARBON CONVERTERS?!
TRY Flop HAIR TONIC

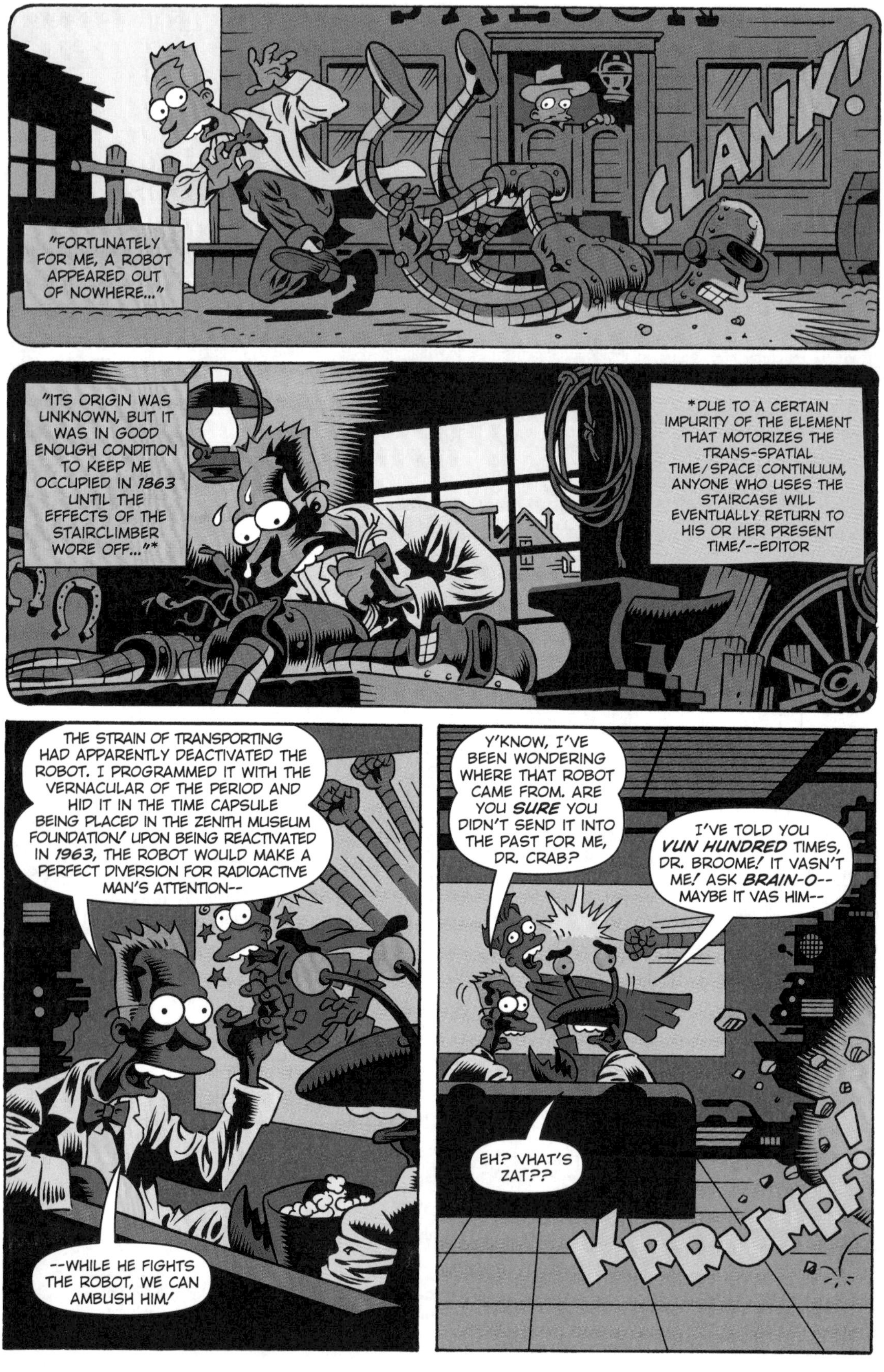
CLANK!
"FORTUNATELY FOR ME, A ROBOT APPEARED OUT OF NOWHERE..."
"ITS ORIGIN WAS UNKNOWN, BUT IT WAS IN GOOD ENOUGH CONDITION TO KEEP ME OCCUPIED IN 1863 UNTIL THE EFFECTS OF THE STAIRCLIMBER WORE OFF..."*
*DUE TO A CERTAIN IMPURITY OF THE ELEMENT THAT MOTORIZES THE TRANS-SPATIAL TIME/SPACE CONTINUUM, ANYONE WHO USES THE STAIRCASE WILL EVENTUALLY RETURN TO HIS OR HER PRESENT TIME!--EDITOR
THE STRAIN OF TRANSPORTING HAD APPARENTLY DEACTIVATED THE ROBOT. I PROGRAMMED IT WITH THE VERNACULAR OF THE PERIOD AND HID IT IN THE TIME CAPSULE BEING PLACED IN THE ZENITH MUSEUM FOUNDATION! UPON BEING REACTIVATED IN 1963, THE ROBOT WOULD MAKE A PERFECT DIVERSION FOR RADIOACTIVE MAN'S ATTENTION--
--WHILE HE FIGHTS THE ROBOT, WE CAN AMBUSH HIM!
Y'KNOW, I'VE BEEN WONDERING WHERE THAT ROBOT CAME FROM. ARE YOU **SURE** YOU DIDN'T SEND IT INTO THE PAST FOR ME, DR. CRAB?
I'VE TOLD YOU **VUN HUNDRED** TIMES, DR. BROOME! IT VASN'T ME! ASK **BRAIN-O**-- MAYBE IT VAS HIM--
EH? VHAT'S ZAT??
KRRUMPF!

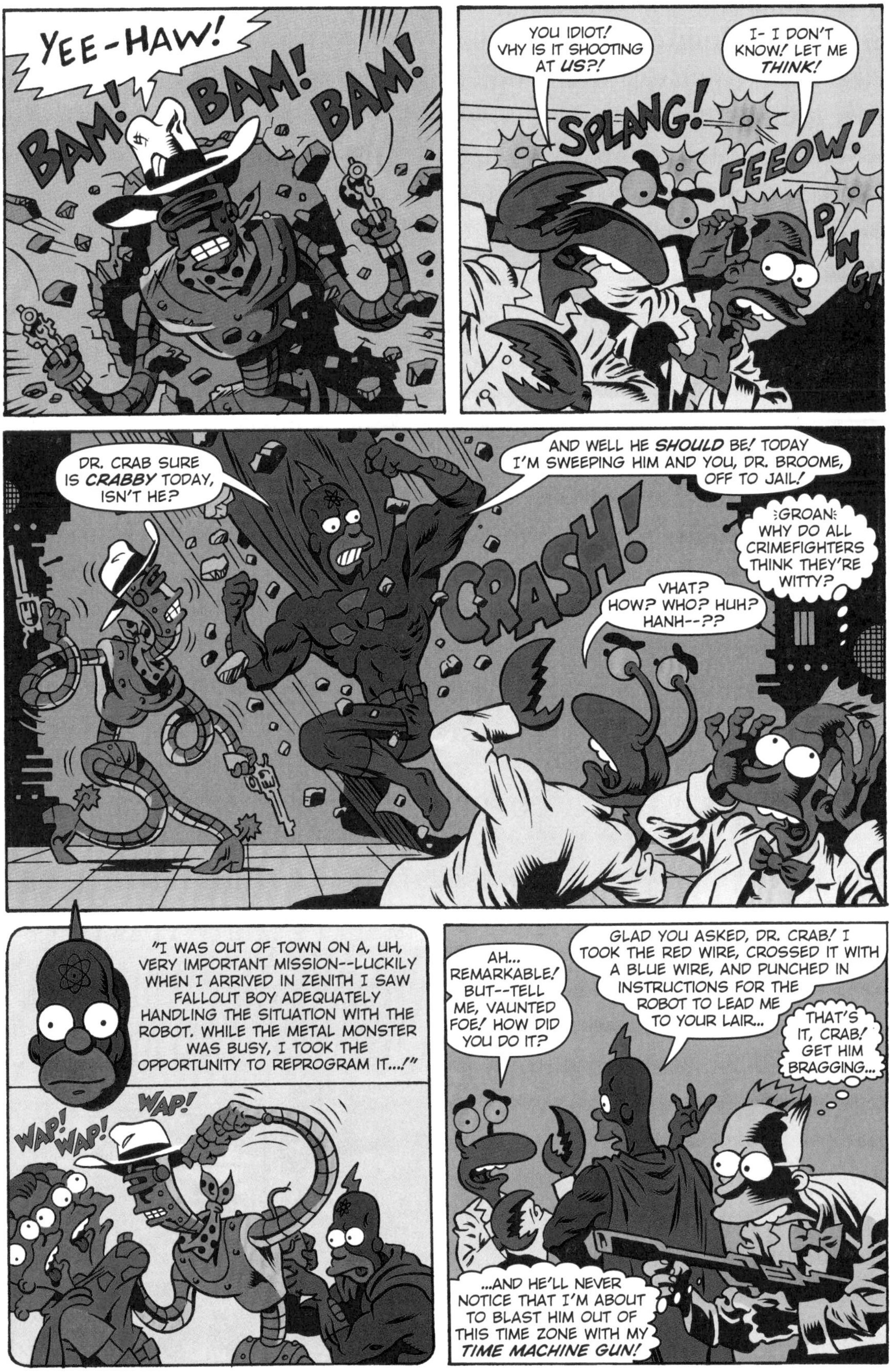
YEE-HAW!
BAM! BAM! BAM!
YOU IDIOT! VHY IS IT SHOOTING AT *US?!*
I- I DON'T KNOW! LET ME *THINK!*
SPLANG!
FEEOW!
PING!
DR. CRAB SURE IS *CRABBY* TODAY, ISN'T HE?
AND WELL HE *SHOULD* BE! TODAY I'M SWEEPING HIM AND YOU, DR. BROOME, OFF TO JAIL!
CRASH!
GROAN WHY DO ALL CRIMEFIGHTERS THINK THEY'RE WITTY?
VHAT? HOW? WHO? HUH? HANH--??
"I WAS OUT OF TOWN ON A, UH, VERY IMPORTANT MISSION--LUCKILY WHEN I ARRIVED IN ZENITH I SAW FALLOUT BOY ADEQUATELY HANDLING THE SITUATION WITH THE ROBOT. WHILE THE METAL MONSTER WAS BUSY, I TOOK THE OPPORTUNITY TO REPROGRAM IT...!"
WAP! WAP! WAP!
AH... REMARKABLE! BUT--TELL ME, VAUNTED FOE! HOW DID YOU DO IT?
GLAD YOU ASKED, DR. CRAB! I TOOK THE RED WIRE, CROSSED IT WITH A BLUE WIRE, AND PUNCHED IN INSTRUCTIONS FOR THE ROBOT TO LEAD ME TO YOUR LAIR...
THAT'S IT, CRAB! GET HIM BRAGGING...
...AND HE'LL NEVER NOTICE THAT I'M ABOUT TO BLAST HIM OUT OF THIS TIME ZONE WITH MY *TIME MACHINE GUN!*

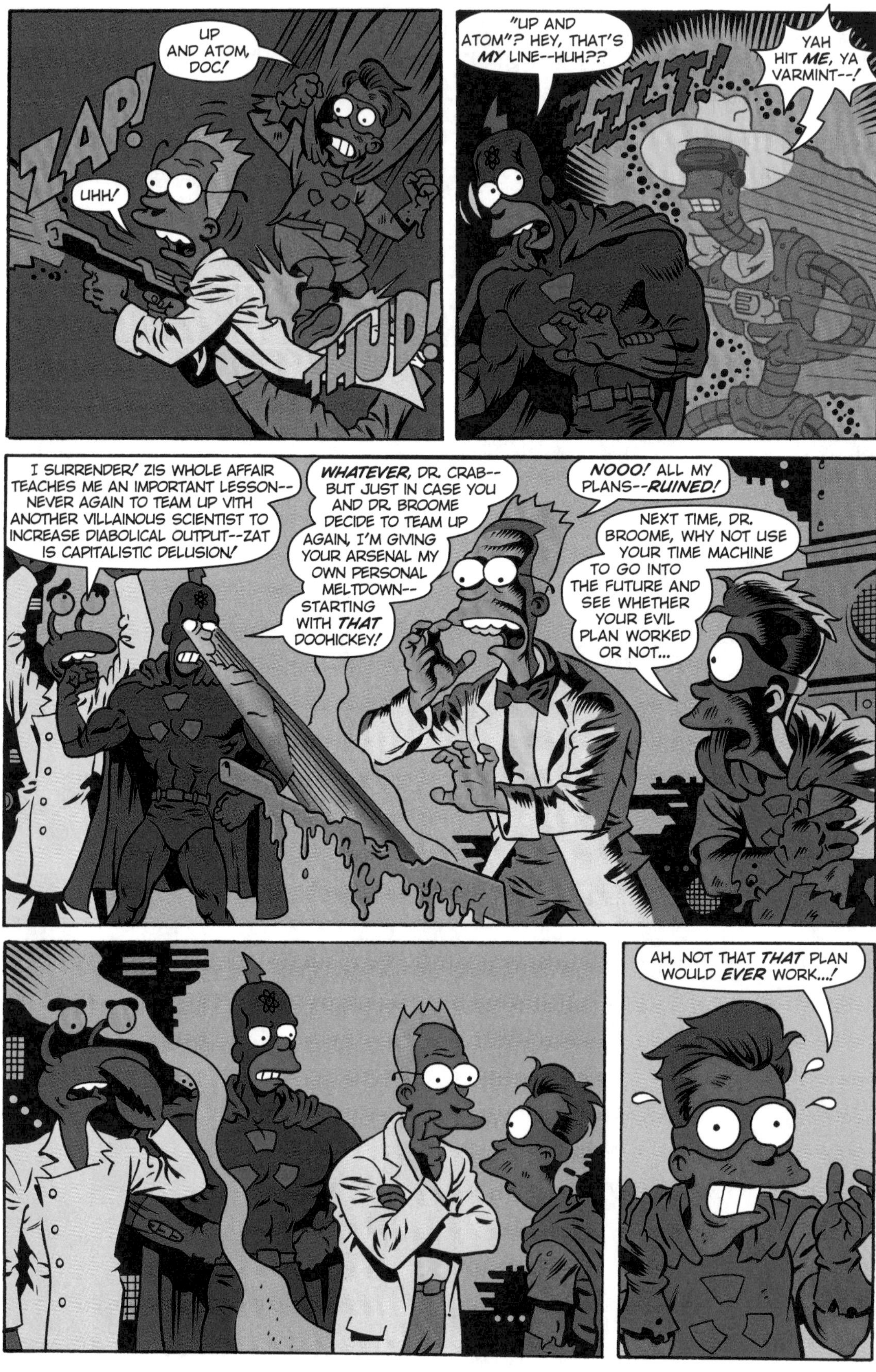
UP AND ATOM, DOC!
ZAP!
UHH!
THUD!
"UP AND ATOM"? HEY, THAT'S *MY* LINE--HUH??
ZIZZT!
YAH HIT *ME*, YA VARMINT--!
I SURRENDER! ZIS WHOLE AFFAIR TEACHES ME AN IMPORTANT LESSON--NEVER AGAIN TO TEAM UP VITH ANOTHER VILLAINOUS SCIENTIST TO INCREASE DIABOLICAL OUTPUT--ZAT IS CAPITALISTIC DELUSION!
WHATEVER, DR. CRAB--BUT JUST IN CASE YOU AND DR. BROOME DECIDE TO TEAM UP AGAIN, I'M GIVING YOUR ARSENAL MY OWN PERSONAL MELTDOWN--STARTING WITH *THAT* DOOHICKEY!
NOOO! ALL MY PLANS--*RUINED!*
NEXT TIME, DR. BROOME, WHY NOT USE YOUR TIME MACHINE TO GO INTO THE FUTURE AND SEE WHETHER YOUR EVIL PLAN WORKED OR NOT...
AH, NOT THAT *THAT* PLAN WOULD *EVER* WORK...!

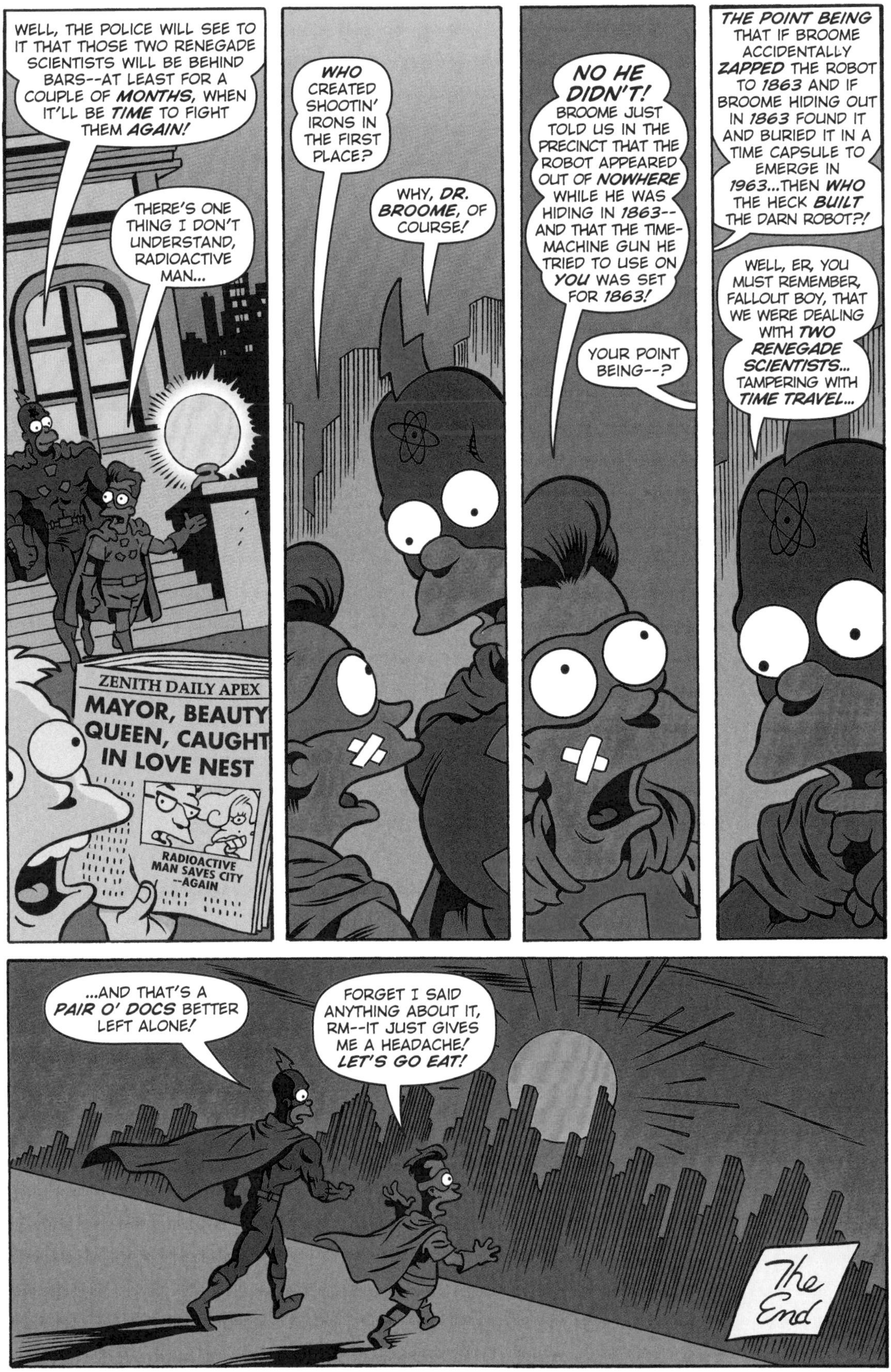
WELL, THE POLICE WILL SEE TO IT THAT THOSE TWO RENEGADE SCIENTISTS WILL BE BEHIND BARS--AT LEAST FOR A COUPLE OF MONTHS, WHEN IT'LL BE TIME TO FIGHT THEM AGAIN!
THERE'S ONE THING I DON'T UNDERSTAND, RADIOACTIVE MAN...
ZENITH DAILY APEX
MAYOR, BEAUTY QUEEN, CAUGHT IN LOVE NEST
RADIOACTIVE MAN SAVES CITY --AGAIN
WHO CREATED SHOOTIN' IRONS IN THE FIRST PLACE?
WHY, DR. BROOME, OF COURSE!
NO HE DIDN'T! BROOME JUST TOLD US IN THE PRECINCT THAT THE ROBOT APPEARED OUT OF NOWHERE WHILE HE WAS HIDING IN 1863--AND THAT THE TIME-MACHINE GUN HE TRIED TO USE ON YOU WAS SET FOR 1863!
YOUR POINT BEING--?
THE POINT BEING THAT IF BROOME ACCIDENTALLY ZAPPED THE ROBOT TO 1863 AND IF BROOME HIDING OUT IN 1863 FOUND IT AND BURIED IT IN A TIME CAPSULE TO EMERGE IN 1963...THEN WHO THE HECK BUILT THE DARN ROBOT?!
WELL, ER, YOU MUST REMEMBER, FALLOUT BOY, THAT WE WERE DEALING WITH TWO RENEGADE SCIENTISTS... TAMPERING WITH TIME TRAVEL...
...AND THAT'S A PAIR O' DOCS BETTER LEFT ALONE!
FORGET I SAID ANYTHING ABOUT IT, RM--IT JUST GIVES ME A HEADACHE! LET'S GO EAT!
The End

FALLOUT SHELTER!

BIG ENOUGH FOR 2-3 KIDS AND A YEAR'S WORTH OF NON-PERISHABLE FOOD!

$1.00 a day for 1,368 days.

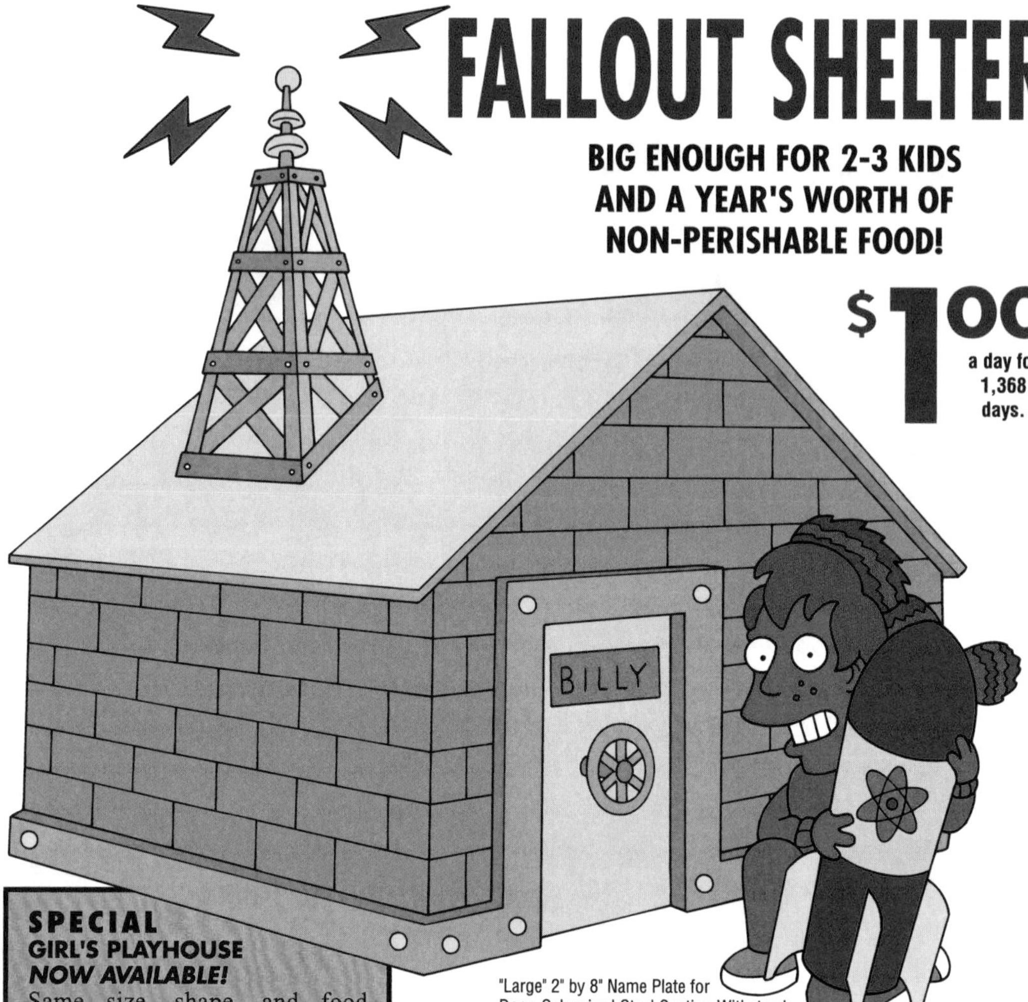

BILLY

SPECIAL
GIRL'S PLAYHOUSE
NOW AVAILABLE!
Same size, shape, and food storage capacity as normal Fallout Shelter, and includes exciting, easy-to-apply can of pink paint. Trés de fille!

FREE "Large" 2" by 8" Name Plate for Door. Galvanized Steel Coating Withstands Any Nuclear Blast. Shelter Can Be Personalized with Child's Name, Date of Birth, Fingerprints, and Epitaph.

Orders Shipped within 24 Hours Barring Declaration of War!

FALLOUT SHELTER
Dept. of Defense, The Pentagon, Washington, D.C. 20301

Please send items checked.

- ☐ **Fallout Shelter @ $1.00** a day for 1,368 days, plus $169.95 postage and handling.
- ☐ **Girl's "Playhouse" @ $1.00** a day for 1,368 days, plus $199.95 postage and handling.
- ☐ **Fallout Shelter or Girl's "Play-house" or Any Combination -- 5 for $4.00** a day for 1,368 days, plus $229.95 postage and handling each.

I enclose: ☐ Cash ☐ Check ☐ Money Order ☐ Weapons for Trade ☐ Russian Secrets

Sorry, No C.O.D.'s!

Name____________________________

Address__________________________

City________________ Zone___ State____

This huge, government-style shelter is a child's dream come true. Size approx. 3 feet high with 23 cubic square feet of space inside and 24 inch thick concrete walls. Complete with 2 cots attached to walls and air mattress that stores away easily. Also comes with HAM radio for hours of listening fun and keeping track of post-apocalyptic doings. Endless hours/days/months of end-of-the-world fun! Big enough for 2-3 kids to "live" in this shelter of their very own. Constructed of bomb-resistant, fallout-safe steel, brick, and mortar. "Easy"-to-read blueprints for "simple" setup.* Shelter lasts forever, withstanding the most atomic of blasts. Flat roof constructed of mutant-resistant concrete. In a youngster's imagination it quickly becomes a GROUND ZERO PLAYHOUSE - MILITIA HEADQUARTERS - or a LIFE-SIZE DOLLHOUSE FOR GIRLS. This king-size shelter is our greatest bargain in years. Your sale price is made possible by buying directly from the factory (i.e. government). We are the largest manufacturers/distributors of "play" fallout shelters in the U.S. They make wonderful gifts. Buy several! Pay for years! Keep the whole neighborhood safe! Are you and your friends prepared for a play "Red Scare" or the real thing? Don't delay--the commies won't! GUARANTEE: Try without risk or obligation for ten days. Let the kids play in and enjoy it. If they are not delighted (or saved from the blast of a nuclear bomb), return for immediate refund.

* Degree in structural engineering required to read blueprints.

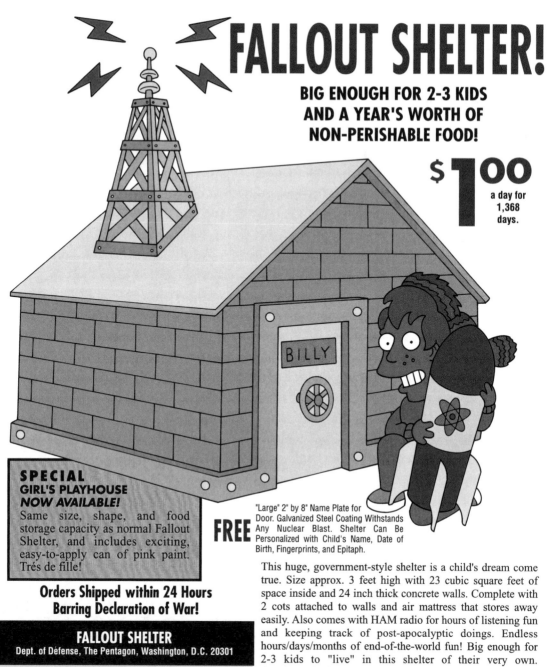

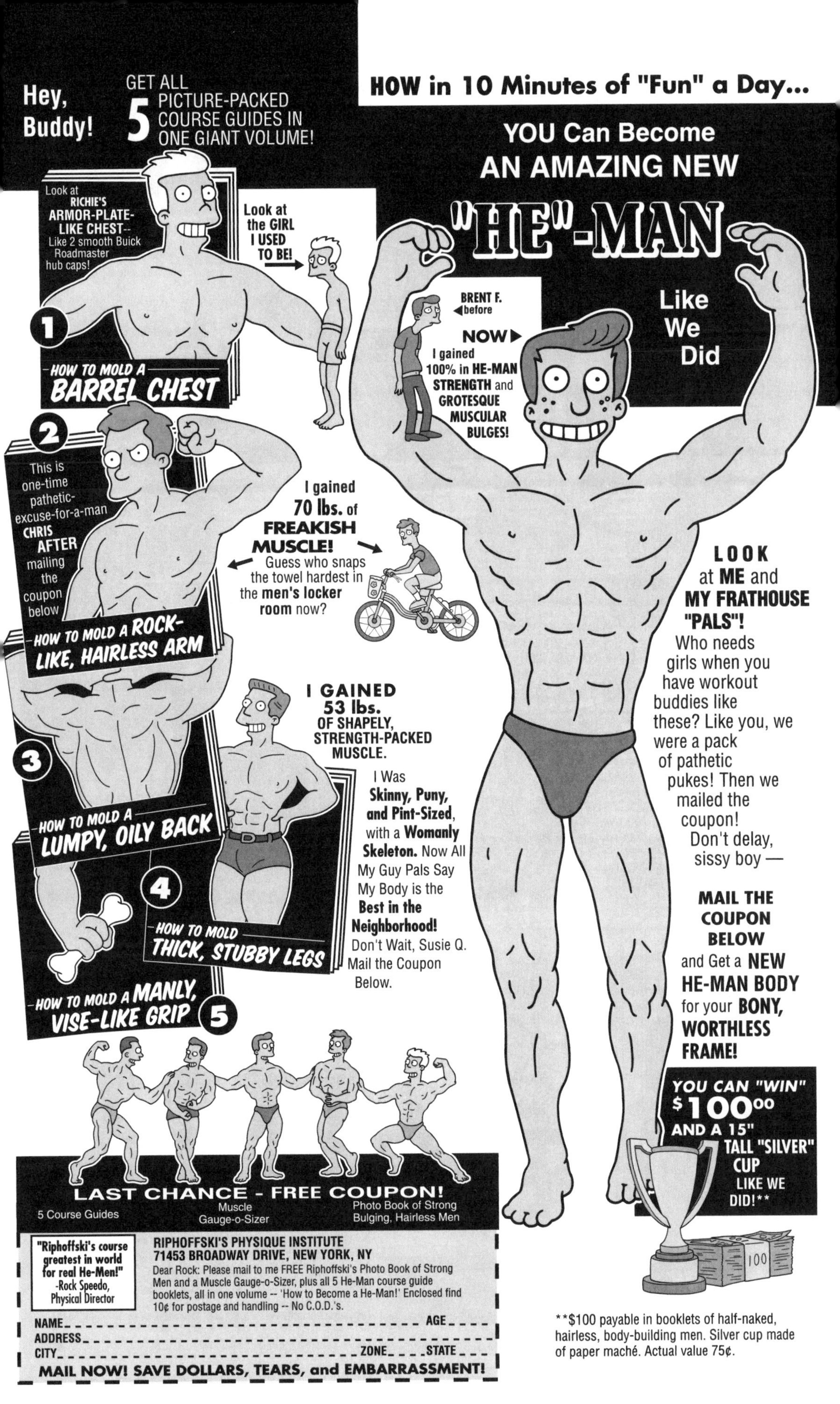

Hey, Buddy!
GET ALL 5 PICTURE-PACKED COURSE GUIDES IN ONE GIANT VOLUME!
HOW in 10 Minutes of "Fun" a Day...
YOU Can Become AN AMAZING NEW "HE"-MAN
Like We Did
Look at RICHIE'S ARMOR-PLATE-LIKE CHEST-- Like 2 smooth Buick Roadmaster hub caps!
Look at the GIRL I USED TO BE!
1
HOW TO MOLD A BARREL CHEST
BRENT F. before
NOW I gained 100% in HE-MAN STRENGTH and GROTESQUE MUSCULAR BULGES!
2
This is one-time pathetic-excuse-for-a-man CHRIS AFTER mailing the coupon below
HOW TO MOLD A ROCK-LIKE, HAIRLESS ARM
I gained 70 lbs. of FREAKISH MUSCLE! Guess who snaps the towel hardest in the men's locker room now?
LOOK at ME and MY FRATHOUSE "PALS"! Who needs girls when you have workout buddies like these? Like you, we were a pack of pathetic pukes! Then we mailed the coupon! Don't delay, sissy boy —
3
HOW TO MOLD A LUMPY, OILY BACK
I GAINED 53 lbs. OF SHAPELY, STRENGTH-PACKED MUSCLE.
I Was Skinny, Puny, and Pint-Sized, with a Womanly Skeleton. Now All My Guy Pals Say My Body is the Best in the Neighborhood! Don't Wait, Susie Q. Mail the Coupon Below.
4
HOW TO MOLD THICK, STUBBY LEGS
MAIL THE COUPON BELOW and Get a NEW HE-MAN BODY for your BONY, WORTHLESS FRAME!
HOW TO MOLD A MANLY, VISE-LIKE GRIP
5
YOU CAN "WIN" $100.00 AND A 15" TALL "SILVER" CUP LIKE WE DID!**
100
LAST CHANCE - FREE COUPON!
5 Course Guides
Muscle Gauge-o-Sizer
Photo Book of Strong Bulging, Hairless Men
"Riphoffski's course greatest in world for real He-Men!" -Rock Speedo, Physical Director
RIPHOFFSKI'S PHYSIQUE INSTITUTE
71453 BROADWAY DRIVE, NEW YORK, NY
Dear Rock: Please mail to me FREE Riphoffski's Photo Book of Strong Men and a Muscle Gauge-o-Sizer, plus all 5 He-Man course guide booklets, all in one volume -- 'How to Become a He-Man!' Enclosed find 10¢ for postage and handling -- No C.O.D.'s.
NAME AGE
ADDRESS
CITY ZONE STATE
MAIL NOW! SAVE DOLLARS, TEARS, and EMBARRASSMENT!
**$100 payable in booklets of half-naked, hairless, body-building men. Silver cup made of paper maché. Actual value 75¢.

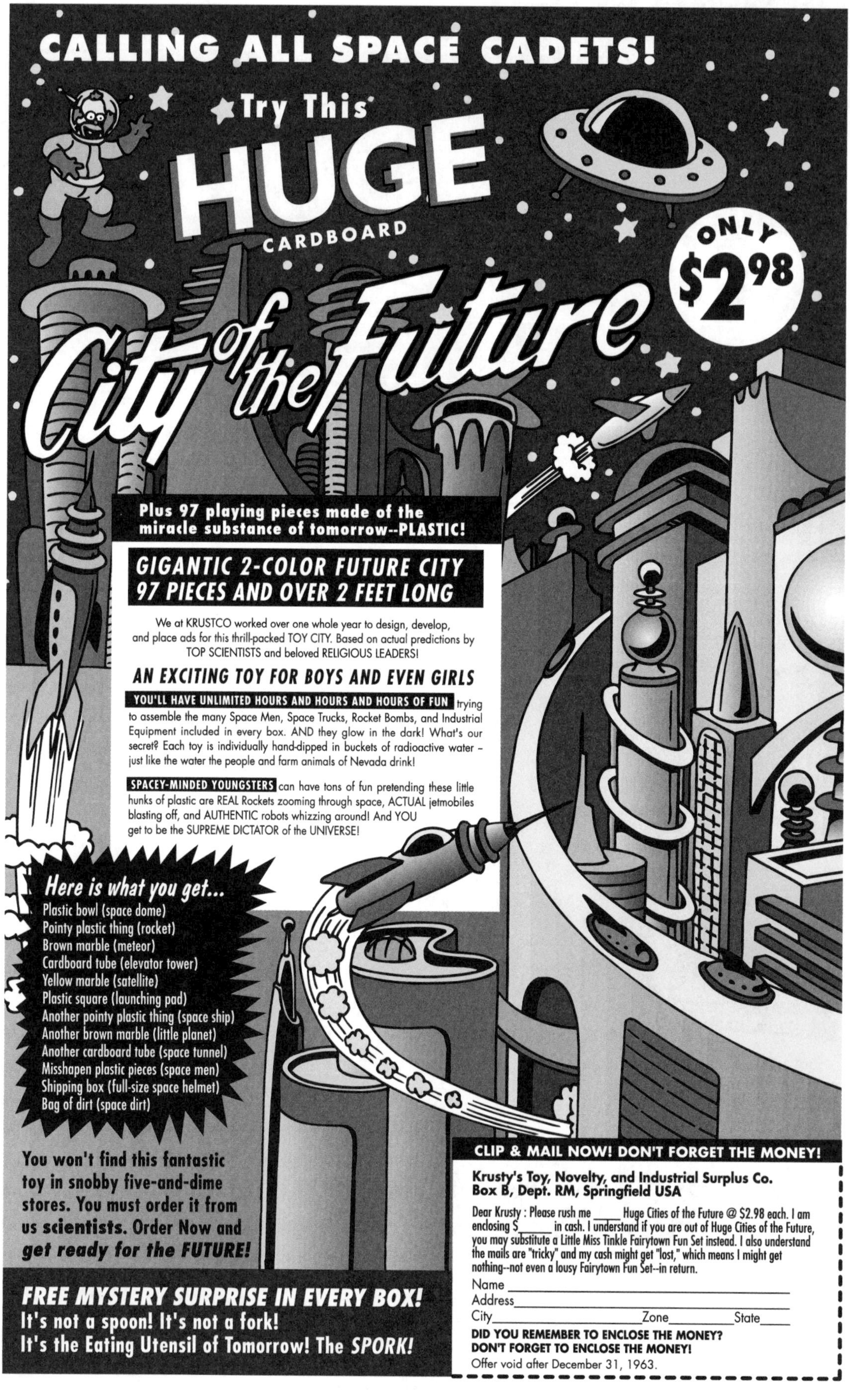

CALLING ALL SPACE CADETS!
Try This
HUGE
CARDBOARD
City of the Future
ONLY $2.98
Plus 97 playing pieces made of the miracle substance of tomorrow--PLASTIC!
GIGANTIC 2-COLOR FUTURE CITY
97 PIECES AND OVER 2 FEET LONG
We at KRUSTCO worked over one whole year to design, develop, and place ads for this thrill-packed TOY CITY. Based on actual predictions by TOP SCIENTISTS and beloved RELIGIOUS LEADERS!
AN EXCITING TOY FOR BOYS AND EVEN GIRLS
YOU'LL HAVE UNLIMITED HOURS AND HOURS AND HOURS OF FUN trying to assemble the many Space Men, Space Trucks, Rocket Bombs, and Industrial Equipment included in every box. AND they glow in the dark! What's our secret? Each toy is individually hand-dipped in buckets of radioactive water – just like the water the people and farm animals of Nevada drink!
SPACEY-MINDED YOUNGSTERS can have tons of fun pretending these little hunks of plastic are REAL Rockets zooming through space, ACTUAL jetmobiles blasting off, and AUTHENTIC robots whizzing around! And YOU get to be the SUPREME DICTATOR of the UNIVERSE!
Here is what you get...
Plastic bowl (space dome)
Pointy plastic thing (rocket)
Brown marble (meteor)
Cardboard tube (elevator tower)
Yellow marble (satellite)
Plastic square (launching pad)
Another pointy plastic thing (space ship)
Another brown marble (little planet)
Another cardboard tube (space tunnel)
Misshapen plastic pieces (space men)
Shipping box (full-size space helmet)
Bag of dirt (space dirt)
You won't find this fantastic toy in snobby five-and-dime stores. You must order it from us scientists. Order Now and get ready for the FUTURE!
FREE MYSTERY SURPRISE IN EVERY BOX!
It's not a spoon! It's not a fork!
It's the Eating Utensil of Tomorrow! The SPORK!
CLIP & MAIL NOW! DON'T FORGET THE MONEY!
Krusty's Toy, Novelty, and Industrial Surplus Co.
Box B, Dept. RM, Springfield USA
Dear Krusty : Please rush me ____ Huge Cities of the Future @ $2.98 each. I am enclosing $______ in cash. I understand if you are out of Huge Cities of the Future, you may substitute a Little Miss Tinkle Fairytown Fun Set instead. I also understand the mails are "tricky" and my cash might get "lost," which means I might get nothing--not even a lousy Fairytown Fun Set--in return.
Name
Address
City
Zone
State
DID YOU REMEMBER TO ENCLOSE THE MONEY?
DON'T FORGET TO ENCLOSE THE MONEY!
Offer void after December 31, 1963.

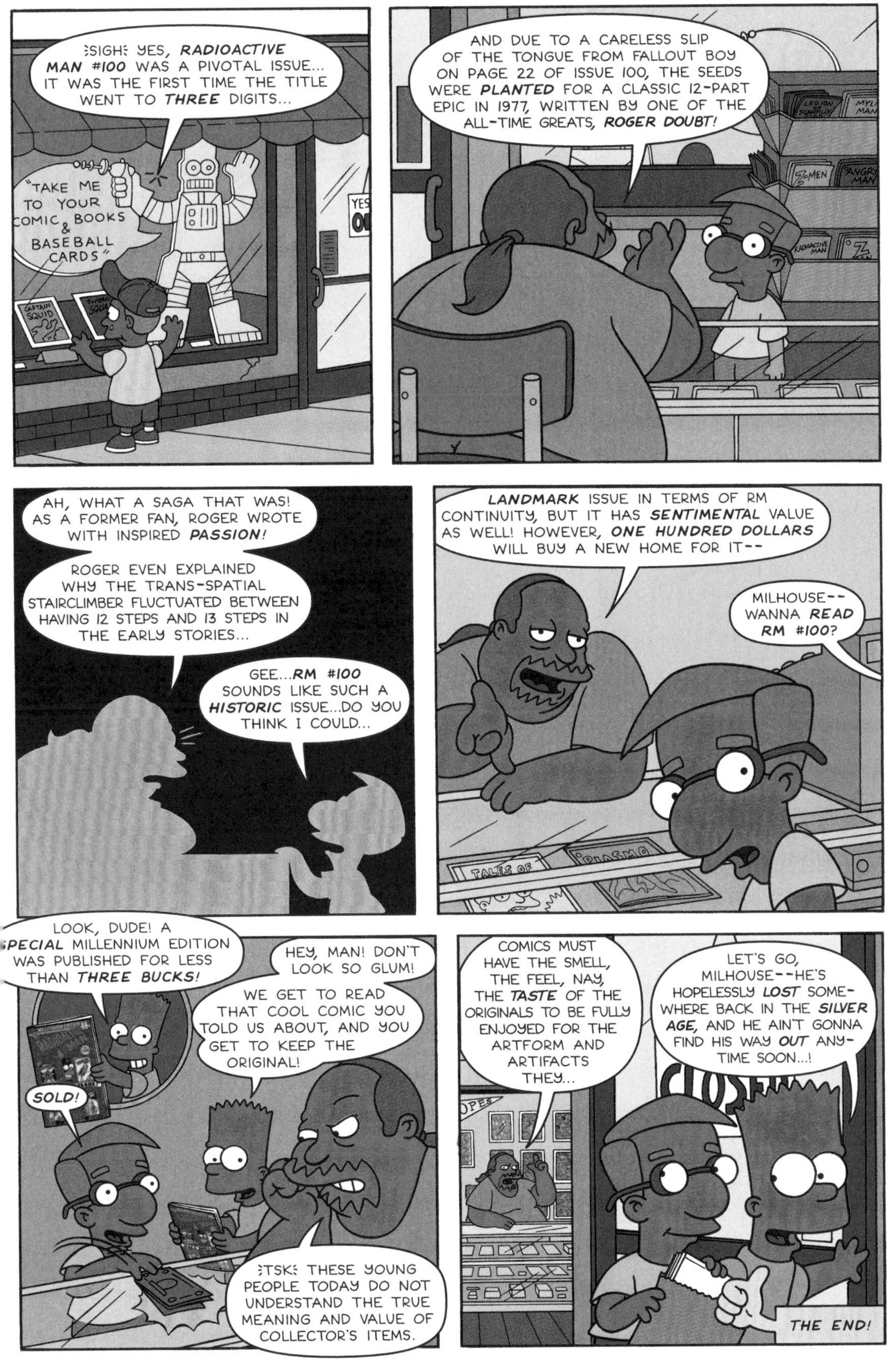
:SIGH: YES, RADIOACTIVE MAN #100 WAS A PIVOTAL ISSUE... IT WAS THE FIRST TIME THE TITLE WENT TO THREE DIGITS...
"TAKE ME TO YOUR COMIC BOOKS & BASEBALL CARDS"
CAPTAIN SQUID
AND DUE TO A CARELESS SLIP OF THE TONGUE FROM FALLOUT BOY ON PAGE 22 OF ISSUE 100, THE SEEDS WERE PLANTED FOR A CLASSIC 12-PART EPIC IN 1977, WRITTEN BY ONE OF THE ALL-TIME GREATS, ROGER DOUBT!
AH, WHAT A SAGA THAT WAS! AS A FORMER FAN, ROGER WROTE WITH INSPIRED PASSION!
ROGER EVEN EXPLAINED WHY THE TRANS-SPATIAL STAIRCLIMBER FLUCTUATED BETWEEN HAVING 12 STEPS AND 13 STEPS IN THE EARLY STORIES...
GEE...RM #100 SOUNDS LIKE SUCH A HISTORIC ISSUE...DO YOU THINK I COULD...
LANDMARK ISSUE IN TERMS OF RM CONTINUITY, BUT IT HAS SENTIMENTAL VALUE AS WELL! HOWEVER, ONE HUNDRED DOLLARS WILL BUY A NEW HOME FOR IT--
MILHOUSE-- WANNA READ RM #100?
TALES OF
PLASMO
LOOK, DUDE! A SPECIAL MILLENNIUM EDITION WAS PUBLISHED FOR LESS THAN THREE BUCKS!
HEY, MAN! DON'T LOOK SO GLUM!
WE GET TO READ THAT COOL COMIC YOU TOLD US ABOUT, AND YOU GET TO KEEP THE ORIGINAL!
SOLD!
:TSK: THESE YOUNG PEOPLE TODAY DO NOT UNDERSTAND THE TRUE MEANING AND VALUE OF COLLECTOR'S ITEMS.
COMICS MUST HAVE THE SMELL, THE FEEL, NAY, THE TASTE OF THE ORIGINALS TO BE FULLY ENJOYED FOR THE ARTFORM AND ARTIFACTS THEY...
LET'S GO, MILHOUSE--HE'S HOPELESSLY LOST SOMEWHERE BACK IN THE SILVER AGE, AND HE AIN'T GONNA FIND HIS WAY OUT ANYTIME SOON...!
THE END!

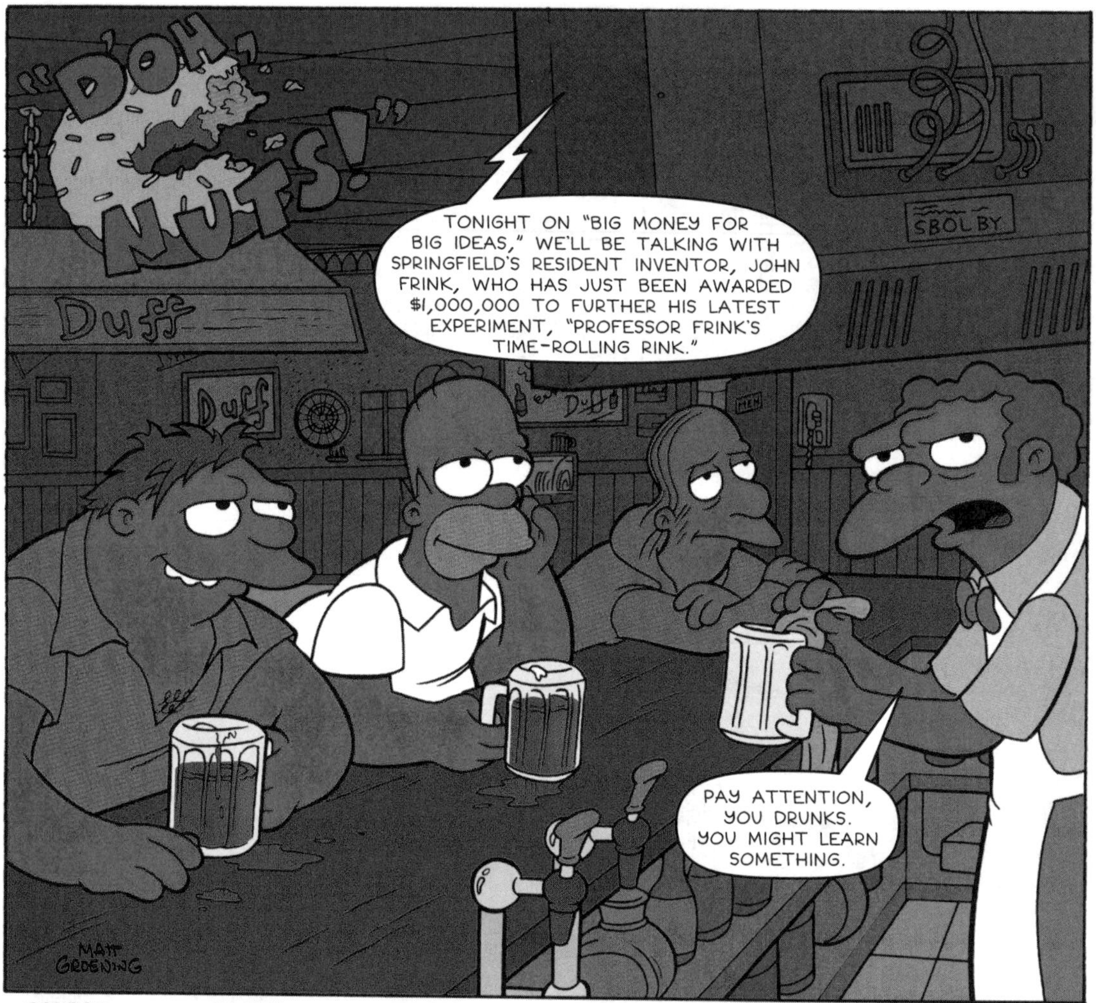
"DOH NUTS!"
Duff
TONIGHT ON "BIG MONEY FOR BIG IDEAS," WE'LL BE TALKING WITH SPRINGFIELD'S RESIDENT INVENTOR, JOHN FRINK, WHO HAS JUST BEEN AWARDED $1,000,000 TO FURTHER HIS LATEST EXPERIMENT, "PROFESSOR FRINK'S TIME-ROLLING RINK."
PAY ATTENTION, YOU DRUNKS. YOU MIGHT LEARN SOMETHING.
MATT GROENING

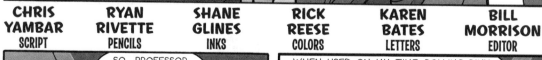

CHRIS YAMBAR SCRIPT | **RYAN RIVETTE** PENCILS | **SHANE GLINES** INKS | **RICK REESE** COLORS | **KAREN BATES** LETTERS | **BILL MORRISON** EDITOR

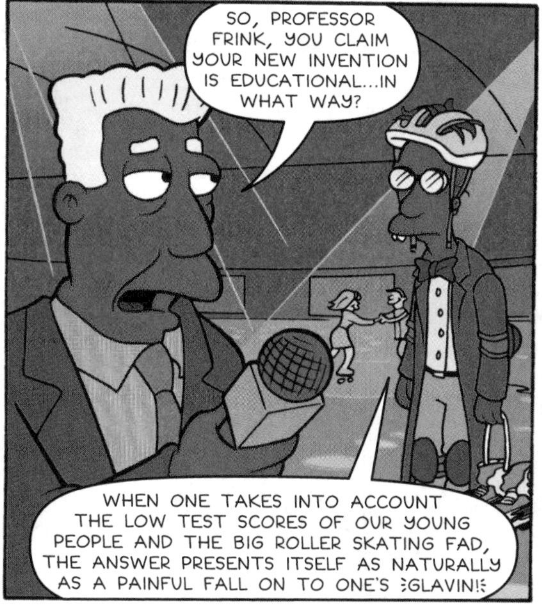
SO, PROFESSOR FRINK, YOU CLAIM YOUR NEW INVENTION IS EDUCATIONAL...IN WHAT WAY?
WHEN ONE TAKES INTO ACCOUNT THE LOW TEST SCORES OF OUR YOUNG PEOPLE AND THE BIG ROLLER SKATING FAD, THE ANSWER PRESENTS ITSELF AS NATURALLY AS A PAINFUL FALL ON TO ONE'S GLAVIN!

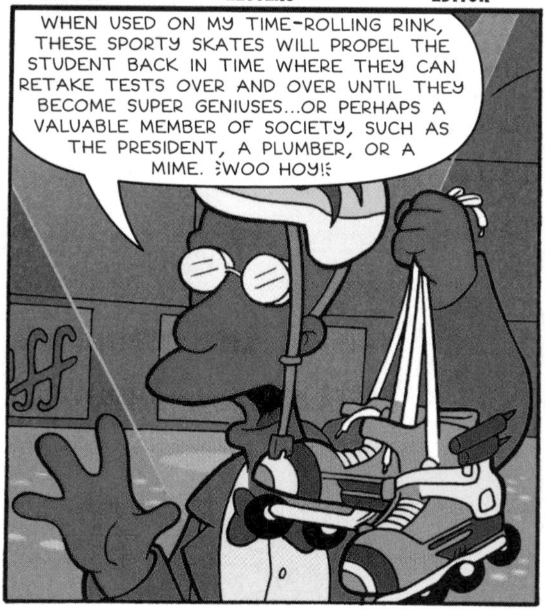
WHEN USED ON MY TIME-ROLLING RINK, THESE SPORTY SKATES WILL PROPEL THE STUDENT BACK IN TIME WHERE THEY CAN RETAKE TESTS OVER AND OVER UNTIL THEY BECOME SUPER GENIUSES...OR PERHAPS A VALUABLE MEMBER OF SOCIETY, SUCH AS THE PRESIDENT, A PLUMBER, OR A MIME. WOO HOY!

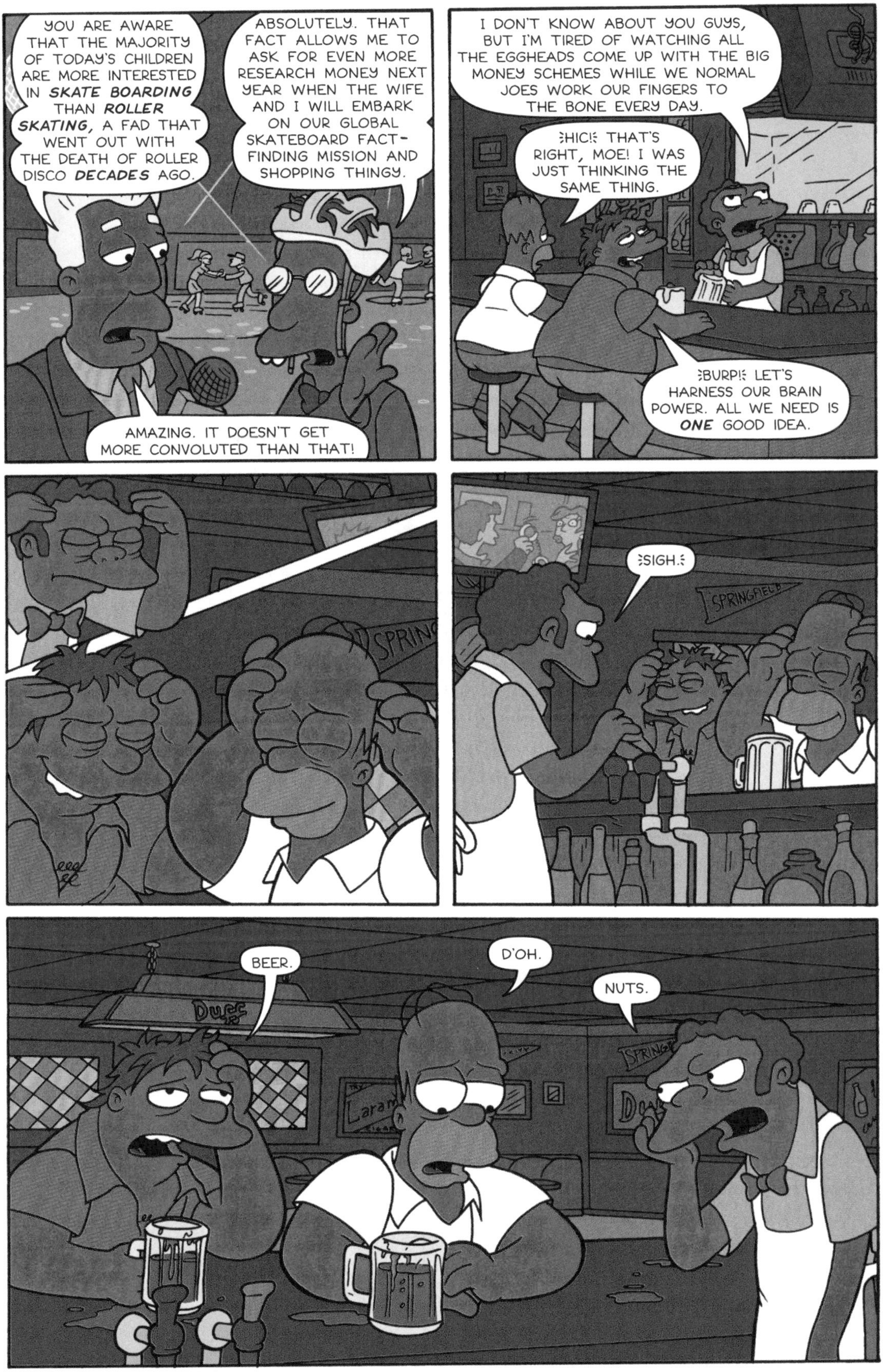
YOU ARE AWARE THAT THE MAJORITY OF TODAY'S CHILDREN ARE MORE INTERESTED IN **SKATE BOARDING** THAN **ROLLER SKATING,** A FAD THAT WENT OUT WITH THE DEATH OF ROLLER DISCO **DECADES** AGO.
ABSOLUTELY. THAT FACT ALLOWS ME TO ASK FOR EVEN MORE RESEARCH MONEY NEXT YEAR WHEN THE WIFE AND I WILL EMBARK ON OUR GLOBAL SKATEBOARD FACT-FINDING MISSION AND SHOPPING THINGY.
AMAZING. IT DOESN'T GET MORE CONVOLUTED THAN THAT!
I DON'T KNOW ABOUT YOU GUYS, BUT I'M TIRED OF WATCHING ALL THE EGGHEADS COME UP WITH THE BIG MONEY SCHEMES WHILE WE NORMAL JOES WORK OUR FINGERS TO THE BONE EVERY DAY.
HIC! THAT'S RIGHT, MOE! I WAS JUST THINKING THE SAME THING.
BURP! LET'S HARNESS OUR BRAIN POWER. ALL WE NEED IS **ONE** GOOD IDEA.
SIGH.
BEER.
D'OH.
NUTS.

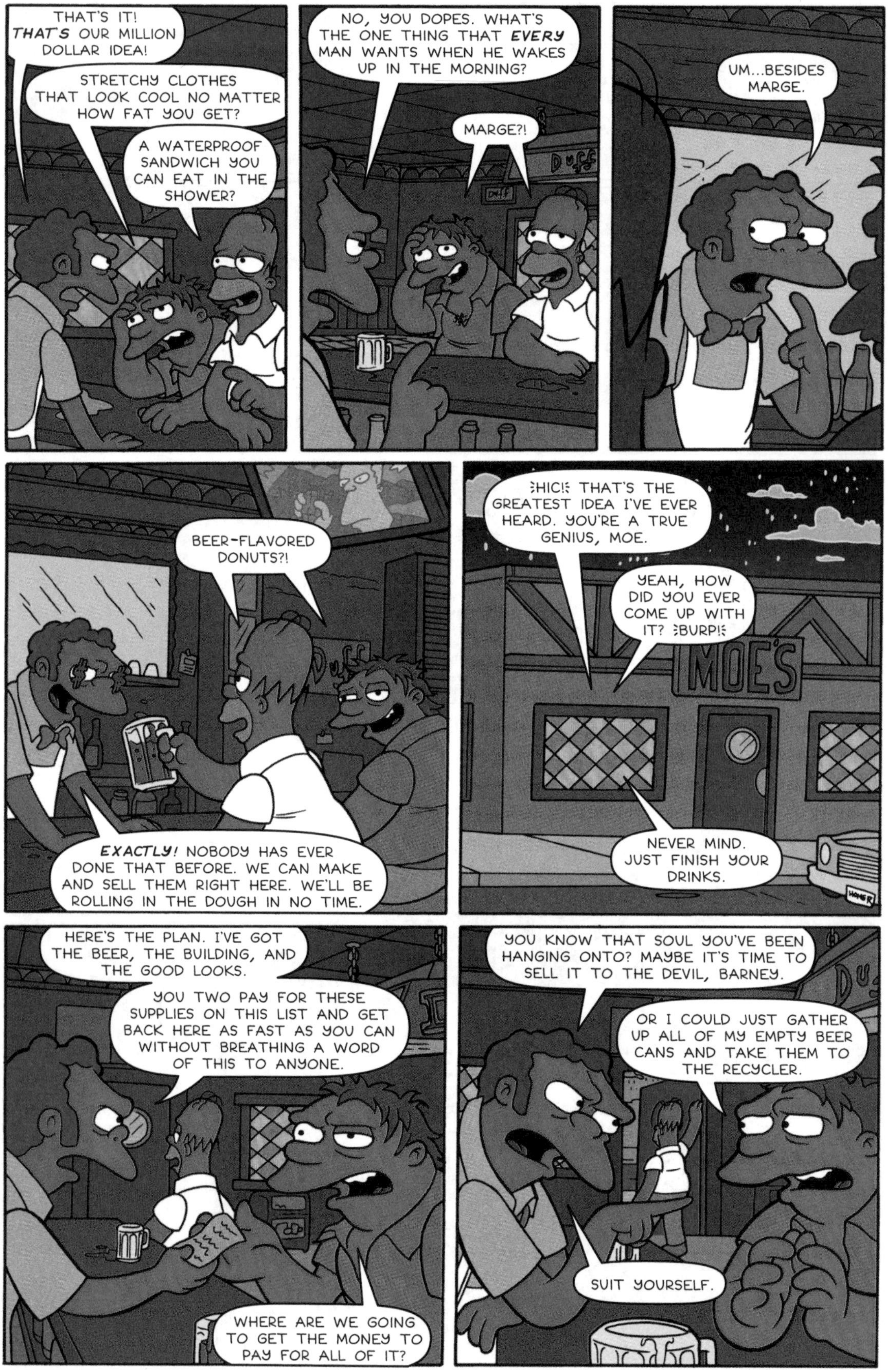
THAT'S IT! *THAT'S* OUR MILLION DOLLAR IDEA!
STRETCHY CLOTHES THAT LOOK COOL NO MATTER HOW FAT YOU GET?
A WATERPROOF SANDWICH YOU CAN EAT IN THE SHOWER?
NO, YOU DOPES. WHAT'S THE ONE THING THAT *EVERY* MAN WANTS WHEN HE WAKES UP IN THE MORNING?
MARGE?!
UM...BESIDES MARGE.
BEER-FLAVORED DONUTS?!
EXACTLY! NOBODY HAS EVER DONE THAT BEFORE. WE CAN MAKE AND SELL THEM RIGHT HERE. WE'LL BE ROLLING IN THE DOUGH IN NO TIME.
HIC! THAT'S THE GREATEST IDEA I'VE EVER HEARD. YOU'RE A TRUE GENIUS, MOE.
YEAH, HOW DID YOU EVER COME UP WITH IT? BURP!
MOE'S
NEVER MIND. JUST FINISH YOUR DRINKS.
HERE'S THE PLAN. I'VE GOT THE BEER, THE BUILDING, AND THE GOOD LOOKS.
YOU TWO PAY FOR THESE SUPPLIES ON THIS LIST AND GET BACK HERE AS FAST AS YOU CAN WITHOUT BREATHING A WORD OF THIS TO ANYONE.
WHERE ARE WE GOING TO GET THE MONEY TO PAY FOR ALL OF IT?
YOU KNOW THAT SOUL YOU'VE BEEN HANGING ONTO? MAYBE IT'S TIME TO SELL IT TO THE DEVIL, BARNEY.
OR I COULD JUST GATHER UP ALL OF MY EMPTY BEER CANS AND TAKE THEM TO THE RECYCLER.
SUIT YOURSELF.

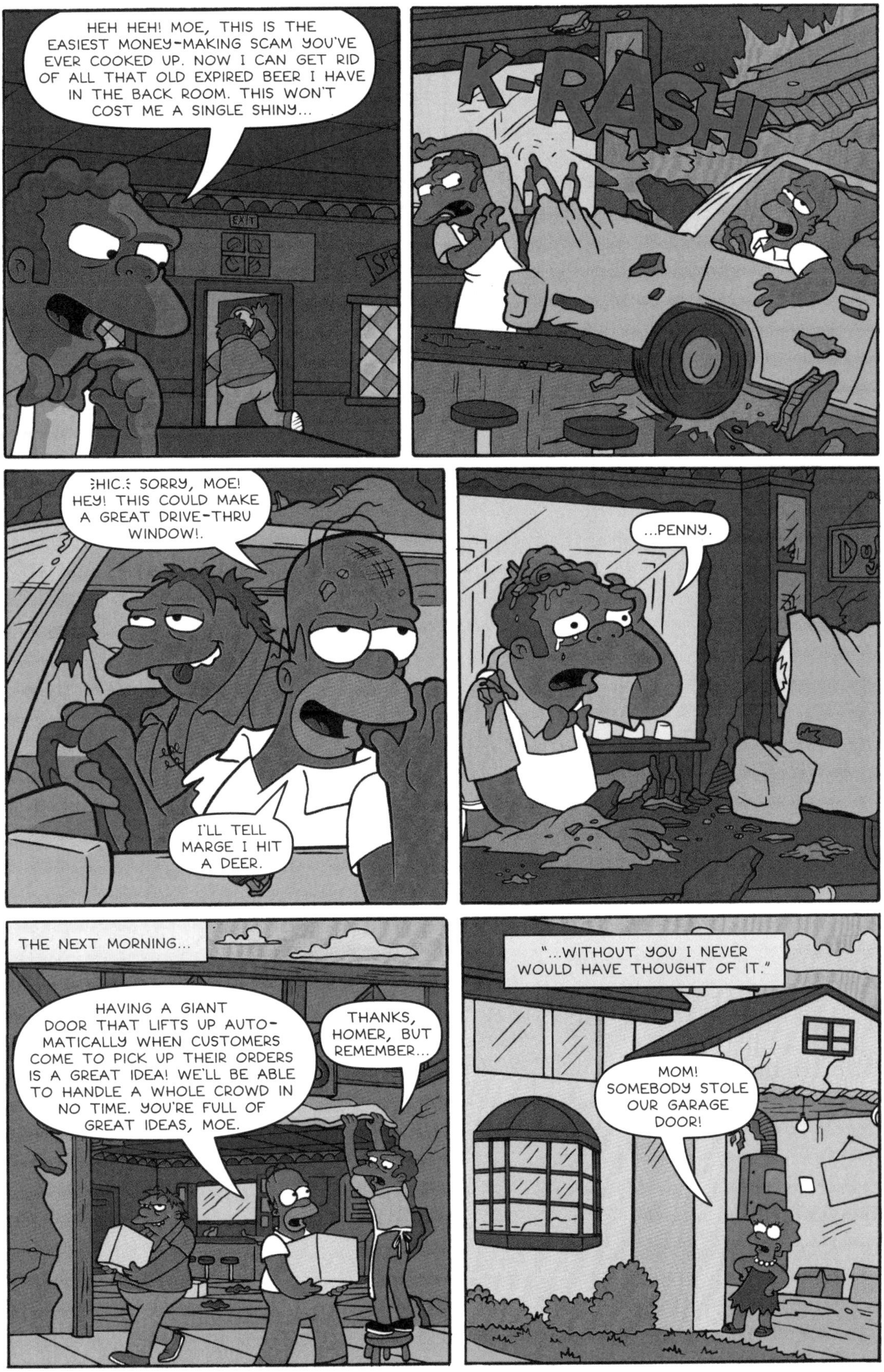
HEH HEH! MOE, THIS IS THE EASIEST MONEY-MAKING SCAM YOU'VE EVER COOKED UP. NOW I CAN GET RID OF ALL THAT OLD EXPIRED BEER I HAVE IN THE BACK ROOM. THIS WON'T COST ME A SINGLE SHINY...
EXIT
K-RASH!
HIC. SORRY, MOE! HEY! THIS COULD MAKE A GREAT DRIVE-THRU WINDOW!.
I'LL TELL MARGE I HIT A DEER.
...PENNY.
THE NEXT MORNING...
HAVING A GIANT DOOR THAT LIFTS UP AUTO-MATICALLY WHEN CUSTOMERS COME TO PICK UP THEIR ORDERS IS A GREAT IDEA! WE'LL BE ABLE TO HANDLE A WHOLE CROWD IN NO TIME. YOU'RE FULL OF GREAT IDEAS, MOE.
THANKS, HOMER, BUT REMEMBER...
"...WITHOUT YOU I NEVER WOULD HAVE THOUGHT OF IT."
MOM! SOMEBODY STOLE OUR GARAGE DOOR!

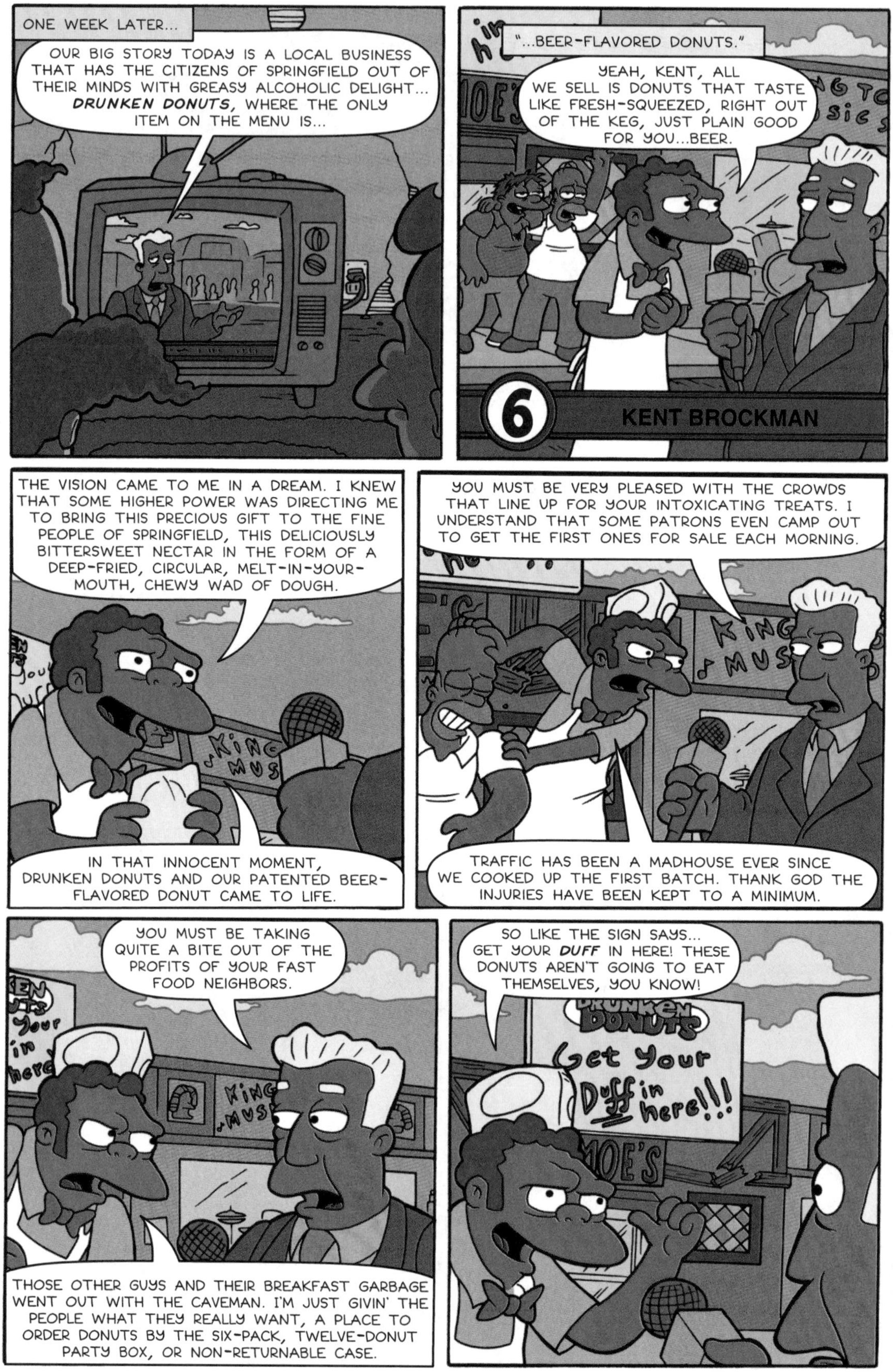

ONE WEEK LATER...
OUR BIG STORY TODAY IS A LOCAL BUSINESS THAT HAS THE CITIZENS OF SPRINGFIELD OUT OF THEIR MINDS WITH GREASY ALCOHOLIC DELIGHT... *DRUNKEN DONUTS*, WHERE THE ONLY ITEM ON THE MENU IS...
"...BEER-FLAVORED DONUTS."
YEAH, KENT, ALL WE SELL IS DONUTS THAT TASTE LIKE FRESH-SQUEEZED, RIGHT OUT OF THE KEG, JUST PLAIN GOOD FOR YOU...BEER.
6
KENT BROCKMAN
THE VISION CAME TO ME IN A DREAM. I KNEW THAT SOME HIGHER POWER WAS DIRECTING ME TO BRING THIS PRECIOUS GIFT TO THE FINE PEOPLE OF SPRINGFIELD, THIS DELICIOUSLY BITTERSWEET NECTAR IN THE FORM OF A DEEP-FRIED, CIRCULAR, MELT-IN-YOUR-MOUTH, CHEWY WAD OF DOUGH.
IN THAT INNOCENT MOMENT, DRUNKEN DONUTS AND OUR PATENTED BEER-FLAVORED DONUT CAME TO LIFE.
YOU MUST BE VERY PLEASED WITH THE CROWDS THAT LINE UP FOR YOUR INTOXICATING TREATS. I UNDERSTAND THAT SOME PATRONS EVEN CAMP OUT TO GET THE FIRST ONES FOR SALE EACH MORNING.
TRAFFIC HAS BEEN A MADHOUSE EVER SINCE WE COOKED UP THE FIRST BATCH. THANK GOD THE INJURIES HAVE BEEN KEPT TO A MINIMUM.
YOU MUST BE TAKING QUITE A BITE OUT OF THE PROFITS OF YOUR FAST FOOD NEIGHBORS.
THOSE OTHER GUYS AND THEIR BREAKFAST GARBAGE WENT OUT WITH THE CAVEMAN. I'M JUST GIVIN' THE PEOPLE WHAT THEY REALLY WANT, A PLACE TO ORDER DONUTS BY THE SIX-PACK, TWELVE-DONUT PARTY BOX, OR NON-RETURNABLE CASE.
SO LIKE THE SIGN SAYS... GET YOUR *DUFF* IN HERE! THESE DONUTS AREN'T GOING TO EAT THEMSELVES, YOU KNOW!
DRUNKEN DONUTS
Get Your Duff in here!!!
MOE'S

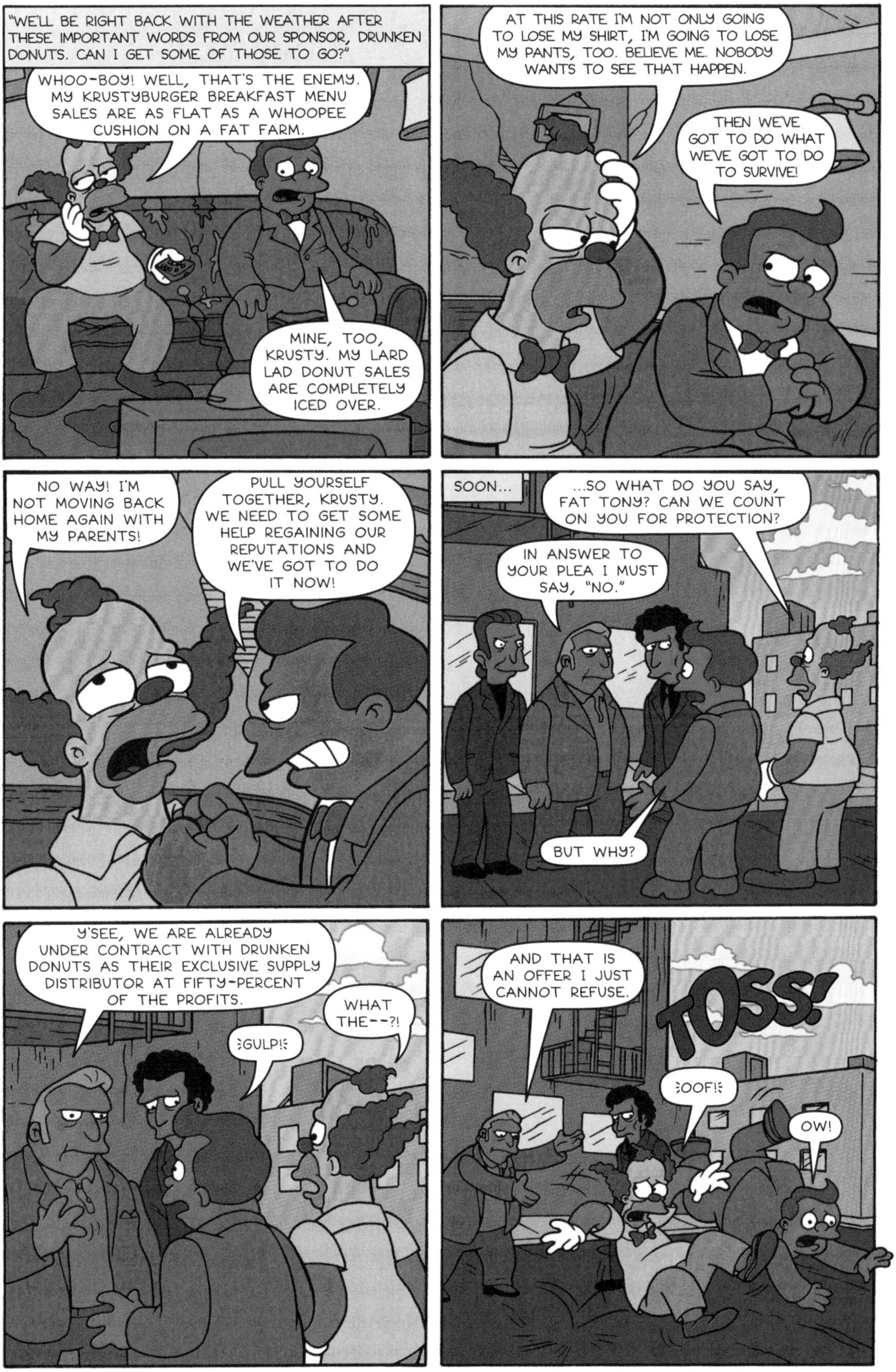

"WE'LL BE RIGHT BACK WITH THE WEATHER AFTER THESE IMPORTANT WORDS FROM OUR SPONSOR, DRUNKEN DONUTS. CAN I GET SOME OF THOSE TO GO?"
WHOO-BOY! WELL, THAT'S THE ENEMY. MY KRUSTYBURGER BREAKFAST MENU SALES ARE AS FLAT AS A WHOOPEE CUSHION ON A FAT FARM.
MINE, TOO, KRUSTY. MY LARD LAD DONUT SALES ARE COMPLETELY ICED OVER.
AT THIS RATE I'M NOT ONLY GOING TO LOSE MY SHIRT, I'M GOING TO LOSE MY PANTS, TOO. BELIEVE ME. NOBODY WANTS TO SEE THAT HAPPEN.
THEN WE'VE GOT TO DO WHAT WE'VE GOT TO DO TO SURVIVE!
NO WAY! I'M NOT MOVING BACK HOME AGAIN WITH MY PARENTS!
PULL YOURSELF TOGETHER, KRUSTY. WE NEED TO GET SOME HELP REGAINING OUR REPUTATIONS AND WE'VE GOT TO DO IT NOW!
SOON...
...SO WHAT DO YOU SAY, FAT TONY? CAN WE COUNT ON YOU FOR PROTECTION?
IN ANSWER TO YOUR PLEA I MUST SAY, "NO."
BUT WHY?
Y'SEE, WE ARE ALREADY UNDER CONTRACT WITH DRUNKEN DONUTS AS THEIR EXCLUSIVE SUPPLY DISTRIBUTOR AT FIFTY-PERCENT OF THE PROFITS.
GULP!
WHAT THE--?!
AND THAT IS AN OFFER I JUST CANNOT REFUSE.
TOSS!
OOF!
OW!

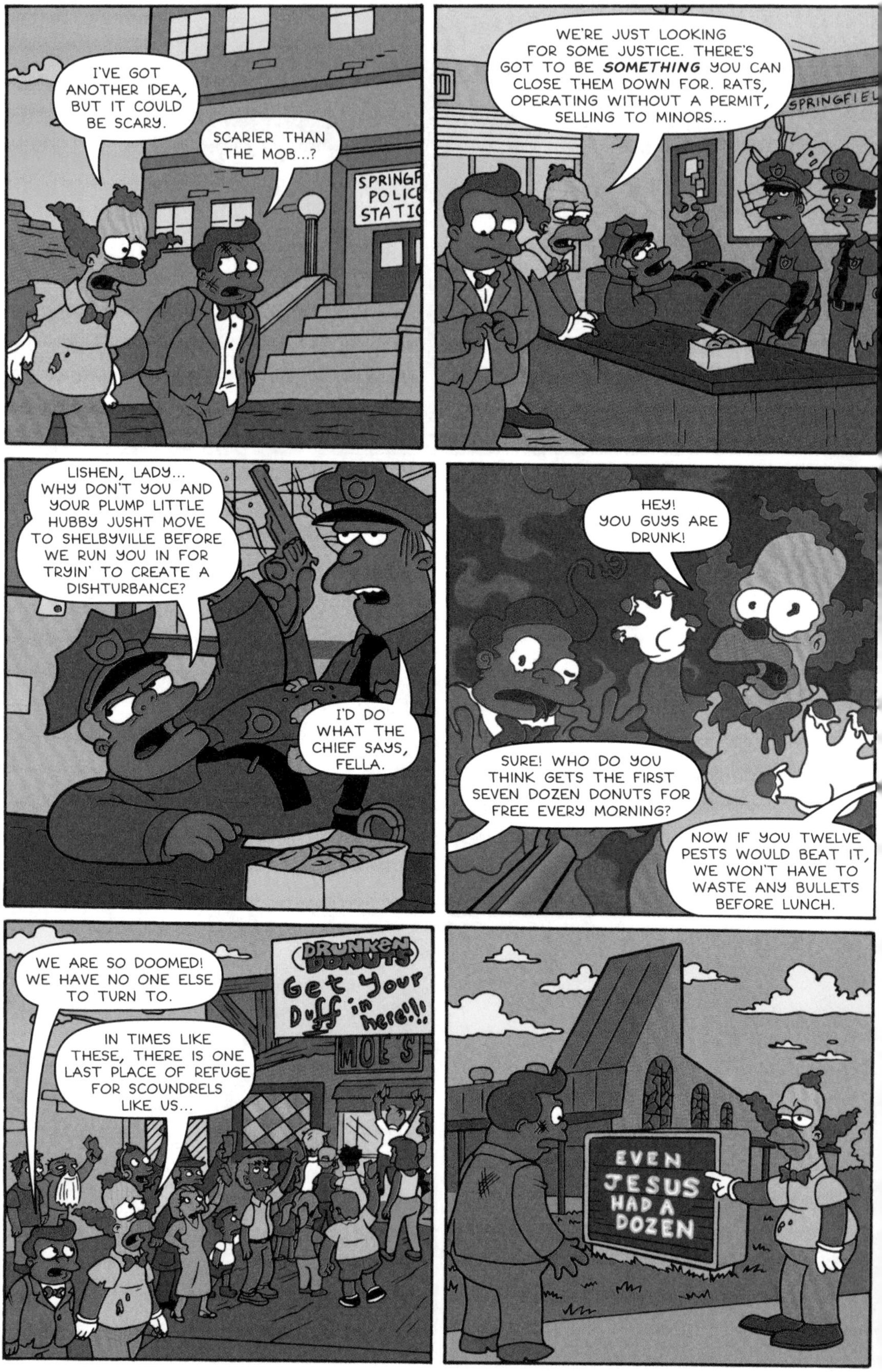
I'VE GOT ANOTHER IDEA, BUT IT COULD BE SCARY.
SCARIER THAN THE MOB...?
SPRINGF POLICE STATIO
WE'RE JUST LOOKING FOR SOME JUSTICE. THERE'S GOT TO BE SOMETHING YOU CAN CLOSE THEM DOWN FOR. RATS, OPERATING WITHOUT A PERMIT, SELLING TO MINORS...
SPRINGFIEL
LISHEN, LADY... WHY DON'T YOU AND YOUR PLUMP LITTLE HUBBY JUSHT MOVE TO SHELBYVILLE BEFORE WE RUN YOU IN FOR TRYIN' TO CREATE A DISHTURBANCE?
I'D DO WHAT THE CHIEF SAYS, FELLA.
HEY! YOU GUYS ARE DRUNK!
SURE! WHO DO YOU THINK GETS THE FIRST SEVEN DOZEN DONUTS FOR FREE EVERY MORNING?
NOW IF YOU TWELVE PESTS WOULD BEAT IT, WE WON'T HAVE TO WASTE ANY BULLETS BEFORE LUNCH.
DRUNKEN DONUTS
Get Your Duff in here!!!
MOE'S
WE ARE SO DOOMED! WE HAVE NO ONE ELSE TO TURN TO.
IN TIMES LIKE THESE, THERE IS ONE LAST PLACE OF REFUGE FOR SCOUNDRELS LIKE US...
EVEN JESUS HAD A DOZEN

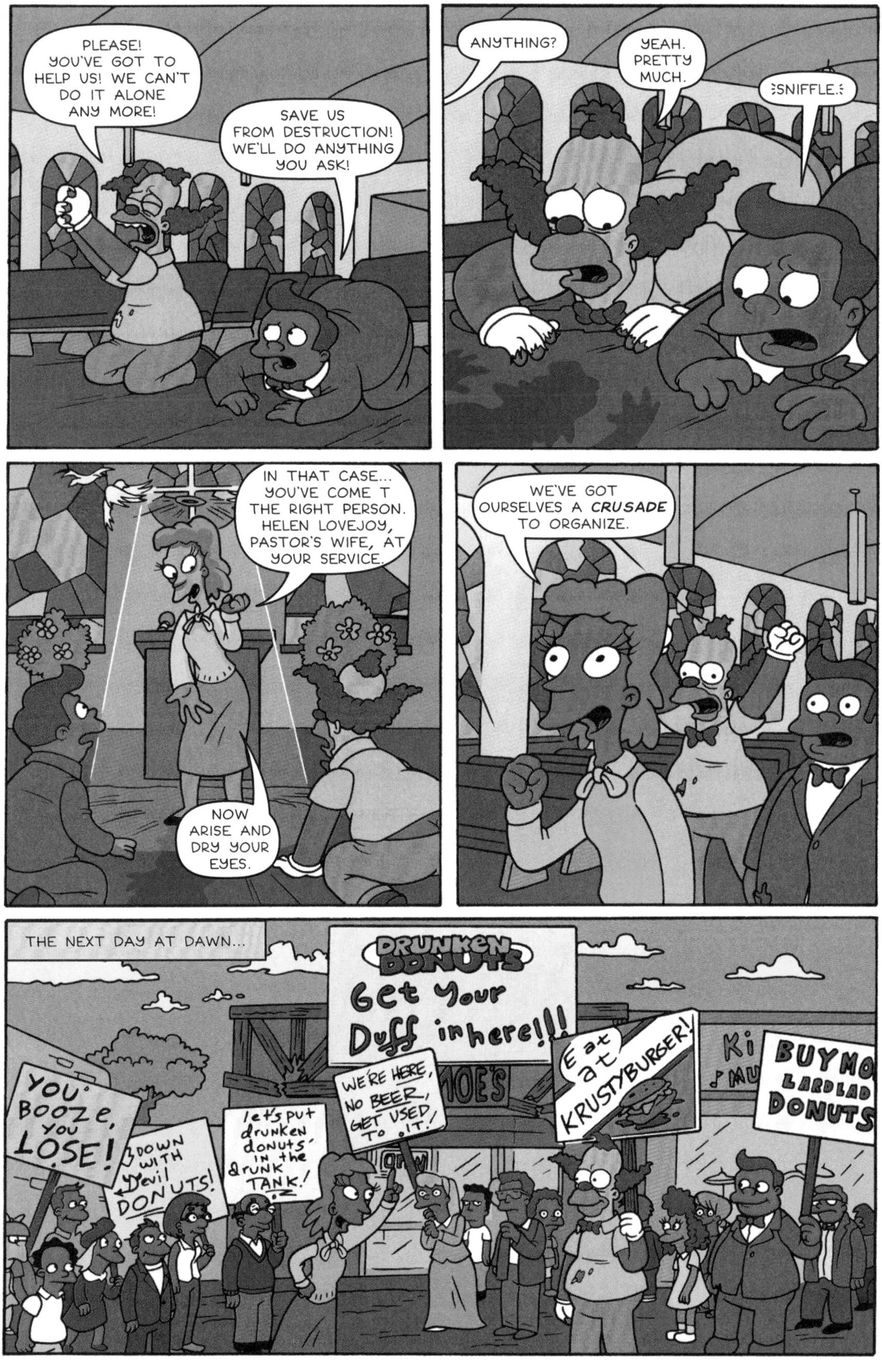
PLEASE! YOU'VE GOT TO HELP US! WE CAN'T DO IT ALONE ANY MORE!
SAVE US FROM DESTRUCTION! WE'LL DO ANYTHING YOU ASK!
ANYTHING?
YEAH. PRETTY MUCH.
SNIFFLE.
IN THAT CASE... YOU'VE COME T THE RIGHT PERSON. HELEN LOVEJOY, PASTOR'S WIFE, AT YOUR SERVICE.
NOW ARISE AND DRY YOUR EYES.
WE'VE GOT OURSELVES A CRUSADE TO ORGANIZE.
THE NEXT DAY AT DAWN...
DRUNKEN DONUTS
Get Your Duff in here!!!
YOU BOOZE, YOU LOSE!
DOWN WITH Devil DONUTS!
let's put drunken donuts in the drunk TANK!
WE'RE HERE, NO BEER, GET USED TO IT!
Eat at KRUSTYBURGER!
BUYMO LARDLAD DONUTS

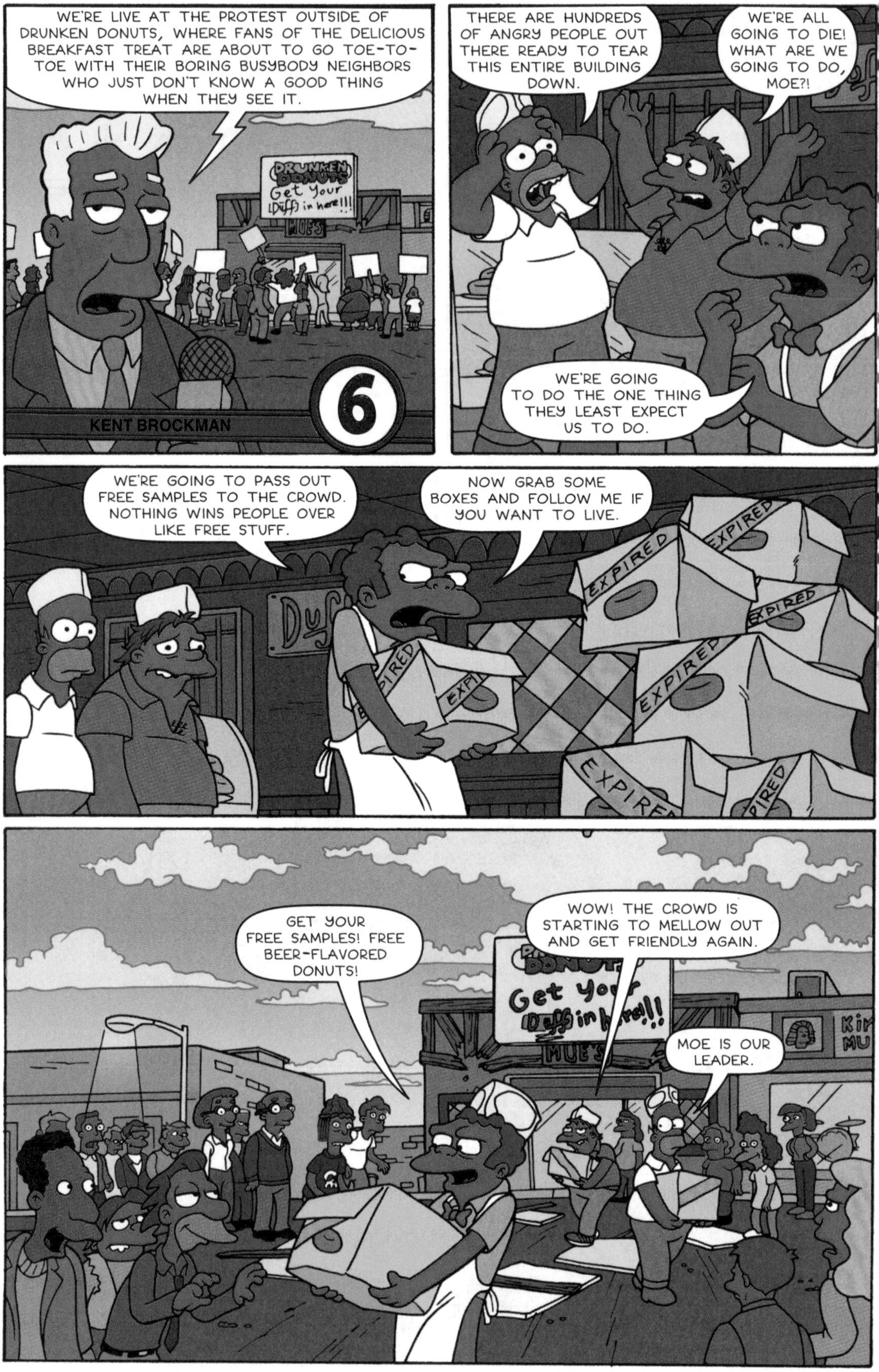
WE'RE LIVE AT THE PROTEST OUTSIDE OF DRUNKEN DONUTS, WHERE FANS OF THE DELICIOUS BREAKFAST TREAT ARE ABOUT TO GO TOE-TO-TOE WITH THEIR BORING BUSYBODY NEIGHBORS WHO JUST DON'T KNOW A GOOD THING WHEN THEY SEE IT.
DRUNKEN DONUTS Get Your Duff in here!!!
MOE'S
6
KENT BROCKMAN
THERE ARE HUNDREDS OF ANGRY PEOPLE OUT THERE READY TO TEAR THIS ENTIRE BUILDING DOWN.
WE'RE ALL GOING TO DIE! WHAT ARE WE GOING TO DO, MOE?!
WE'RE GOING TO DO THE ONE THING THEY LEAST EXPECT US TO DO.
WE'RE GOING TO PASS OUT FREE SAMPLES TO THE CROWD. NOTHING WINS PEOPLE OVER LIKE FREE STUFF.
NOW GRAB SOME BOXES AND FOLLOW ME IF YOU WANT TO LIVE.
EXPIRED
GET YOUR FREE SAMPLES! FREE BEER-FLAVORED DONUTS!
WOW! THE CROWD IS STARTING TO MELLOW OUT AND GET FRIENDLY AGAIN.
Get your Duffs in here!!
MOE'S
MOE IS OUR LEADER.

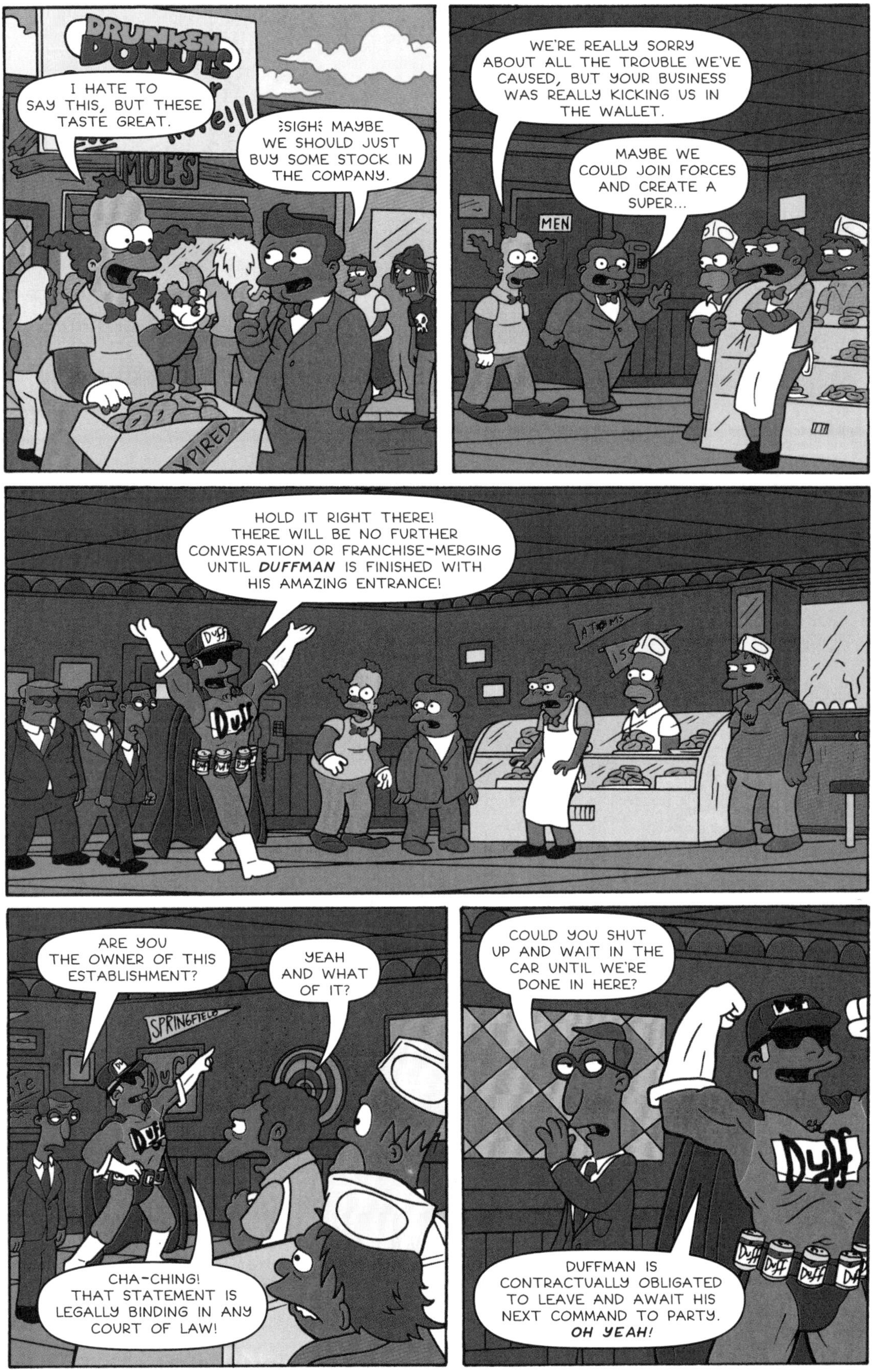
DRUNKEN DONUTS
I HATE TO SAY THIS, BUT THESE TASTE GREAT.
MOE'S
SIGH MAYBE WE SHOULD JUST BUY SOME STOCK IN THE COMPANY.
WE'RE REALLY SORRY ABOUT ALL THE TROUBLE WE'VE CAUSED, BUT YOUR BUSINESS WAS REALLY KICKING US IN THE WALLET.
MAYBE WE COULD JOIN FORCES AND CREATE A SUPER...
MEN
HOLD IT RIGHT THERE! THERE WILL BE NO FURTHER CONVERSATION OR FRANCHISE-MERGING UNTIL ***DUFFMAN*** IS FINISHED WITH HIS AMAZING ENTRANCE!
DUFF
ARE YOU THE OWNER OF THIS ESTABLISHMENT?
YEAH AND WHAT OF IT?
SPRINGFIELD
CHA-CHING! THAT STATEMENT IS LEGALLY BINDING IN ANY COURT OF LAW!
COULD YOU SHUT UP AND WAIT IN THE CAR UNTIL WE'RE DONE IN HERE?
DUFFMAN IS CONTRACTUALLY OBLIGATED TO LEAVE AND AWAIT HIS NEXT COMMAND TO PARTY. ***OH YEAH!***
DUFF

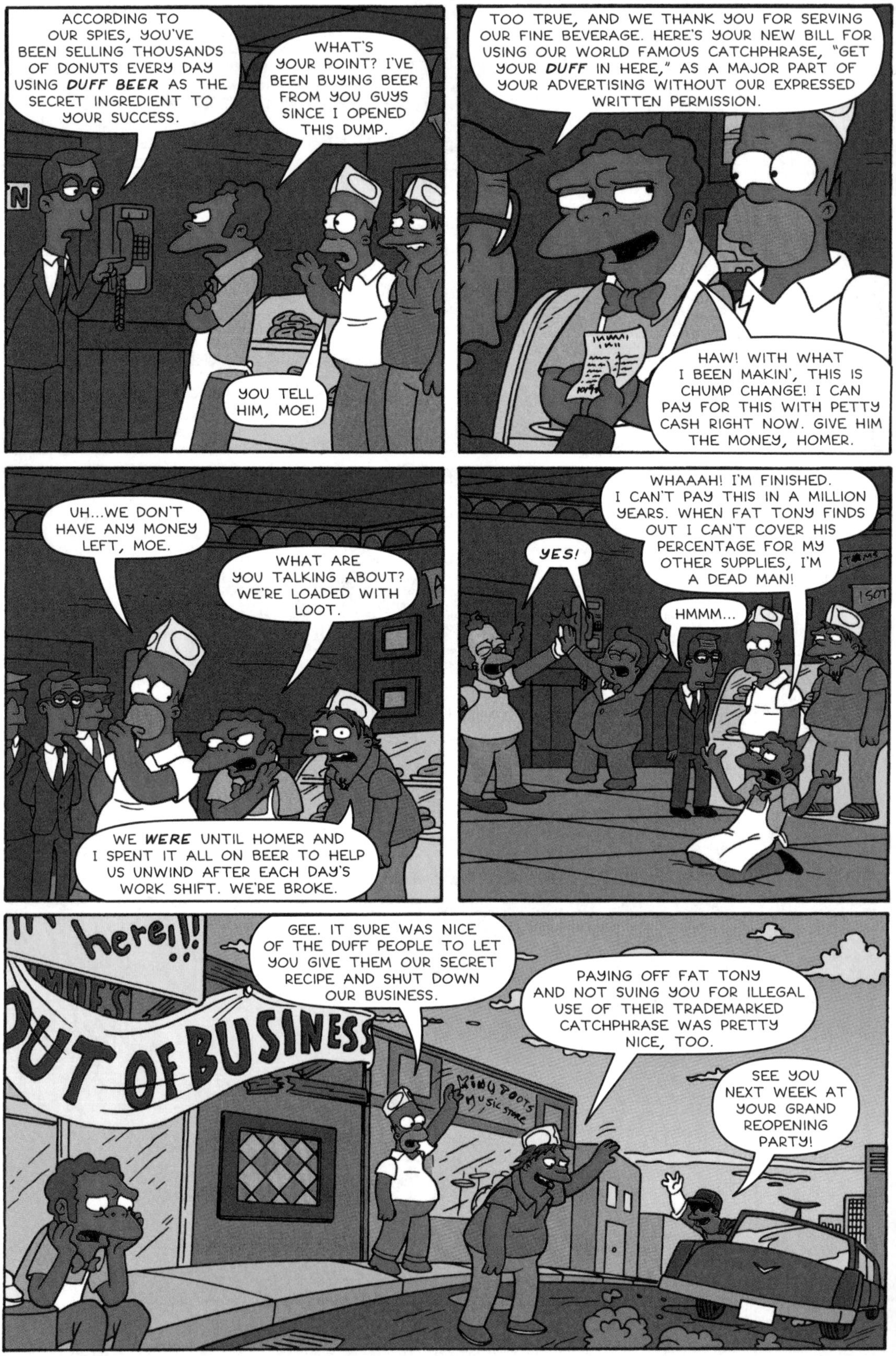
ACCORDING TO OUR SPIES, YOU'VE BEEN SELLING THOUSANDS OF DONUTS EVERY DAY USING ***DUFF BEER*** AS THE SECRET INGREDIENT TO YOUR SUCCESS.
WHAT'S YOUR POINT? I'VE BEEN BUYING BEER FROM YOU GUYS SINCE I OPENED THIS DUMP.
YOU TELL HIM, MOE!
TOO TRUE, AND WE THANK YOU FOR SERVING OUR FINE BEVERAGE. HERE'S YOUR NEW BILL FOR USING OUR WORLD FAMOUS CATCHPHRASE, "GET YOUR ***DUFF*** IN HERE," AS A MAJOR PART OF YOUR ADVERTISING WITHOUT OUR EXPRESSED WRITTEN PERMISSION.
HAW! WITH WHAT I BEEN MAKIN', THIS IS CHUMP CHANGE! I CAN PAY FOR THIS WITH PETTY CASH RIGHT NOW. GIVE HIM THE MONEY, HOMER.
UH...WE DON'T HAVE ANY MONEY LEFT, MOE.
WHAT ARE YOU TALKING ABOUT? WE'RE LOADED WITH LOOT.
WE ***WERE*** UNTIL HOMER AND I SPENT IT ALL ON BEER TO HELP US UNWIND AFTER EACH DAY'S WORK SHIFT. WE'RE BROKE.
WHAAAH! I'M FINISHED. I CAN'T PAY THIS IN A MILLION YEARS. WHEN FAT TONY FINDS OUT I CAN'T COVER HIS PERCENTAGE FOR MY OTHER SUPPLIES, I'M A DEAD MAN!
YES!
HMMM...
here!!
OUT OF BUSINESS
GEE. IT SURE WAS NICE OF THE DUFF PEOPLE TO LET YOU GIVE THEM OUR SECRET RECIPE AND SHUT DOWN OUR BUSINESS.
PAYING OFF FAT TONY AND NOT SUING YOU FOR ILLEGAL USE OF THEIR TRADEMARKED CATCHPHRASE WAS PRETTY NICE, TOO.
SEE YOU NEXT WEEK AT YOUR GRAND REOPENING PARTY!

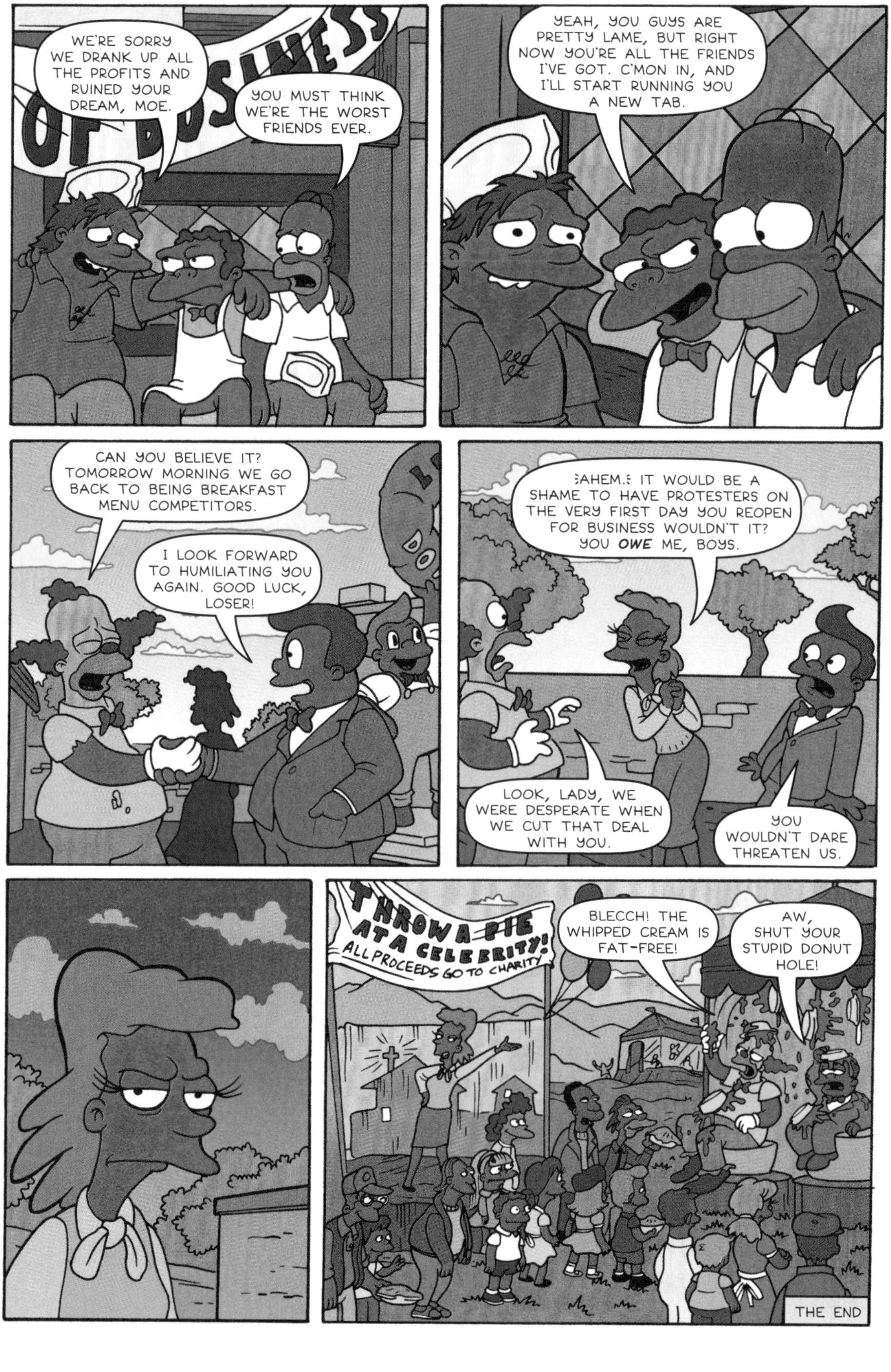
OF BUSINESS
WE'RE SORRY WE DRANK UP ALL THE PROFITS AND RUINED YOUR DREAM, MOE.
YOU MUST THINK WE'RE THE WORST FRIENDS EVER.
YEAH, YOU GUYS ARE PRETTY LAME, BUT RIGHT NOW YOU'RE ALL THE FRIENDS I'VE GOT. C'MON IN, AND I'LL START RUNNING YOU A NEW TAB.
CAN YOU BELIEVE IT? TOMORROW MORNING WE GO BACK TO BEING BREAKFAST MENU COMPETITORS.
I LOOK FORWARD TO HUMILIATING YOU AGAIN. GOOD LUCK, LOSER!
:AHEM.: IT WOULD BE A SHAME TO HAVE PROTESTERS ON THE VERY FIRST DAY YOU REOPEN FOR BUSINESS WOULDN'T IT? YOU **OWE** ME, BOYS.
LOOK, LADY, WE WERE DESPERATE WHEN WE CUT THAT DEAL WITH YOU.
YOU WOULDN'T DARE THREATEN US.
THROW A PIE AT A CELEBRITY! ALL PROCEEDS GO TO CHARITY
BLECCH! THE WHIPPED CREAM IS FAT-FREE!
AW, SHUT YOUR STUPID DONUT HOLE!
THE END

ITCHY & SCRATCHY in FACE-LIFT FELINE

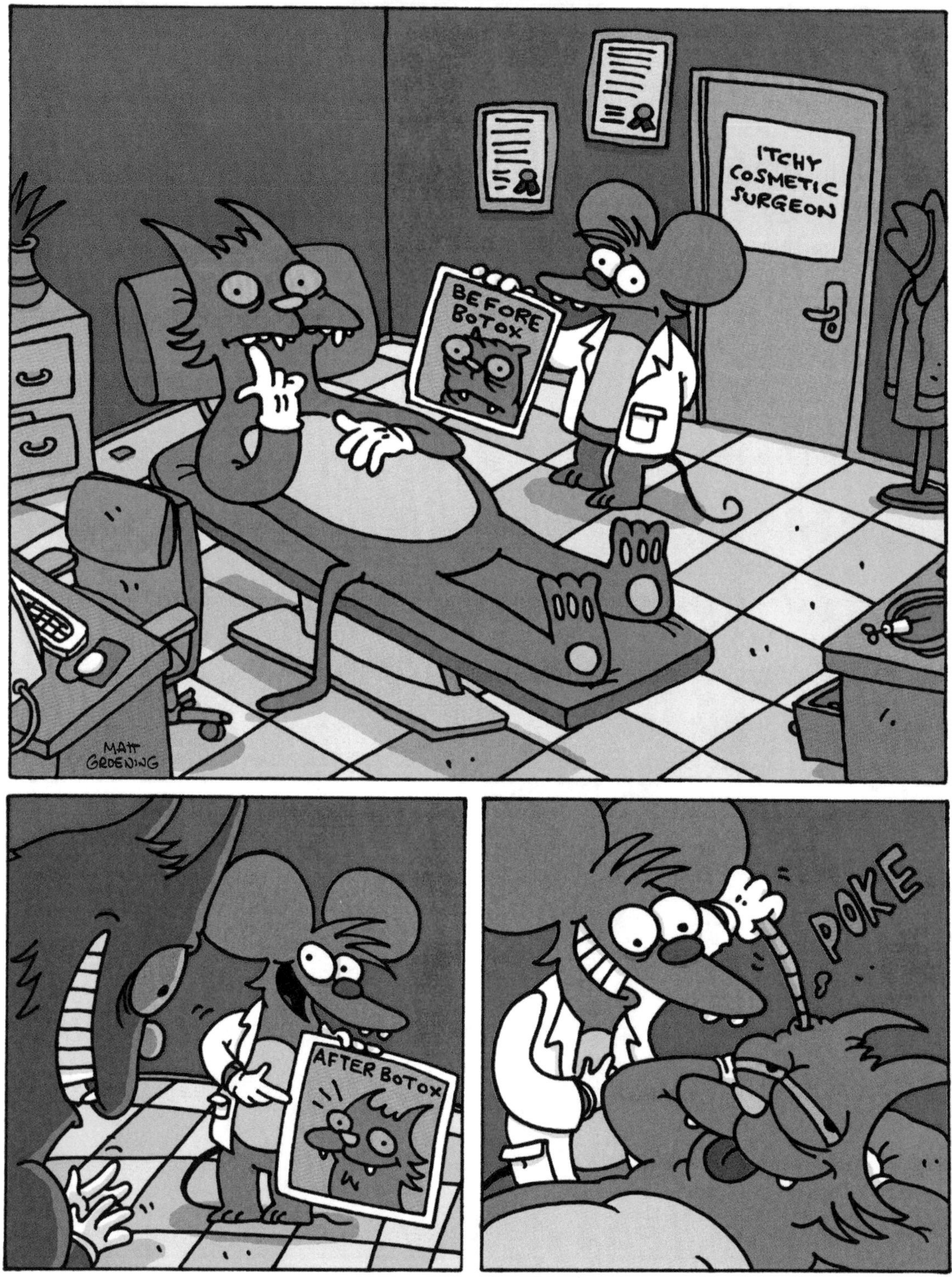
ITCHY COSMETIC SURGEON
BEFORE BOTOX
MATT GROENING
AFTER BOTOX
POKE

DEAN RANKINE
STORY & ART

KAREN BATES
LETTERS

BILL MORRISON
EDITOR

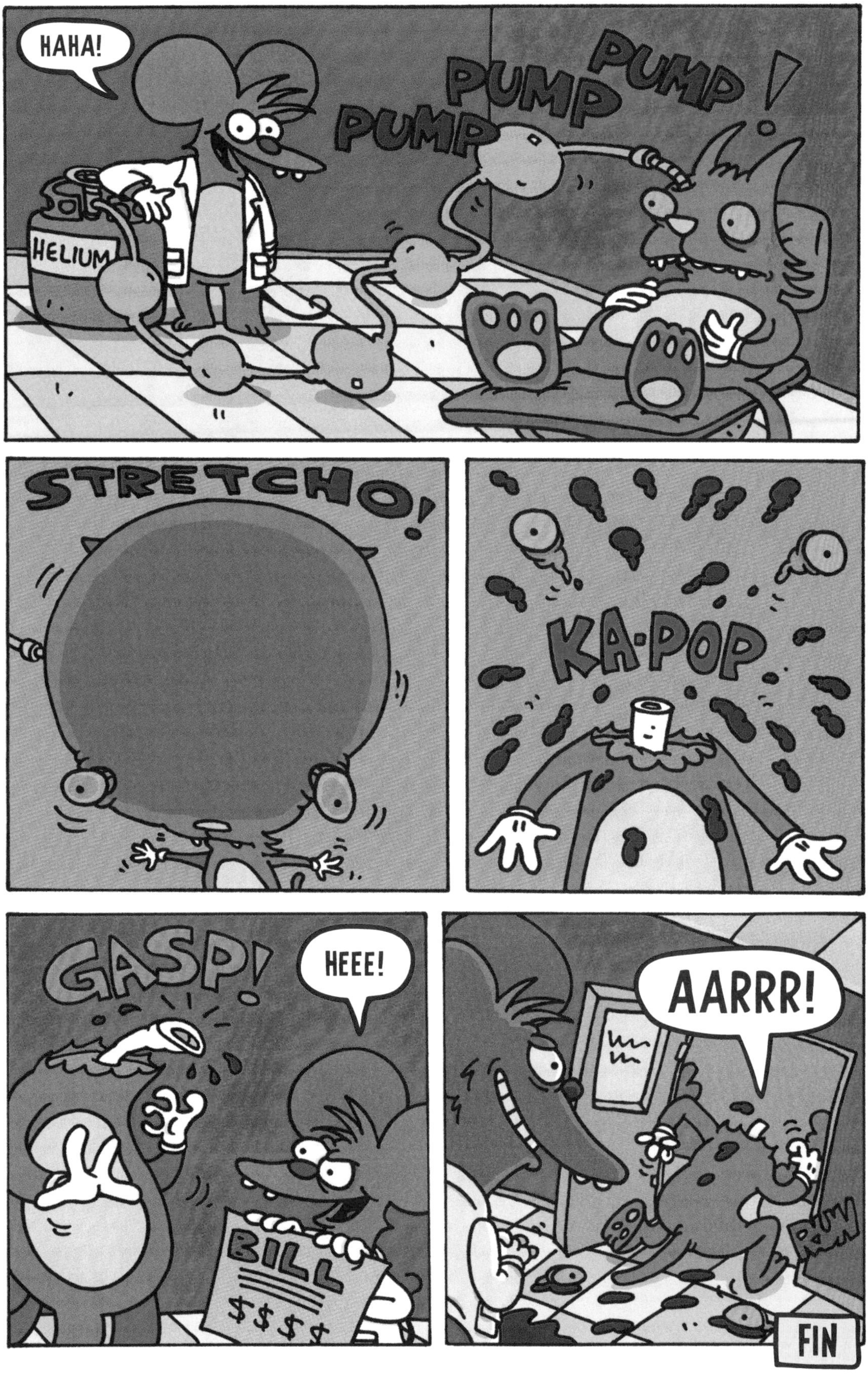
HAHA!
PUMP
PUMP
PUMP!
HELIUM
STRETCHO!
KA-POP
GASP!
HEEE!
BILL
$$$$
AARRR!
RAW
FIN

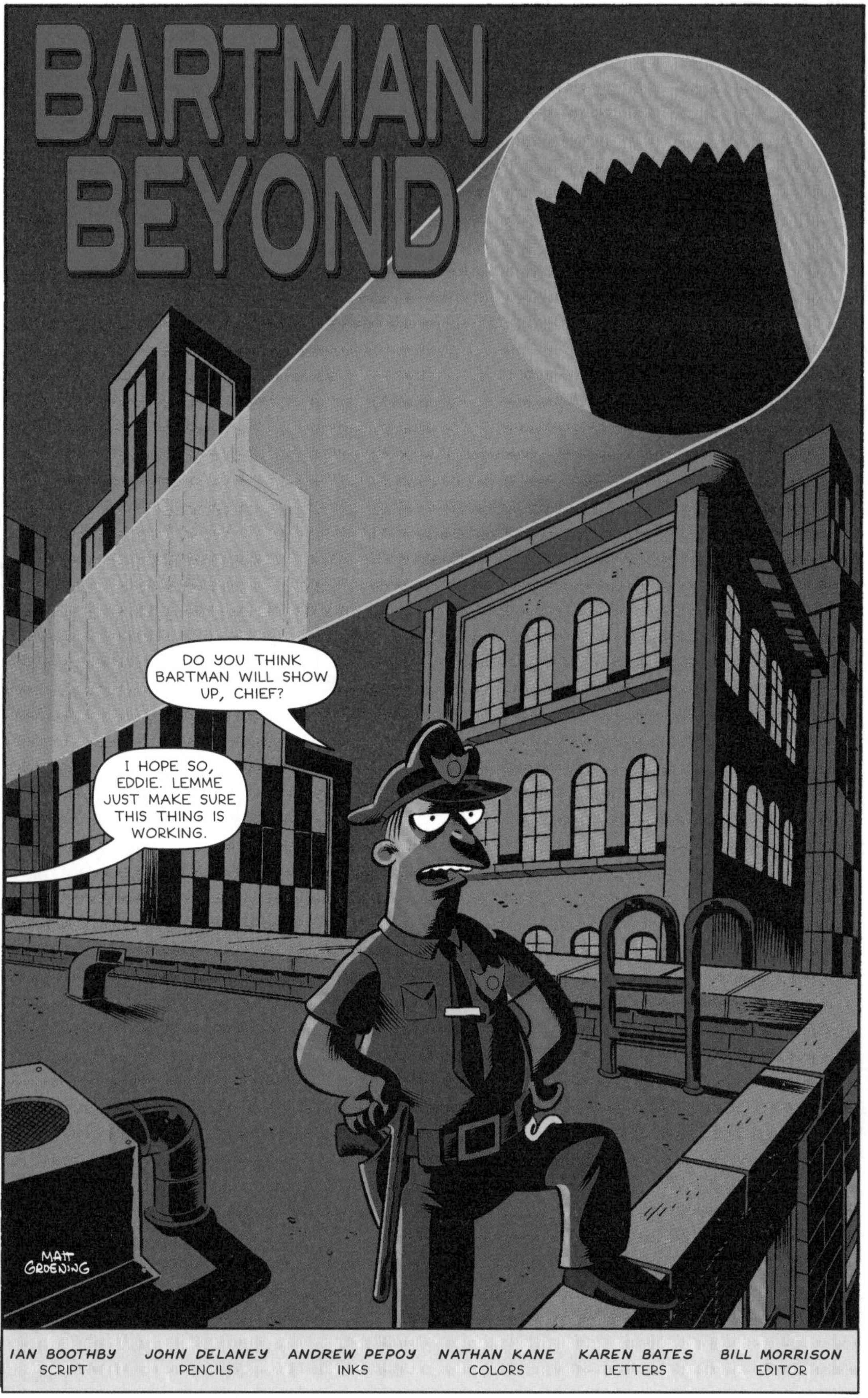
BARTMAN BEYOND
DO YOU THINK BARTMAN WILL SHOW UP, CHIEF?
I HOPE SO, EDDIE. LEMME JUST MAKE SURE THIS THING IS WORKING.
MATT GROENING

IAN BOOTHBY SCRIPT *JOHN DELANEY* PENCILS *ANDREW PEPOY* INKS *NATHAN KANE* COLORS *KAREN BATES* LETTERS *BILL MORRISON* EDITOR

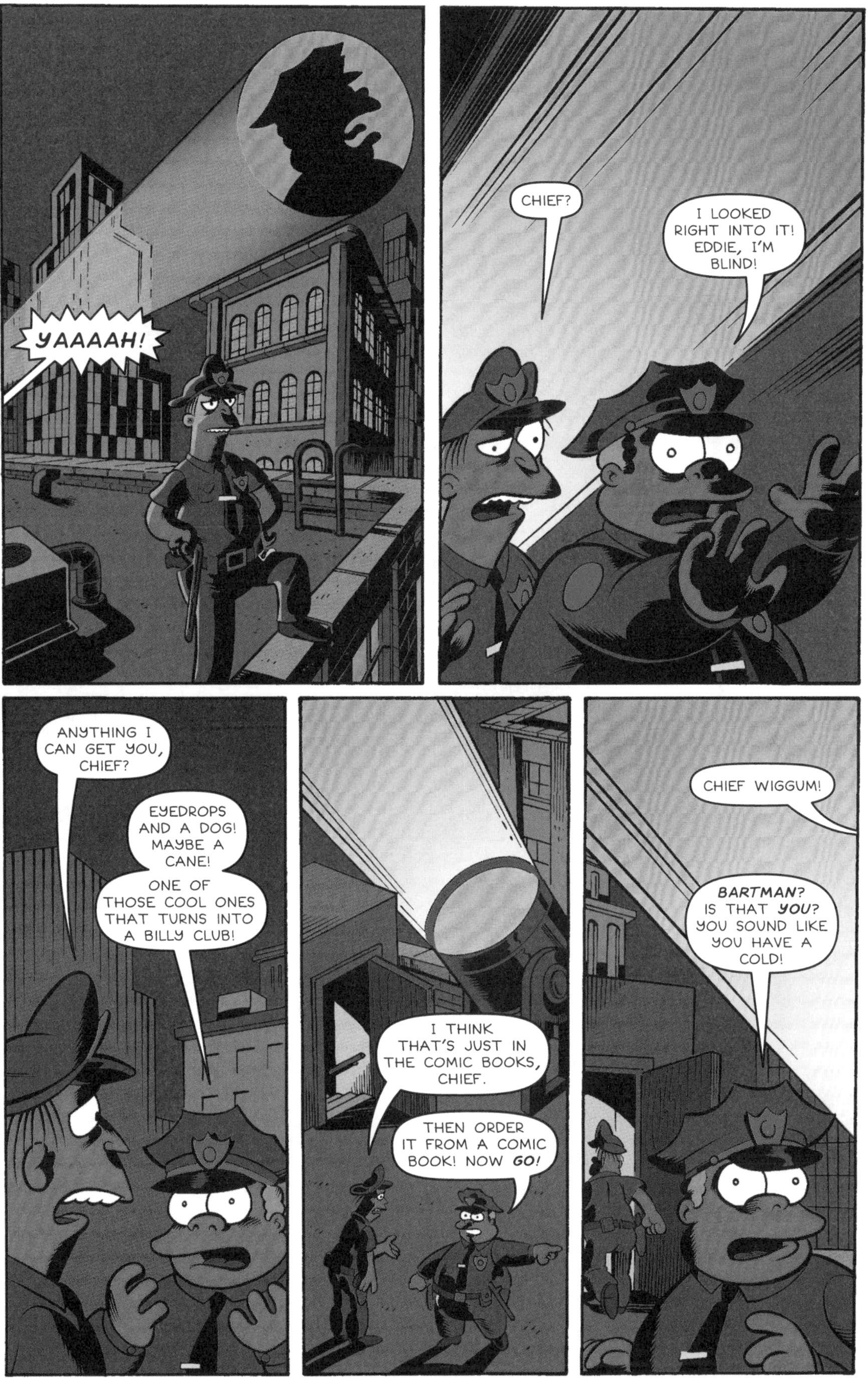
YAAAAH!
CHIEF?
I LOOKED RIGHT INTO IT! EDDIE, I'M BLIND!
ANYTHING I CAN GET YOU, CHIEF?
EYEDROPS AND A DOG! MAYBE A CANE!
ONE OF THOSE COOL ONES THAT TURNS INTO A BILLY CLUB!
I THINK THAT'S JUST IN THE COMIC BOOKS, CHIEF.
THEN ORDER IT FROM A COMIC BOOK! NOW GO!
CHIEF WIGGUM!
BARTMAN? IS THAT YOU? YOU SOUND LIKE YOU HAVE A COLD!

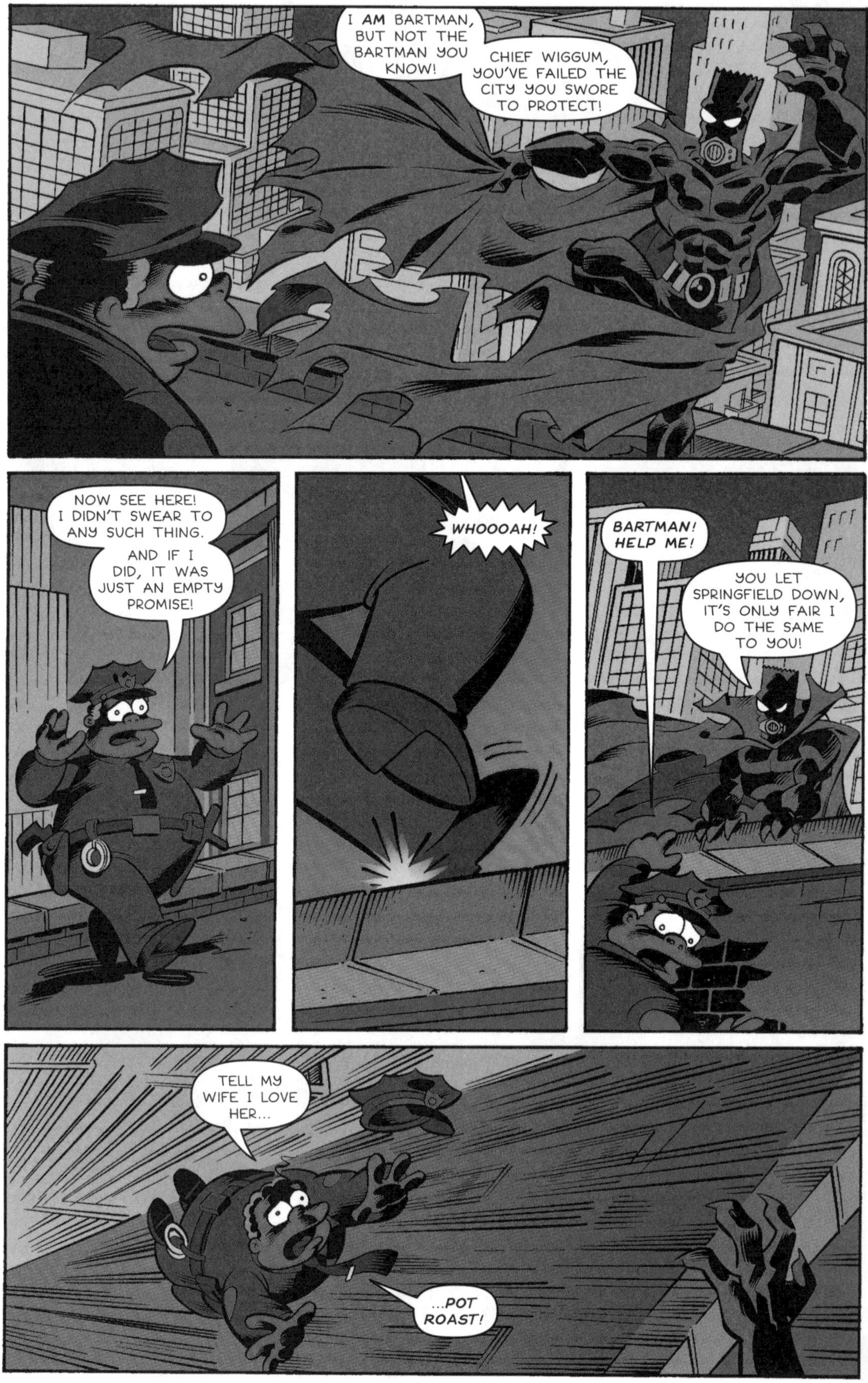
I **AM** BARTMAN, BUT NOT THE BARTMAN YOU KNOW!
CHIEF WIGGUM, YOU'VE FAILED THE CITY YOU SWORE TO PROTECT!
NOW SEE HERE! I DIDN'T SWEAR TO ANY SUCH THING.
AND IF I DID, IT WAS JUST AN EMPTY PROMISE!
WHOOOAH!
BARTMAN! HELP ME!
YOU LET SPRINGFIELD DOWN, IT'S ONLY FAIR I DO THE SAME TO YOU!
TELL MY WIFE I LOVE HER...
...***POT ROAST!***

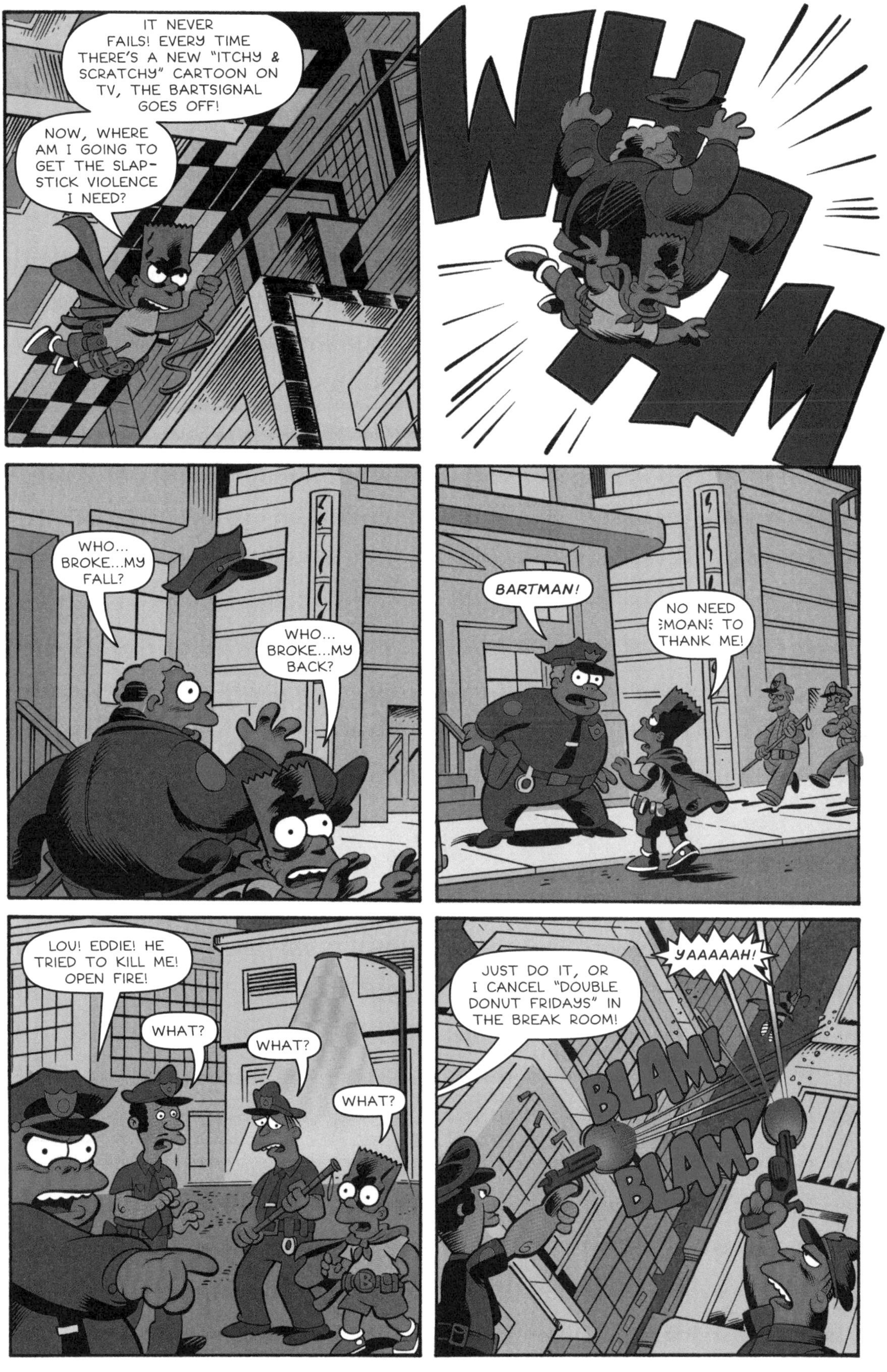

IT NEVER FAILS! EVERY TIME THERE'S A NEW "ITCHY & SCRATCHY" CARTOON ON TV, THE BARTSIGNAL GOES OFF!
NOW, WHERE AM I GOING TO GET THE SLAP-STICK VIOLENCE I NEED?
WHHUMM
WHO... BROKE...MY FALL?
WHO... BROKE...MY BACK?
BARTMAN!
NO NEED ⁝MOAN⁝ TO THANK ME!
LOU! EDDIE! HE TRIED TO KILL ME! OPEN FIRE!
WHAT?
WHAT?
WHAT?
JUST DO IT, OR I CANCEL "DOUBLE DONUT FRIDAYS" IN THE BREAK ROOM!
YAAAAAH!
BLAM!
BLAM!

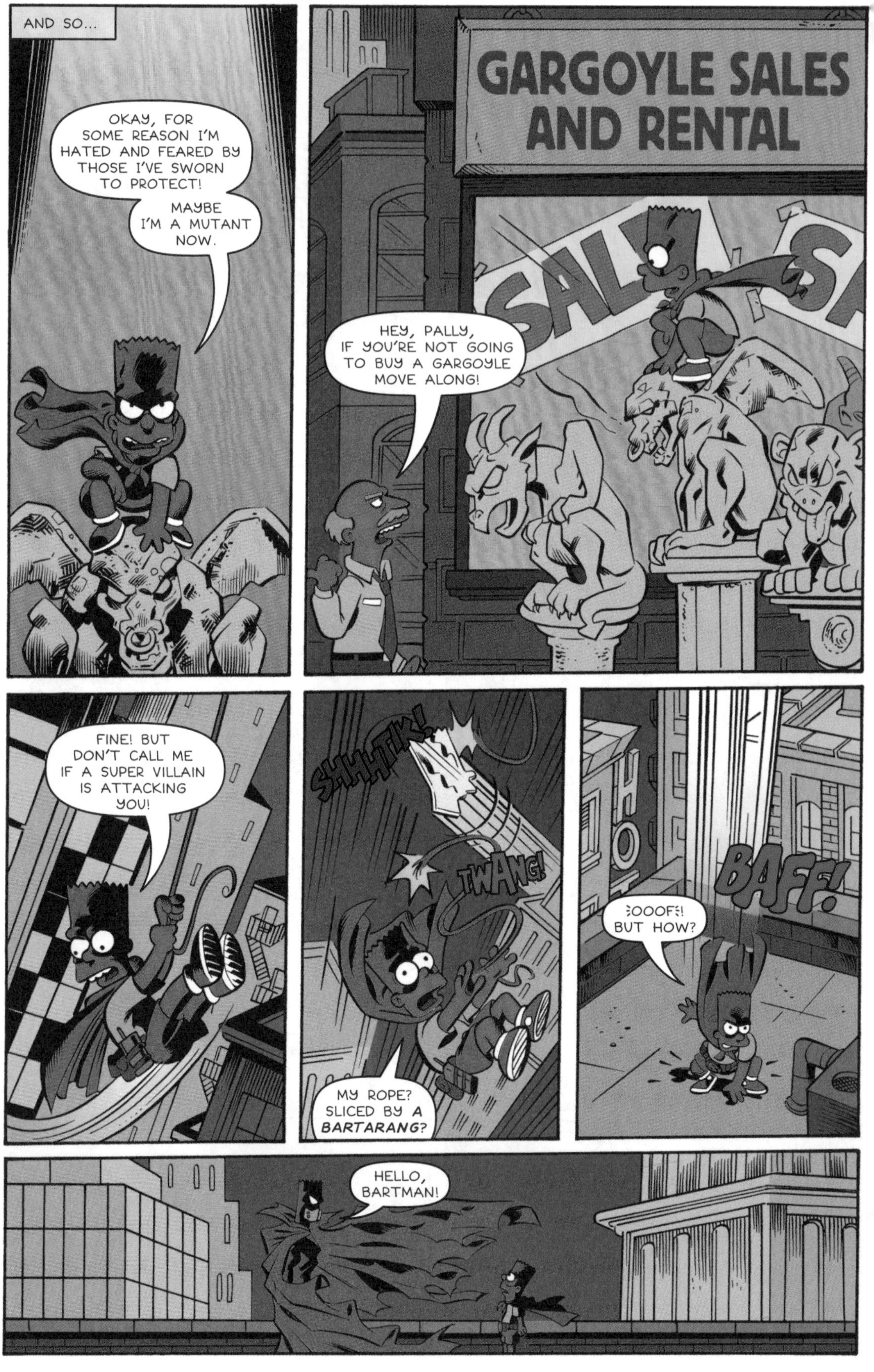
AND SO...
OKAY, FOR SOME REASON I'M HATED AND FEARED BY THOSE I'VE SWORN TO PROTECT!
MAYBE I'M A MUTANT NOW.
GARGOYLE SALES AND RENTAL
HEY, PALLY, IF YOU'RE NOT GOING TO BUY A GARGOYLE MOVE ALONG!
FINE! BUT DON'T CALL ME IF A SUPER VILLAIN IS ATTACKING YOU!
SHHHTIK!
TWANG!
MY ROPE? SLICED BY A BARTARANG?
BAFF!
OOOF! BUT HOW?
HELLO, BARTMAN!

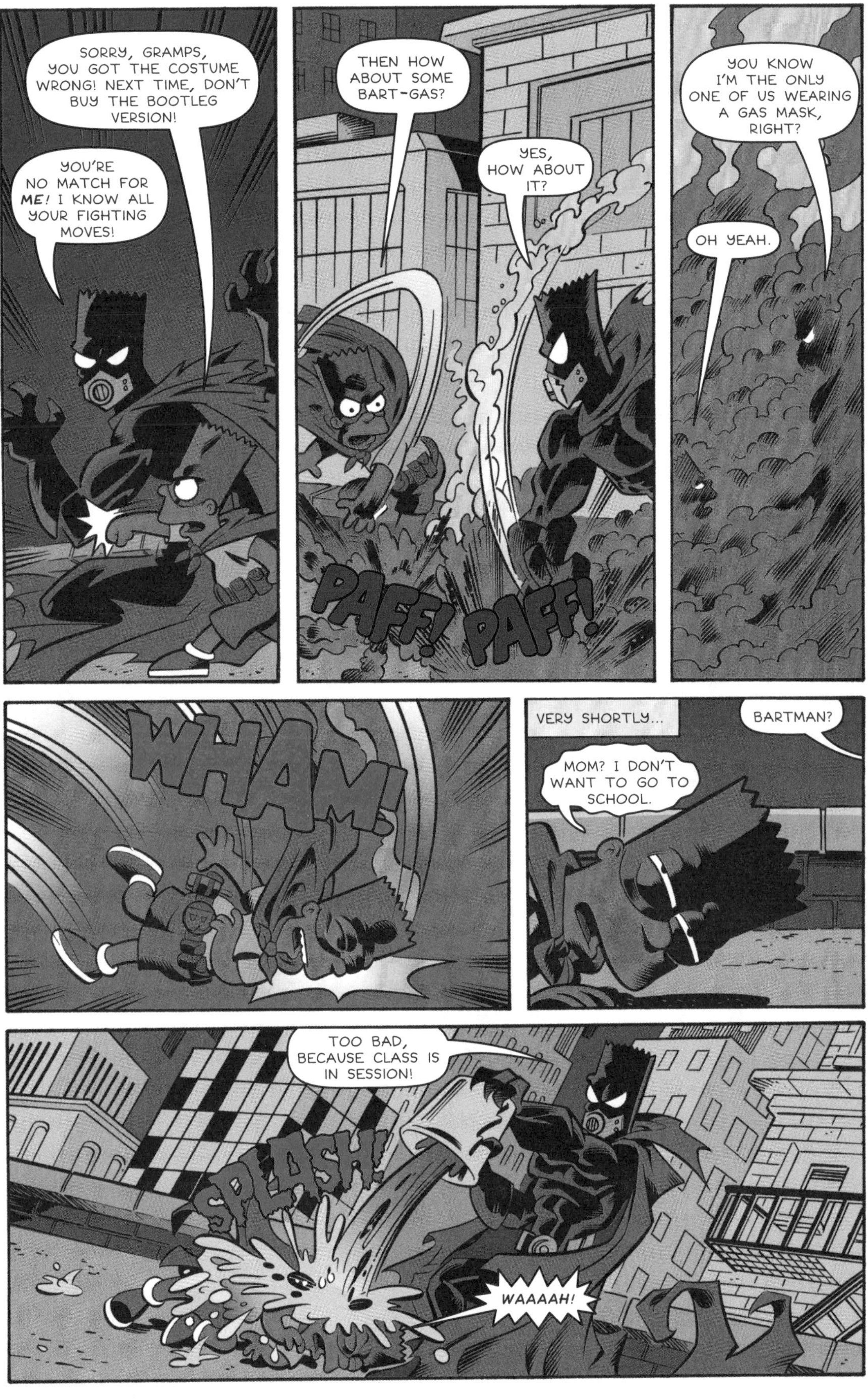
SORRY, GRAMPS, YOU GOT THE COSTUME WRONG! NEXT TIME, DON'T BUY THE BOOTLEG VERSION!
YOU'RE NO MATCH FOR ME! I KNOW ALL YOUR FIGHTING MOVES!
THEN HOW ABOUT SOME BART-GAS?
YES, HOW ABOUT IT?
PAFF! PAFF!
YOU KNOW I'M THE ONLY ONE OF US WEARING A GAS MASK, RIGHT?
OH YEAH.
WHAM!
VERY SHORTLY...
BARTMAN?
MOM? I DON'T WANT TO GO TO SCHOOL.
TOO BAD, BECAUSE CLASS IS IN SESSION!
SPLASH!
WAAAAH!

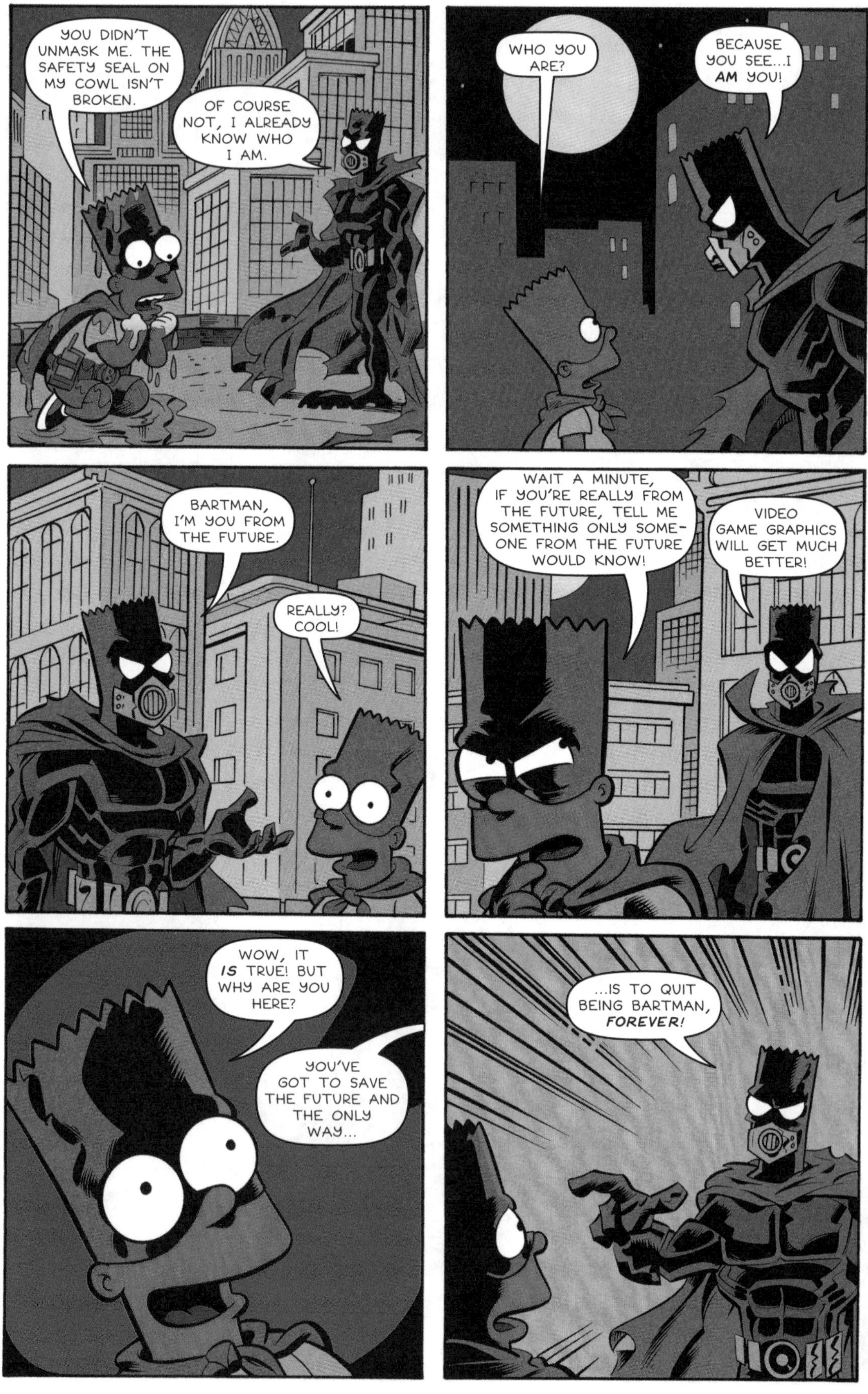
YOU DIDN'T UNMASK ME. THE SAFETY SEAL ON MY COWL ISN'T BROKEN.
OF COURSE NOT, I ALREADY KNOW WHO I AM.
WHO YOU ARE?
BECAUSE YOU SEE...I **AM** YOU!
BARTMAN, I'M YOU FROM THE FUTURE.
REALLY? COOL!
WAIT A MINUTE, IF YOU'RE REALLY FROM THE FUTURE, TELL ME SOMETHING ONLY SOME-ONE FROM THE FUTURE WOULD KNOW!
VIDEO GAME GRAPHICS WILL GET MUCH BETTER!
WOW, IT ***IS*** TRUE! BUT WHY ARE YOU HERE?
YOU'VE GOT TO SAVE THE FUTURE AND THE ONLY WAY...
...IS TO QUIT BEING BARTMAN, ***FOREVER***!

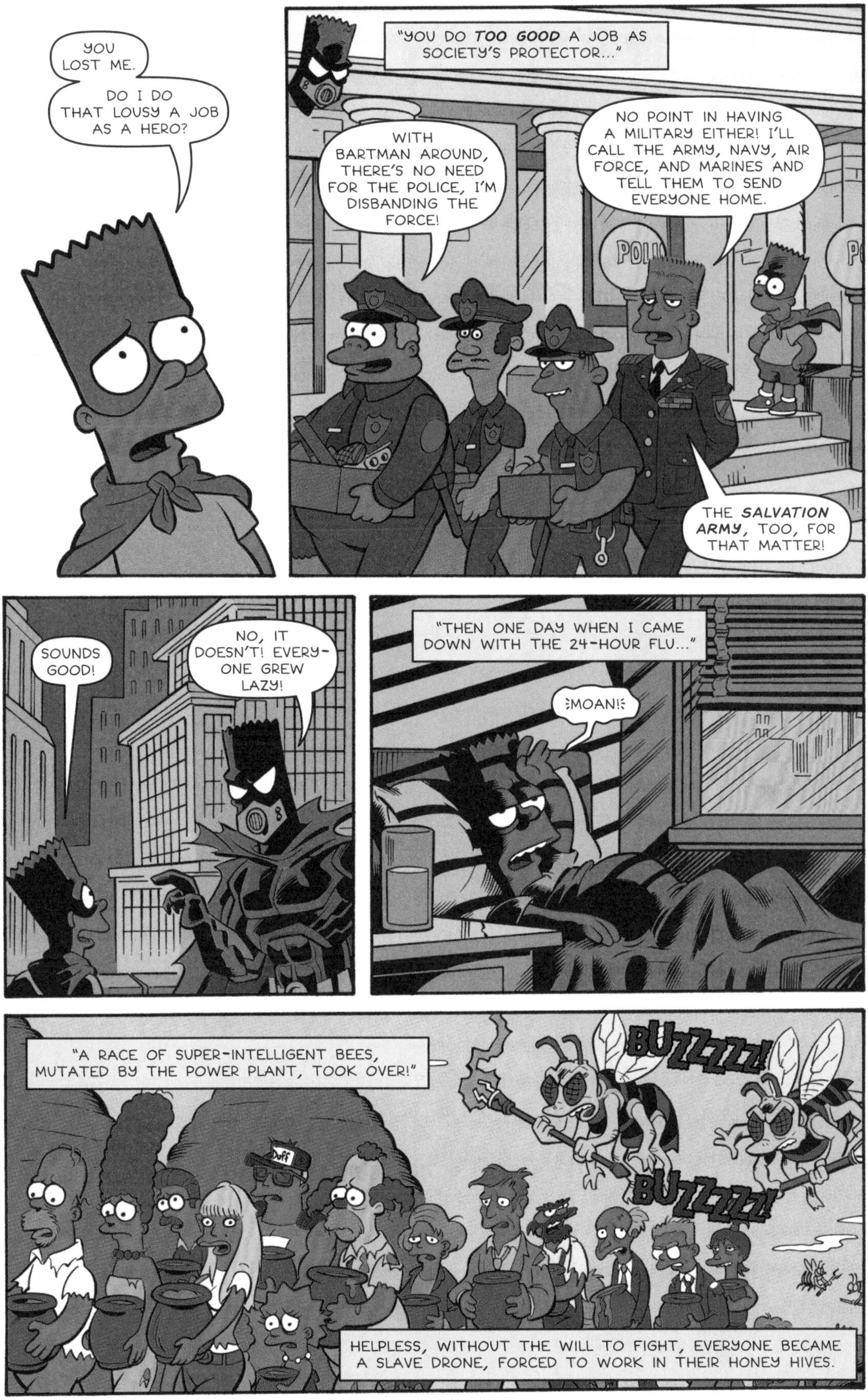
YOU LOST ME.
DO I DO THAT LOUSY A JOB AS A HERO?
"YOU DO TOO GOOD A JOB AS SOCIETY'S PROTECTOR..."
WITH BARTMAN AROUND, THERE'S NO NEED FOR THE POLICE, I'M DISBANDING THE FORCE!
NO POINT IN HAVING A MILITARY EITHER! I'LL CALL THE ARMY, NAVY, AIR FORCE, AND MARINES AND TELL THEM TO SEND EVERYONE HOME.
THE SALVATION ARMY, TOO, FOR THAT MATTER!
SOUNDS GOOD!
NO, IT DOESN'T! EVERY-ONE GREW LAZY!
"THEN ONE DAY WHEN I CAME DOWN WITH THE 24-HOUR FLU..."
MOAN!
"A RACE OF SUPER-INTELLIGENT BEES, MUTATED BY THE POWER PLANT, TOOK OVER!"
BUZZZZZ!
BUZZZZZ!
HELPLESS, WITHOUT THE WILL TO FIGHT, EVERYONE BECAME A SLAVE DRONE, FORCED TO WORK IN THEIR HONEY HIVES.

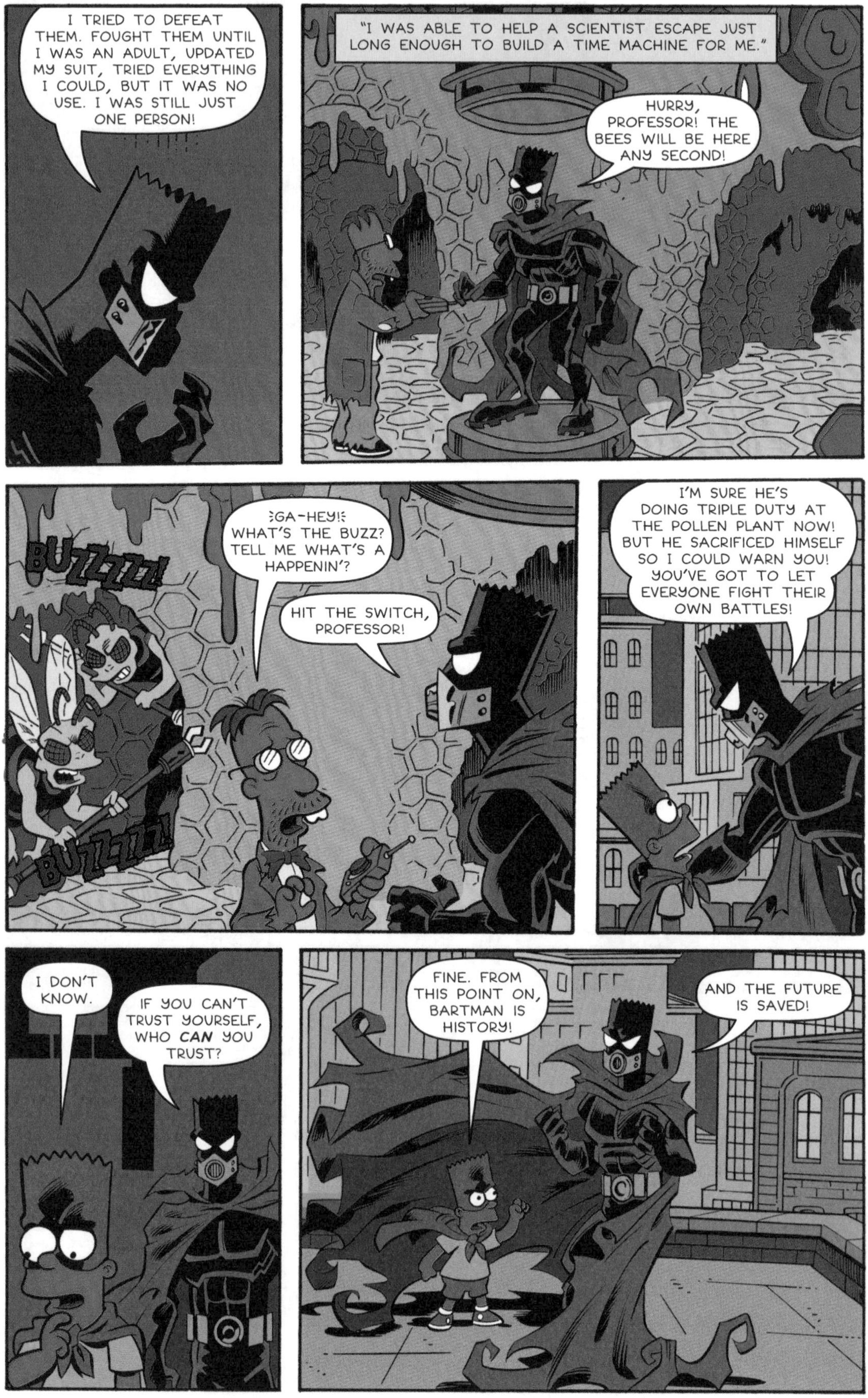
I TRIED TO DEFEAT THEM. FOUGHT THEM UNTIL I WAS AN ADULT, UPDATED MY SUIT, TRIED EVERYTHING I COULD, BUT IT WAS NO USE. I WAS STILL JUST ONE PERSON!
"I WAS ABLE TO HELP A SCIENTIST ESCAPE JUST LONG ENOUGH TO BUILD A TIME MACHINE FOR ME."
HURRY, PROFESSOR! THE BEES WILL BE HERE ANY SECOND!
BUZZZZZZ!
GA-HEY! WHAT'S THE BUZZ? TELL ME WHAT'S A HAPPENIN'?
HIT THE SWITCH, PROFESSOR!
BUZZZZZ!
I'M SURE HE'S DOING TRIPLE DUTY AT THE POLLEN PLANT NOW! BUT HE SACRIFICED HIMSELF SO I COULD WARN YOU! YOU'VE GOT TO LET EVERYONE FIGHT THEIR OWN BATTLES!
I DON'T KNOW.
IF YOU CAN'T TRUST YOURSELF, WHO CAN YOU TRUST?
FINE. FROM THIS POINT ON, BARTMAN IS HISTORY!
AND THE FUTURE IS SAVED!

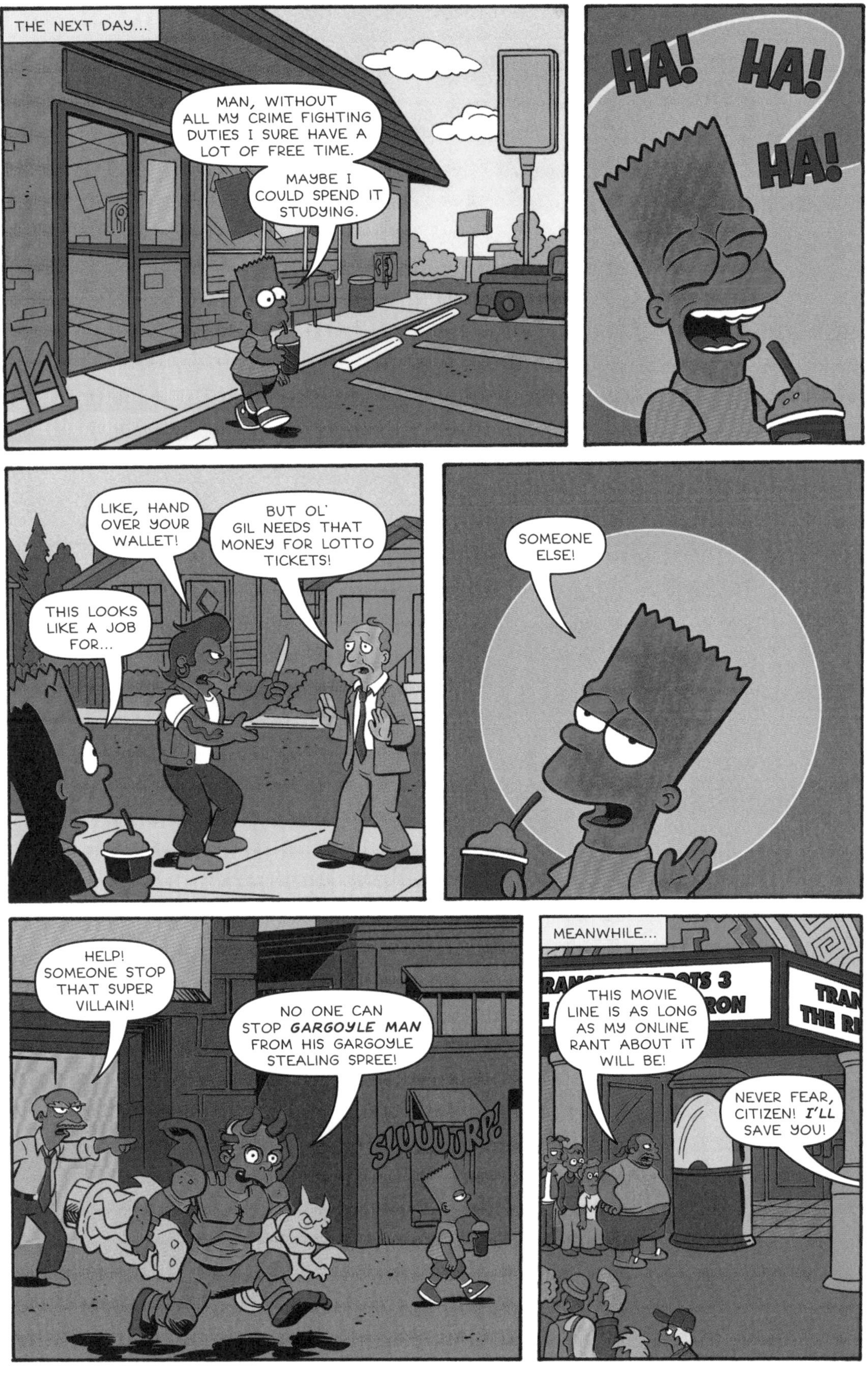
THE NEXT DAY...
MAN, WITHOUT ALL MY CRIME FIGHTING DUTIES I SURE HAVE A LOT OF FREE TIME.
MAYBE I COULD SPEND IT STUDYING.
HA! HA! HA!
THIS LOOKS LIKE A JOB FOR...
LIKE, HAND OVER YOUR WALLET!
BUT OL' GIL NEEDS THAT MONEY FOR LOTTO TICKETS!
SOMEONE ELSE!
HELP! SOMEONE STOP THAT SUPER VILLAIN!
NO ONE CAN STOP *GARGOYLE MAN* FROM HIS GARGOYLE STEALING SPREE!
SLUUUURP!
MEANWHILE...
THIS MOVIE LINE IS AS LONG AS MY ONLINE RANT ABOUT IT WILL BE!
NEVER FEAR, CITIZEN! *I'LL* SAVE YOU!

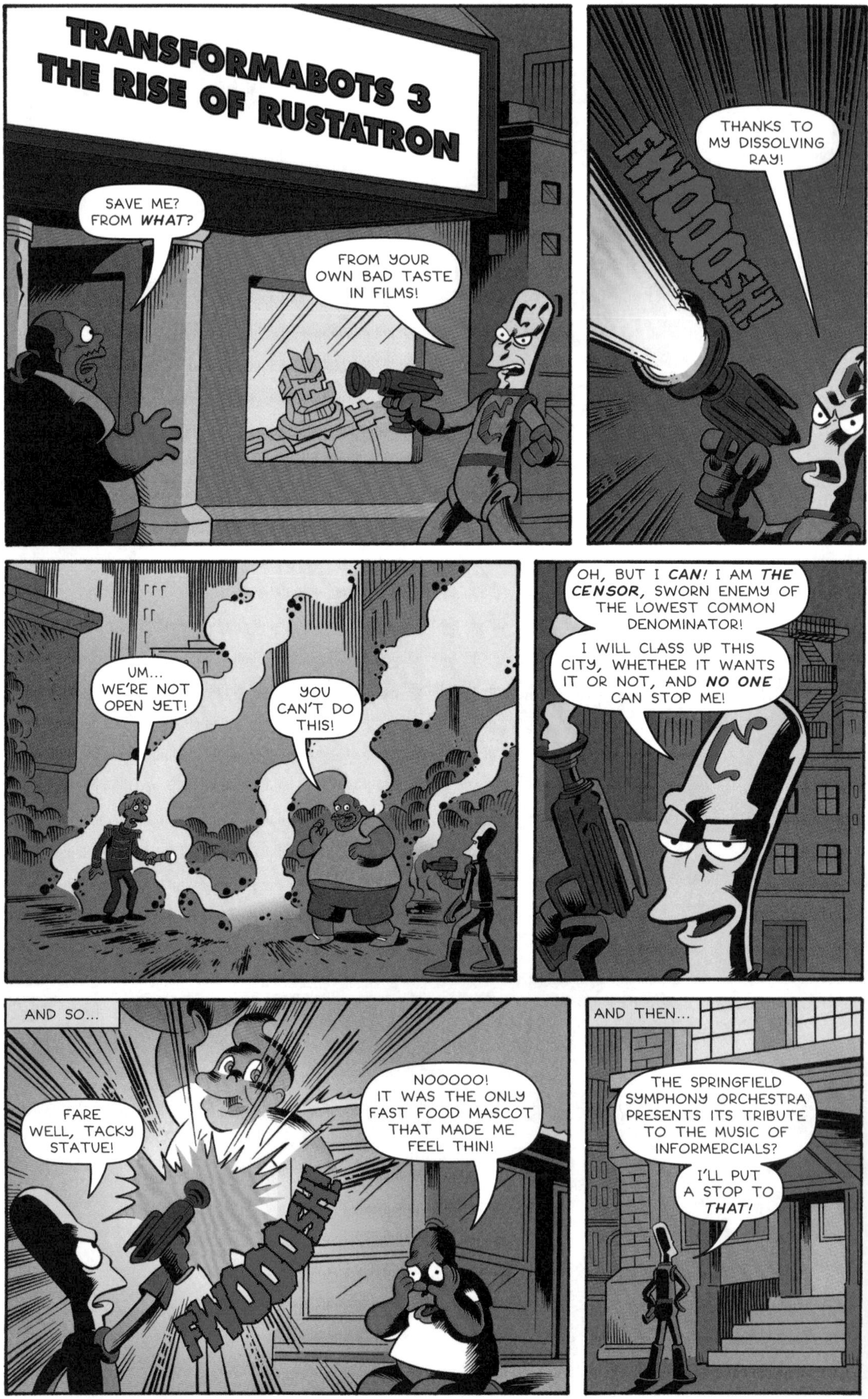

TRANSFORMABOTS 3 THE RISE OF RUSTATRON
SAVE ME? FROM *WHAT*?
FROM YOUR OWN BAD TASTE IN FILMS!
FWOOOSH!
THANKS TO MY DISSOLVING RAY!
UM... WE'RE NOT OPEN YET!
YOU CAN'T DO THIS!
OH, BUT I *CAN!* I AM *THE CENSOR,* SWORN ENEMY OF THE LOWEST COMMON DENOMINATOR!
I WILL CLASS UP THIS CITY, WHETHER IT WANTS IT OR NOT, AND *NO ONE* CAN STOP ME!
AND SO...
FARE WELL, TACKY STATUE!
FWOOOSH!
NOOOOO! IT WAS THE ONLY FAST FOOD MASCOT THAT MADE ME FEEL THIN!
AND THEN...
THE SPRINGFIELD SYMPHONY ORCHESTRA PRESENTS ITS TRIBUTE TO THE MUSIC OF INFORMERCIALS?
I'LL PUT A STOP TO *THAT!*

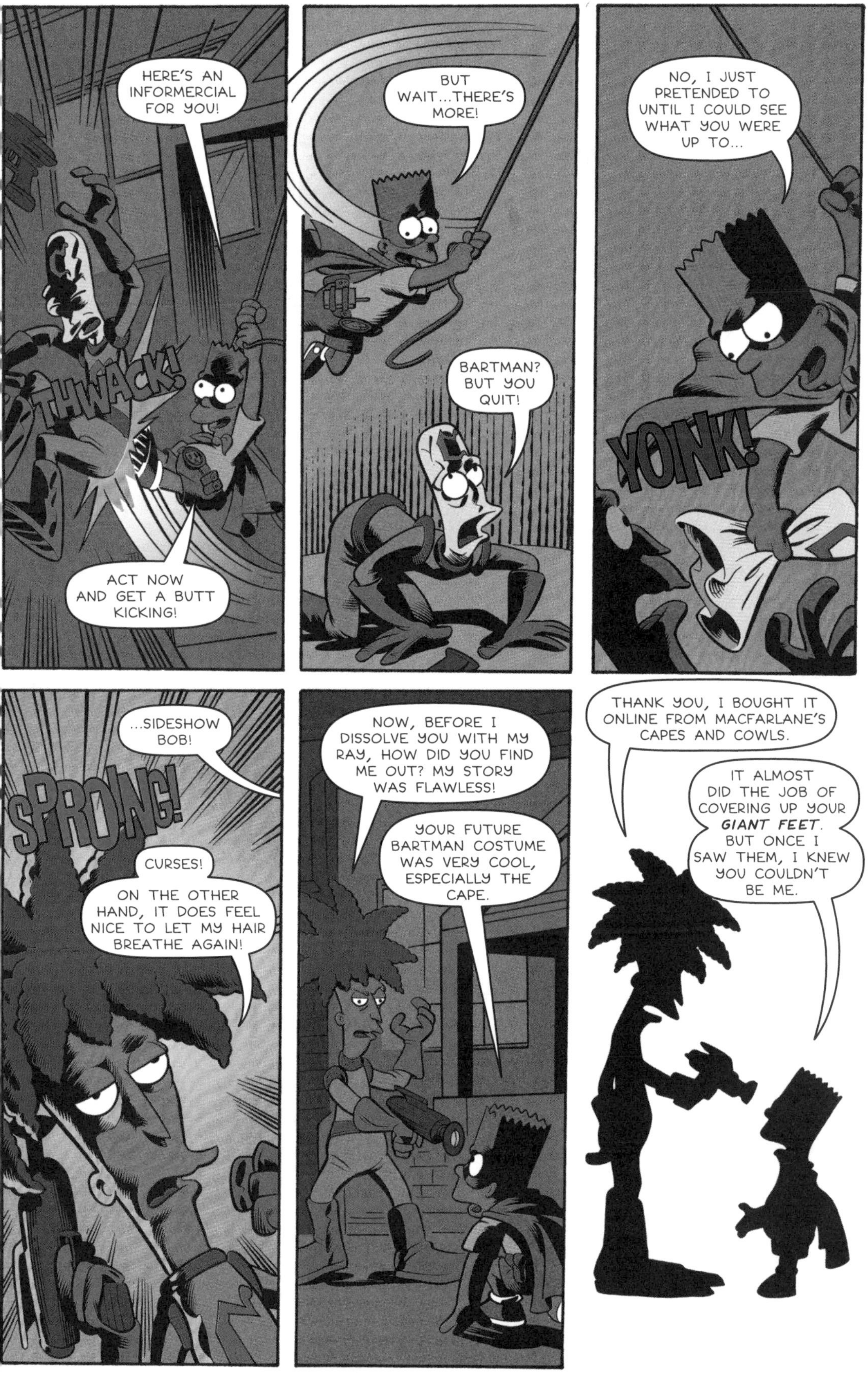
HERE'S AN INFORMERCIAL FOR YOU!
THWACK!
ACT NOW AND GET A BUTT KICKING!
BUT WAIT...THERE'S MORE!
BARTMAN? BUT YOU QUIT!
NO, I JUST PRETENDED TO UNTIL I COULD SEE WHAT YOU WERE UP TO...
YOINK!
...SIDESHOW BOB!
SPROING!
CURSES!
ON THE OTHER HAND, IT DOES FEEL NICE TO LET MY HAIR BREATHE AGAIN!
NOW, BEFORE I DISSOLVE YOU WITH MY RAY, HOW DID YOU FIND ME OUT? MY STORY WAS FLAWLESS!
YOUR FUTURE BARTMAN COSTUME WAS VERY COOL, ESPECIALLY THE CAPE.
THANK YOU, I BOUGHT IT ONLINE FROM MACFARLANE'S CAPES AND COWLS.
IT ALMOST DID THE JOB OF COVERING UP YOUR GIANT FEET. BUT ONCE I SAW THEM, I KNEW YOU COULDN'T BE ME.

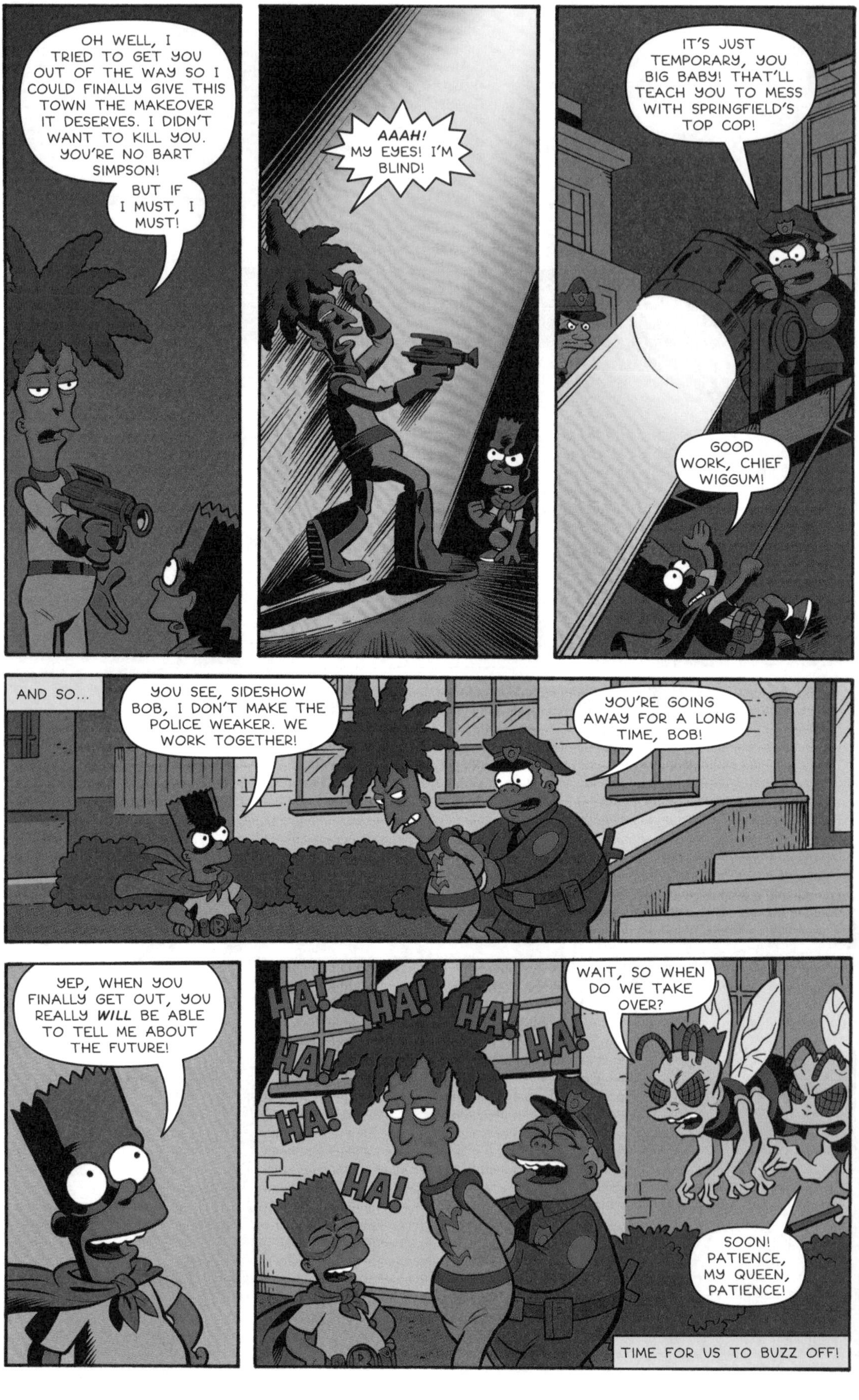
OH WELL, I TRIED TO GET YOU OUT OF THE WAY SO I COULD FINALLY GIVE THIS TOWN THE MAKEOVER IT DESERVES. I DIDN'T WANT TO KILL YOU. YOU'RE NO BART SIMPSON!
BUT IF I MUST, I MUST!
AAAH! MY EYES! I'M BLIND!
IT'S JUST TEMPORARY, YOU BIG BABY! THAT'LL TEACH YOU TO MESS WITH SPRINGFIELD'S TOP COP!
GOOD WORK, CHIEF WIGGUM!
AND SO...
YOU SEE, SIDESHOW BOB, I DON'T MAKE THE POLICE WEAKER. WE WORK TOGETHER!
YOU'RE GOING AWAY FOR A LONG TIME, BOB!
YEP, WHEN YOU FINALLY GET OUT, YOU REALLY WILL BE ABLE TO TELL ME ABOUT THE FUTURE!
HA! HA! HA! HA! HA! HA! HA!
WAIT, SO WHEN DO WE TAKE OVER?
SOON! PATIENCE, MY QUEEN, PATIENCE!
TIME FOR US TO BUZZ OFF!

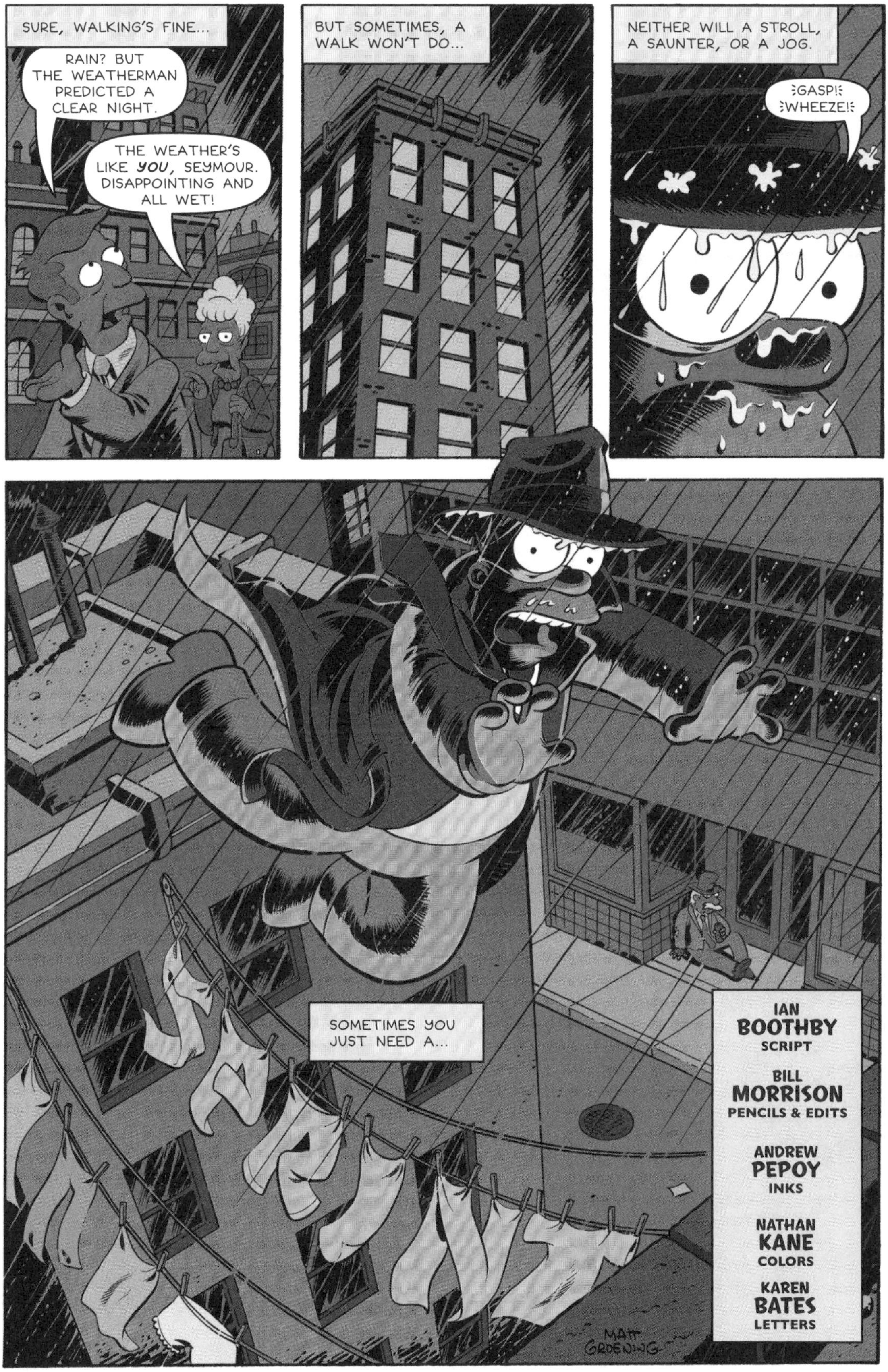
SURE, WALKING'S FINE...
RAIN? BUT THE WEATHERMAN PREDICTED A CLEAR NIGHT.
THE WEATHER'S LIKE ***YOU***, SEYMOUR. DISAPPOINTING AND ALL WET!
BUT SOMETIMES, A WALK WON'T DO...
NEITHER WILL A STROLL, A SAUNTER, OR A JOG.
GASP! WHEEZE!
SOMETIMES YOU JUST NEED A...
IAN
BOOTHBY
SCRIPT
BILL
MORRISON
PENCILS & EDITS
ANDREW
PEPOY
INKS
NATHAN
KANE
COLORS
KAREN
BATES
LETTERS
MATT GROENING

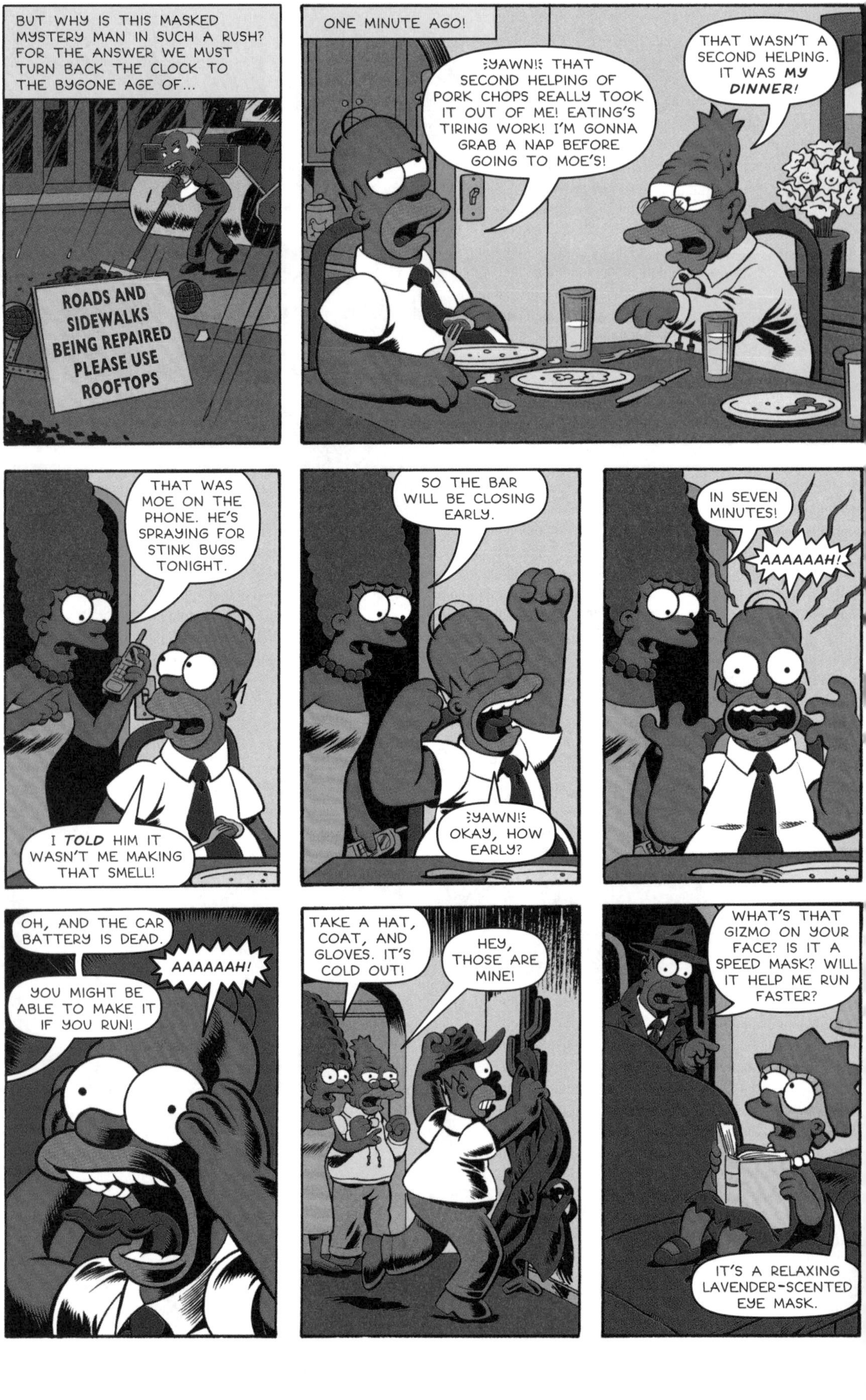

BUT WHY IS THIS MASKED MYSTERY MAN IN SUCH A RUSH? FOR THE ANSWER WE MUST TURN BACK THE CLOCK TO THE BYGONE AGE OF...
ROADS AND SIDEWALKS BEING REPAIRED PLEASE USE ROOFTOPS
ONE MINUTE AGO!
:YAWN!: THAT SECOND HELPING OF PORK CHOPS REALLY TOOK IT OUT OF ME! EATING'S TIRING WORK! I'M GONNA GRAB A NAP BEFORE GOING TO MOE'S!
THAT WASN'T A SECOND HELPING. IT WAS MY DINNER!
THAT WAS MOE ON THE PHONE. HE'S SPRAYING FOR STINK BUGS TONIGHT.
I TOLD HIM IT WASN'T ME MAKING THAT SMELL!
SO THE BAR WILL BE CLOSING EARLY.
:YAWN!: OKAY, HOW EARLY?
IN SEVEN MINUTES!
AAAAAAH!
OH, AND THE CAR BATTERY IS DEAD.
AAAAAAH!
YOU MIGHT BE ABLE TO MAKE IT IF YOU RUN!
TAKE A HAT, COAT, AND GLOVES. IT'S COLD OUT!
HEY, THOSE ARE MINE!
WHAT'S THAT GIZMO ON YOUR FACE? IS IT A SPEED MASK? WILL IT HELP ME RUN FASTER?
IT'S A RELAXING LAVENDER-SCENTED EYE MASK.

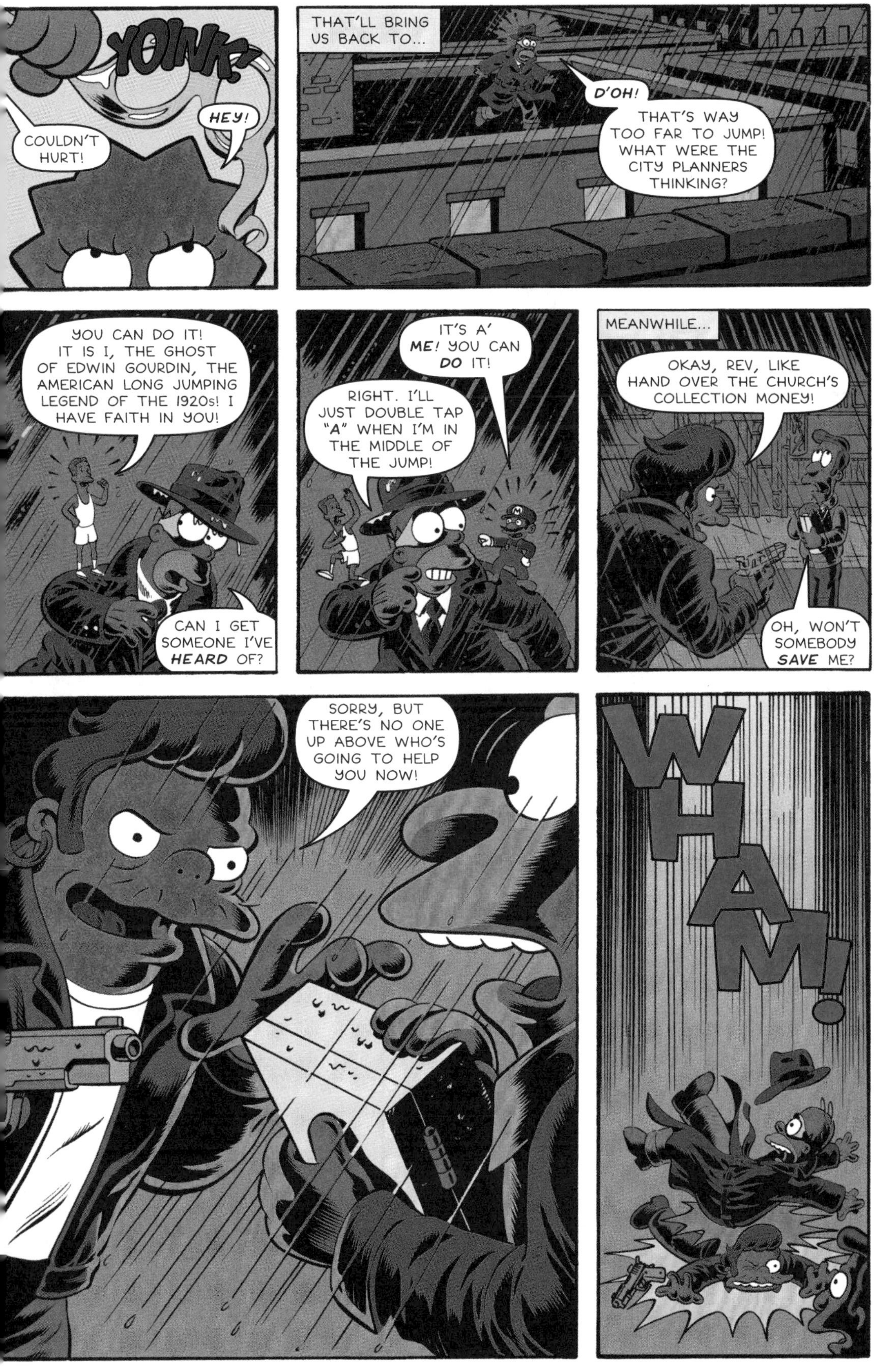
YOINK!
COULDN'T HURT!
HEY!
THAT'LL BRING US BACK TO...
D'OH!
THAT'S WAY TOO FAR TO JUMP! WHAT WERE THE CITY PLANNERS THINKING?
YOU CAN DO IT! IT IS I, THE GHOST OF EDWIN GOURDIN, THE AMERICAN LONG JUMPING LEGEND OF THE 1920s! I HAVE FAITH IN YOU!
CAN I GET SOMEONE I'VE **HEARD** OF?
IT'S A' **ME**! YOU CAN **DO** IT!
RIGHT. I'LL JUST DOUBLE TAP "**A**" WHEN I'M IN THE MIDDLE OF THE JUMP!
MEANWHILE...
OKAY, REV, LIKE HAND OVER THE CHURCH'S COLLECTION MONEY!
OH, WON'T SOMEBODY **SAVE** ME?
SORRY, BUT THERE'S NO ONE UP ABOVE WHO'S GOING TO HELP YOU NOW!
WHAM!

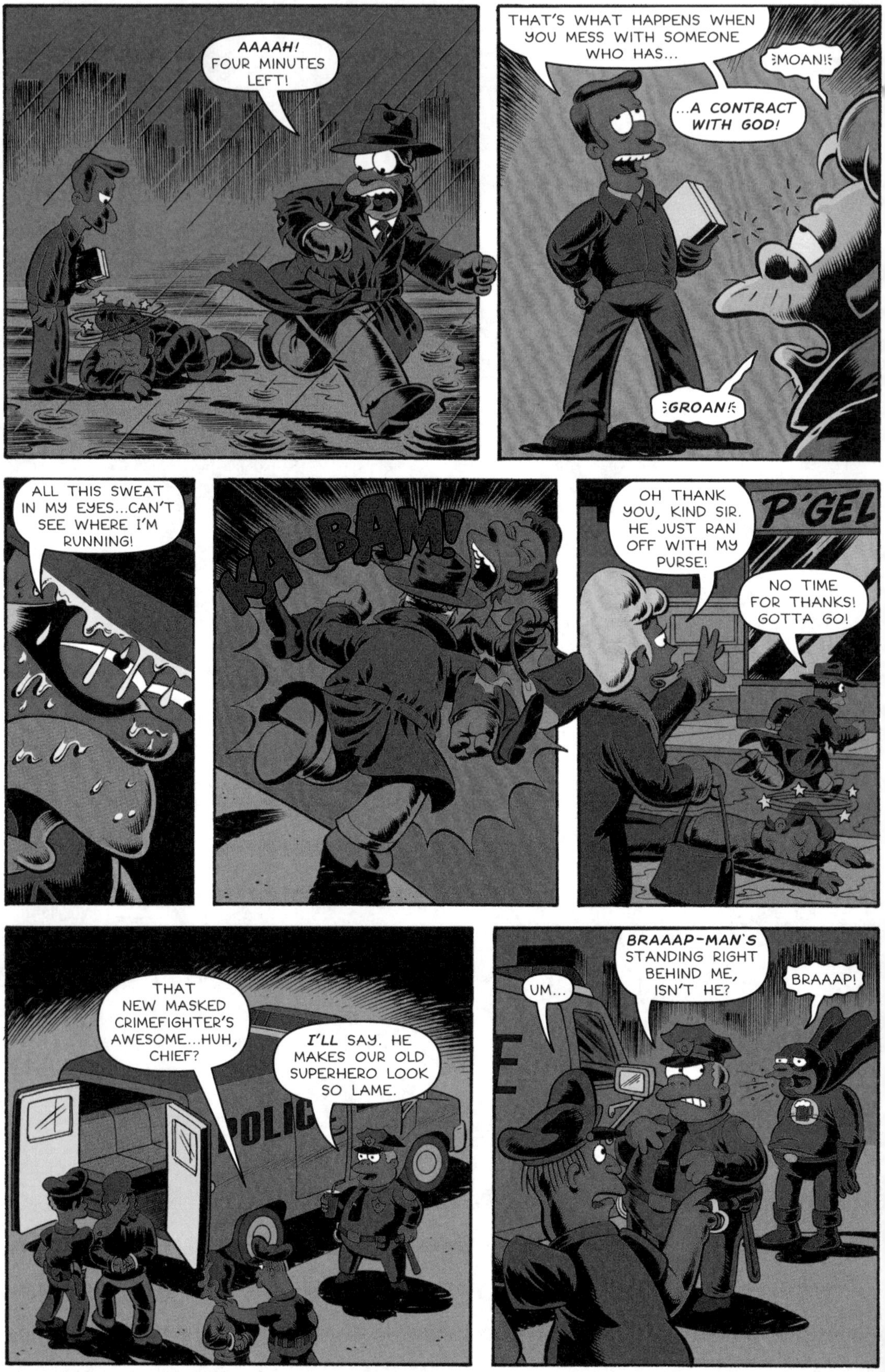
AAAAH! FOUR MINUTES LEFT!
THAT'S WHAT HAPPENS WHEN YOU MESS WITH SOMEONE WHO HAS...
...A CONTRACT WITH GOD!
MOAN!
GROAN!
ALL THIS SWEAT IN MY EYES...CAN'T SEE WHERE I'M RUNNING!
KA-BAM!
OH THANK YOU, KIND SIR. HE JUST RAN OFF WITH MY PURSE!
P'GEL
NO TIME FOR THANKS! GOTTA GO!
THAT NEW MASKED CRIMEFIGHTER'S AWESOME...HUH, CHIEF?
I'LL SAY. HE MAKES OUR OLD SUPERHERO LOOK SO LAME.
POLIC
UM...
BRAAAP-MAN'S STANDING RIGHT BEHIND ME, ISN'T HE?
BRAAAP!

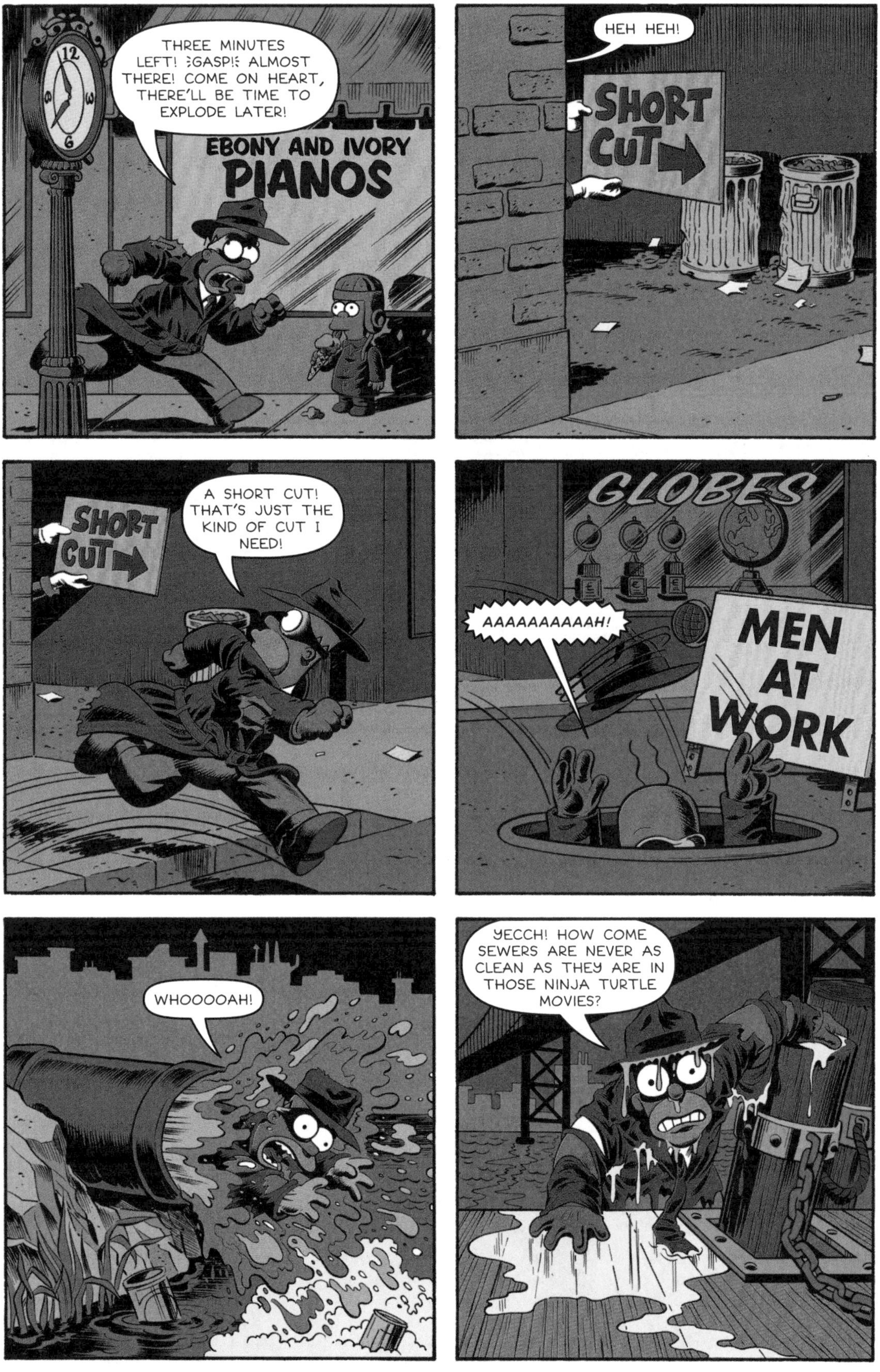
THREE MINUTES LEFT! ;GASP!; ALMOST THERE! COME ON HEART, THERE'LL BE TIME TO EXPLODE LATER!
EBONY AND IVORY PIANOS
HEH HEH!
SHORT CUT
SHORT CUT
A SHORT CUT! THAT'S JUST THE KIND OF CUT I NEED!
GLOBES
AAAAAAAAAAH!
MEN AT WORK
WHOOOOAH!
YECCH! HOW COME SEWERS ARE NEVER AS CLEAN AS THEY ARE IN THOSE NINJA TURTLE MOVIES?

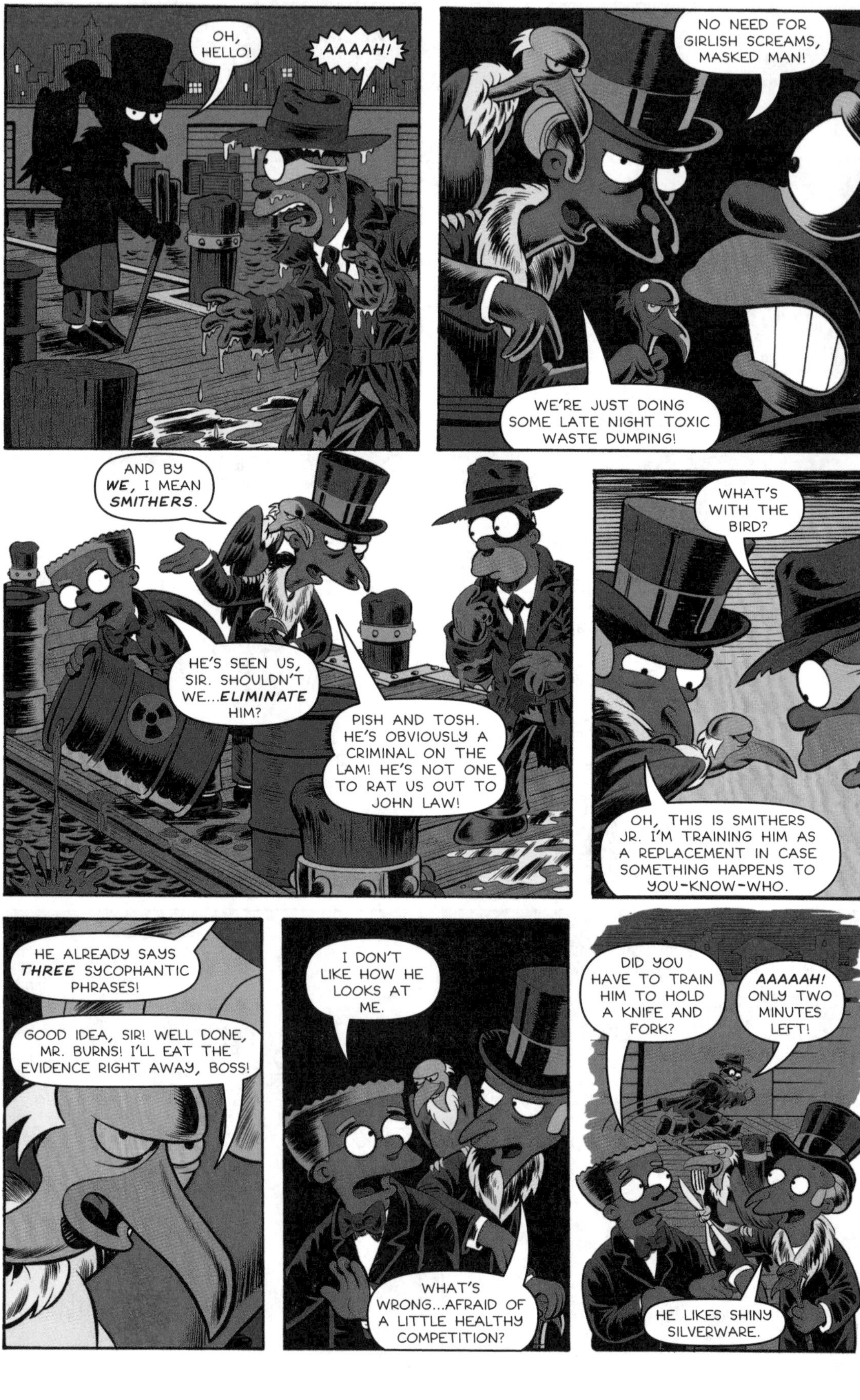

OH, HELLO!
AAAAH!
NO NEED FOR GIRLISH SCREAMS, MASKED MAN!
WE'RE JUST DOING SOME LATE NIGHT TOXIC WASTE DUMPING!
AND BY WE, I MEAN SMITHERS.
HE'S SEEN US, SIR. SHOULDN'T WE...ELIMINATE HIM?
PISH AND TOSH. HE'S OBVIOUSLY A CRIMINAL ON THE LAM! HE'S NOT ONE TO RAT US OUT TO JOHN LAW!
WHAT'S WITH THE BIRD?
OH, THIS IS SMITHERS JR. I'M TRAINING HIM AS A REPLACEMENT IN CASE SOMETHING HAPPENS TO YOU-KNOW-WHO.
HE ALREADY SAYS THREE SYCOPHANTIC PHRASES!
GOOD IDEA, SIR! WELL DONE, MR. BURNS! I'LL EAT THE EVIDENCE RIGHT AWAY, BOSS!
I DON'T LIKE HOW HE LOOKS AT ME.
WHAT'S WRONG...AFRAID OF A LITTLE HEALTHY COMPETITION?
DID YOU HAVE TO TRAIN HIM TO HOLD A KNIFE AND FORK?
AAAAAH! ONLY TWO MINUTES LEFT!
HE LIKES SHINY SILVERWARE.

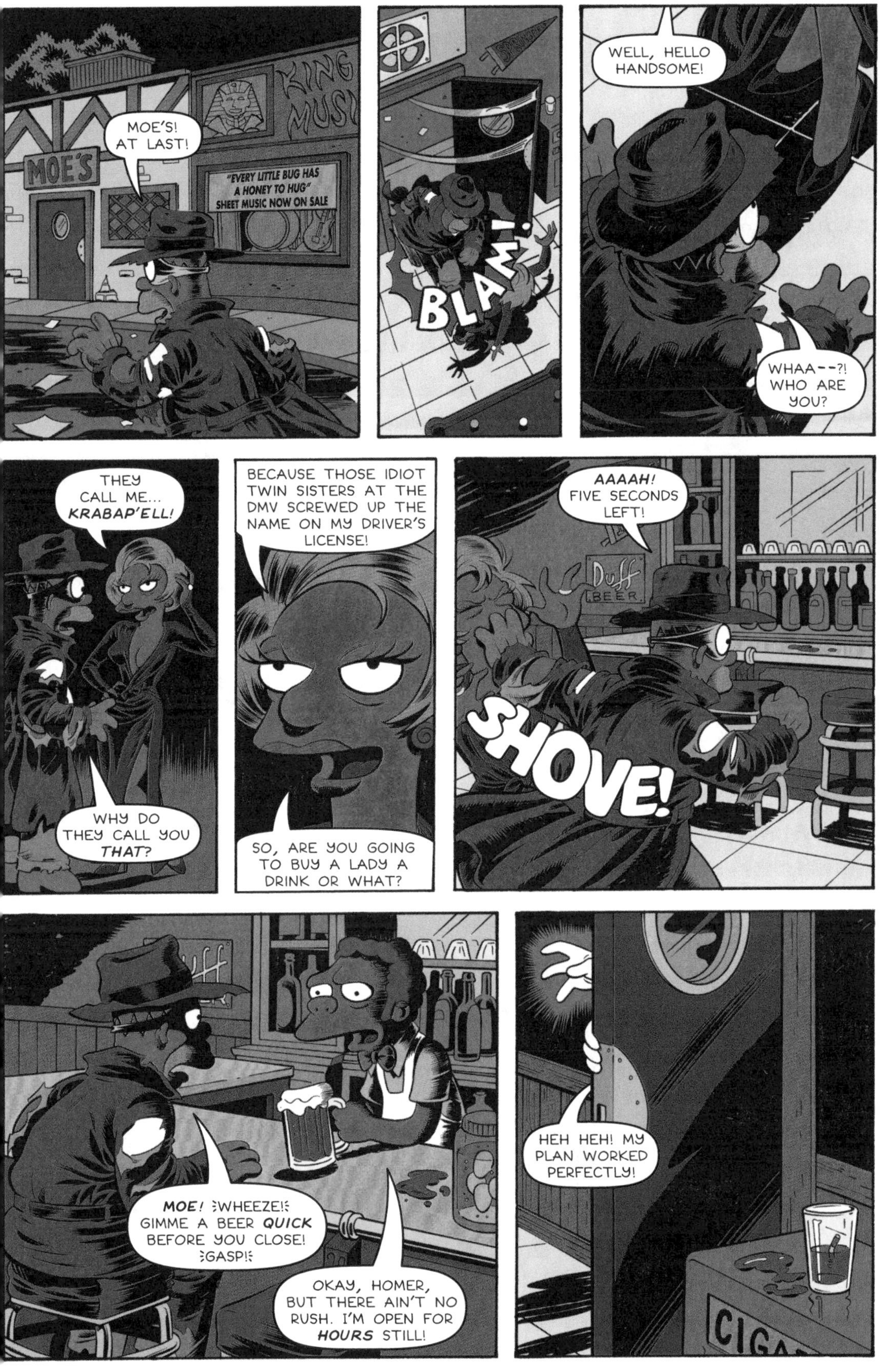
MOE'S! AT LAST!
MOE'S
KING MUSI
"EVERY LITTLE BUG HAS A HONEY TO HUG" SHEET MUSIC NOW ON SALE
BLAM!
WELL, HELLO HANDSOME!
WHAA--?! WHO ARE YOU?
THEY CALL ME... KRABAP'ELL!
WHY DO THEY CALL YOU THAT?
BECAUSE THOSE IDIOT TWIN SISTERS AT THE DMV SCREWED UP THE NAME ON MY DRIVER'S LICENSE!
SO, ARE YOU GOING TO BUY A LADY A DRINK OR WHAT?
AAAAH! FIVE SECONDS LEFT!
Duff BEER
SHOVE!
MOE! WHEEZE! GIMME A BEER QUICK BEFORE YOU CLOSE! GASP!
OKAY, HOMER, BUT THERE AIN'T NO RUSH. I'M OPEN FOR HOURS STILL!
HEH HEH! MY PLAN WORKED PERFECTLY!
CIGA

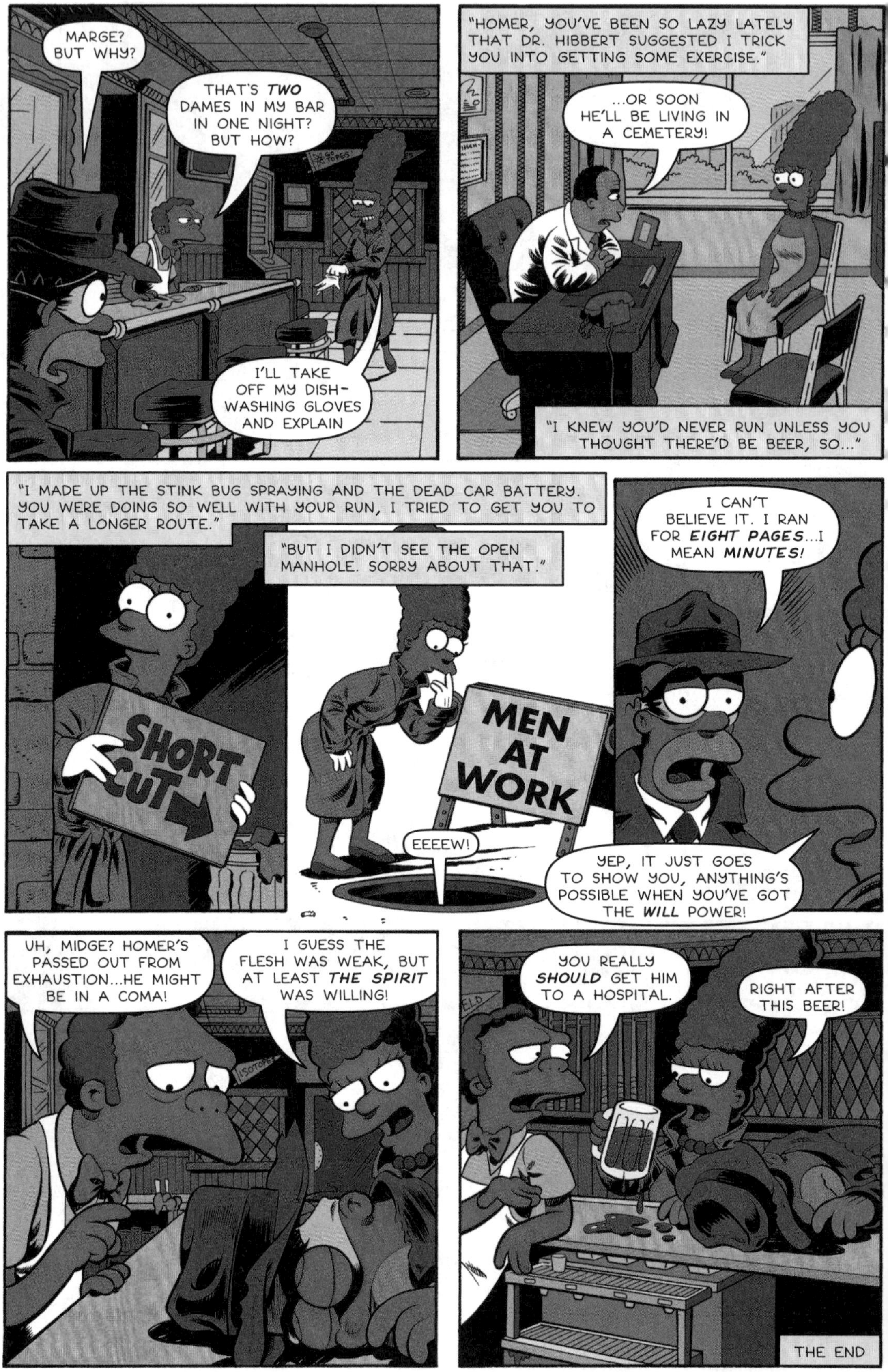
MARGE? BUT WHY?
THAT'S TWO DAMES IN MY BAR IN ONE NIGHT? BUT HOW?
I'LL TAKE OFF MY DISH-WASHING GLOVES AND EXPLAIN
"HOMER, YOU'VE BEEN SO LAZY LATELY THAT DR. HIBBERT SUGGESTED I TRICK YOU INTO GETTING SOME EXERCISE."
...OR SOON HE'LL BE LIVING IN A CEMETERY!
"I KNEW YOU'D NEVER RUN UNLESS YOU THOUGHT THERE'D BE BEER, SO..."
"I MADE UP THE STINK BUG SPRAYING AND THE DEAD CAR BATTERY. YOU WERE DOING SO WELL WITH YOUR RUN, I TRIED TO GET YOU TO TAKE A LONGER ROUTE."
SHORT CUT
"BUT I DIDN'T SEE THE OPEN MANHOLE. SORRY ABOUT THAT."
MEN AT WORK
EEEEW!
I CAN'T BELIEVE IT. I RAN FOR EIGHT PAGES...I MEAN MINUTES!
YEP, IT JUST GOES TO SHOW YOU, ANYTHING'S POSSIBLE WHEN YOU'VE GOT THE WILL POWER!
UH, MIDGE? HOMER'S PASSED OUT FROM EXHAUSTION...HE MIGHT BE IN A COMA!
I GUESS THE FLESH WAS WEAK, BUT AT LEAST THE SPIRIT WAS WILLING!
YOU REALLY SHOULD GET HIM TO A HOSPITAL.
RIGHT AFTER THIS BEER!
THE END

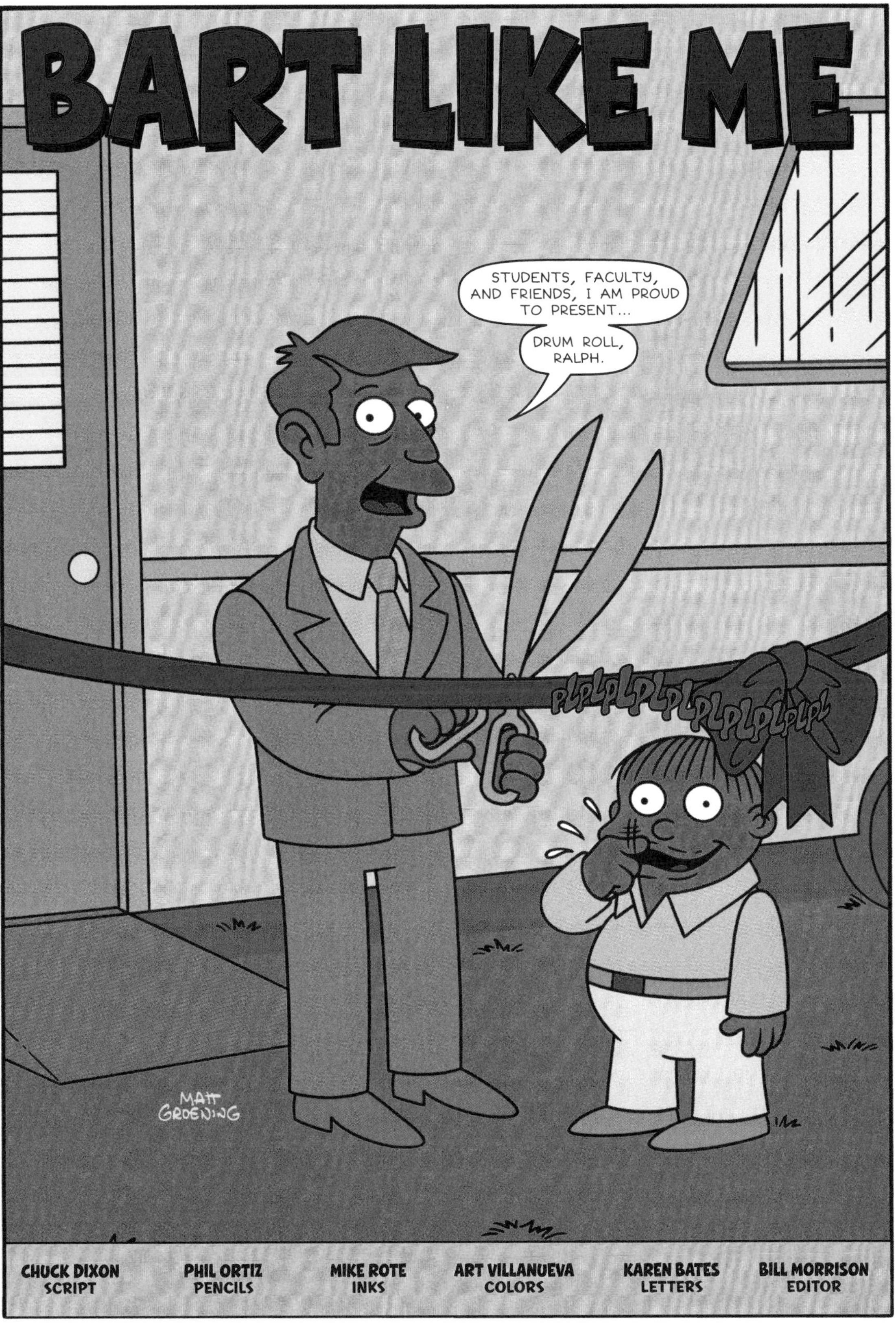
BART LIKE ME
STUDENTS, FACULTY, AND FRIENDS, I AM PROUD TO PRESENT...
DRUM ROLL, RALPH.
MATT GROENING

CHUCK DIXON SCRIPT
PHIL ORTIZ PENCILS
MIKE ROTE INKS
ART VILLANUEVA COLORS
KAREN BATES LETTERS
BILL MORRISON EDITOR

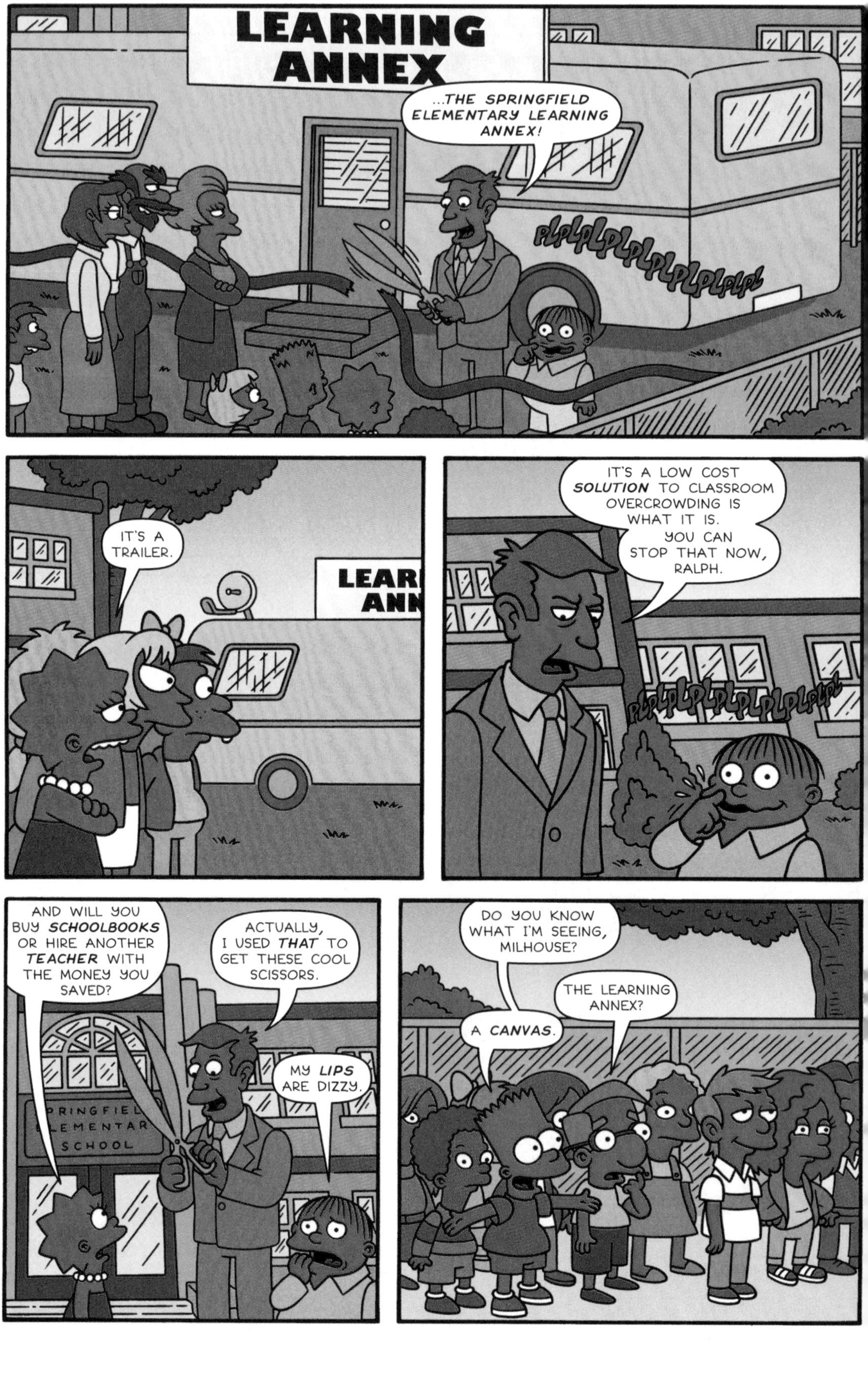
LEARNING ANNEX
...THE SPRINGFIELD ELEMENTARY LEARNING ANNEX!
PLPLPLPLPLPLPLPLPLPLPL
IT'S A TRAILER.
IT'S A LOW COST SOLUTION TO CLASSROOM OVERCROWDING IS WHAT IT IS.
YOU CAN STOP THAT NOW, RALPH.
PLPLPLPLPLPLPLPLPLPL
AND WILL YOU BUY SCHOOLBOOKS OR HIRE ANOTHER TEACHER WITH THE MONEY YOU SAVED?
ACTUALLY, I USED THAT TO GET THESE COOL SCISSORS.
MY LIPS ARE DIZZY.
DO YOU KNOW WHAT I'M SEEING, MILHOUSE?
A CANVAS.
THE LEARNING ANNEX?

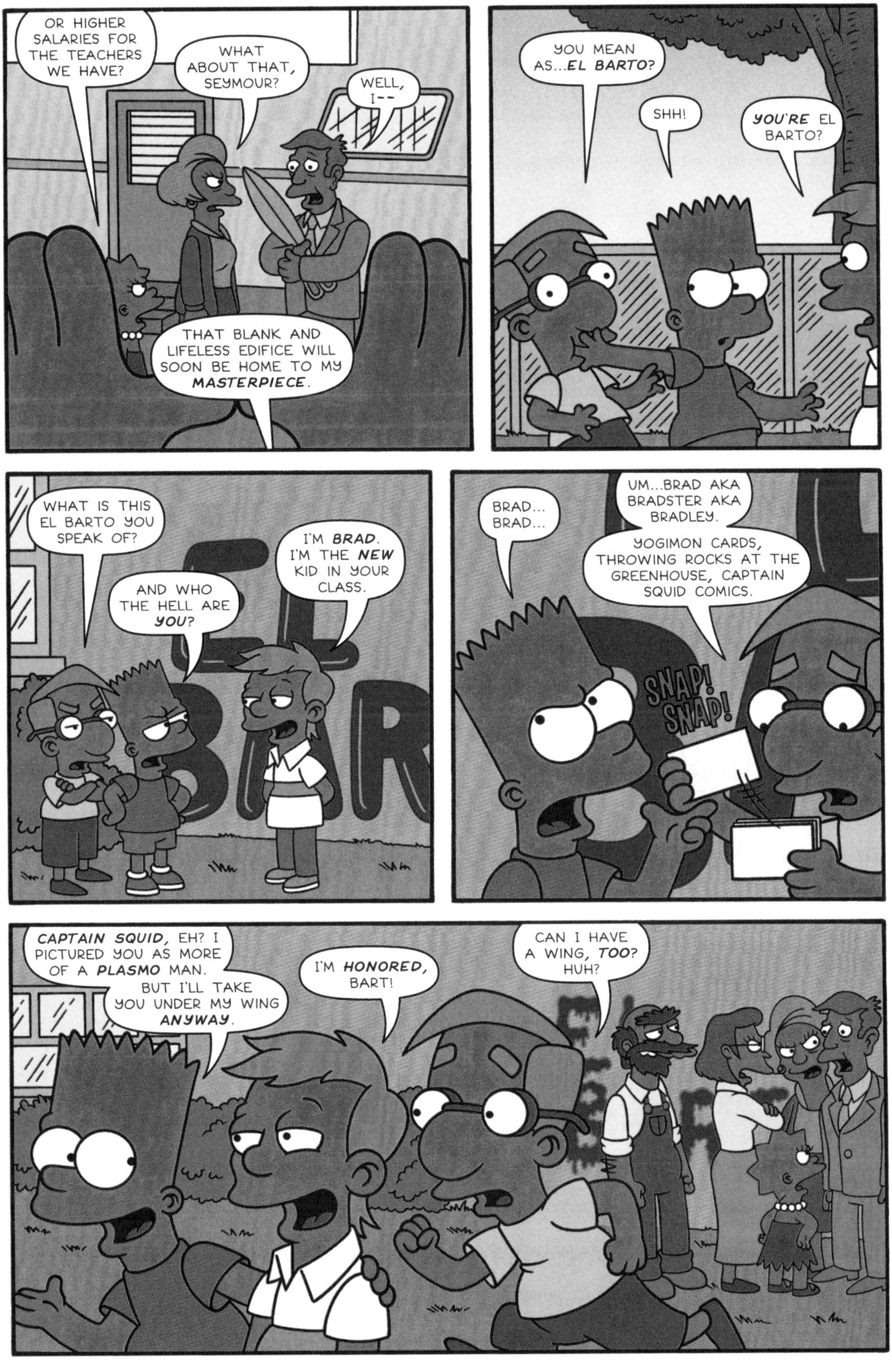
OR HIGHER SALARIES FOR THE TEACHERS WE HAVE?
WHAT ABOUT THAT, SEYMOUR?
WELL, I--
THAT BLANK AND LIFELESS EDIFICE WILL SOON BE HOME TO MY **MASTERPIECE**.
YOU MEAN AS...**EL BARTO?**
SHH!
YOU'RE EL BARTO?
WHAT IS THIS EL BARTO YOU SPEAK OF?
AND WHO THE HELL ARE **YOU?**
I'M **BRAD**. I'M THE **NEW** KID IN YOUR CLASS.
BRAD... BRAD...
UM...BRAD AKA BRADSTER AKA BRADLEY.
YOGIMON CARDS, THROWING ROCKS AT THE GREENHOUSE, CAPTAIN SQUID COMICS.
SNAP! SNAP!
CAPTAIN SQUID, EH? I PICTURED YOU AS MORE OF A **PLASMO** MAN.
BUT I'LL TAKE YOU UNDER MY WING **ANYWAY**.
I'M **HONORED,** BART!
CAN I HAVE A WING, **TOO?** HUH?

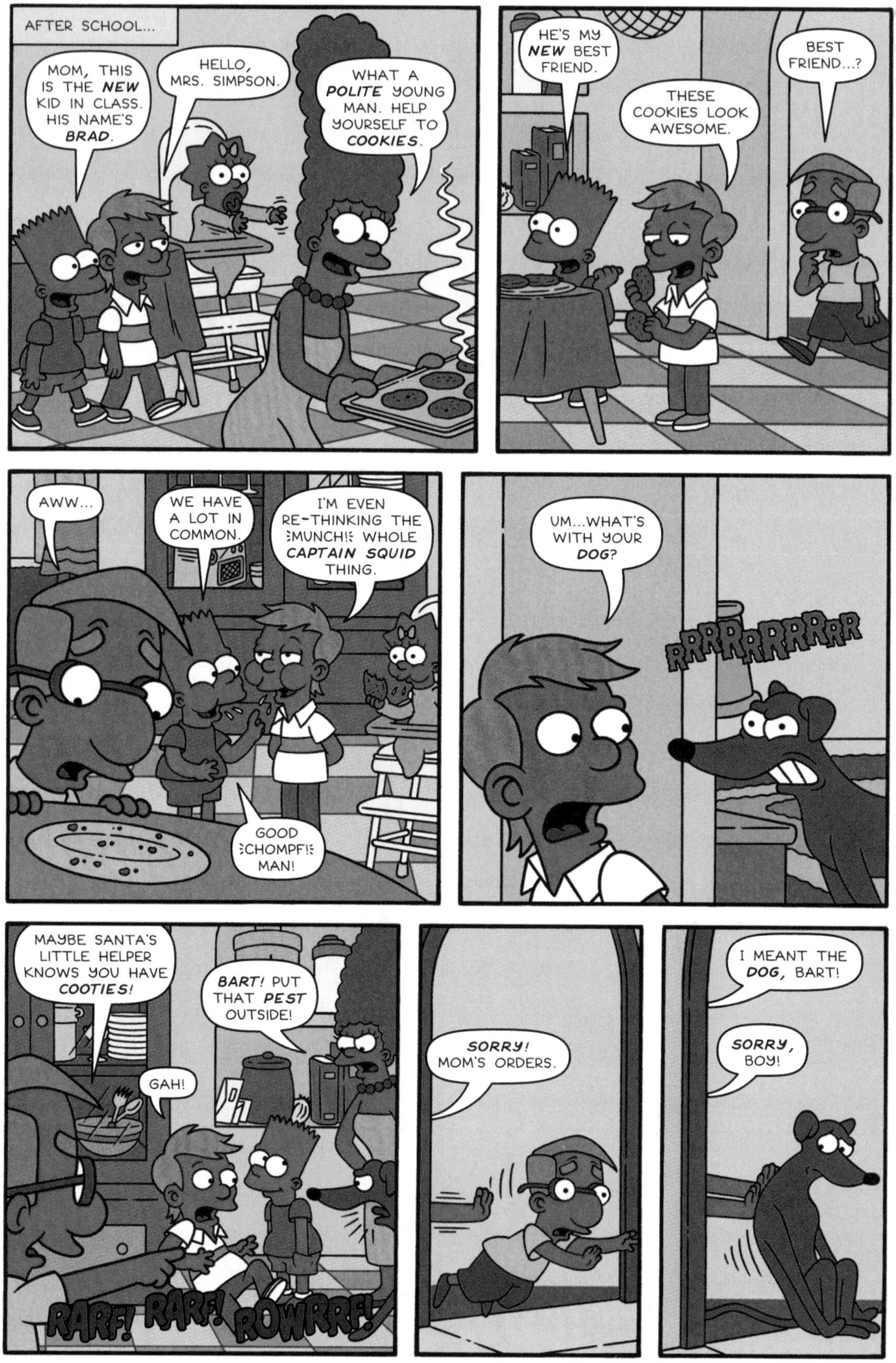
AFTER SCHOOL...
MOM, THIS IS THE NEW KID IN CLASS. HIS NAME'S BRAD.
HELLO, MRS. SIMPSON.
WHAT A POLITE YOUNG MAN. HELP YOURSELF TO COOKIES.
HE'S MY NEW BEST FRIEND.
THESE COOKIES LOOK AWESOME.
BEST FRIEND...?
AWW...
WE HAVE A LOT IN COMMON.
I'M EVEN RE-THINKING THE MUNCH! WHOLE CAPTAIN SQUID THING.
GOOD CHOMPF! MAN!
UM...WHAT'S WITH YOUR DOG?
RRRRRRRRRRR
MAYBE SANTA'S LITTLE HELPER KNOWS YOU HAVE COOTIES!
BART! PUT THAT PEST OUTSIDE!
GAH!
RARF! RARF! ROWRRF!
SORRY! MOM'S ORDERS.
I MEANT THE DOG, BART!
SORRY, BOY!

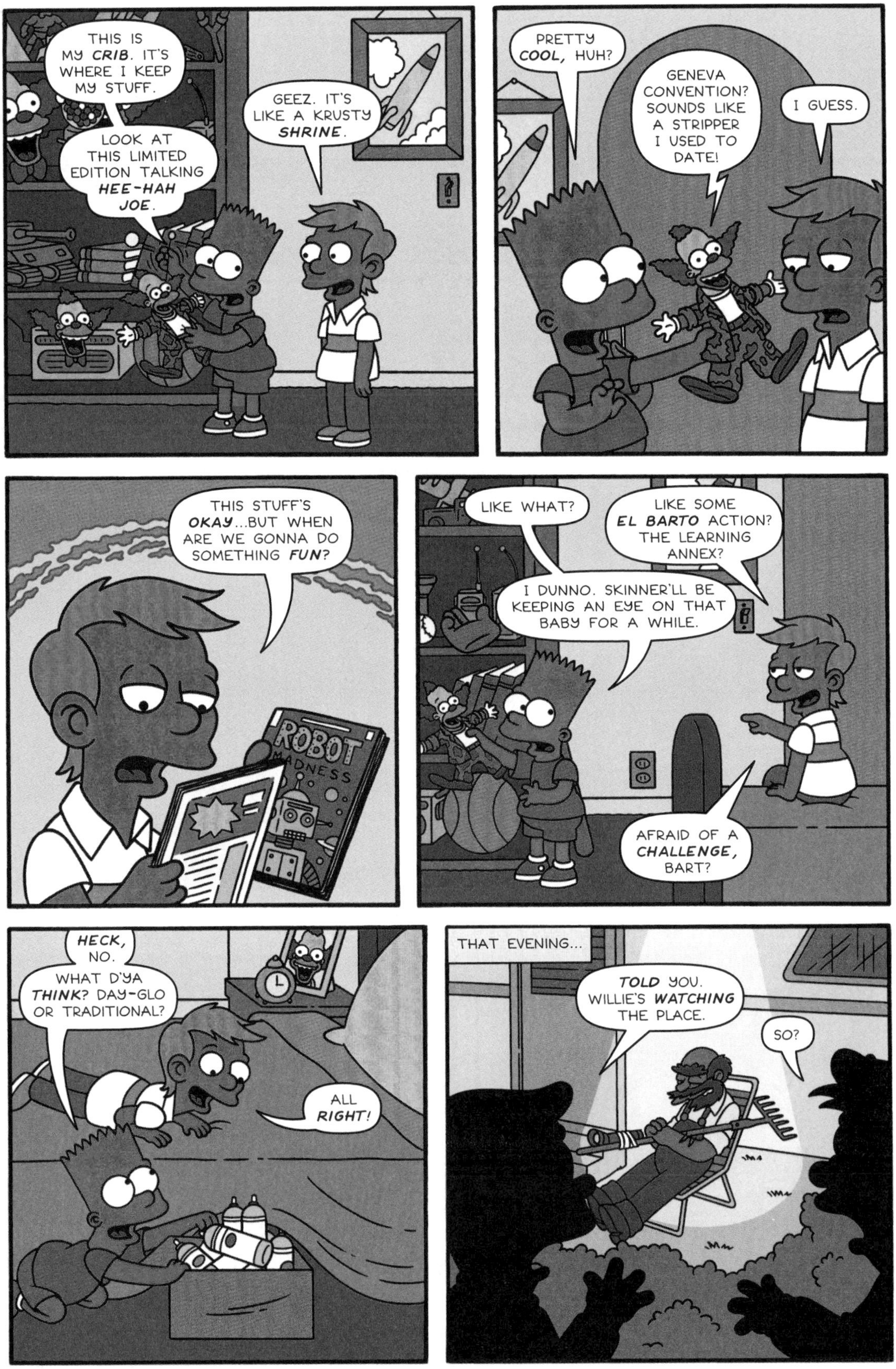

THIS IS MY **CRIB**. IT'S WHERE I KEEP MY STUFF.
LOOK AT THIS LIMITED EDITION TALKING **HEE-HAH JOE**.
GEEZ. IT'S LIKE A KRUSTY **SHRINE**.
PRETTY **COOL**, HUH?
GENEVA CONVENTION? SOUNDS LIKE A STRIPPER I USED TO DATE!
I GUESS.
THIS STUFF'S **OKAY**...BUT WHEN ARE WE GONNA DO SOMETHING **FUN**?
ROBOT MADNESS
LIKE WHAT?
LIKE SOME **EL BARTO** ACTION? THE LEARNING ANNEX?
I DUNNO. SKINNER'LL BE KEEPING AN EYE ON THAT BABY FOR A WHILE.
AFRAID OF A **CHALLENGE**, BART?
HECK, NO.
WHAT D'YA **THINK**? DAY-GLO OR TRADITIONAL?
ALL **RIGHT**!
THAT EVENING...
TOLD YOU. WILLIE'S **WATCHING** THE PLACE.
SO?

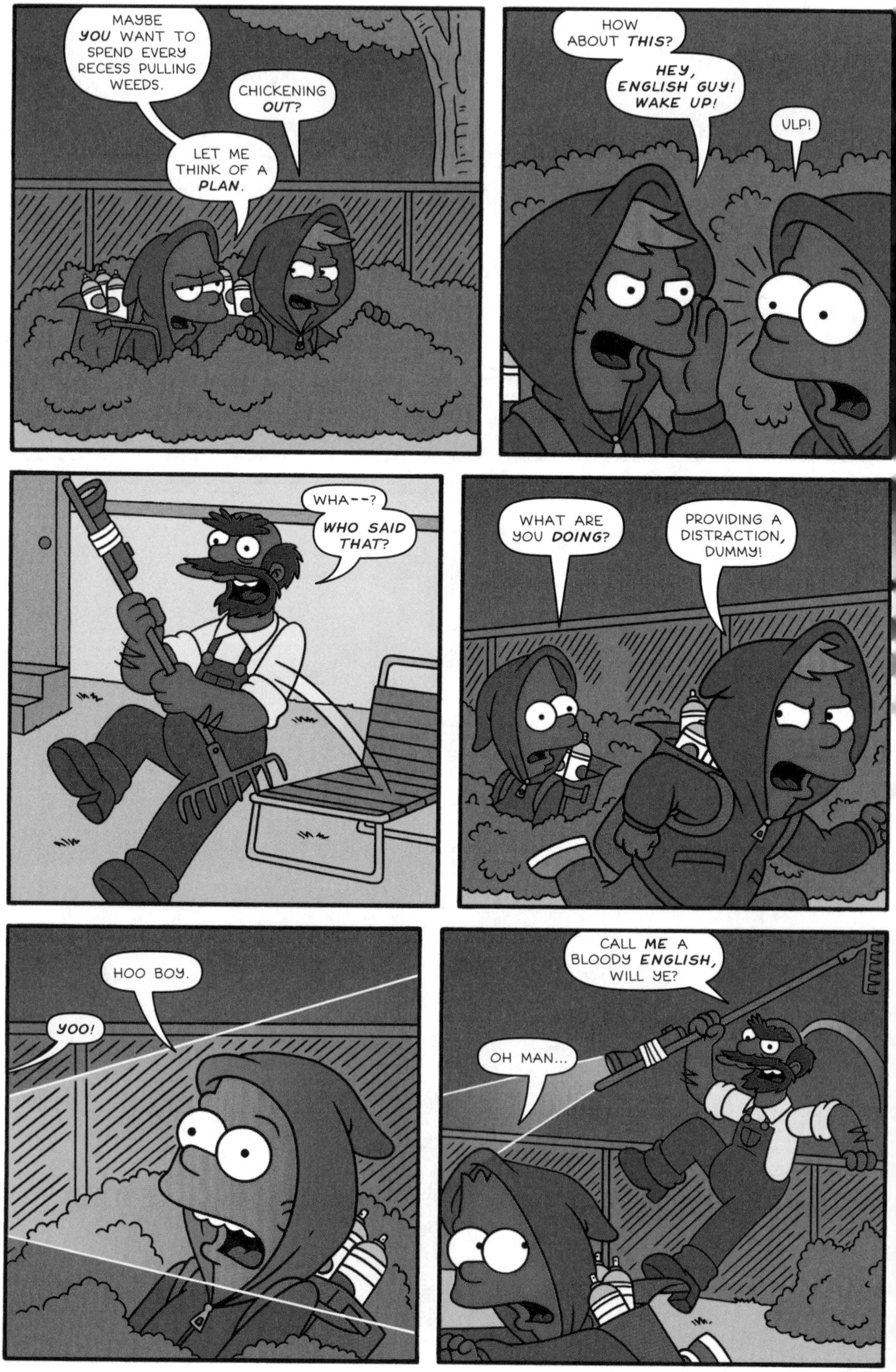
MAYBE YOU WANT TO SPEND EVERY RECESS PULLING WEEDS.
CHICKENING OUT?
LET ME THINK OF A PLAN.
HOW ABOUT THIS?
HEY, ENGLISH GUY! WAKE UP!
ULP!
WHA--? WHO SAID THAT?
WHAT ARE YOU DOING?
PROVIDING A DISTRACTION, DUMMY!
HOO BOY.
YOO!
CALL ME A BLOODY ENGLISH, WILL YE?
OH MAN...

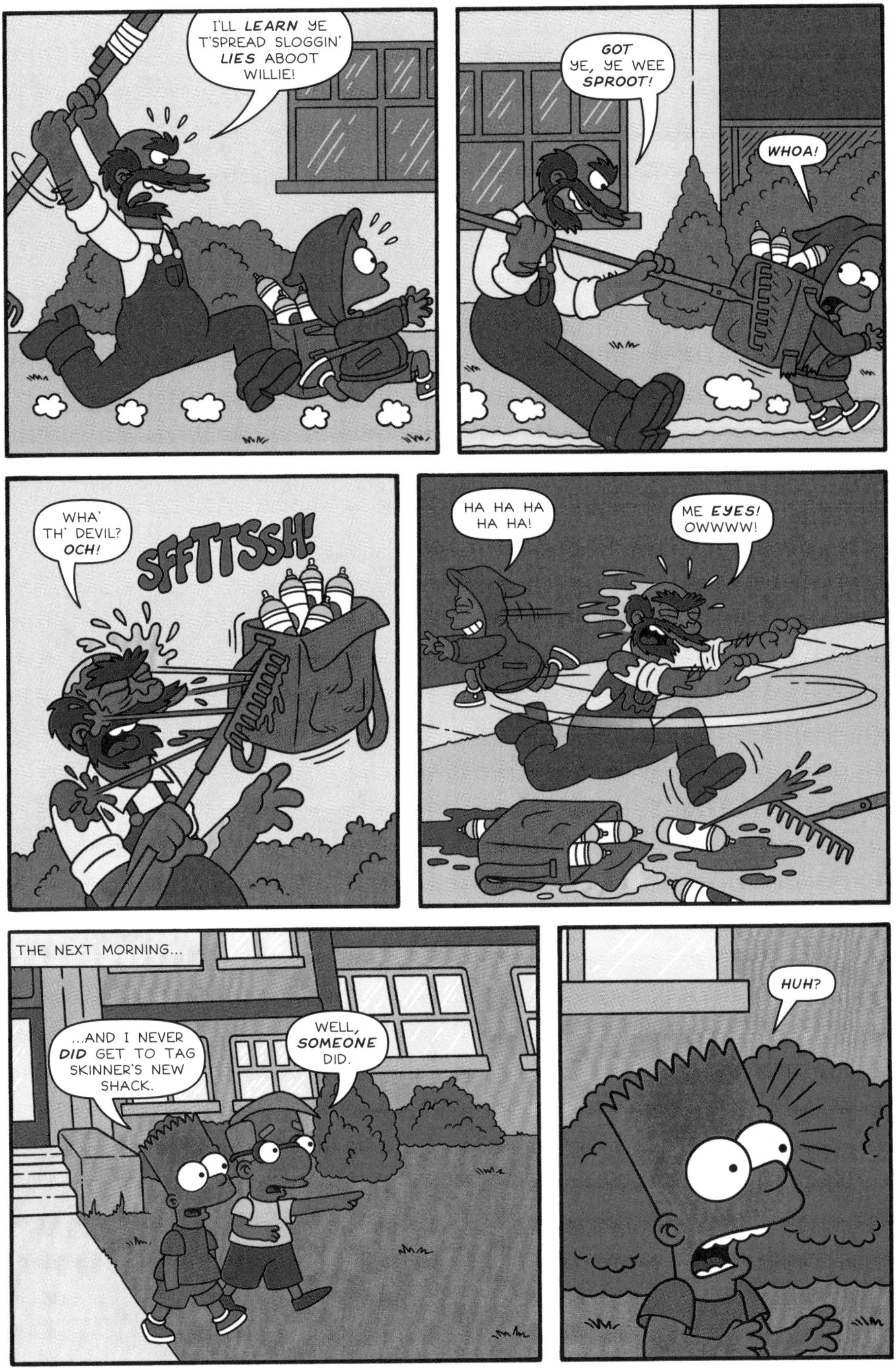
I'LL LEARN YE T'SPREAD SLOGGIN' LIES ABOOT WILLIE!
GOT YE, YE WEE SPROOT!
WHOA!
WHA' TH' DEVIL? OCH!
SFFTTSSH!
HA HA HA HA HA!
ME EYES! OWWWW!
THE NEXT MORNING...
...AND I NEVER DID GET TO TAG SKINNER'S NEW SHACK.
WELL, SOMEONE DID.
HUH?

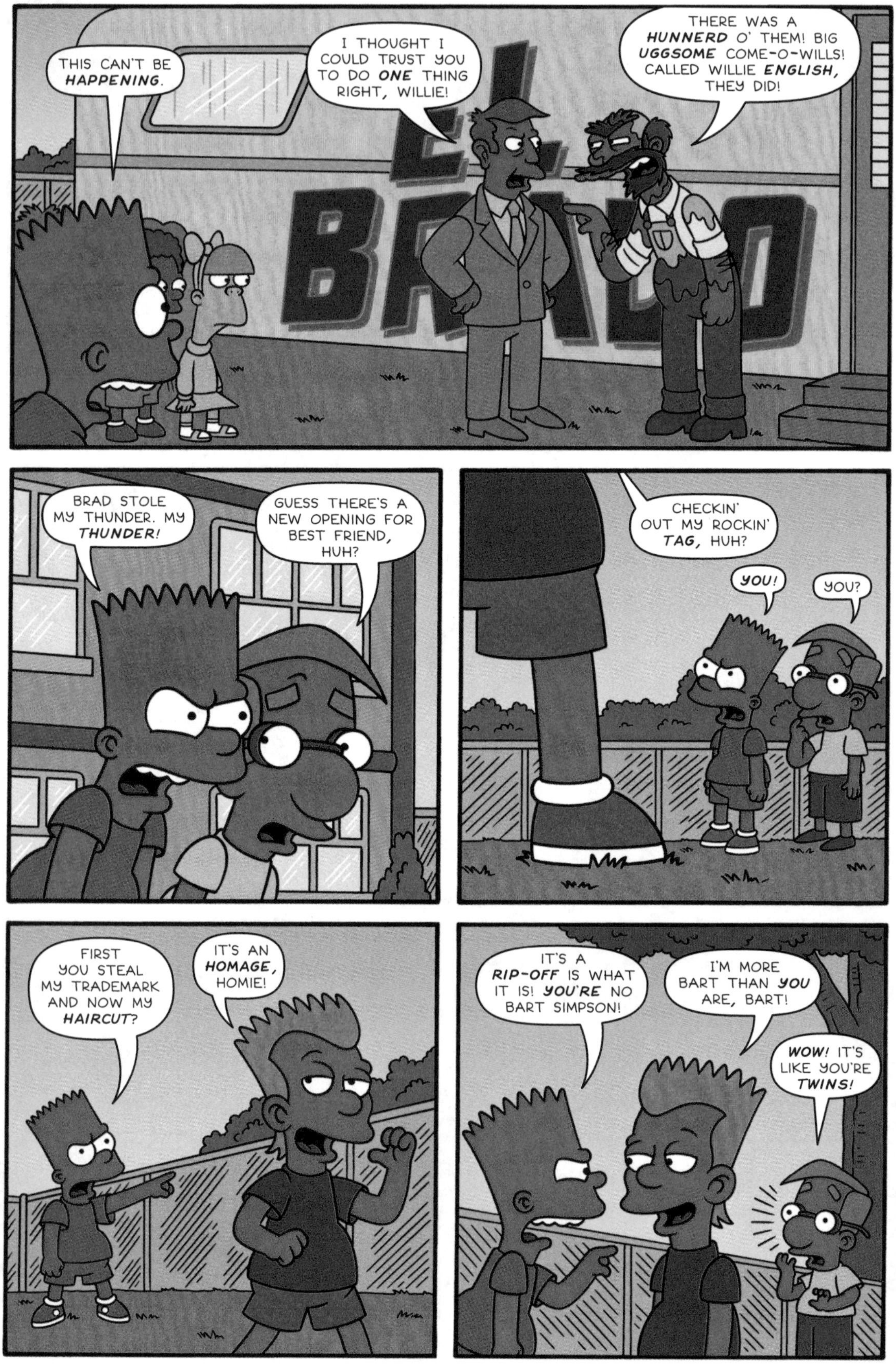
THIS CAN'T BE HAPPENING.
I THOUGHT I COULD TRUST YOU TO DO ONE THING RIGHT, WILLIE!
THERE WAS A HUNNERD O' THEM! BIG UGGSOME COME-O-WILLS! CALLED WILLIE ENGLISH, THEY DID!
BRAD STOLE MY THUNDER. MY THUNDER!
GUESS THERE'S A NEW OPENING FOR BEST FRIEND, HUH?
CHECKIN' OUT MY ROCKIN' TAG, HUH?
YOU!
YOU?
FIRST YOU STEAL MY TRADEMARK AND NOW MY HAIRCUT?
IT'S AN HOMAGE, HOMIE!
IT'S A RIP-OFF IS WHAT IT IS! YOU'RE NO BART SIMPSON!
I'M MORE BART THAN YOU ARE, BART!
WOW! IT'S LIKE YOU'RE TWINS!

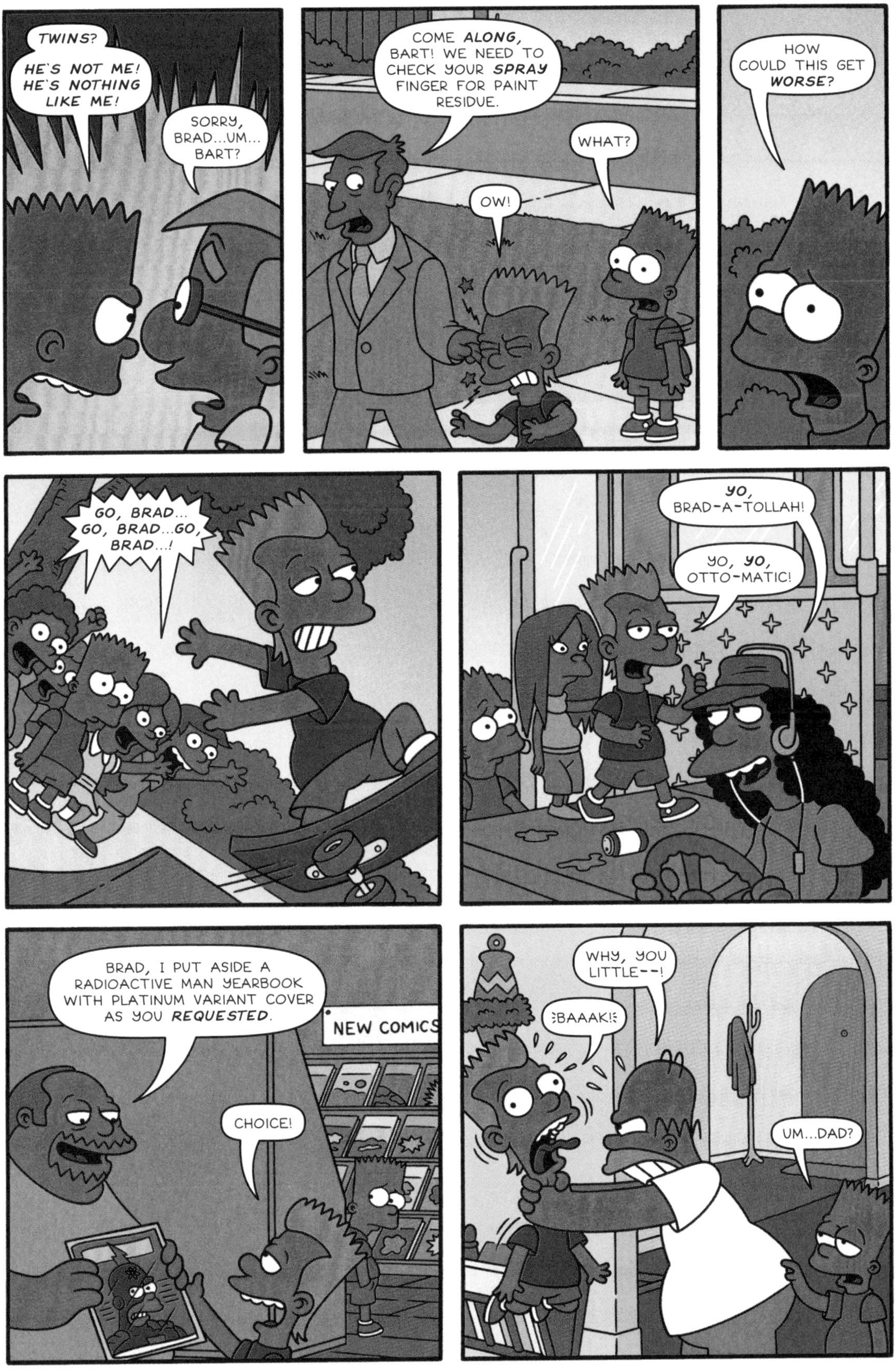
TWINS?
HE'S NOT ME! HE'S NOTHING LIKE ME!
SORRY, BRAD...UM... BART?
COME ALONG, BART! WE NEED TO CHECK YOUR SPRAY FINGER FOR PAINT RESIDUE.
OW!
WHAT?
HOW COULD THIS GET WORSE?
GO, BRAD... GO, BRAD...GO, BRAD...!
YO, BRAD-A-TOLLAH!
YO, YO, OTTO-MATIC!
BRAD, I PUT ASIDE A RADIOACTIVE MAN YEARBOOK WITH PLATINUM VARIANT COVER AS YOU REQUESTED.
NEW COMICS
CHOICE!
WHY, YOU LITTLE--!
BAAAK!
UM...DAD?

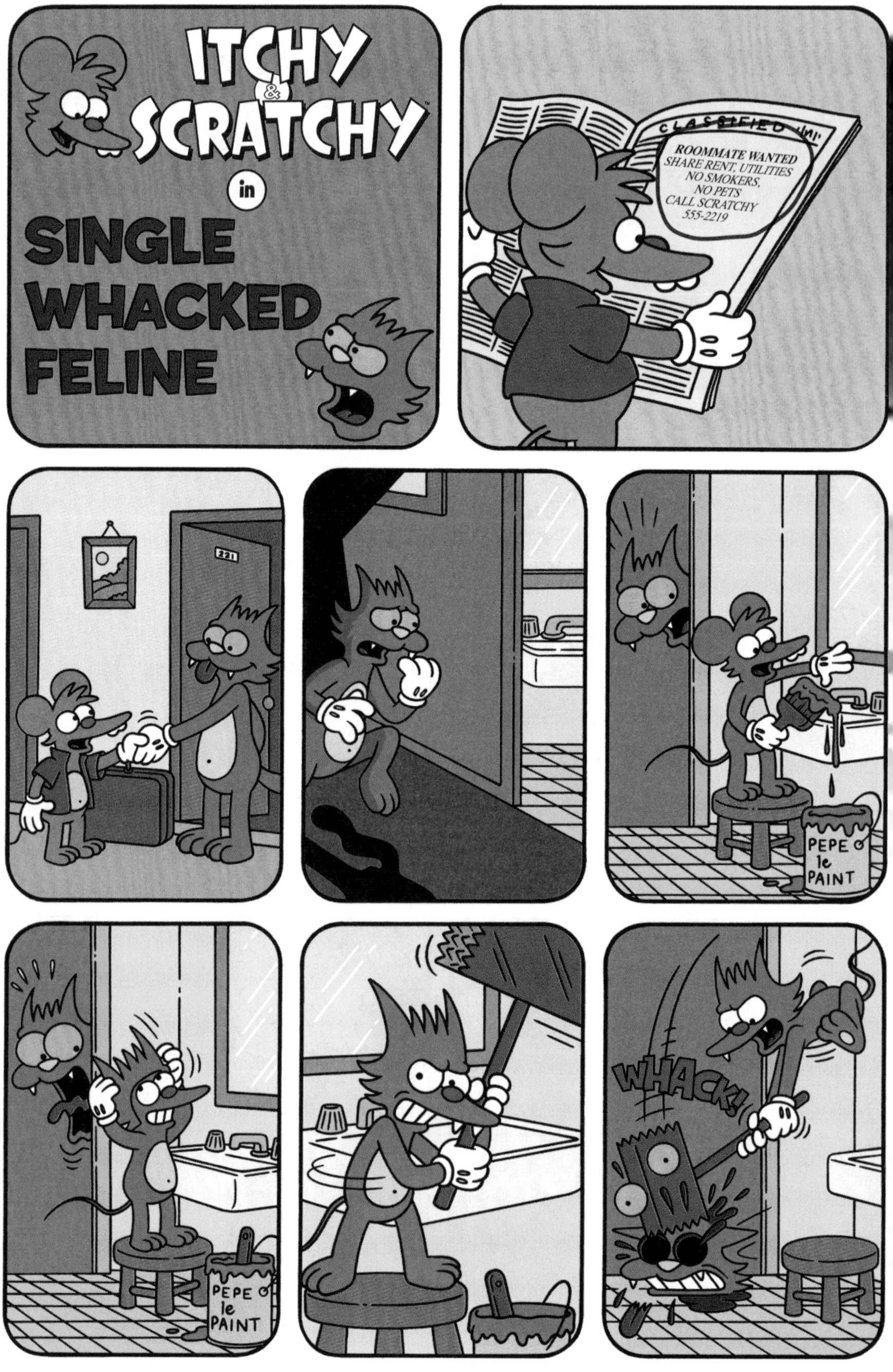
ITCHY & SCRATCHY
in
SINGLE WHACKED FELINE
CLASSIFIED
ROOMMATE WANTED
SHARE RENT, UTILITIES
NO SMOKERS,
NO PETS
CALL SCRATCHY
555-2219
221
PEPE le PAINT
PEPE le PAINT
WHACK!

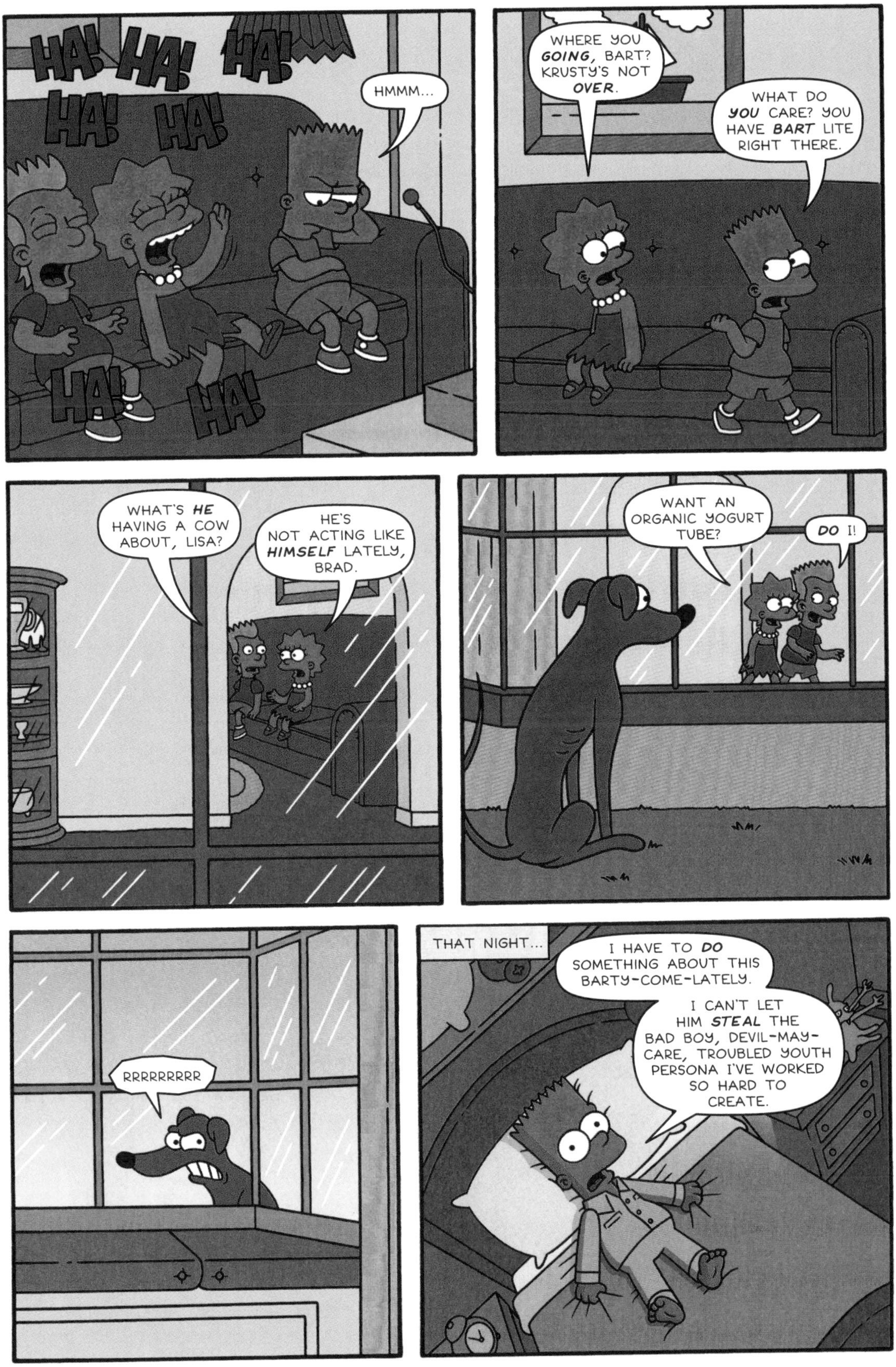
HA! HA! HA!
HA! HA!
HMMM...
HA! HA!
WHERE YOU GOING, BART? KRUSTY'S NOT OVER.
WHAT DO YOU CARE? YOU HAVE BART LITE RIGHT THERE.
WHAT'S HE HAVING A COW ABOUT, LISA?
HE'S NOT ACTING LIKE HIMSELF LATELY, BRAD.
WANT AN ORGANIC YOGURT TUBE?
DO I!
RRRRRRRRR
THAT NIGHT...
I HAVE TO DO SOMETHING ABOUT THIS BARTY-COME-LATELY.
I CAN'T LET HIM STEAL THE BAD BOY, DEVIL-MAY-CARE, TROUBLED YOUTH PERSONA I'VE WORKED SO HARD TO CREATE.

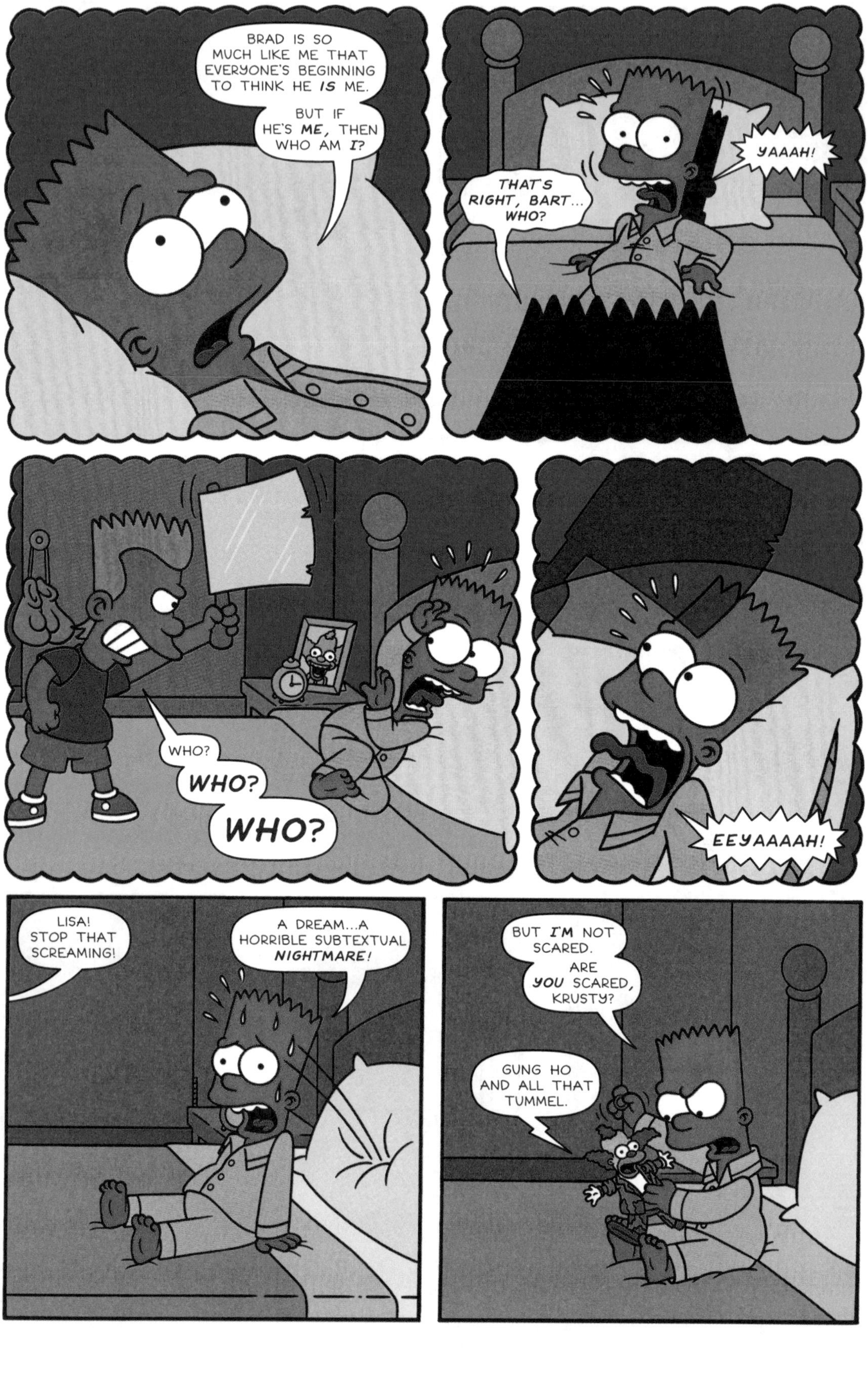
BRAD IS SO MUCH LIKE ME THAT EVERYONE'S BEGINNING TO THINK HE *IS* ME.
BUT IF HE'S **ME**, THEN WHO AM *I*?
THAT'S RIGHT, BART... WHO?
YAAAH!
WHO?
WHO?
WHO?
EEYAAAAH!
LISA! STOP THAT SCREAMING!
A DREAM...A HORRIBLE SUBTEXTUAL ***NIGHTMARE!***
BUT ***I'M*** NOT SCARED.
ARE ***YOU*** SCARED, KRUSTY?
GUNG HO AND ALL THAT TUMMEL.

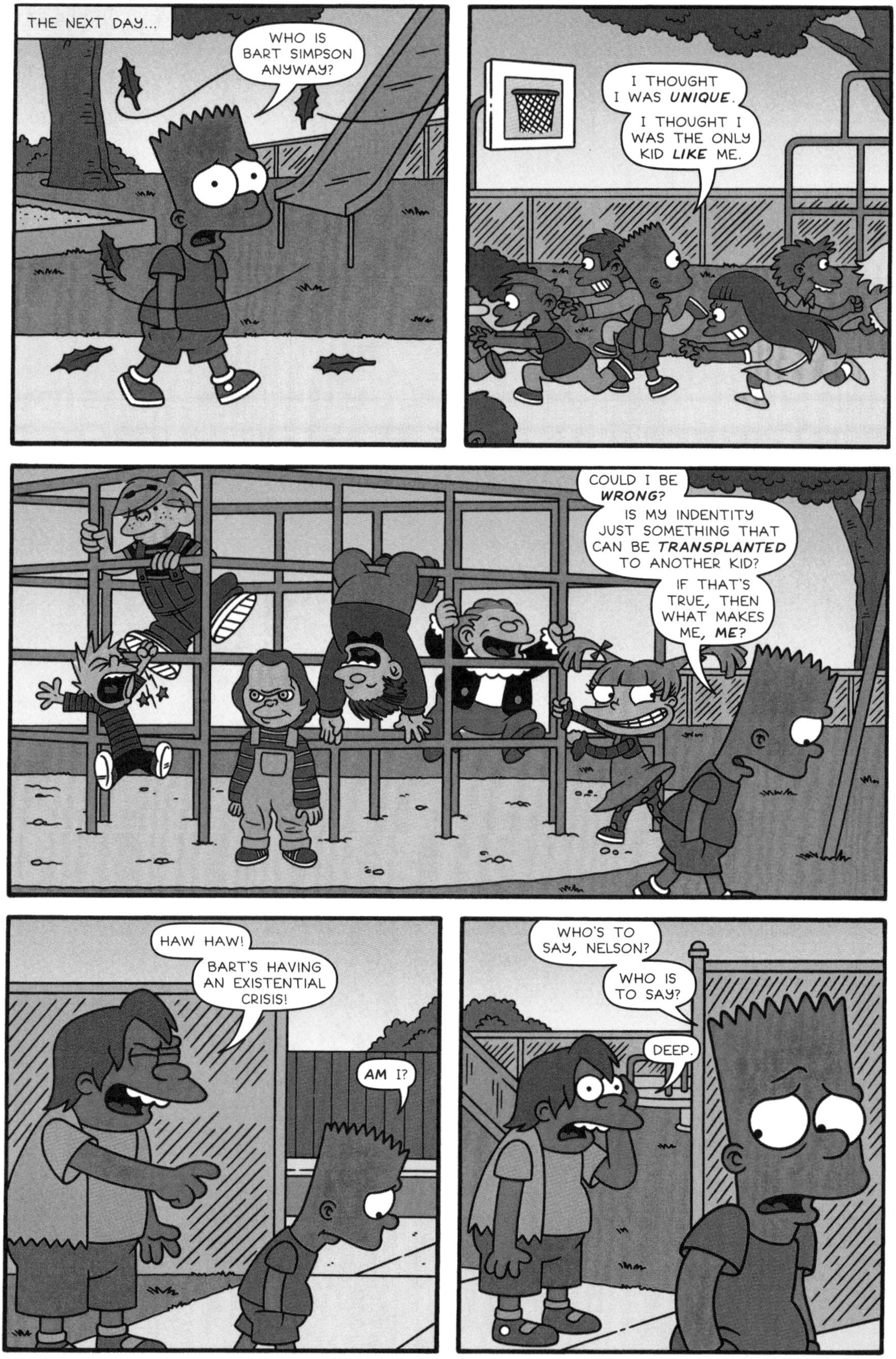
THE NEXT DAY...
WHO IS BART SIMPSON ANYWAY?
I THOUGHT I WAS UNIQUE.
I THOUGHT I WAS THE ONLY KID LIKE ME.
COULD I BE WRONG?
IS MY INDENTITY JUST SOMETHING THAT CAN BE TRANSPLANTED TO ANOTHER KID?
IF THAT'S TRUE, THEN WHAT MAKES ME, ME?
HAW HAW!
BART'S HAVING AN EXISTENTIAL CRISIS!
AM I?
WHO'S TO SAY, NELSON?
WHO IS TO SAY?
DEEP.

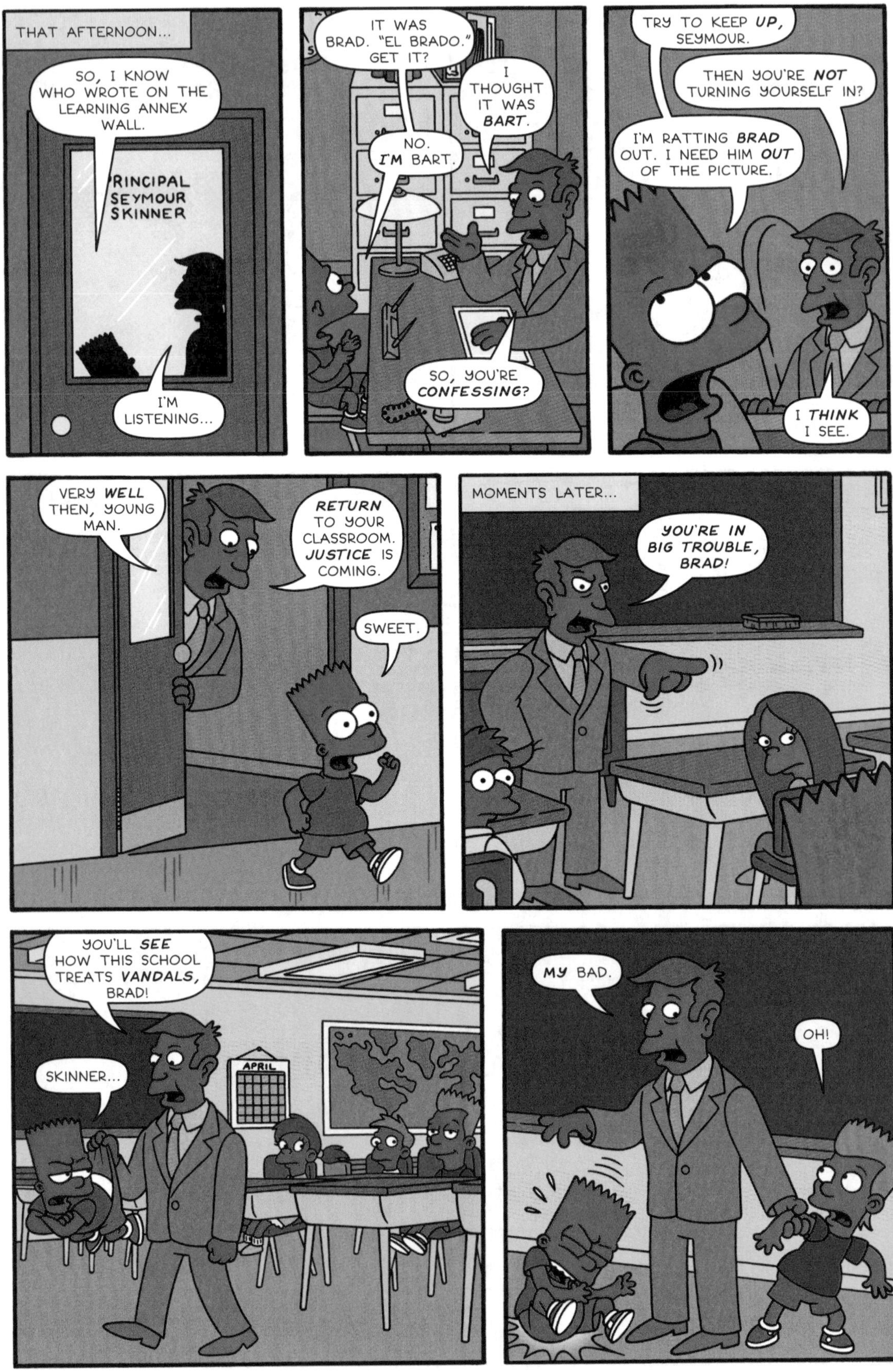

THAT AFTERNOON...
SO, I KNOW WHO WROTE ON THE LEARNING ANNEX WALL.
PRINCIPAL SEYMOUR SKINNER
I'M LISTENING...
IT WAS BRAD. "EL BRADO." GET IT?
I THOUGHT IT WAS BART.
NO. I'M BART.
SO, YOU'RE CONFESSING?
TRY TO KEEP UP, SEYMOUR.
THEN YOU'RE NOT TURNING YOURSELF IN?
I'M RATTING BRAD OUT. I NEED HIM OUT OF THE PICTURE.
I THINK I SEE.
VERY WELL THEN, YOUNG MAN.
RETURN TO YOUR CLASSROOM. JUSTICE IS COMING.
SWEET.
MOMENTS LATER...
YOU'RE IN BIG TROUBLE, BRAD!
YOU'LL SEE HOW THIS SCHOOL TREATS VANDALS, BRAD!
SKINNER...
APRIL
MY BAD.
OH!

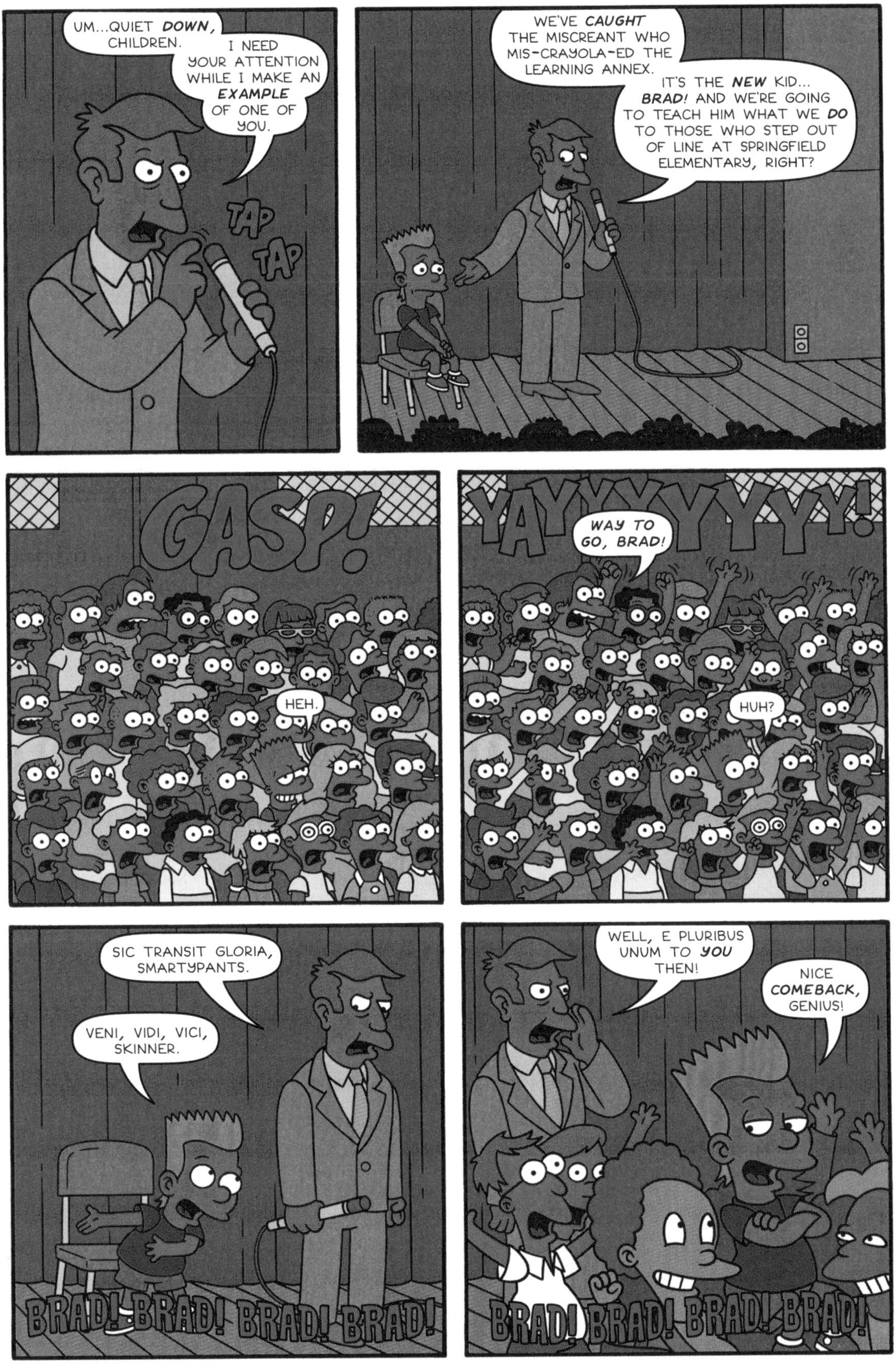
UM...QUIET DOWN, CHILDREN.
I NEED YOUR ATTENTION WHILE I MAKE AN EXAMPLE OF ONE OF YOU.
TAP TAP
WE'VE CAUGHT THE MISCREANT WHO MIS-CRAYOLA-ED THE LEARNING ANNEX.
IT'S THE NEW KID... BRAD! AND WE'RE GOING TO TEACH HIM WHAT WE DO TO THOSE WHO STEP OUT OF LINE AT SPRINGFIELD ELEMENTARY, RIGHT?
GASP!
HEH.
YAYYYYYYY!
WAY TO GO, BRAD!
HUH?
SIC TRANSIT GLORIA, SMARTYPANTS.
VENI, VIDI, VICI, SKINNER.
BRAD! BRAD! BRAD! BRAD!
WELL, E PLURIBUS UNUM TO YOU THEN!
NICE COMEBACK, GENIUS!
BRAD! BRAD! BRAD! BRAD!

AFTER SCHOOL...

MAN, I TRY TO WREAK VENGEANCE ON BRAD AND WIND UP MAKING HIM A *HERO*.

IT'S ALMOST LIKE HE'S *RUBBER* AND YOU'RE *GLUE*... TO QUOTE THE CLASSICS.

THERE'S BRAD *NOW*.

AND HE'S GETTING IN THAT *CAR*.

SO, YOU'RE A *NARRATOR* NOW?

WHERE YOU *GOING*, BART?

BRAD KNOWS MY WHOLE LIFE, AND I KNOW *NADA* ABOUT HIM.

I'M GOING TO SHOW *HIM* THAT A LITTLE KNOWLEDGE IS A DANGEROUS THING.

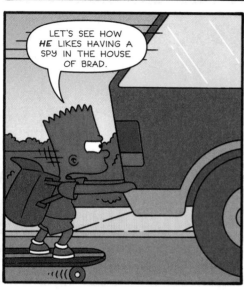

LET'S SEE HOW *HE* LIKES HAVING A SPY IN THE HOUSE OF BRAD.

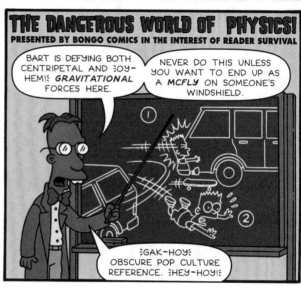

THE DANGEROUS WORLD OF PHYSICS!

PRESENTED BY BONGO COMICS IN THE INTEREST OF READER SURVIVAL

BART IS DEFYING BOTH CENTRIPETAL AND ≥OY-HEM!≤ *GRAVITATIONAL* FORCES HERE.

NEVER DO THIS UNLESS YOU WANT TO END UP AS A *MCFLY* ON SOMEONE'S WINDSHIELD.

≥GAK-HOY≤ OBSCURE POP CULTURE REFERENCE. ≥HEY-HOY!≤

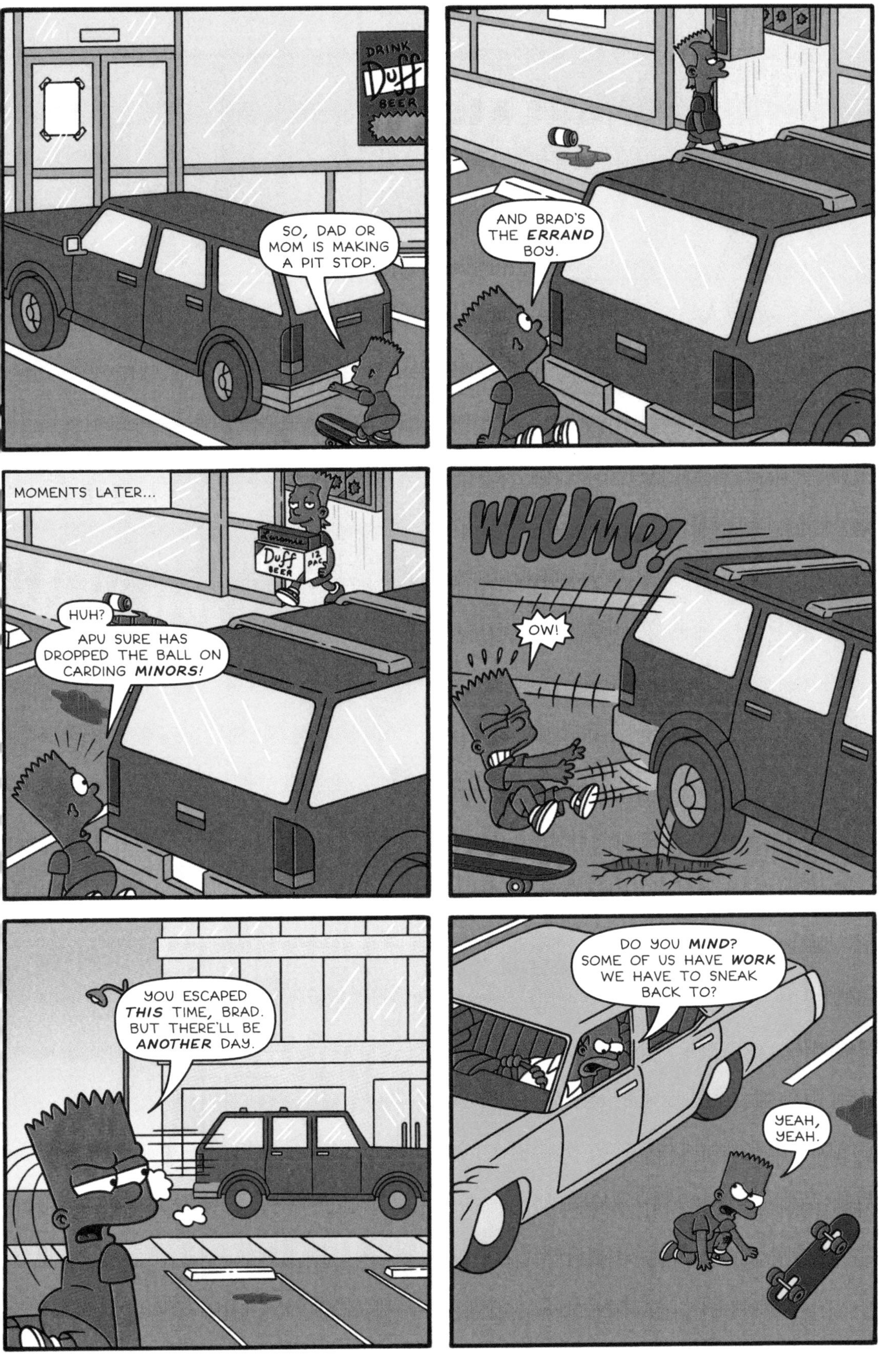
SO, DAD OR MOM IS MAKING A PIT STOP.
AND BRAD'S THE ERRAND BOY.
MOMENTS LATER...
HUH?
APU SURE HAS DROPPED THE BALL ON CARDING MINORS!
WHUMP!
OW!
YOU ESCAPED THIS TIME, BRAD. BUT THERE'LL BE ANOTHER DAY.
DO YOU MIND? SOME OF US HAVE WORK WE HAVE TO SNEAK BACK TO?
YEAH, YEAH.

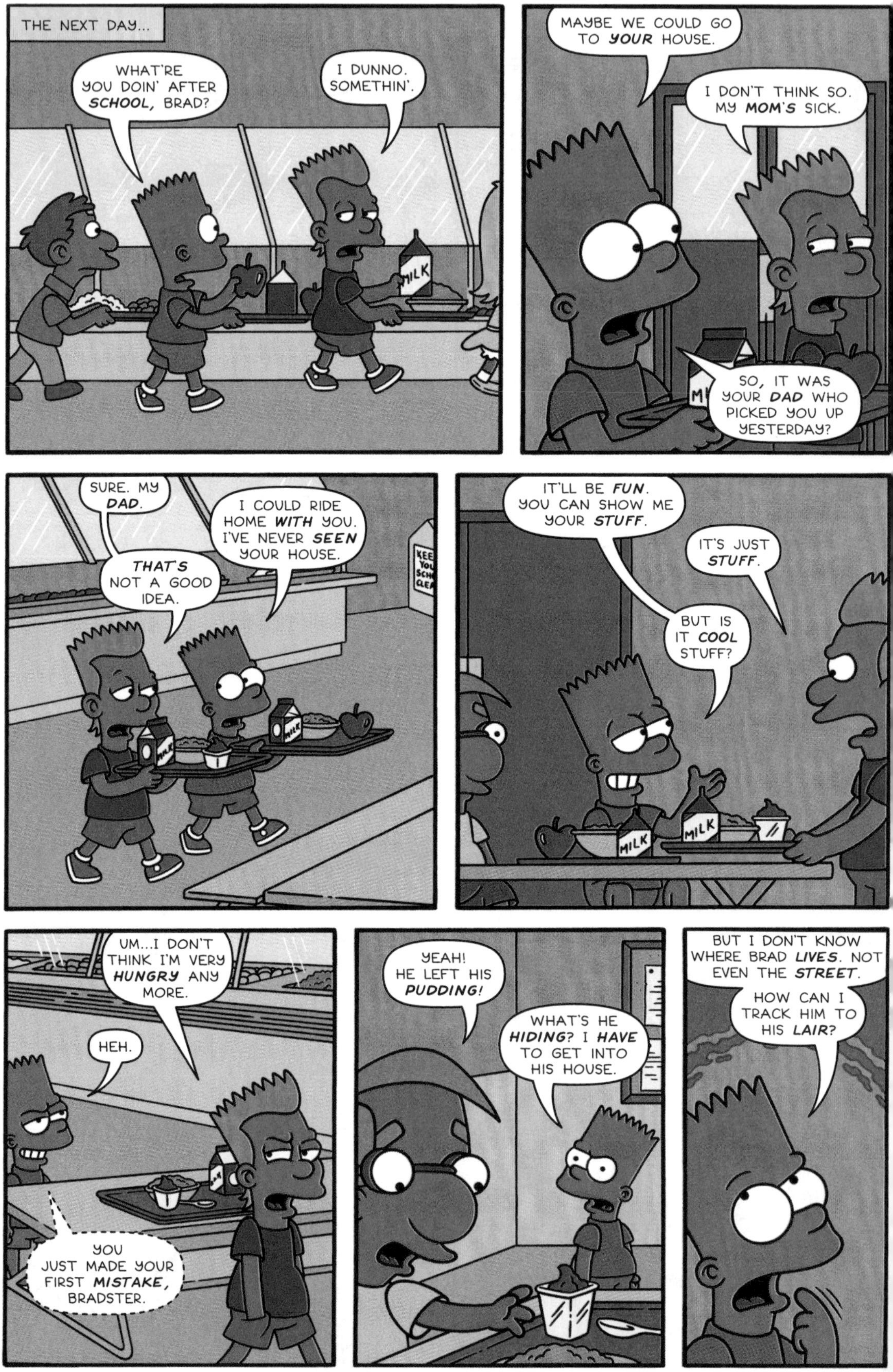
THE NEXT DAY...
WHAT'RE YOU DOIN' AFTER **SCHOOL,** BRAD?
I DUNNO. SOMETHIN'.
MAYBE WE COULD GO TO **YOUR** HOUSE.
I DON'T THINK SO. MY **MOM'S** SICK.
SO, IT WAS YOUR **DAD** WHO PICKED YOU UP YESTERDAY?
MILK
SURE. MY **DAD**.
I COULD RIDE HOME **WITH** YOU. I'VE NEVER **SEEN** YOUR HOUSE.
THAT'S NOT A GOOD IDEA.
MILK
IT'LL BE **FUN**. YOU CAN SHOW ME YOUR **STUFF**.
IT'S JUST **STUFF**.
BUT IS IT **COOL** STUFF?
MILK
UM...I DON'T THINK I'M VERY **HUNGRY** ANY MORE.
HEH.
YOU JUST MADE YOUR FIRST **MISTAKE,** BRADSTER.
YEAH! HE LEFT HIS **PUDDING!**
WHAT'S HE **HIDING?** I **HAVE** TO GET INTO HIS HOUSE.
BUT I DON'T KNOW WHERE BRAD **LIVES**. NOT EVEN THE **STREET**.
HOW CAN I TRACK HIM TO HIS **LAIR?**

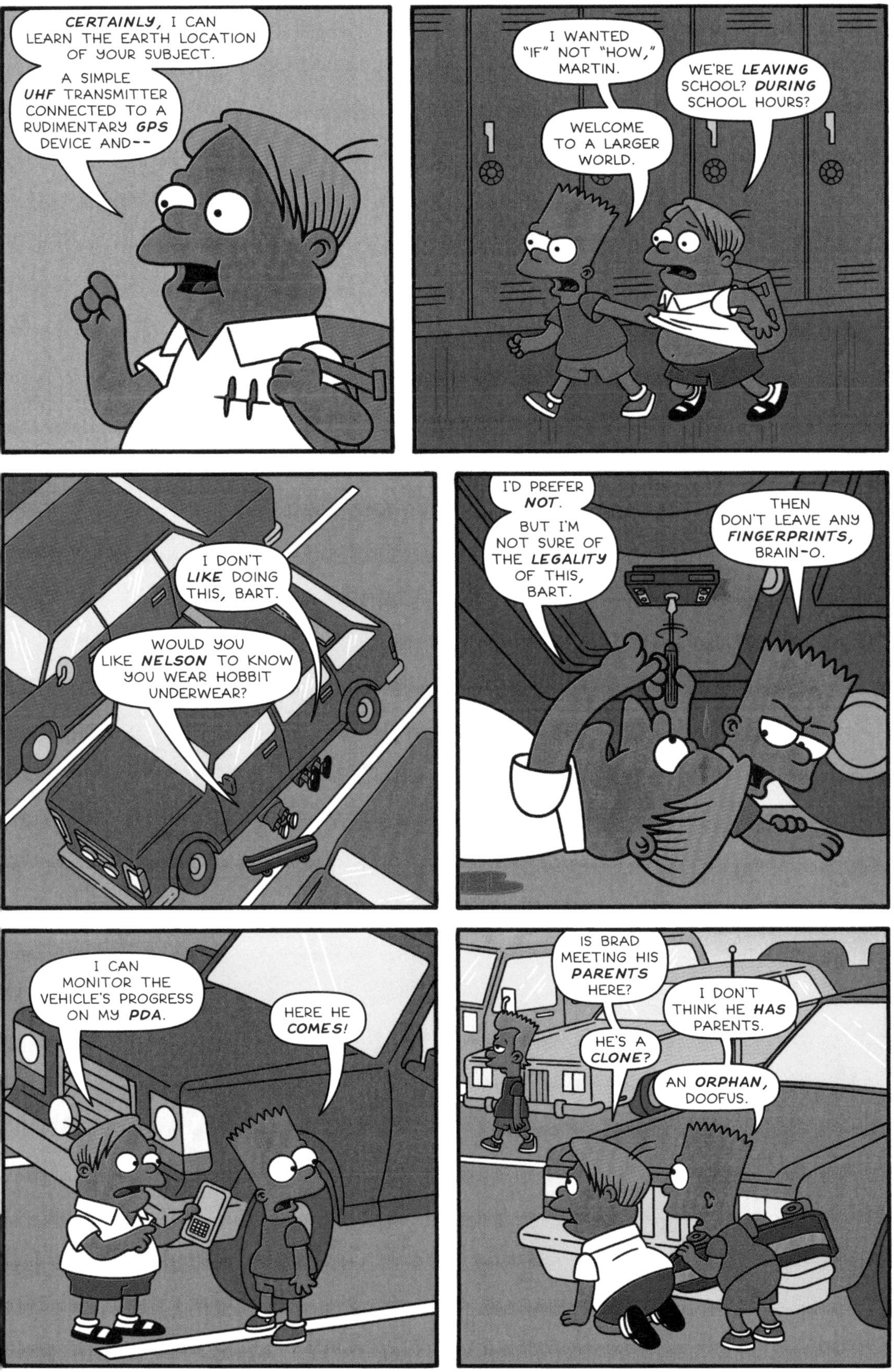
CERTAINLY, I CAN LEARN THE EARTH LOCATION OF YOUR SUBJECT.
A SIMPLE UHF TRANSMITTER CONNECTED TO A RUDIMENTARY GPS DEVICE AND--
I WANTED "IF" NOT "HOW," MARTIN.
WELCOME TO A LARGER WORLD.
WE'RE LEAVING SCHOOL? DURING SCHOOL HOURS?
I DON'T LIKE DOING THIS, BART.
WOULD YOU LIKE NELSON TO KNOW YOU WEAR HOBBIT UNDERWEAR?
I'D PREFER NOT.
BUT I'M NOT SURE OF THE LEGALITY OF THIS, BART.
THEN DON'T LEAVE ANY FINGERPRINTS, BRAIN-O.
I CAN MONITOR THE VEHICLE'S PROGRESS ON MY PDA.
HERE HE COMES!
IS BRAD MEETING HIS PARENTS HERE?
I DON'T THINK HE HAS PARENTS.
HE'S A CLONE?
AN ORPHAN, DOOFUS.

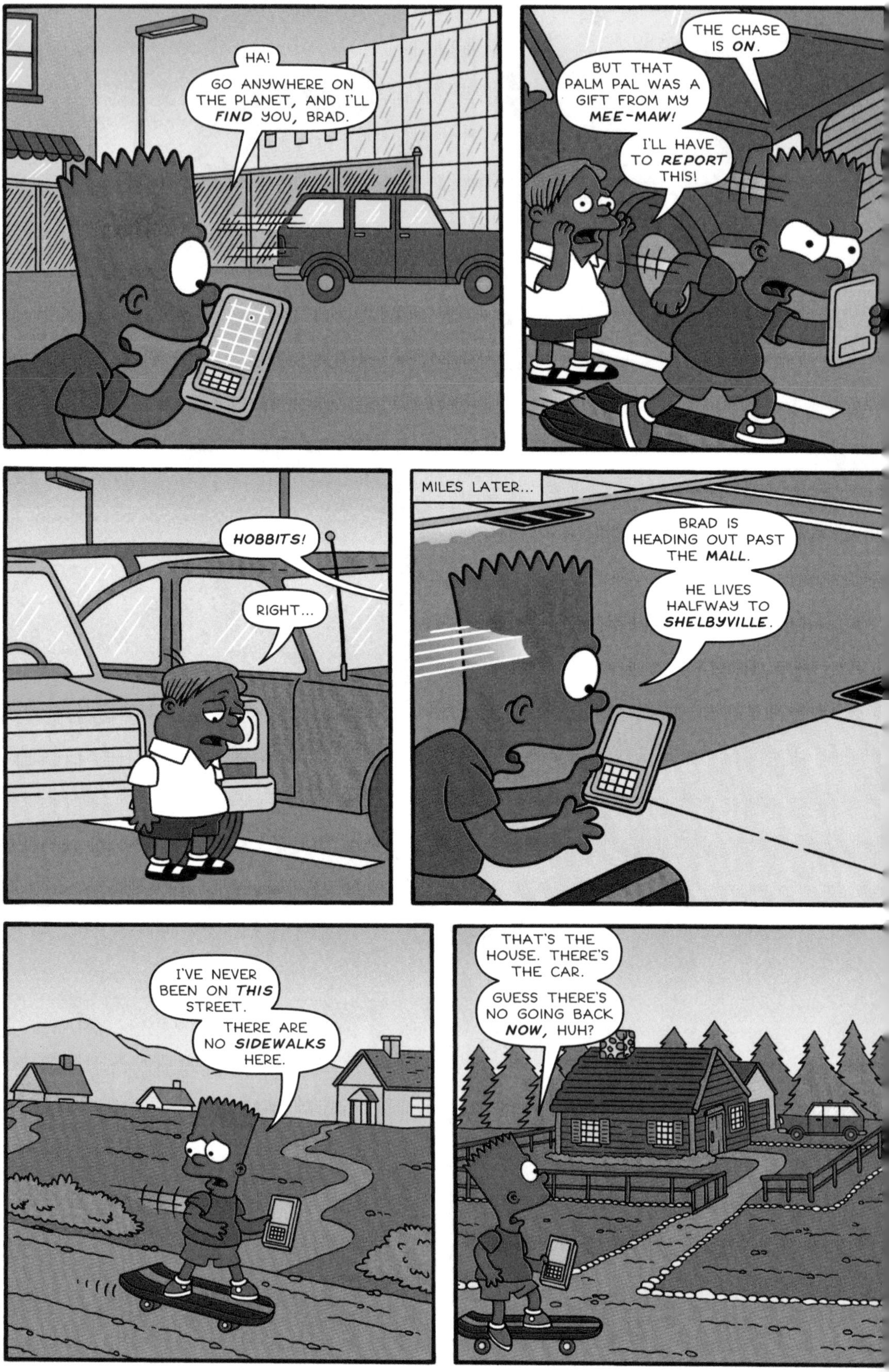
HA!
GO ANYWHERE ON THE PLANET, AND I'LL FIND YOU, BRAD.
THE CHASE IS ON.
BUT THAT PALM PAL WAS A GIFT FROM MY MEE-MAW!
I'LL HAVE TO REPORT THIS!
HOBBITS!
RIGHT...
MILES LATER...
BRAD IS HEADING OUT PAST THE MALL.
HE LIVES HALFWAY TO SHELBYVILLE.
I'VE NEVER BEEN ON THIS STREET.
THERE ARE NO SIDEWALKS HERE.
THAT'S THE HOUSE. THERE'S THE CAR.
GUESS THERE'S NO GOING BACK NOW, HUH?

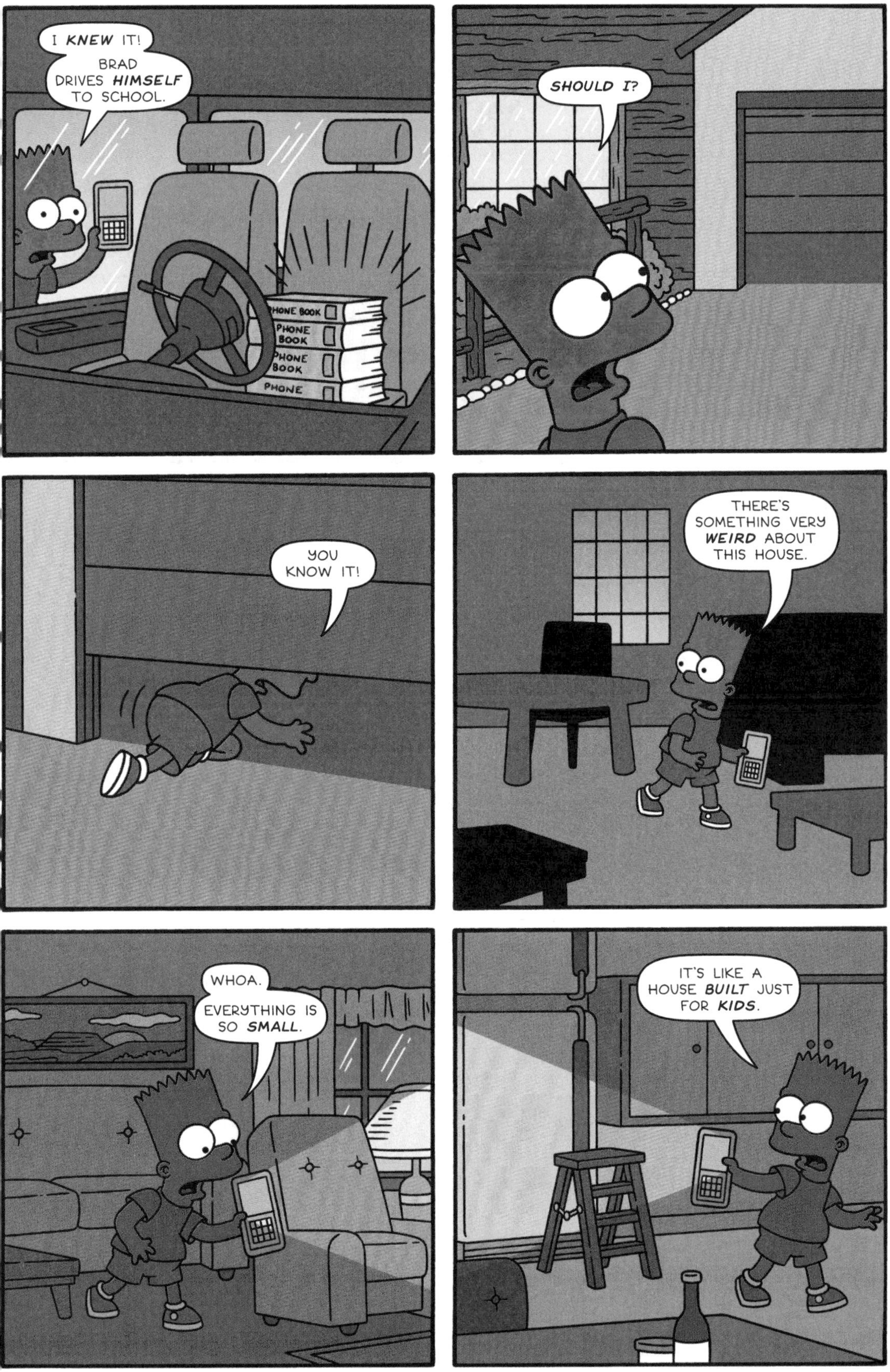
I KNEW IT! BRAD DRIVES HIMSELF TO SCHOOL.
PHONE BOOK
PHONE BOOK
PHONE BOOK
PHONE
SHOULD I?
YOU KNOW IT!
THERE'S SOMETHING VERY WEIRD ABOUT THIS HOUSE.
WHOA.
EVERYTHING IS SO SMALL.
IT'S LIKE A HOUSE BUILT JUST FOR KIDS.

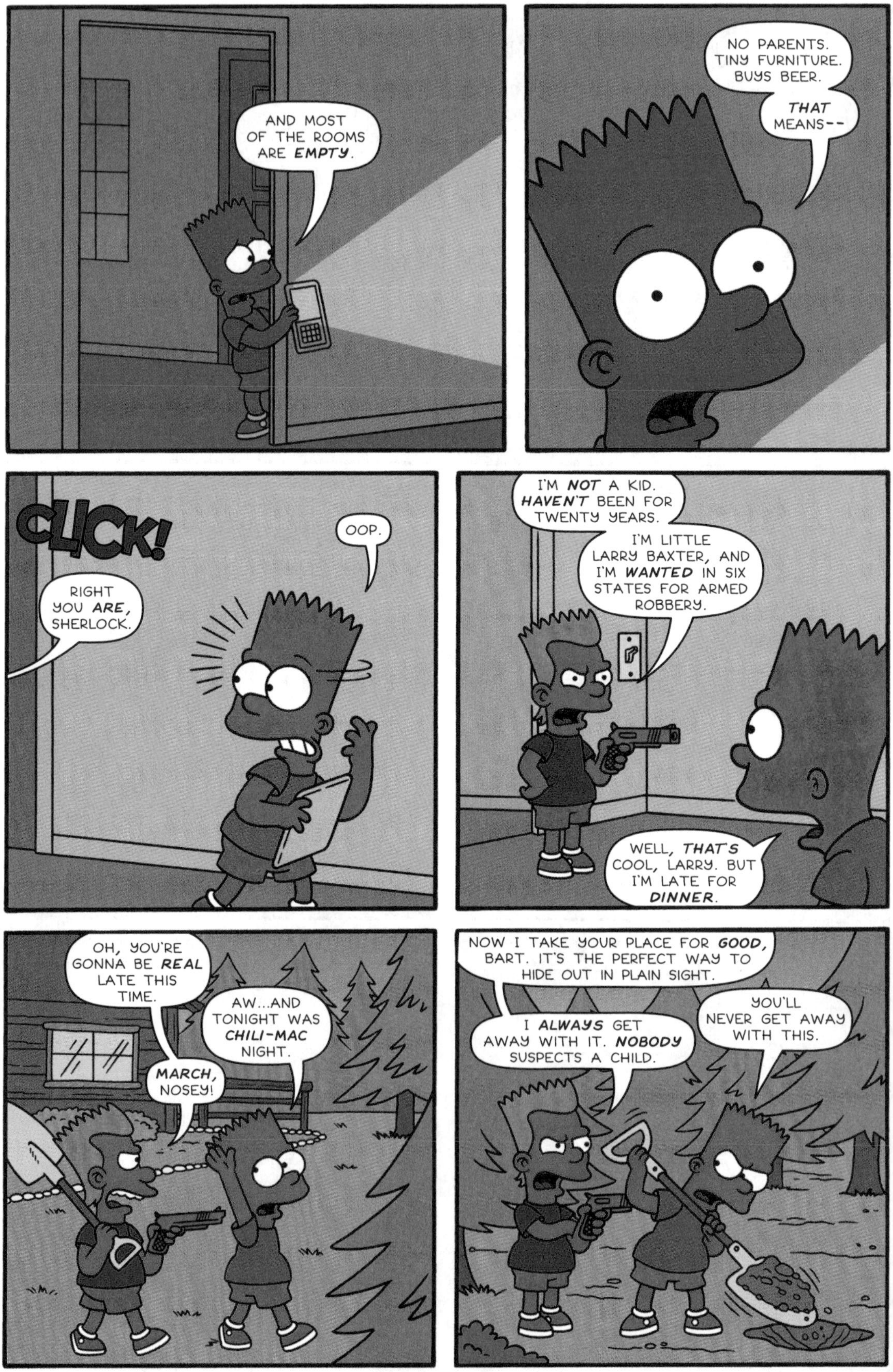
AND MOST OF THE ROOMS ARE EMPTY.
NO PARENTS. TINY FURNITURE. BUYS BEER.
THAT MEANS--
CLICK!
OOP.
RIGHT YOU ARE, SHERLOCK.
I'M NOT A KID. HAVEN'T BEEN FOR TWENTY YEARS.
I'M LITTLE LARRY BAXTER, AND I'M WANTED IN SIX STATES FOR ARMED ROBBERY.
WELL, THAT'S COOL, LARRY. BUT I'M LATE FOR DINNER.
OH, YOU'RE GONNA BE REAL LATE THIS TIME.
AW...AND TONIGHT WAS CHILI-MAC NIGHT.
MARCH, NOSEY!
NOW I TAKE YOUR PLACE FOR GOOD, BART. IT'S THE PERFECT WAY TO HIDE OUT IN PLAIN SIGHT.
YOU'LL NEVER GET AWAY WITH THIS.
I ALWAYS GET AWAY WITH IT. NOBODY SUSPECTS A CHILD.

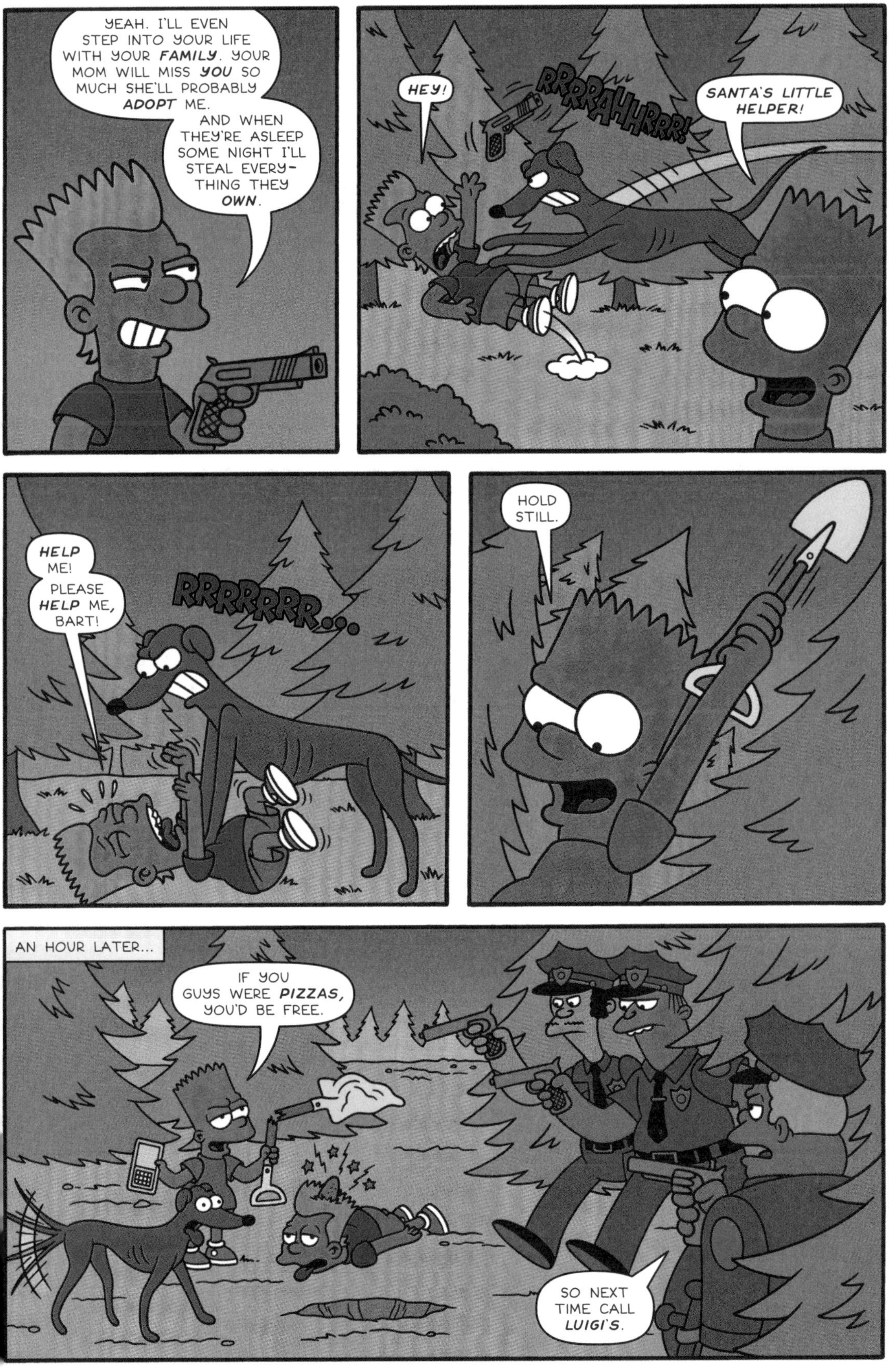
YEAH. I'LL EVEN STEP INTO YOUR LIFE WITH YOUR FAMILY. YOUR MOM WILL MISS YOU SO MUCH SHE'LL PROBABLY ADOPT ME.
AND WHEN THEY'RE ASLEEP SOME NIGHT I'LL STEAL EVERY-THING THEY OWN.
HEY!
RRRRAHHRRR!
SANTA'S LITTLE HELPER!
HELP ME!
PLEASE HELP ME, BART!
RRRRRRR...
HOLD STILL.
AN HOUR LATER...
IF YOU GUYS WERE PIZZAS, YOU'D BE FREE.
SO NEXT TIME CALL LUIGI'S.

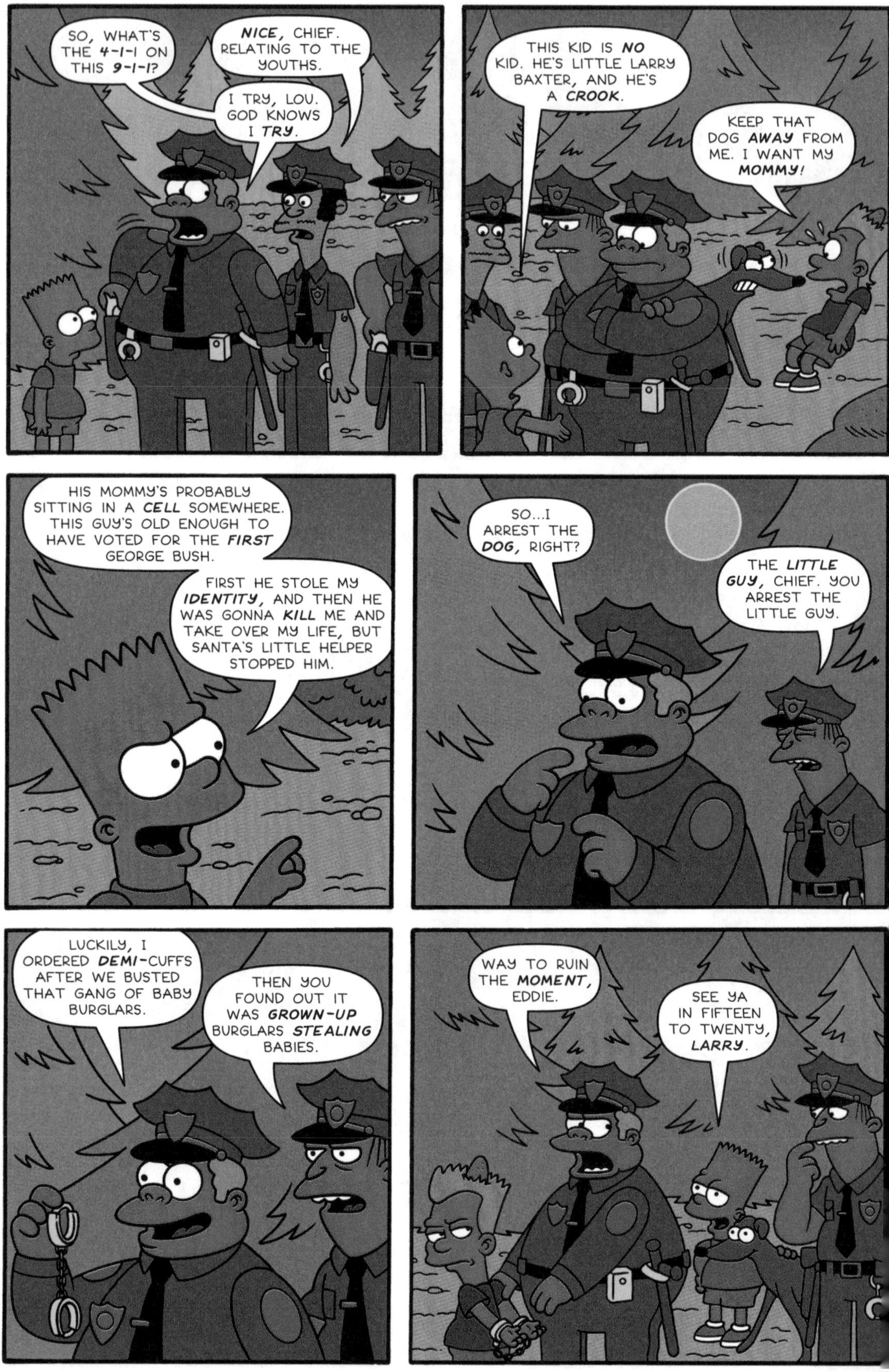
SO, WHAT'S THE 4-1-1 ON THIS 9-1-1?
NICE, CHIEF. RELATING TO THE YOUTHS.
I TRY, LOU. GOD KNOWS I TRY.
THIS KID IS NO KID. HE'S LITTLE LARRY BAXTER, AND HE'S A CROOK.
KEEP THAT DOG AWAY FROM ME. I WANT MY MOMMY!
HIS MOMMY'S PROBABLY SITTING IN A CELL SOMEWHERE. THIS GUY'S OLD ENOUGH TO HAVE VOTED FOR THE FIRST GEORGE BUSH.
FIRST HE STOLE MY IDENTITY, AND THEN HE WAS GONNA KILL ME AND TAKE OVER MY LIFE, BUT SANTA'S LITTLE HELPER STOPPED HIM.
SO...I ARREST THE DOG, RIGHT?
THE LITTLE GUY, CHIEF. YOU ARREST THE LITTLE GUY.
LUCKILY, I ORDERED DEMI-CUFFS AFTER WE BUSTED THAT GANG OF BABY BURGLARS.
THEN YOU FOUND OUT IT WAS GROWN-UP BURGLARS STEALING BABIES.
WAY TO RUIN THE MOMENT, EDDIE.
SEE YA IN FIFTEEN TO TWENTY, LARRY.

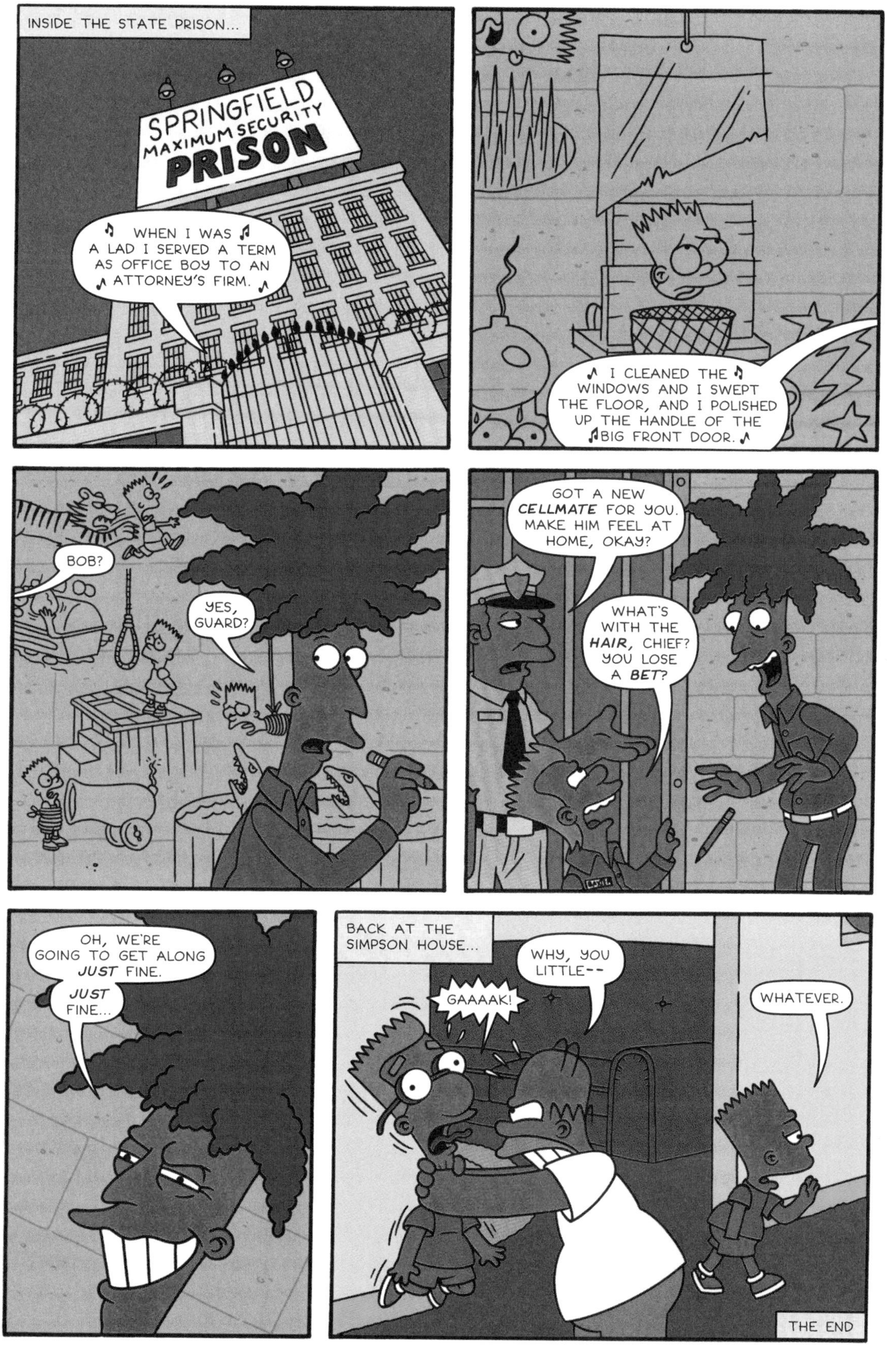
INSIDE THE STATE PRISON...
SPRINGFIELD MAXIMUM SECURITY PRISON
♪ WHEN I WAS ♫ A LAD I SERVED A TERM AS OFFICE BOY TO AN ♪ ATTORNEY'S FIRM. ♪
♪ I CLEANED THE ♫ WINDOWS AND I SWEPT THE FLOOR, AND I POLISHED UP THE HANDLE OF THE ♫BIG FRONT DOOR. ♪
BOB?
YES, GUARD?
GOT A NEW **CELLMATE** FOR YOU. MAKE HIM FEEL AT HOME, OKAY?
WHAT'S WITH THE **HAIR,** CHIEF? YOU LOSE A **BET**?
OH, WE'RE GOING TO GET ALONG **JUST** FINE.
JUST FINE...
BACK AT THE SIMPSON HOUSE...
WHY, YOU LITTLE--
GAAAAK!
WHATEVER.
THE END

HEY THERE, YA BUNCHA YAHOOS! I'M ALL OUT OF BAR NUTS AND THE LOVE TESTER'S ON THE FRITZ, SO IF YOU AIN'T GONNA ORDER SOME SUDS...MAYBE YOU SHOULD TRY YOUR LUCK WITH THE NEXT

BUSY HANDS PAPERCRAFT PROJECT!

THAT'S RIGHT...IT'S AN ITTY-BITTY VERSION OF MOE'S TAVERN! BUT IF YOU WANT THE REAL THING (COMPLETE WITH THE ROACHES, THE RATS, AND THE DANK) THEN COME DOWN TO THE REAL THING FOR HAPPY HOUR FROM 5:00-5:30 P.M.

WHAT YOU WILL NEED:
- Scissors, adhesive tape, and a straight edge (such as a ruler).
- An ability to fold along straight lines.
- An additional "mint condition" copy of this book secured elsewhere!

1. Cut out figures and bases.
2. Cut along the dotted line at the base of each figure and also the center of each curved base. (Be careful not to cut too far!)
3. Connect base to figure as shown (Fig. 1).
4. Before cutting out the shapes, use a ruler and a slightly rounded metal tool (like the edge of a key) to first score, and then fold lightly along all the interior lines (this will make final folds much easier).
5. Cut along the exterior shape. Make sure to cut all the way to where the walls, the roof, and the flaps lines meet (Fig. 2). Also, carefully cut along the dotted lines on the roof, being careful to limit your cuts to the length of the lines.

Fig. 1

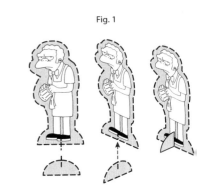

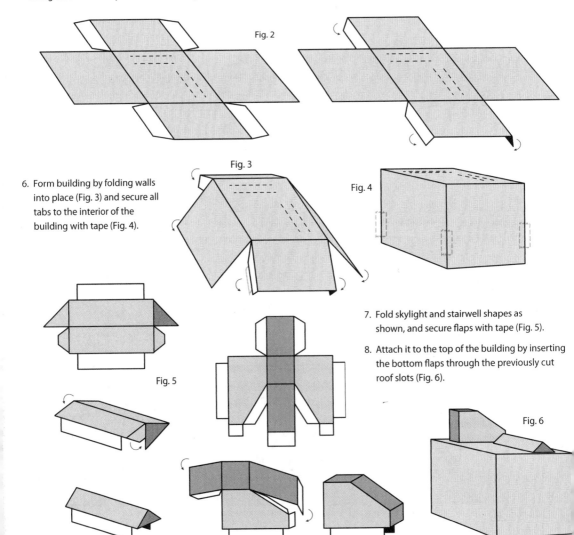

Fig. 2

Fig. 3

6. Form building by folding walls into place (Fig. 3) and secure all tabs to the interior of the building with tape (Fig. 4).

Fig. 4

Fig. 5

7. Fold skylight and stairwell shapes as shown, and secure flaps with tape (Fig. 5).

8. Attach it to the top of the building by inserting the bottom flaps through the previously cut roof slots (Fig. 6).

Fig. 6